# HANNS EISLER AND HIS CIRCLE IN REPUBLICAN SPAIN

# HANNS EISLER AND HIS CIRCLE IN REPUBLICAN SPAIN

## MUSIC, ANTIFASCISM, WAR

*Diego Alonso Tomás*

THE BOYDELL PRESS

First published 2026
The Boydell Press, Woodbridge

ISBN 978 1 83765 317 1 (hardback); 978 1 83765 318 8 (paperback)


The open access version of this publication was funded by the Deutsche Forschungsgemeinschaft (German Research Foundation). The finalization of the publication and copyright costs were supported by the grant RYC2021-033651-I, supported by the MCIN/AEI (10.13039/501100011033) and the European Union NextGenerationEU/PRTR.

The Boydell Press is an imprint of Boydell & Brewer Ltd
and of Boydell & Brewer Inc.
website: www.boydellandbrewer.com

Our Authorised Representative for product safety in the EU is Easy Access System Europe – Mustamäe tee 50, 10621 Tallinn, Estonia, gpsr.requests@easproject.com

A CIP catalogue record for this book is available from the British Library

Für Markus,

mit Liebe und Dankbarkeit

# Contents

*List of Figures* viii
*List of Musical Examples* x
*Acknowledgements* xiii
*Abbreviations* xv

Introduction 1

I. HANNS EISLER AND SPANISH ANTIFASCISM

1 Barcelona, 1936: The Comintern, the ISCM, and the People's Olympiad 29
2 Eisler in Wartime Spain. A Re-Examination in Light of New Sources 59
3 The *Peasant Cantata* from the *German Symphony*: A Response to the Spanish War 85

II. RECEPTION AND INFLUENCE

4 Battle Songs in Times of Peace and War 107
5 Musical and Political Progressivism: Emulating the *Solidarity Song* 139
6 Critical Theories of Music and Historiographical Narratives 181

Epilogue: Memorialisation of the Spanish War 204

APPENDICES

*Battle Songs by Spanish Communist Composers* 227
*Otto Mayer-Serra's Writings in Germany and Spain* 233

*Select Bibliography* 243
*Index* 259

# List of Figures


I.1 GDR Minister of Transport Erwin Kramer presents Eisler with the Beimler Medal (17 July 1956). 2

I.2 The Beimler Medal (1956). 2

I.3 Catalogue of the KdA music publishing house Verlag für Neue Musik (ca. 1932). 11

1.1 Loose-leaf edition of Eisler and Sagarra's *Himne per a l'Olimpíada Popular* (1936). 42

1.2 Vocal melody of *La Marianne de 1883.* 45

1.3 Cover for a French edition of Souëtre and Trafiers's *La Marianne* (Paris: Hayard, ca. 1902). 46

1.4 Poster showing the figure of Marianne as an allegory for the French Republic (left) and the Spanish Republic (right), ca. 1931, artist unknown. 47

1.5 End of *Hymne per a l'Olimpíada Popular* (1936). 53

1.6 Lewy, Fritz: advertising poster of the People's Olympiad (1936). 54

1.7 Programme of the People's Olympiad's opening ceremony, 19 July 1936. 56

2.1 Hanns Eisler in Spain with the German volunteers of the International Brigades. 62

2.2 Wartime edition of Oropesa's vocal line and lyrics for *Himno del 5º Cuerpo* (ca. 1938). 64

2.3 Sheet containing the lyrics of *In Spanien ist Revolution* (ca. 1937). 75

2.4 Eisler with a group of interbrigadists, almost certainly in Murcia. 77

2.5 Renn's markings of the lyrics's rhythmic structures in the drafts for *Drüben in Deutschland herrscht Not* (ca. 1937). 79

3.1 José Renau, *Cartel. Decreto 7 octubre 1936* (1936). 97

3.2 "Siwe", *Campesinos. La tierra es vuestra. P.O.U.M.* (ca. 1936). 98

3.3 Joan Miró, *Aidez l'Espagne* (1937). 99

3.4 José Renau, *L'Agriculture espagnole reposait sur: Des salaires misérable, Une inique reparation de la terre* (1937). 100

4.1 The Proletarian Orchestra and Choirs Rehearsing. 113

4.2 The Proletarian Choir conducted by Ataulfo Argenta. 113

4.3 Example of a programme for an *acto* held in Murcia on 15 March 1937 116.

4.4 Choir of the Altavoz del Frente in the Madrid studios of Unión Radio, ca. October 1936. 118

4.5 Spanish arrangement for wind band of Eisler's *Comintern Song.* 119

4.6 Programme for Busch's concert on 15 September 1937 in Barcelona's Casal de la Cultura. 132

4.7 *Marcha del Quinto Regimiento,* as published in the *International Revolutionary Songbook,* edited by Mayer-Serra for the Propaganda Agency of the Catalan Government. 134

4.8 Edition of the French version of Eisler's *Marcha del Quinto Regimiento,* published by Editions Sociales Internationales as a loose leaflet in Paris (1937). 135

5.1 Title page to the wartime edition of Tapia and Bacarisse's *Canto a la marina* (1936) by Francisco Mateos. 150

5.2 Manuel Albero, *Interior of the "Exposición homenaje a la aviación" (Exhibition in homage to aviation),* photography, Madrid, January 1938. 163

5.3 Josep Renau, poster *Hoy más que nunca, Victoria* (ca. 1936). 163

5.4 Jesús García Leoz's manuscript draft for *Himno a "La Gloriosa"* ca. 1938). 164

5.5 Opening of Falla's *Himno marcial* (1937). 177

5.6 Republican Propaganda train being painted with the antifascist slogan "All against Fascism". 178

5.7 Josep Renau, *Industria de guerra, potente palanca de la victoria* (*Military Industry, Powerful Lever of Victory*), 1937. 179

6.1 Beginning of the lyrics invented by Schering for the second movement of Beethoven's Fifth Symphony. 189

6.2 Theme and first variation from Rodolfo Halffter's *Para la tumba de Lenin* (1937), as published in 1937 by the Comissariat de Propaganda. 196

7.1 Brecht's "Fotoepigrame" about the Spanish Civil War. 216

7.2 Hanns Eisler, *Marsch des Fünften Regiments,* in *Soldaten singen. Liederbuch der Nationalen Volksarmee* (1957). 220

# List of Musical Examples


| | | |
|---|---|---|
| I.1 | Beginning of Meyer's *Kampflied gegen Hitler.* © Arbeiterlied-Archiv of the AdK. | 13 |
| 1.1 | Comparison of the vocal melody for the refrain from Trafier's *La Marianne populaire* and the vocal melody from Eisler's "March of the People's Olympiad". | 49 |
| 1.2 | Excerpt from the *Comintern Song* (bb. 17–20). © by Deutscher Verlag für Musik Leipzig. | 50 |
| 2.1 | *No pasarán* as notated by Palacio in 1974. © HEA of the AdK | 67 |
| 2.2 | *Das Lied vom 7. Januar.* Motivic organisation. © by Deutscher Verlag für Musik Leipzig. | 71 |
| 2.3 | Sprechchor "Wer für den Kommunismus kämpft" (Those who fight for communism), no. 3b from Eisler's *Die Massnahme,* op. 20 (1931). © by Deutscher Verlag für Musik Leipzig. | 79 |
| 3.1 | Hanns Eisler, *Peasant Cantata,* bb. 173–189. © by Deutscher Verlag für Musik Leipzig. | 91 |
| 3.2 | Joseph Haydn, "Agnus Dei" of the *Missa in tempore belli* (1796). | 92 |
| 3.3 | *Bauernlied* (*Peasant Song*) in Bittner's *Der Bergsee* (Act II, bb. 7–14, following rehearsal number 13). | 94 |
| 3.4 | *Bauernliedchen* (bb. 219–226) (piano reduction from *Lieder und Kantaten,* p. 100). © by Deutscher Verlag für Musik Leipzig. | 95 |
| 4.1 | Hanns Eisler, *Vier Stücke für gemischten Chor,* op. 13, mov. 1 (bb. 18–22). © by Deutscher Verlag für Musik Leipzig. | 110 |
| 4.2 | Opening of *Marxa de l'Exèrcit Popular.* | 127 |
| 4.3 | Closing of *Marxa de l'Exèrcit Popular.* | 128 |
| 4.4 | Final bars of Meyer's *Kampflied gegen Hitler* (1933). © Arbeiterlied-Archiv of the AdK. | 128 |
| 5.1 | *Solidarity Song,* section A (setting of the main refrain), as published by Universal Edition, bb. 1–10. © C.F. Peters GmbH & Co. KG, Leipzig und Deutscher Verlag für Musik Leipzig | 141 |

5.2 *Solidarity Song*, section B, verse (bb. 11–22) followed by the final chorus, A' (bb. 23–31). © C.F. Peters GmbH & Co. KG, Leipzig und Deutscher Verlag für Musik Leipzig 142

5.3 Villatoro, *Himno a Thaelmann*, section C, bb. 35–48. Source: Fundación Juan March Library (FJML). 147

5.4 Alternative notation for the first phrases of section C. Source: FJML. 147

5.5 Opening of *Himno a Thaelmann* (bb. 1–12). Source: FJML. 147

5.6 Leaps of a perfect fourth in the openings to the *Solidarity Song* and the *Himno a Thaelmann*. Source: FJML. 148

5.7 Villatoro, *Himno a Thelmann*, section B, bb. 19–33. Source: FJML. 148

5.8 Final bars of Bacarisse's *Canto a la Marina* (bb. 112–119). © Real Academia de Bellas Artes de San Fernando, Madrid. 152

5.9 Modal mixture for setting an allusion to the Soviet Union, *Canto a la Marina*, bb. 72–79. © Real Academia de Bellas Artes de San Fernando, Madrid. 152

5.10 Opening of *Los campesinos.* 155

5.11 Closing bars of *Los campesinos.* 155

5.12 Beginning of the verse section, *Venguemos a los caídos* (bb. 9–16). 158

5.13 Closing of Palacio's *Venguemos a los caídos.* 158

5.14 End of *Canto nocturno en las trincheras* (bb. 35–42). 160

5.15 End of section A (bb. 13–19) of *Canto nocturno en las trincheras.* 161

5.16 *Himno a "La Gloriosa",* bb. 7–23. 165

5.17 Closing of *Himno a "La Gloriosa" (*bb. 42–47). 165

5.18 Closing of *Juventudes proletarias* (bb. 33–40). 167

5.19 Similar motifs open the verse section of the *Solidarity Song* (bb. 11–13) and *Juventudes proletarias* (bb. 9–13). 167

5.20 Closing section of *Alerta* (bb. 42–59). The boxes enclose subsets of the octatonic collection. 171

5.21 Carl Sands (Charles Seeger), *Mount The Barricades.* 172

5.22 Aaron Copland, *Into The Streets May First! Workers Songbook,* vol. 2, pp. 6–7. © Aaron Copland Fund for Music. 173

5.23 Alan Bush, *Make Your Meaning Clear!* (1939). Source: The Workers' Music Association, London, 1939. 174

5.24 Beginning of Francisco Moraleda's *Canción del falangista* (ca. 1936). 176

7.1 Hanns Eisler, topoi of death and sadness in *Spanisches Liedchen 1937* (bb. 5–13). © by Deutscher Verlag für Musik Leipzig 207

7.2 Paul Dessau, *Mein Bruder war ein Flieger* for voice and guitar (from *5 Kinderlieder*, 1949), bb. 1–11. © Hofmeister Musikverlag. 207

7.3 *Song of the Hostages* from *Hangmen Also Die.* As given in *Hanns Eisler Complete Edition*, Breitkopf & Härtel, 2002. 209

7.4 Ernst H. Meyer, third cue of the film score for *Wo du hin gehst.* 213

7.5 Hanns Eisler, *Bilder aus der Kriegsfibel*, second movement, bb. 19–28 (piano reduction from *Lieder und Kantaten*, vol. 10, p. 38). © by Deutscher Verlag für Musik Leipzig 217

7.6 Hanns Eisler, *Lied der Tankisten*, 1956 (bb. 5–10). © by Deutscher Verlag für Musik Leipzig 222

7.7 Eisler's *Spanien*, closing section. © by Deutscher Verlag für Musik Leipzig 224

7.8 Closing bars to the version of *Spanien* recorded by Busch, as arranged by Andre Asriel and Hans Hauska. © by Deutscher Verlag für Musik Leipzig 224

# Acknowledgements

This book would not have been possible without the generosity and expertise of numerous colleagues, organisations, and institutions. Most of the research for this book was carried out with the support of a fellowship funded by the Deutsche Forschungsgemeinschaft (German Research Foundation). My project was hosted by the Department of Musicology at Humboldt University in Berlin, where Arne Stollberg and other members of the institute offered crucial support and provided invaluable academic advice. The final stage of my research was funded by the grant RYC2021-033651-I, supported by MCIN/AEI (10.13039/501100011033) and the European Union NextGenerationEU/PRTR.

I would like to extend my gratitude to the many Eisler scholars who have generously shared their insights and opinions regarding specific aspects of my research. I am particularly thankful to Peter Deeg for his expert guidance on sources relevant to my research topic and for his numerous comments on intriguing facets of Eisler's biography. Tobias Fasshauer offered perceptive critiques of earlier versions of several chapters for this book; our discussions on interwar German music were especially enriching. Johannes C. Gall kindly advised me after reviewing the first draft of my project proposal and provided valuable feedback on several studies concerning Eisler's and Mayer-Serra's activities in Spain. Knud Breyer provided constructive feedback on an earlier version of my chapter discussing the reception of Eisler's music in Spain. I also appreciate the contributions of Eva Moreda, María Cáceres, and Pilar Ramos, who shared their ideas during the initial conception and development of my project. My gratitude extends to Francesc Cortès and Albert Fontelles for their insights into Catalan interwar music. Nicholas de Lange kindly shared his knowledge of 20th-century Jewish history and culture. Lidia López brought several Spanish films featuring Eisler's music as a soundtrack to my attention. I gained new and valuable insights into my research topic through conversations with Michael Christoforidis, Samuel Llano, Peter Schweinhardt, Steffen Just, Hartmut Fladt, Martin Elste, Enrique Mejías, Carola Schramm, Gemma Pérez Zalduondo, Lucía Cotarelo, Ana Vega Toscano, and Marco Antonio de la Ossa.

I am deeply appreciative of the expert assistance I have received from various individuals and institutions in locating a wealth of primary sources pertinent to my research. The completion of substantial portions of this book would not have been feasible without the invaluable research support provided by Otto Mayer-Serra's family. I would like to extend my gratitude to his daughter, Isabel Olmsted, as well as Daniela Gleizer, Carlos Elizondo, and the rest of the musicologist's family for sharing significant information and primary sources regarding their relative's life. I also wish to thank Carola Schramm and Christof

Kugler for granting me access to primary sources related to Ernst Buch. My appreciation extends to the staff of the Archiv der Akademie der Künste in Berlin (particularly Peter Deeg), the Jewish Museum Berlin (especially Ulrike Neuwirth), the Centro Documental de la Memoria Histórica in Salamanca (notably Víctor García Herrero), the music section of the Biblioteca de Cataluña (particularly Rosa Montalt and Margarida Ullate), the Biblioteca Pavelló de la República in Barcelona, the historical archive of the Communist Party of Spain, the archive of the University of Greifswald (especially Dirk Alvermann), the DEFA Stiftung in Berlin, the Real Academia de Bellas Artes de San Fernando in Madrid, and the Archivo Real y General de Navarra in Pamplona.

Several individuals generously assisted me with the translation and analysis of lyrics, poems, legal documents, and texts in Catalan and Russian. I extend my gratitude to Anna Betlem Borrull, Pau Sanchis i Ferrer, Albert Fontelles, and Carles Cárcamo for their contributions to the analysis and translation of Josep Maria de Sagarra's *Himne per a l'Olimpíada Popular*. I am also grateful to Julio E. Marco-Franco and Sophia Belik for their translations of various Russian sources, and to Josep Ramon Llagostera and Purificació Perona for their invaluable assistance in securing the publication rights for the images in the book..

My deepest gratitude goes to those who have consistently supported and assisted me throughout this and other academic and personal endeavours: my parents and my partner, Markus.

# Abbreviations

| | |
|---|---|
| AdK | Akademie der Künste, Berlin (Academy of the Arts, Berlin) |
| AdF | Altavoz del Frente (Loudspeaker of the Front) |
| ASM | Assotsiatsiia sovremennoi muzykt (Association of Contemporary Music) |
| CPSU | Communist Party of the Soviet Union |
| DEFA | Deutsche Film AG |
| KdA | Kampfgemeinschaft der Arbeitersänger (Fighting Union of Working-Class Singers) |
| KPD | Kommunistische Partei Deutschlands (Communist Party of Germany) |
| GDR | German Democratic Republic |
| FDJ | Freie Deutsche Jugend (Free German Youth) |
| HEA | Hanns-Eisler-Archiv of the Akademie der Künste |
| ISCM | International Society for Contemporary Music |
| IMO | International Music Office |
| IMS | International Musicological Society |
| IOC | International Olympic Committee |
| PCE | Partido Comunista de España (Communist Party of Spain) |
| PSUC | Partit Socialista Unificat de Catalunya (Unified Socialist Party of Catalonia) |
| SED | Sozialistische Einheitspartei Deutschlands (Socialist Unity Party of Germany) |
| UE | Universal Edition, Vienna. |
| USC | Unió Socialista de Catalunya (Socialist Union of Catalonia) |

All translations, where otherwise unspecified, are the author's own.

# Introduction

On 18 July 1956, the Council of Ministers of the German Democratic Republic awarded the Austrian composer Hanns Eisler along with 630 other East German citizens with the Hans Beimler Medal as part of the official celebrations in East Berlin marking the 20th anniversary of the beginning of the Spanish Civil War (Fig. I.1). They conferred this decoration "in recognition of the outstanding services rendered by German antifascists among the International Brigades in active support of the Spanish struggle for freedom".[1] This commemoration was one of many initiatives in the early GDR celebrating the participation in the Spanish war by several thousand German communists, most of them volunteer soldiers, and a few – including Eisler – as cultural propagandists. The Spanish conflict was remembered as the first great battle of communism against fascism, the direct precursor to the defeat of Nazism in the Second World War and, ultimately, as a crucial milestone in the "prehistory" of the socialist German Democratic Republic.[2]

The "services" for which Eisler was decorated consisted of a brief collaboration as a composer with the German volunteers of the International Brigades. This second and last visit to Spain occurred in January 1937, a few months after his first stay in the country in April 1936 to attend the 14th Festival of the International Society for Contemporary Music (ISCM) held in Barcelona. Although it is questionable whether Eisler himself regarded those services as truly "outstanding", his collaboration with the German volunteers served the GDR's institutional propaganda by integrating one of the country's leading composers and the author of its national anthem into the young state's narrative of their "antifascist-democratic" past. In the following decades, and even after German reunification, the legendary status of the International Brigades rendered it difficult to critically address Eisler's collaboration with Spanish antifascism. Thus,

1 "in Anerkennung der hervorragenden Verdienste, die sich deutsche Antifaschisten in den Internationalen Brigaden bei der aktiven Unterstützung des spanischen Freiheitskampfes erworben haben", in "Verordnung über die Stiftung der 'Hans Beimler-Medaille' beschlossen am 17. Mai 1956". This decree is partially reproduced in: *Pasaremos. Deutsche Antifaschisten im national-revolutionären Kampf des spanischen Volkes*, ed. Militärakademie "Friedrich Engels" (Berlin: Deutscher Militärverlag, 1966), 349.

2 On the GDR's strategies and processes regarding the historical memory of the Spanish Civil War, see Josie McLellan, *Antifascism and Memory in East Germany. Remembering the International Brigades 1945–1989* (Oxford: Oxford University Press, 2004); and Wolfgang Asholt, Rüdiger Reinecke, and Susanne Schlünder, eds., *Der spanische Bürgerkrieg in der DDR. Strategien intermedialer Erinnerungsbildung* (Frankfurt am Main: Vervuert, 2009).

Fig. I.1. GDR Minister of Transport Erwin Kramer presents Eisler with the Beimler Medal, together with a certificate of the award (pictured), on 17 July 1956. Kramer was selected to present this medal because he himself had fought in the Spanish Civil War (source: HEA 10346).
Published with kind permission.

Fig. I.2. The Beimler Medal (Source: https://www.numisbids.com/n.php?p=lot&sid=684&lot=1995 [Accessed 20 June 2025]).

his participation in the Spanish war has often been described as heroic, or as a logical decision for an artist with such a high degree of antifascist commitment.[3]

This book demonstrates how Eisler's links with Republican Spain and Spanish antifascism were more multifaceted and, in general, less epic than previously asserted. The study focuses on his collaboration with antifascist groups in pre-Francoist Spain, the reception of his compositional and theoretical output there, and the impact of the Spanish Civil War on his vocal and symphonic music. His activities in Spain are examined in relation to the work of several German communist musicians from his circle who also collaborated with Spanish antifascism. These include the Marxist music historian and composer Ernst Hermann Meyer, the communist singer Ernst Busch, the writer Ludwig Renn, and, in particular, the musicologist Otto Mayer, now better known as Mayer-Serra.

The present monograph extends recent international efforts to reconsider Eisler's political and artistic initiatives during his long exile as well as his influence as a composer and thinker outside of German-speaking countries.[4] This study adds to a growing body of literature on music and war that avoid centring national or hagiographic paradigms, aiming to provide a more critical appraisal of war and antifascism as cultural systems that operated across national boundaries in the early twentieth century.[5] My examination relies heavily on unpublished materials

3 See, for instance, Ludwig Renn, *Der spanische Krieg* (Aufbau: Berlin, 1955); Carlos Palacio, "Erinnerungen an Hanns Eisler in Spanien", in *Hanns Eisler heute*, ed. Manfred Grabs (Berlin: Akademie der Künste, 1974), 67–69; Jürgen Schebera, *Hanns Eisler im USA-Exil. Zu den politischen ästhetischen und kompositorischen Positionen des Komponisten 1938 bis 1948* (Berlin: Akademie Verlag, 1978), 44; Jürgen Schebera, *Hanns Eisler. Eine Biographie in Texten, Bildern und Dokumenten* (Mainz: Schott, 1998), 146.

4 Recent studies on Eisler's activities and influence beyond Austria and Germany include: Horst Weber, *I am not a hero. I am a composer. Hanns Eisler in Hollywood* (Hildesheim: Olms, 2012); Caled Boyd, *They Called me an alien. Hanns Eisler's American Years, 1935–1948.* PhD diss., Arizona University, 2013; Oliver Dahin and Erik Levi, *Eisler in England. Proceedings of the International Hanns Eisler Conference, London 2010* (Wiesbaden: Breitkopf & Härtel, 2014); Peter Schweinhardt, ed., *Eisler Mitteilungen 42 (Eisler und die Niederlande)* (Saarbrücken: Pfau, 2006); Peter Schweinhardt, ed., *Eisler Mitteilungen 37 (Eisler und die Schweiz)* (Saarbrücken: Pfau, 2005); Manuel Dourado Bastos, "Brasiliens Landlose entdecken Hanns Eisler", in *Eisler-Mitteilungen 50* (Die Nummer 50), ed. Peter Schweinhardt (Saarbrücken: Pfau, 2010), 30–31; Roberto Kolb, "Hanns Eisler, Silvestre Revueltas und die mexikanische Kampfliedkultur", in *Hanns Eisler. Ein Komponist ohne Heimat?*, ed. Hartmut Krones (Vienna: Böhlau. 2012), 133–149; Fernando Beyer, "Hanns Eisler in Mexico City," *Eisler Mitteilungen* 66 (2018): 4–11; and Antonia Teibler, "Erstfunde mexikanischer Dokumente zu Hanns Eislers Gastprofessur am Conservatorio Nacional de Música in México D. F.," in *Hanns Eisler, Ein Komponist ohne Heimat?*, ed. Hartmut Krones (Vienna: Böhlau 2012), 117–132.

5 See, for instance, Josephine Grant Morag, "On Music and War", *Transposition* [online 2020], hors-série 2. Available from: http://journals.openedition.org/transposition/4469 [Accessed 23 August 2022]; Annegret Fauser, *Sounds of War. Music in the United States during World War II* (Oxford: Oxford University Press, 2013).

preserved mainly in German, Spanish, Mexican, and US archives. The analytical approach to these sources draws on perspectives influenced less by Cold War narratives and chooses instead to privilege accounts of the subject that consider both the emphatically transnational dimension of antifascism in the 1930s, as well as the prominent movements of peripheral nationalism and national identity in Spain, most especially Catalanism. In doing so, the study sheds light on one of the least examined aspects of the otherwise oft-analysed Republican period in Spanish culture: the musical propaganda initiatives organised in Spain by regional, national, and supranational communist organisations, including the Unified Socialist Party of Catalonia (PSUC), the Communist Party of Spain (PCE), and the Communist International or Comintern, the supranational governing body of all national communist parties, established by Lenin in 1919 (also known as the Third International).

## Rewriting Music History

Eisler's two brief visits to Spain took place shortly after he became the composer of "proletarian music" par excellence, as well as a leading Marxist music theorist. From around 1927 onwards, he began to apply Karl Marx and Friedrich Engels' theory of society and history, or "historical materialism", to the study of past and present musical practices and repertoires. Working within a relatively large circle of young, Berlin-based Marxist intellectuals, he analysed the relationship between historic socio-economic orders and changes in "bourgeois" and "proletarian" music. At the centre of the circle's interests were what musicologists now term the "musical canon" of eighteenth- and nineteenth-century Western music, along with the functions of music in previous and contemporary societies, the commodity character of music under the capitalist system, and the impact of new technologies on music, particularly radio. One of their primary aims was to rewrite traditional narratives of music history, which Eisler considered "falsified" in the interests of the bourgeoisie. Their ultimate goal was to better understand how contemporary musical culture could be transformed to be more egalitarian and thus, more aligned with the principles of socialism.[6] Lenin's contributions to Marxist theory and the incipient studies on musical sociology by Max Weber and other German theorists influenced these discussions. This was the first time that musical commentators followed the example of literary scholars, who had been applying Marxist approaches to literary history since the late nineteenth century.[7]

6 Hanns Eisler, "Einiges über das Verhalten der Arbeiter-Sänger und -Musiker in Deutschland", in *Hanns Eisler. Gesammelte Schriften 1921–1935*, ed. Tobias Fasshauer and Günter Mayer (Wiesbaden: Breitkopf & Härtel, 2007), 221.

7 Günter Mayer has thoroughly examined Eisler's thought in the 1930s in *Weltbild. Notenbild. Zur Dialektik des musikalischen Materials* (Leipzig: Philipp Reclam, 1978),

The main theses of the critical theory of music developed by Eisler in the final years of the Weimar Republic are summarised in the manuscript of a lecture he gave in 1931. This illuminating essay – later published as *Die Erbauer einer neuen Musikkultur* (*The Builders of a New Musical Culture*) – is now regarded as one of the foundational texts of Marxist music historiography.[8] Independent of Eisler and his circle, Theodor W. Adorno wrote the essay *Zur gesellschaftlichen Lage der Musik* (*On the Social Situation of Music*), though apparently sometime after Eisler's.[9] In contrast to Eisler, Adorno equated non-tonal modernism with political radicalism, arguing that the public's hostility towards the music of Arnold Schoenberg and his school was a consequence of its supposed political dimension. Eisler harshly criticised Adorno's essay for its lack of explicit commitment to the workers' movement.[10] As Eisler scholars Tobias Fasshauer and Günter Mayer have pointed out, both essays are "the first significant documents of a historically-materially orientated, and inasmuch historically new quality of, music sociology and music aesthetics".[11]

Starting in 1928, Eisler lectured on music history from a perspective rooted in historical materialism at the Marxistische Arbeiterschule (Marxist Workers' School) in Berlin, among other venues. This school for adult workers had opened in 1926 on the initiative of the Communist Party of Germany, the KPD.[12] Eisler founded a study group in 1931 with some former attendees of those lectures and other Marxist intellectuals. The group met every few weeks in his Berlin apartment to discuss aspects of music history and aesthetics, taking dialectical materialism as their guiding theoretical position. Their aim was to overcome the conservative, idealistic, and non-sociological approaches of music studies within institutional musicology.[13] Among the many attendees

---

93–375. For further insights, see also Tobias Fasshauer and Günter Mayer's preface to *Hanns Eisler. Gesammelte Schriften 1921–1935*, XVII–XXIV.

8 Hanns Eisler, "Die Erbauer einer neuen Musikkultur" (1931), in *Hanns Eisler. Gesammelte Schriften 1921–1935*, 132–151.

9 Theodor W. Adorno, "Zur gesellschaftlichen Lage der Musik", in *Zeitschrift für Sozialforschung* 1 (1932): 103–124 and 356–378. The article is re-printed in Theodor W. Adorno, *Gesammelte Schriften* vol. 18, ed. Rolf Tiedemann (Frankfurt am Main: Shurkampf, 1984), 729–777.

10 Hanns Eisler, "Zur Krise der bürgerliche Musik", in *Hanns Eisler. Gesammelte Schriften 1921–1935*, 170.

11 "die ersten bedeutenden Dokumente einer historisch-materialistisch orientierten und insofern geschichtlich neuen Qualität von Musiksoziologie und Musikästhetik". Fasshauer and Mayer, Preface, XXII.

12 For information on the Berlin Marxist Workers' School, see Gabriele Gerhard-Sonnenberg, *Marxistische Arbeiterbildung in der Weimarer Zeit* (Cologne: Pahl-Rugenstein, 1976).

13 The project is mentioned in Hanns Eisler, "Die Fortschritte in der Arbeitermusikbewegung", in *Hanns Eisler. Gesammelte Schriften 1921–1935*, 109, and Hanns Eisler, "Die Erbauer einer neuen Musikkultur" [1931], in *Hanns*

at these meetings were the philosophers Hannah Arendt and Günther Anders, the playwright and poet Bertolt Brecht, the historian and social scientist Hermann Duncker, and the musicologists Manfred Bukofzer, Edwin von der Nüll, Heinrich Jacoby, and Otto Mayer.[14] The latter was the only member of the group who went into exile in Spain after the Nazi takeover.

Otto Mayer was born to Jewish parents in Berlin in 1904.[15] He studied musicology from 1922 to 1926 at the Friedrich-Wilhelms-Universität, now the Humboldt-Universität zu Berlin. In mid-1929, he defended his doctoral thesis on the Romantic piano sonata at the University of Greifswald, in north Germany.[16] The socio-economic and political difficulties resulting from the Wall Street Crash fuelled his interest in class struggle, broader Marxist philosophy, and communism. It was around that time that he came into close contact with Eisler's circle. Years later, while in exile in Spain, he recalled his former membership in this group:

> Eisler is an excellent music teacher and masters issues of counterpoint like few others. No one knows how to analyse a Bach fugue or a Beethoven sonata like him, and no one knows how to discuss the problems of revo-

---

*Eisler. Gesammelte Schriften 1921–1935,* 132. See also Inge Lammel, *Arbeiterlied – Arbeitergesang. Hundert Jahre Arbeitermusikkultur in Deutschland* (Berlin: Hentrich & Hentrich, 2002), 256.

14 I have deduced the list of attendees from Ernst Hermann Meyer, "Meine Erlebnisse mit Hanns Eisler" (Eisler-Abend Pankow Rathaus. 4 October 1968); note kept at the Ernst-Hermann-Meyer archive, sig. 156, p. 1; Brennecke and Hansen, *Ernst Hermann Meyer. Kontraste. Konflikte,* 100; Meyer, "Begegnungen mit Hanns Eisler", document from 1978 kept at the Ernst-Hermann-Meyer archive, sig. 161, pp. 3, 4; and Anon., *Protokoll Arbeitsgemeinschaft "Über dialektischen Materialismus und Musik". 15 November 1931* (Minutes of the study group "On dialectical materialism and music"), HEA (AdK), sig. 2580.

15 Until very recently, it was widely believed that Mayer-Serra was born in Barcelona, as stated in the principal music encyclopaedias, including *The New Grove Dictionary of Music and Musicians*. This assertion is a fabrication created by Mayer-Serra at the end of the civil war, when he was compelled to leave Spain. The Jewish musicologist attempted to present himself as a Spaniard, a strategy designed to evade repatriation to Nazi Germany and facilitate his emigration to the Americas, like many Spaniards. The original birth certificate, issued by the registrar's office in Berlin-Mitte, is dated 19 June 1904 (Landesarchiv Berlin, folder P-Rep-521, No. 817). Documents relating to Mayer's ancestry are housed in the family archive, as well as in the archive of the Jewish Museum Berlin, under the reference "Outline Descendant Report for Moritz Otto Mayer", Sammlung Gabriel–Salomonis, K1034, Mp. 5.

16 His PhD thesis, entitled *Die romantische Klaviersonate. Eine formal-stilistische Untersuchung* (The Romantic Sonata for Piano: Formal and Stylistic Analysis), was never published; the manuscript is lost; see *Promotionsbuch der Philosophischen Fakultät Greifswald*; and Richard Schaal, *Verzeichnis deutschsprachiger musikwissenschaftlicher Dissertationen 1861–1960* (Kassel: Bärenreiter, 1963), 84.

> lutionary art and the function of music within social movements like him. We, young musicologists, conductors of workers' choirs, writers, and composers, meet [sic] regularly with him at his home in order to analyse the great problems in the historical evolution of our art through the method of historical materialism, or to discuss the norms of our practical work within the cultural organizations of the proletarian movement.[17]

Ernst H. Meyer was a key figure in Eisler's Berlin circle and was quite close to Otto Mayer at the time. He and Mayer shared not only the same surname (though differently spelled) but also similar intellectual and social backgrounds: they were nearly the same age, both grew up in Berlin as the sons of wealthy, assimilated Jewish families involved in cultural pursuits, studied musicology at the same university, were interested in the artistic potential of radio, and were active as conductors of workers' choirs. However, only Meyer developed a career as a composer alongside his work as a musicologist. He took composition lessons in the early 1930s with Paul Hindemith, Eisler, and others. Meyer became something of a mentor to Otto Mayer regarding issues related to music historiography, music sociology, and communist activism.[18]

## Militant music

While Eisler was developing the foundations of Marxist musical historiography in Berlin, he also collaborated intensively as a composer alongside the German

[17] "...Eisler és un excel·lent professor de música i domina els problemes contrapúntics com pocs. Ningú no sap, com ell, analitzar una fuga de Bach o una sonata de Beethoven, però ningú no sap també com ell discutir els problemes de l'art revolucionari i de la funció de la música dintre els moviments socials. Regularment ens reunim amb ell a casa seva joves musicòlegs, directors de cors populars, escriptors i compositors per a analitzar per mitjà del mètode del materialisme històric els grans problemes de l'evolució històrica del nostre art o per a discutir les normes del nostre treball pràctic dintre les organitzacions culturals del moviment proletari." Otto Mayer, "Hanns Eisler. Un gran músic revolucionari", *Mirador* 400 (24 December 1936): 7. The minutes from only two of the several meetings held at Eisler's home have survived. Mayer-Serra is not listed among the discussants at these specific meetings. If he did attend, it was only as part of the audience; an "attendance list" referenced in the minutes has not survived. The minutes are housed at the HEA of the AdK under the following references: Anon., *Protokoll vom 15. November 1931*, and Anon., *Aufgestellte Thesen in der Sitzung vom 6. Dezember 1931* (HEA, sig. 2783).

[18] On the Mayer–Meyer relationship see the letters from Otto Mayer to Ernst Hermann Meyer from the period 1933–1938, kept at the Ernst-Hermann-Meyer-Archive (AdK), no catalogue number. For an account of Meyer's life and work, see Mathias Hansen, *Ernst Hermann Meyer. Das kompositorische und theoretische Werk* (Leipzig: EB Deutscher Verlag für Musik, 1976); and Dietrich Brennecke and Mathias Hansen, eds., *Ernst Hermann Meyer – Kontraste. Konflikte. Erinnerungen. Gespräche. Kommentare* (Berlin: Neue Musik, 1979).

communist movement, which was then of unparalleled size and importance in Europe. Between 1927 and his exile in 1933, he composed a large number of overtly political one-part songs, polyphonic choral works, and musical theatre scores. In communist circles, such pieces were referred to as "revolutionary music" or *Kampfmusik* (militant music). This output was largely in response to the new policy of the German Communist Party (KPD) regarding culture. From 1927 onwards, the party sought to develop a more politically radical culture, and to create more effective propaganda for workers than the style of address promoted by the Social Democratic Party (SPD), then the other major German workers' party. As Eisler pointed out, these pieces of "militant music" were composed for the only instrument that all workers possess: their own voice. Stylistically, these compositions were more innovative than the German workers' songs of the nineteenth century; such songs, known as *Tendenzlieder*, were still sung in the 1920s. The lyrics for the new communist "militant music" no longer promised an allegorical, or far-flung liberation of the proletariat, but rather called explicitly for active struggle against capitalism and fascism. The aim of these vocal pieces, as Eisler explained, was to politically "activate" the workers, who should sing them at demonstrations and other political events rather than passively listen to them from their seats at a concert hall. As a bourgeois institution – he warned – the concert was "useless for the purposes of the revolutionary working class. It can only offer non-committal pleasures and make the listener passive".[19]

One of the intended functions for new "militant music" was to instruct workers in Marxist thought by representing "the teachings of the classic theorists and agitators in great scenes and images".[20] Eisler and Bertolt Brecht's didactic plays *Die Mutter* (*The Mother*, 1931) and *Die Maßnahme* (*The Measures Taken*, 1930) are exemplary of this category. "Militant music" also served the more immediate needs of communist propaganda by conveying messages directly related to specific, timely political issues.[21] The main genres that took on this function included the political ballad and the *Kampflied* or battle song.

The lyrics of Eisler's ballads denounced certain injustices of capitalist, militaristic, racist, and patriarchal class society. Well-known examples include the antimilitarist *Ballade vom Soldaten* (*Ballad of the Soldier*, 1928), the *Ballade zum § 218* (a 1929 song protesting against the German law banning abortion),

19 "Die Konzertform, die sich im Zeitalter der Bourgeoisie ausbildete ist für die Zwecke der revolutionären Arbeiterschaft unbrauchbar. Sie kann nur unverbindliche Genüsse bieten und den Hörer passiv machen". Hanns Eisler, "Die Fortschritte in der Arbeitermusikbewegung", in *Hanns Eisler. Gesammelte Schriften 1921–1935*, 109–110.

20 "die Lehre der Klassiker und der Propagandisten in grossen Bildern", Hanns Eisler, "Die Kunst als Lehrmeisterin im Klassenkampf", in *Hanns Eisler. Gesammelte Schriften 1921–1935*, 131

21 Eisler, "Die Erbauer einer neuen Musikkultur" (1931), in *Hanns Eisler. Gesammelte Schriften 1921–1935*, 150–151.

and *Stempellied. Lied der Arbeitlosen* (*Stamp Song: Song of the Unemployed*, 1929). These and similar political songs were mainly sung in theatres or cabarets, or at political events, often by amateur singers. Some were recorded and marketed. A few of them became popular in workers' circles.[22]

Battle songs represented a new type of one-part communist propaganda marching song, one with more incisive lyrics and compositional style than either the *Tendenzlieder* or the contrafacta of soldiers' songs from the First World War sung by communist militants in the early 1920s.[23] For Eisler, these new battle songs were "the real folk song of the proletariat".[24] Among his best-known battle songs of the Weimar period are the anthem of the Communist International or *Kominternlied* (*Comintern Song*, 1929), *Der rote Wedding* (*The Red* [Berlin district] *Wedding*, 1931), the *Solidaritätslied* (*Solidarity Song*, 1931), and *Der heimlische Aufmarsch* (*The Secret Deployment*, 1932). A large number of young German communist composers, including Ernst H. Meyer, Stefan Wolpe, and Manfred Bukofzer, also created pro-communist battle songs during this period, often taking Eisler's innovative battle songs as a model. Unlike Eisler's songs, most of the battle songs by the communist composers of his circle have since passed into oblivion among performers as well as musicologists.[25]

The new communist battle songs were often transmitted orally. They were sung *a cappella* at demonstrations and other political events, frequently in public spaces. Some were also sung on stage, sometimes with piano accompaniment, and occasionally as part of a so-called *Chor-Montage* (choral montage), a scripted sequence of battle songs sung by a workers' choir, though often joined by the audience as well, interspersed with short political speeches, occasional instrumental pieces, and projected documentary images. As the political dimension of the lyrics was of fundamental importance, sheets of lyrics were occasionally distributed to invited audiences to sing along.[26]

22 Peter Deeg and Jürgen Schebera, "Hanns Eisler auf Schallplatte", *Eisler-Mitteilungen* 59 (2015), 8–11.

23 On the song repertoires sung by communist militants in the Weimar era see Boris Voigt, "Arbeitergesang zwischen bildungsbürgerlichem Ideal, Gemeinschaftskonstitution und proletarischem Kampf. Die Liedersammlungen des deutschen Arbeiter-Sängerbundes in der Zeit der Weimarer Republik", *International Review of the Aesthetics and Sociology of Music* 51, no. 1 (June 2020): 59–100.

24 "das eigentliche Volkslied des Proletariats", Eisler, "Einiges über das Verhalten", 225.

25 For information on this repertoire of interwar German communist battle songs, see Inge Lammel, *Arbeiterlied–Arbeitergesang. Hundert Jahre Arbeitermusikkultur in Deutschland. Aufsätze und Vorträge aus 40 Jahren 1959–1998* (Berlin: Hentrich & Hentrich 2002), 115–119. Lammel included many of these songs in several songbooks she published, including *Das Arbeiterlied* (Leipzig: Philipp Reclam, 1980); and *Und weil der Mensch ein Mensch ist* (Leipzig: VEB Deutscher Verlag für Musik, 1986).

26 On this type of performance see Hanns Eisler, "Neue Methode der Kampfmusik" (1932), in *Hanns Eisler: Gesammelte Schriften, 1921–1935*, 155–156; Werner Fuhr,

In the last two years of the Weimar Republic, many of these songs were performed by workers' choirs affiliated with the main association of communist musicians in Weimar Germany, the Kampfgemeinschaft der Arbeitersänger (Fighting Union of Working-Class Singers) or KdA. This union of workers' choral societies was founded in 1931 as a communist splinter group from the reformist, social-democratic Deutscher Arbeiter-Sängerbund (German Workers' Federation of Singers).[27] The KdA's declared objective was to transform the workers' singing movement into an instrument of communist and antifascist propaganda.[28] To this end, the KdA founded new choirs, organised *Montages*, and fostered collaborations between choirs and agitprop groups. Unlike the socialist Deutscher Arbeiter-Sängerbund, which favoured a repertoire of choral works with minimal political content, the KdA promoted the singing of overtly political pieces outside of the "bourgeois" concert hall, at demonstrations and other political events, typically in public spaces.

Eisler and Ernst H. Meyer were the most prominent figures within the KdA. The latter was the editor-in-chief of the monthly periodical of the KdA, the *Kampfmusik* (Militant Music). Otto Mayer was among the numerous musicians in Eisler's circle who conducted KdA-associated workers' choirs during the later phase of the Weimar Republic. He conducted an unspecified workers' choir founded in Buch, a small working-class suburb to the north of Berlin.[29] As no historical sources seem to survive from this choir, I infer that this ensemble was one among many short-lived groups created in the early 1930s on the initiative of the KdA, disbanding by early 1933 at the latest. The type of repertoire sung by this and other KdA choirs can be gleaned from the catalogue published around 1932 by the KdA publishing house as shown below in Figure I.3. The compositions are divided into "single-part battle-songs" (Einstimmige Kampflieder), pieces for male choir (Männerchöre), and pieces for mixed choir (Gem. Chöre).[30]

---

*Proletarische Musik in Deutschland (1928–1933)* (Göppingen: Alfred Kümmerle, 1977), 209; Werner Kaden, *Signale des Aufbruchs. Musik im Spiegel der "Roten Fahne"* (Berlin: Neue Musik, 1988), 149; Inge Lammel, "Kampflied und 'Tendenzlied' in der Arbeiterchorbewegung", in *Arbeiterlied – Arbeitergesang*, 115–136.

27 Lammel, *Arbeiterlied – Arbeitergesang*, 125.

28 "Resolution zur 1. Arbeitskonferenz der KdAS 1931", in *Kampfmusik*, Nr. 5, Juni 1931; cited in Lammel, *Arbeiterlied – Arbeitergesang*, 126.

29 Letter from Otto Mayer to Ernst Hermann Meyer 27 July 1933 (Ernst-Hermann-Meyer-Archive at the Akademie der Künste, Berlin; no catalogue number).

30 On the KdA choral ensembles see Ernst Hermann Meyer, "Aus der 'Kampfgemeinschaft der Arbeitersänger'", in *Sinn und Form. Beiträge zur Literatur*. Sonderheft Hanns Eisler (Berlin: Rütten und Loening, 1964), 152–160. On the KdA's broader repertoire and activities consult Lammel, *Arbeiterlied – Arbeitergesang*, 125 and 252–259; and Kaden, *Signale des Aufbruchs*, 24–54. For an insider's perspective on the KdA, see Hanns Eisler, "Geschichte der deutschen Arbeitermusikbewegung seit 1848" [1934], in *Hanns Eisler. Gesammelte Schriften, 1921–1935*, 191–203.

# VERLAGS=VERZEICHNIS

## VERLAG FÜR NEUE MUSIK

### Einstimmige Lieder

| | | | |
|---|---|---|---|
| K. Rankl | Einheitsfrontlied | Singstimme | -.05 |
| | | Klavierstimme | -.10 |
| | Arbeiter der Welt erwacht | " | -.20 |
| Stefan Wolpe | * Links den Kurs | " | -.05 |
| | * Antikriegslied | " | -.05 |
| | * Es wird die neue Welt geboren | " | -.05 |
| | R.S.J. Rotes Spartakiadelied | " | -.20 |
| Karl Vollmer | Das Lied vom roten Aufbau } | " | |
| A. Davidenko | Schlagen wollte man uns } | " | -.10 |
| Hanns Eisler | Kampflied der J.A.H. | " | -.10 |
| | Stempellied | " | -.20 |
| | Der heimliche Aufmarsch | " | -.20 |
| Manfred Bukofzer | Kampfbundlied | " | -.05 |
| * * * | Lied der R.G.O. | " | -.20 |
| Lebedinez | Traktoristenlied | " | -.10 |
| Wlademir Vogel | Jungpionierenschritt | Kl. Trommel, loses Becken | -.10 |
| E.H. Meyer | * Solidarität | Singstimme | -.10 5 |
| | * Auf die Straße | " | -.10 5 |

### Männerchöre

| | | | |
|---|---|---|---|
| Karl Rankl | Das Lied vom Abbau | Partitur | -.20 |
| Lied v. H. Eisler f. Männerchor bearb. v. K. Rankl | * Spartakus 1919 | " | -.20 |
| | | Singstimme | -.05 |
| Karl Vollmer | Der Erwerbslosenmarsch | Partitur | -.20 |
| | | Singstimme | -.10 |

### Gem. Chöre

| | | | |
|---|---|---|---|
| Szabo | Sowjetstern sei die Parole, Werk für Gem. Chor (a capella in sechs Sätzen). | Partitur | -.50 |
| | | Singstimme | -.15 |
| Hans Schroeder | Stalin spricht, vierstimmiger gem. a capella Chor. | Partitur | -.40 |
| | | Singstimme | -.10 |
| Karl Vollmer | Spätsommerlied | Partitur | -.20 |
| | | Singstimme | -.10 |
| | Gelöbnis der Betriebsarbeiter | Partitur | -.20 |
| | | Singstimme | -.10 |
| | Dann gibt es Arbeit | Partitur | -.10 |
| A. Koster | Es marschiert eine Riesenarmee | Partitur | -.10 |
| H. Eisler bearb. v. Rankl | * Spartakus 1919 | " | -.20 |
| | | Singstimme | -.10 5 |
| K. Rankl | * Chorstück f. Naturschwärmer | Partitur | -.20 |
| | | Singstimme | -.05 |

* Neuerscheinungen!

Zu beziehen durch: Richard Gierschner Berlin O.17, Breslauer Str. 14.

Auf alle im eigenen Verlag erschienenen Lieder b. Abnahme v. 20 Stimmen 25% Rabatt. Außerdem vermitteln wir sämtl. in der Universal-Edition erschienenen Eisler-Chöre.

Fig. I.3. Catalogue of the KdA music publishing house Verlag für Neue Musik, ca. 1932. Source: Arbeiter-Lied-Archiv, sig. 2438. Published with kind permission.

The now-forgotten *Kampflied gegen Hitler* (*Battle Song against Hitler*), from early 1933, offers an illustrative example of the unison propaganda marching songs produced in the early 1930s by composers in Eisler's circle that were sung by choirs close to the KdA. Ex. I.1 shows the beginning of the song. The lyrics, by the Berlin-born writer Erwin Fritz Bernhard Albrecht, emphasise workers' identity as an organised collective, urging them to join the communist ranks, rather than the Nazis. Based on this text, I propose that the *Kampflied gegen Hitler* was created as a campaign song for the German Communist Party to use during the electoral campaign leading up to the March 1933 German federal election, which took place shortly after the Reichstag fire.[31] The lyrics' first stanza and refrain read:

Prolet, Beamter, Bauer, Angestellter!
Der Feind kürzt euch die Löhne und Gehälter!
Der Feind hat feine Wagen,
der Feind füllt sich den Magen!
Wir haben nichts als bittere Not zu tragen!

*Refrain*
Kein Hitler, kein schwarzweißrotes Band
hilft uns aus unseren Nöten!
Reicht endlich euch die Bruderhand,
ihr kämpfenden Proleten!
Uns kann nicht Thyssen noch Prinz Auwi befreien
Darum schließen wir die roten Kämpferreih'n
Die rote Front sprengt unsere Fesseln entzwei
Der Kommunismus macht uns frei!
[two stanzas follow]

Proletarian, civil servant, peasant, employee!
The enemy is cutting your wages and salaries!
The enemy has fine cars,
the enemy fills his stomach!
We have nothing but bitter misery to bear!

*Refrain*
No Hitler, no black-white-red ribbon[32]
will help us leave our misery!
Extend at last the hand of brotherhood,
you fighting proletarians!
Thyssen or Prince Auwi[33] cannot liberate us
That's why we join the Red Fighter Columns
The red front shall burst our shackles to pieces
Communism will set us free!
[two stanzas follow]

31 I am grateful to Peter Deeg for drawing my attention to the song's probable connection to the election campaign.

32 The colours of the Third Reich's heraldry, as well as those of the "Kampffront Schwarz-Weiß-Rot," an electoral alliance of disparate conservative parties formed on 11 February 1933.

33 German businessman Franz Thyssen (1873–1951) and Prince August Wilhelm of Prussia (1887–1949), commonly known by his popular nickname "Auwi", both

Ex. I.1. Beginning of Meyer's *Kampflied gegen Hitler.* Source: Akademie der Künste, Berlin, Arbeiterlied-Archiv Nr. 3167.

## Taking Action

Among the approximately 50,000 people who left Germany in 1933 to escape Nazi repression were virtually all the members of Eisler's circle of Marxist musicians. Eisler fled to Austria in January 1933 while Ernst H. Meyer to France, in May. Otto Mayer also left Berlin around that May together with his partner Karin Gaster. They had begun preparing for their exile months in advance. Five days after Adolf Hitler was sworn in as Chancellor of Germany, Mayer obtained a Spanish diplomatic passport through the mediation of the influential Spanish communist politician Manuel Serra i Moret.[34] Twenty years Mayer's senior, Serra was an influential socialist politician in Catalonia at that time. The passport is the earliest document to record the Spanish politician's first surname "Serra" as Mayer's second surname. The addition of the second surname suggests that Otto Mayer likely intended to pass himself off as a Spanish or half-Spanish relative of the politician, following the Spanish tradition of using two surnames, with the first derived from one's father, and the second from one's mother. When the civil war ended, Mayer permanently adopted the first surname of the politician, whose help had been crucial for him in Spain.[35] Manuel Serra's biographers have not documented any significant links between the politician and Germany. How, when and where he and Otto Mayer met and became friends remains unknown.[36] Before meeting him, Mayer-Serra

supported National Socialism in 1933.

34 Otto Mayer, Passport, No. F694, issued by the Spanish Ministry of Foreign Affairs in Figueras on 4 February 1933 (family archive).

35 Throughout this book, I use the composite surname "Mayer-Serra", by which the musicologist has been known internationally ever since. The only exception is the references to documents he signed or published under his birth surname, Mayer.

36 On Manuel Serra's life and work, see Antoni Jutglar, ed., *Manuel Serra i Moret.*

and Gaster lacked any significant ties to Spain. They had no apparent Spanish relatives or Sephardic ancestry by which they might have facilitated asylum there.[37] Neither spoke Spanish or Catalan, and Mayer-Serra had not shown any prior interest in the country or its culture.[38] Their decision to move to Spain instead of another, more prosperous American or Western European country was seemingly motivated by the help offered by the Catalan politician and by the fact that Spain, unlike other countries, did not require a permit to work as part of their application for asylum.

In his first surviving letters to his friend Ernst H. Meyer, dated some three months after settling in Barcelona, Mayer-Serra lamented his lack of financial means and confused state of mind: "We follow with great attention all the events, announcements, laws, etc. [in Germany] and the sobriety of these reports cannot hide from us the horror of what is actually happening".[39] As for the Spanish communist movement, he explained that the situation was bleak: the Spanish Communist Party was politically insignificant; the Communist Catalan-nationalist party Bloque Obrero y Campesino (Workers' and Peasants' Bloc) was larger and better organised but opposed the Comintern: "The people in the [socialist and anarcho-syndicalist] trade unions are just as ghastly and stuffy as in Germany and have no idea about politics, let alone Marxism."[40]

Mayer-Serra expressed his desire to organise musical propaganda activities in Barcelona similar to those he and his colleagues had promoted in Berlin: "Nothing is closer to my heart now than to work entirely and intensively in politics, but, my dear, do we really still have the unwavering drive to join any party with full sails?"[41] He also acknowledged his fears and doubts, including some ominous thoughts:

---

*Introducción al "Manifiesto comunista" y otros escritos* (Barcelona: Anthropos, 1984), 7–103; Miquel-Àngel Velasco Martín, *Manuel Serra i Moret* (Vic: Patronat d'Estudis Ausonencs, 2009); and Ricard Alcaraz i González, *La Unió Socialista de Catalunya (1923–1936)* (Barcelona: Magrana, 1987).

37 Email from Mayer-Serra's daughter Isabel Olmsted to the author, 17 February 2019.

38 On Mayer-Serra's lack of knowledge of Spanish musicology in mid-1933, see his "Mossèn Higini Anglès. Un gran musicòleg català", *Mirador* 249 (9 November 1933): 8.

39 "Wir verfolgen mit grosser Aufmerksamkeit alle Vorgänge, Bekanntmachungen, Gesetze usw. und die Nüchternheit dieser Nachrichten kann uns nicht über die Grauenhaftigkeit der eigentlichen Geschehnisse hinwegtäuschen". Letter from Otto Mayer to Ernst H. Meyer, 27 July 1933 (Ernst-Hermann-Meyer-Archive. AdK, no catalogue number).

40 "Die Leute in den Gewerkschaften sind genau so grässlich und spießig wie in Deutschland und haben von Politik, geschweige denn von Marxismus, keinen blassen Dunst." Letter from Otto Mayer to Ernst H. Meyer, 22 August 1933 (Ernst-Hermann-Meyer-Archive (AdK), no catalogue number).

41 "Mir liegt auch nichts näher, als jetzt mit aller Intensivität politisch wirken zu wollen, aber, mein Lieber, haben wir denn wirklich noch den ungebrochenen Elan, um uns mit vollen Segeln irgend einer Partei anzuschliessen?" Letter from Otto Mayer to Ernst H.

...this is what I am asking you here: in the face of a completely deadlocked situation [in Spain], in the face of all the symptoms that point to a none too distant collapse of the republican government and to a breakthrough of reactionary and clerical forces: should we once again engage with all the fire of our idealism and act as if this world could really be ours [communists'] soon? After all that we have been through, can we create a choir again and raise hopes and aspirations through our songs? In short, can we re-create that eschatological mood in which, if we are honest and if we interpret the symptoms correctly, we simply can no longer believe? You write that there is no more compromise and no more mercy. You talk about taking action and intervening in the world. What does the German collapse teach us if not that the commitment of so many individual militants cannot remedy the problem itself, because the objective situation simply overrides us. It is difficult for me to say this, but I have to ask you a very urgent question, and I await an equally urgent answer from you in a joyous moment: Doesn't it seem that, in this time of the last desperate struggle by capitalism for its continued existence, our time has simply not yet come? Isn't it a waste of precious energy when the communists in Germany now simply allow themselves to be slaughtered? The slogan, however broadly interpreted, that a lost battle is better than complete inaction, is really not enough here... Maybe you know the answer to this whole load of pessimism. It probably won't prevent me from doing what I think deep down is wrong [i.e., communist activism] and from seeking political effectiveness here.[42]

---

Meyer, 22 August 1933 (Ernst-Hermann-Meyer-Archive (AdK), no catalogue number).

42 "Aber, das frage ich Dich hier, sollen wir uns noch einmal angesichts einer völlig verfahrenen Situation, angesichts all der Symptome, die auf einen nicht mehr sehr fernen Zusammenbruch der republikanischen Regierung und auf einen Durchbruch reaktionärer und klerikaler Kräfte deuten – sollen wir uns da noch einmal mit den ganzen Temperamenten unseres Idealismus einsetzen und so tun, als ob diese Welt wirklich sobald unser sein könnte? Können wir es, nach all dem, was wir erlebt haben, verantworten, sei es auch nur wieder einen Chor zusammenzubringen und durch unsere Lieder Hoffnungen und Sehnsüchte, kurz jene eschatologische Stimmung wieder zu erzeugen, an die wir doch eigentlich, wenn wir ehrlich sind und wenn wir die Symptome richtig interpretieren, ganz einfach selber nicht glauben dürfen. Du schreibst, Kompromisse und Pardon gibt es nicht mehr. Du sprichst von Hineinspringen, Eigreifen in diese Welt. Was lehrt uns denn der deutsche Zusammenbruch anders, als dass der Einsatz noch so viel einzelner Kämpfer die Sache selbst nicht retten kann, weil die objektive Situation einfach über uns weggeht. Es ist mir schwer, das, auszusprechen, aber ich muss Dich doch einmal ganz eindringlich fragen, und erwarte in einer glücklichen Stunde von Dir darauf eine eben so eindringliche Antwort: Scheint es nicht so, als ob in dieser Zeit des letzten verzweifelten Ringens des Kapitalismus um seine Weiterexistenz einfach unsere Zeit noch nicht gekommen ist? Ist es nicht eine Vergeudung wertvoller Energien, wenn die Kommunisten jetzt in Deutschland sich einfach abschlachten lassen? Dafür reicht doch wirklich die noch so weitherzig interpretierte Parole nicht aus, dass eine verlorene Schlacht besser als

The political activities in which Mayer-Serra wanted to engage included the creation of a workers' choir similar to the one he had conducted in Berlin, lecturing workers on the power of music for political "activation", and even the publication of a Spanish translation of Hitler's *Mein Kampf* (*My Struggle*), consisting of annotated excerpts from the book that compared Hitler's ideas "with today's reality: [through] newspaper clippings, reports, legal texts, etc.":

> You see, I am moving in all directions. I am fully aware that I am becoming deeply involved in politics and, as you know from your own activity. I will certainly also be entangled in all kinds of controversies – here even more so than in Berlin, but I believe I have no other choice. I would rather experience an end with horror in a few years than remain unable to do anything in the meantime.[43]

In the same letter, Mayer-Serra asked Meyer to send him handwritten copies of "all our unison songs" to Barcelona. He would then translate them into Catalan. Mayer-Serra specifically requested six songs that he remembered as particularly effective, including Eisler's *Kampflied für die IAH* (*Battle Song for the Internationale Arbeiterhilfe*, 1931), *Solidarity Song* (1931), and *Der heimliche Aufmarsch* (*The Secret Deployment*, 1930), as well as Meyer's own *Auf die Straße!* (*To the Streets!*, 1932).[44] All these songs had been part of the KdA repertoire. A few weeks later, Mayer-Serra received an unknown number of handwritten songs from Meyer. With these scores in hand, Mayer-Serra wrote back to Meyer, expressing his gratitude: "I can now try to organise something here [...] an extraordinarily impressive *Montage* can be made".[45] We do not

völlige Untätigkeit ist... Vielleicht weisst du Antwort auf diesen ganzen Haufen von Pessimismus. Er wird mich wahrscheinlich nicht hindern können, trotzdem das zu tun, was ich innerlich für falsch halte und hier politische Wirksamkeit zu suchen". Letter from Otto Mayer to Ernst H. Meyer, 22 August 1933 (Ernst-Hermann-Meyer-Archive (AdK), no catalogue number).

43 "Ausserdem möchte ich gerne eine spanische Übersetzung von Hitlers "Mein Kampf" in die Wege leiten und verhandele gerade darüber. (Auszüge mit Gegenüberstellungen aus der heutigen Wirklichkeit, Zeitungsausschnitten, Berichte, Gesetztexte, etc.) / Du siehst ich rege mich nach allen Seiten hin. Ich bin mir vollkommen darüber klar, dass ich sehr stark ins Politische hineinkomme und mich bestimmt auch, das weisst Du ja von Deiner eigenen Tätigkeit her, hier noch viel mehr als in Berlin in allerlei Gegensätzlichkeiten begeben werde, aber meines Erachtens bleibt mir nichts anderes übrig. Ich will dann lieber nach ein paar Jahren ein Ende mit Schrecken erleben, als die ganze Zwischenzeit nichts unternehmen zu können." Letter from Otto Mayer to Ernst H. Meyer, 27 July 1933 (Ernst-Hermann-Meyer-Archive (AdK), no catalogue number).

44 Letter from Otto Mayer to Ernst Hermann Meyer, July 27 1933 (Ernst-Hermann-Meyer-Archive at the Akademie der Künste, Berlin; no catalogue number). On this repertory see my "Transnational Networks of Communist Musical Propaganda in the Spanish Civil War", *Journal of War & Culture Studies*, 14, no. 4 (2021): 1–25.

45 "Ich kann nun versuchen, organisatorisch hier etwas aufzubauen. Schon aus den bis jetzt vorhandene Melodien lässt sich eine ausserordentlich eindrucksvolle Montage

know which songs Meyer then sent to Mayer-Serra, except for Meyer's *Kampflied gegen Hitler* (*Battle Song against Hitler*), which Mayer-Serra praised in his reply.[46]

Since Mayer-Serra's personal papers from his time in Spain are lost, it remains difficult to ascertain whether he actually tried to establish a workers' choir in Barcelona, created any Catalan versions of the German battle-songs, or organised anything similar to the *Montages* formerly promoted by communist musicians in Berlin. The lack of coverage for such events in the Catalan press suggests he probably did not succeed in doing so. He certainly failed to publish an annotated version of *Mein Kampf*, as the only surviving Spanish version of Hitler's book distributed in Spain was published in 1935 by the central publishing house of the Nazi Party in Munich.[47]

These attempts failed in part due to Mayer-Serra's need to keep a low profile as a communist activist so as not to jeopardise the position as music journalist he achieved from late 1933 onwards at some important "bourgeois" periodicals, including the *Mirador*, then one of the most renowned Catalan journals. More importantly, the lack of a solid network of Spanish communist organisations made any form of communist activism much more difficult than it had been in Weimar Berlin. It was not until the beginning of the civil war, in the new, largely pro-communist context that emerged on the Republican side, that he was able to widely apply the methods of German communist musical propaganda in Spain and disseminate international repertoires of battle songs. He carried out this work mainly in his capacity as head of the music department in the Comissariat de Propaganda de la Generalitat de Catalunya (Propaganda Agency of the Catalan Government), and as secretary of propaganda for the music department of the communist-controlled Casal de la Cultura (House of Culture), both in Barcelona.

During the war, Mayer-Serra combined this work with his regular activities as a music journalist, mainly for two important periodicals controlled by the Catalan communist party PSUC. Occasionally, he also published in other reputable Spanish periodicals, including the journal of the wartime governmental organisation Consejo Central de la Música (Central Music Council). In a few of his prewar writings and in most of his wartime articles, he outlined aspects of a Marxist historiography of music based on Eisler's critical theories of music. In the history of Spanish and Catalan musicology, these writings are significant for being the first and practically the only studies to elaborate on certain aspects of a historical-materialist narrative of music history. They were the main channel through which some of Eisler's main historiographical positions became known in Republican Spain.

---

machen", letter from Otto Mayer to Ernst Hermann Meyer, 22 August 1933 (Ernst-Hermann-Meyer-Archive at the Akademie der Künste, Berlin, no catalogue number).

46 Letter from Otto Mayer to Ernst Hermann Meyer, 22 August 1933 (Ernst-Hermann-Meyer-Archive at the Akademie der Künste, Berlin, no catalogue number).

47 Adolf Hitler, *Mi lucha* (Barcelona: Casa Editorial Araluce, 1935).

## Eisler and Spanish Antifascism

After fleeing Germany in 1933, Eisler and Mayer-Serra met again in April 1936 in Barcelona. The composer had travelled to the city to attend the 14th Festival of the International Society of Contemporary Music. Spain was then undergoing significant political changes that brought great hope to the left. A few weeks earlier, the PCE had first entered government as part of a democratically elected left-wing coalition, the Frente Popular. As a result, the Comintern and the Comintern-affiliated PCE began that spring to wield significant political influence in Spain for the very first time. According to Mayer-Serra, Eisler was particularly optimistic about this political context in Spain.[48]

In Barcelona, Eisler came into contact with Catalan communist activists and learned about efforts to organise the so-called "People's Olympiad" in the city. These proletarian "Olympic Games" were scheduled to be held that July at the Montjuïc stadium, as a protest against the International Olympic Committee's decision to hold the official Games in Nazi Germany. Backed by the Comintern-supported sports organisation Red Sport International, the People's Olympiad was one of the most significant antifascist events organised in Spain before the civil war. Eisler decided to compose a marching song as a musical emblem for the Games. The organising committee received the score a few weeks later from London, where Eisler had gone for work. The renowned Catalan poet Josep María de Sagarra provided lyrics to the song. Eisler and Sagarra's *Himne per a l'Olimpíada Popular* (*Hymn for the People's Olympiad*) – as the piece was titled – can be considered the proletarian, antifascist counterpart to the fundamentally different *Olympische Hymne* (*Olympic Hymn*) created shortly before by Richard Strauss and Robert Lubahn for the official Berlin Games.

Over 17–18 July, three months after Eisler's visit to Barcelona, a group of right-wing generals staged a coup d'état with the backing of an alliance between Spanish fascists ("Falangists") and conservatives. The People's Olympiad, scheduled to begin on 19 July, was cancelled at the last moment. The workers' militias, especially the anarchist CNT-FAI, took political control in part of the Republican zone. These militias were joined by some of the foreign athletes who had travelled to Barcelona for the proletarian Games. Echoing a widely held view on the left, the PSUC organ *Treball* declared that the aim of these "revolutionary militias" was to guarantee "a new form of human coexistence that does not make men devour each other, as happened with the capitalist formula that we have just destroyed".[49]

The coup quickly succeeded in several medium-sized Spanish cities, but failed in Madrid, Barcelona, or other major urban centres, which remained under government control. This marked the beginning of a civil war that would

48 Mayer, "Hanns Eisler. Un gran músic revolucionari".

49 "una nova forma de convivéncia humana que no fací devorar els homes uns als altres, com passava amb la fórmula capitalista que acabem de trencar pel mig", Anon., "L'autoritat de les Milícies Populars", *Treball* (8 June 1936): 3.

last nearly three years. Supporters of the Republican government, both in Spain and abroad, viewed the war as a battle between fascist tyranny and democratic freedom. Conversely, supporters of the rebels saw it as a struggle against communist and anarchist hordes, defending Christian civilisation and the capitalist order. Throughout this book, I use "Republican(s)" to refer to all groups and individuals in Spain who supported the government during the war, including socialists, communists, and anarcho-syndicalists – some of whom were not ideologically republican. By "rebels" (rather than "Nationalists" or "Francoists"), I denote those who rebelled against the democratically elected government of the Second Republic, or who supported that rebellion within Spain.

The PCE and its Catalan branch, the PSUC, formed the backbone of antifascist resistance in Republican Spain. Both parties advocated order and discipline at the front lines as well as on the home front, prioritising the subordination of socialist revolution to the goal of victory in the war. They called for restraint in the face of what they viewed as anarchist excesses, such as forced collectivisation, and supported transforming the workers' militias into a more professional "People's Army". Moreover, these parties became one of the most powerful and well-organised engines of antifascist propaganda throughout wartime Spain.

The Spanish Civil War was an intrinsically international phenomenon, even down to its origins. Nazi Germany and fascist Italy provided military support to the rebels from the very beginning. The Soviet Union, then beginning the "Great Terror", assisted the Spanish Republic with military experts and war materiel starting in the autumn of 1936. This support significantly increased the appeal of the Comintern, the PCE, and communist ideology in Republican Spain. From October 1936, Soviet and Comintern support helped form the International Brigades. This army was composed of foreign volunteer soldiers, commanded by communist militants and organised into battalions, almost always grouped by language affinity. In total, approximately 35,000 interbrigadists fought in Spain, though no more than 15–20,000 were present at any one time. About a third of these troops died in the war. Most interbrigadists were young, communist-aligned manual workers from Europe and the United States, though there was also a significant number of intellectuals and artists. Roughly one-fifth of the interbrigadists came from Jewish backgrounds. Among the German-speaking military units, the Thälmann Battalion was particularly prominent; Ludwig Renn, a friend of Eisler's since his time in Berlin, served as one of the battalion's commanders.[50]

50 The bibliography on the history of the International Brigades is now extensive. For insights into the musical practices and repertoires of the International Brigades, see Javier Pérez, *La música en las brigadas internacionales. Las canciones como estrategia de guerra* (PhD diss., Universidad de Castilla-La Mancha, 2014); Joaquina Labajo, "Compartiendo canciones y utopías. El caso de los voluntarios Internacionales en la Guerra Civil española", *Trans. Revista Transcultural de Música* 8 (2004) (accessed online); "La práctica de una memoria sostenible. El repertorio de las canciones internacionales durante la guerra civil española", *ARBOR. Ciencia, Pensamiento y Cultura* 187 (2011): 847–856.

One of the primary motivations for most of these foreign volunteers was their despair at the failure of the democratic powers to oppose an increasingly aggressive international fascist movement. An American volunteer named Gene Wolman summed up his reasoning in July 1937, shortly before his death at the front: "For the first time in history, for the first time since Fascism began systematically throttling and rending all we hold dear, we are getting the opportunity to fight back". In Spain, "finally the oppressed of the Earth are united, here finally we have weapons, here we can fight back. Here, even if we lose [...] in the fight itself, in the weakening of Fascism, we will have won".[51] Although Eisler probably thought along similar lines, his visit may not have been entirely based on his own initiative; rather, Ludwig Renn appears to have requested his presence.

The scarcity of effective composers in Spain capable of producing Eisler's highly regarded sort of propaganda battle songs prompted Renn, and potentially other communist propagandists active in the country, to pull strings in order to bring the composer to Spain. Battle songs were urgently needed by the Republican side for live performances at the front lines, on the home front, and for the dissemination of propaganda via the then-new sound technologies: radio, sound films, and large loudspeakers in public spaces.[52] To address this lack of appropriate propaganda songs, Spanish and Catalan versions of many pre-existing foreign battle songs were quickly created, including some by Eisler. Additionally, a significant number of foreign antifascist composers, especially from Central Europe and the Soviet Union, composed new propaganda songs for specific use in Spain.[53] Spanish communist composers also responded to appeals by communist-led groups to compose new antifascist battle songs. Among them were renowned art-music composers, like Rodolfo Halffter and Salvador Bacarisse, as well as others who were less prominent as composers yet more deeply involved in communist propaganda, including Joaquín Villatoro and Carlos Palacio. Many of these composers emulated Eisler's battle song style in their propaganda war songs. A substantial number drew inspi-

51 Wolman's letter is reproduced in Peter N. Carroll, *The Odyssey of the Abraham Lincoln Brigade. Americans in the Spanish Civil War* (Stanford: Stanford University Press, 1994), 74.

52 In spite of the importance of these technologies almost no research on their use in Spain for the dissemination of musical propaganda has been carried out. A general study of the role of radio in this war is Alan Davies, "The First Radio War. Broadcasting in the Spanish Civil War", *Historical Journal of Film, Radio and Television* 19, no. 4 (1999): 473–513.

53 Except for Revueltas' *Mexico en España* (Mexico in Spain), the contexts for these songs' creation or use as propaganda in Spain are still to be studied in detail. On Revueltas' *Mexico en España* see Luís Velasco-Pufleau, "The Spanish Civil War in the work of Silvestre Revueltas", in *Music and Francoism*, eds. Gemma Pérez Zalduondo and German Gan Quesada (Turnhout: Brepols, 2013), 321–347; and Roberto Kolb-Neuhaus, *Silvestre Revueltas. Sounds of a Political Passion.* (Oxford: Oxford University Press, 2023), 77–78 and 519–530.

ration from his most iconic battle song, the *Solidarity Song*, using it as a primary compositional model.

Eisler's mission in wartime Spain was thus to serve as a composer, not a soldier, working with the International Brigades and other antifascist groups in the country. The Comintern actively supported the initiative. During his twelve-day stay, he visited Barcelona, Valencia, Madrid, Murcia, and Alicante. In Madrid, he collaborated artistically with only one Spaniard, the communist poet José Herrera Petere. They created the battle song *No pasarán* (*They Shall Not Pass*), which is one of Eisler's lesser-known pieces. Petere also wrote new lyrics for Eisler's unused Olympic song. The new version, entitled *Marcha del Quinto Regimiento* (*March of the Fifth Regiment*), played an important role in civil war-related propaganda both in Spain and internationally. Additionally, Eisler also set to music a poem by Renn that they entitled *Das Lied vom 7. Januar* (*The Song of 7 January*). Composed for voice and squeezebox, this elegy memorialised the tragic events of that date during Eisler's stay, when almost the entire Thälmann battalion was killed on the Madrid front. This slow ballad is one of the few songs written for soldiers in Spain that musically conveys the deep trauma of war.

The Spanish war had a significant impact on Eisler's creative output even before his active participation in the conflict. In early January 1937, shortly before he travelled to Spain, he completed his earliest work inspired by, or in response to, the war: the twelve-tone *Bauernkantate* (*Peasant Cantata*) for solo bass, two speakers, choir, and symphonic orchestra, composed in Paris. The figure of the revolutionary peasant, a common symbol of Spanish antifascism at the time, plays a central role in this composition. Eisler's artistic interest in the Spanish Civil War continued well beyond the conflict, especially after his settlement in the GDR. He became one of many East German creators who contributed various works to the historical remembrance of the war as a milestone in antifascist history and to the glorification of the German interbrigadists' resistance. However, in his later years, Eisler expressed increasing dissatisfaction with the GDR's growing tendency to propagandistically idealise the Spanish war.

## The Issues

My discussion of Eisler's relationship with Spanish culture and politics is structured in two main parts. The first examines his artistic and political initiatives in connection with Republican Spain before, during, and shortly after his two brief visits to the country, in April 1936 and January 1937. The second part investigates the reception and influence of his music and ideas in Spain, with particular emphasis on the civil war period.

Chapter 1 focuses on Eisler's political engagement with two international initiatives organised in Barcelona in 1936, both of which involved the Comintern. The first was the hosting of the 14th Festival of the International Society for Contemporary Music (ISCM) in the city. The chapter analyses Eisler's vigorous but ultimately unsuccessful attempts to shift the location of the 1936 festival to Moscow, aiming to enhance Soviet influence within the ISCM. It explores the political significance the festival acquired as a result of these efforts and discusses how this failure signalled the collapse of Eisler's broader ambitions to forge connections between Soviet and Western European musical institutions and to integrate the musical avant-garde into the Comintern's antifascist Popular Front strategy. The second initiative was the organisation of the antifascist "People's Olympiad". The chapter examines Eisler's engagement with the event's organisers and the context in which he and Josep Maria de Sagarra composed the Olympich "anthem", entitled *Himne per a l'Olimpíada Popular*. The chapter analyses how Eisler linked this marching song to the Popular Front and the Communist International, notably through his adaptation of the nineteenth-century French workers' song *La Marianne populaire* (1883) and his quotation of the *Comintern Song* (1929). The chapter concludes by considering the role of the *Himne* in the promotion of the People's Olympiad and its exclusion from the event's spectacular opening ceremony, in which Catalan folklore ultimately dominated.

Chapter 2 re-examines Eisler's collaborations with German volunteers in the International Brigades, as well as with members of the communist Fifth Regiment of Popular Militias and other affiliated organisations in Spain. Drawing primarily on previously unpublished sources, the chapter adopts a perspective shaped less by GDR-era narratives than earlier studies. It outlines the motivations and circumstances surrounding Eisler's wartime visit to Spain and provides an account of his principal activities while in the country. The chapter also analyses Eisler's collaboration with José Herrera Petere in Madrid, particularly in the creation of *No pasarán* and the *Marcha del Quinto Regimiento*. It then turns to *Das Lied vom 7. Januar*, examining its compositional context, stylistic features, and early performance history. This ballad was premiered at a concert organised by Eisler and Ludwig Renn for the few surviving victims of the massacre referenced in the title. For this concert, held in Murcia, Eisler, Renn, and their collaborators also prepared a number of antifascist works, including spoken-word pieces for a so-called "speaking choir" (*Sprechchor*). The chapter concludes with an exploration of this concert, during which German and Spanish soldiers exchanged performances of their respective antifascist musical traditions.

Chapter 3 presents the first sustained argument that the *Bauernkantate* (*Peasant Cantata*) was conceived as a creative response to the Spanish war. Shortly after completing the work, Eisler decided to incorporate it as the eighth movement of his *Deutsche Sinfonie* (*German Symphony*), one of the most powerful vocal-symphonic compositions written by German exiles during the Nazi era as a condemnation of fascism. Although the symphony has been extensively analysed, the connection between the *Peasant Cantata* and Spain has remained largely unexamined. In his comprehensive study of the symphony, Eisler scholar Thomas Phleps dismissed any such connection, asserting that the

Spanish war played no role in the cantata: "As banal as it may sound," he concluded, "the title *German Symphony* already entitles us to this conclusion, and a further discussion seems superfluous."[54] While musicologists Kyung-Boon Lee and Gerd Rienäcker have been more receptive to the possibility of a link between the cantata and the Spanish war, the precise nature of this connection has not yet been explored in depth. In a 2009 essay, Rienäcker speculated whether the cantata might represent a veiled "chronicle of Spain in 1936".[55] This chapter answers Rienäcker's question affirmatively. It demonstrates that the *Peasant Cantata* functions both as an allegory of the ongoing "peasant revolution" in a "feudal" Spain and as an indictment of the early bombing campaigns carried out by the Condor Legion in Madrid.

Chapter 4 opens the second part of the book. The essay explores Robert Gerhard's advocacy of Eisler's atonal and proletarian music in 1930s Catalonia. The Catalan composer was the only Spaniard who had studied under Schoenberg and who knew of Eisler's music in relative depth. In 1931, Gerhard called for performances of Eisler's works such as *Die Maßnahme* (*The Measures Taken*), and his choral works for workers, to be organised in Barcelona. Such appeals had no impact at all, largely because of the lack of influence of the communist movement in Spain. The only works by Eisler played regularly in Republican Spain were his most popular battle songs, that is, the pieces that provided the most immediate functionality as propaganda. The chapter examines the reception of these songs, before and particularly during the civil war. The study focuses on the work of many individuals that contributed to the dissemination of *Marcha del Quinto Regimiento, No pasarán, Das Lied vom 7. Januar*, and the Spanish and Catalan versions of Eisler's *Comintern Song* and *Einheitsfrontlied* (*Song of the United Front*). These included Carlos Palacio and José Herrera Petere, as well as members of the communist Orquesta y Coros Proletarios de Madrid, the Communist Party of Spain, and the Barcelona Casal de la Cultura. The study discusses the means of dissemination for these songs, including musical editions, recordings, sound films, and concerts held live or broadcast over radio. The chapter explores the two earliest recordings of the *Song of the United Front,* which were made in wartime Spain, as well as Busch's key role in the Spanish reception of Eisler's political ballads. The study also showcases how Ernst. H. Meyer, then in London, was almost certainly the author of the

[54] "Im Kontext der Sinfonie allerdings spielt ein wie auch immer gelagerter Bezug der Kantate zum spanischen Bürgerkrieg eine untergeordnete, letztlich keine Rolle. Eine Feststellung, wozu uns – so banal es klingen mag – bereits der Titel DEUTSCHE SINFONIE berechtigt und eine weitergehende Diskussion überflüssig scheint." Thomas Phleps, *Hanns Eislers Deutsche Sinfonie. Ein Beitrag zur Ästhetik des Widerstands* (Kassel: Bärenreiter, 1988), 359.

[55] Gerd Rienäcker, "Die 'Bauernkantate'. Eine Chronik über Spanien 1936?", in *Der spanische Bürgerkrieg in der DDR. Strategien intermedialer Erinnerungsbildung*, eds. Wolfgang Asholt, Rüdiger Reinecke, and Susanne Schlünder (Frankfurt am Main: Vervuert, 2009).

anthem of the Republican "Popular Army", which quickly became one of the best-known battle songs in Catalonia during the war.

Chapter 5 examines the influence of Eisler's music on Spanish communist composers of battle songs. This study analyses the emulation and reinterpretation of distinctive elements found in the *Solidarity Song* across seven Spanish battle songs composed between 1933 and 1938. The chapter demonstrates that the reasons why these composers emulated Eisler's most innovative battle song lie in an association between modernism and leftist politics. Such an association was the result of a then prevalent understanding of the history of music and the history of politics as ever-advancing teleological processes. The tendency to align musical and political progressivism within the battle song genre was not unique to Spain, but part of a wider international trend. To contextualise the Spanish case, the chapter compares the selected works with modernist battle songs from the 1930s by composers such as Alan Bush and Aaron Copland, among others associated with international communist movements. The Spanish repertoire is also contrasted with two propaganda anthems composed by Fernando Moraleda and Manuel de Falla – both sympathetic to the rebel faction. As was typical among composers aligned with the rebels, both opted for a markedly conservative musical idiom, sharply divergent from the stylistic approaches of most antifascist battle songs of the period. The chapter concludes by situating the corpus of Spanish modernist battle songs within the aesthetic frameworks promoted by the Communist Pary of Spain and affiliated organisations during the civil war, highlighting their commitment to a modernist musical language as a vehicle for revolutionary propaganda.

Chapter 6 studies the reception of Eisler's critical theories of music in Republican Spain through the writings of Otto Mayer-Serra. The focus is on the articles in which Mayer-Serra discussed aspects of the historiographical and aesthetic theories developed by the composer and his circle of Marxist thinkers in the early 1930s. Central to Mayer-Serra's narratives of music history was an understanding of classicism and Romanticism as the respective antecedents of the socialist Self and the capitalist-bourgeois Other. A consequence of this perspective was their opposition to Schoenberg's expressionism, alongside a defence of the modernist anti-romantic tendencies of the interwar period. The chapter outlines Mayer-Serra's challenge to "bourgeois" accounts of music history, using his reinterpretation of Beethoven's symphonic music as a case study – not as a precursor of Romanticism, but as an embodiment of enlightened, pro-socialist, and antifascist values. I then elaborate on Mayer-Serra's discourses regarding the proletarianisation of musical modernism in the future socialist society. The chapter also addresses the tensions that arose during the civil war between Mayer-Serra's defence of modernism as a historical necessity and the aesthetic conservatism officially promoted in the Soviet Union, the Republic's main ally during the war. The study concludes with a discussion of the scope and influence of Mayer-Serra's theories of music history both in Spain and abroad.

The epilogue provides a concise examination of the various forms of musical memorialisation of the civil war following Eisler's final stay in Spain. It discusses his 1937 twelve-tone song about the Condor Legion *Spanisches Liedchen 1937*, as well as his reworking of the *Marcha del Quinto Regimiento* in the score for Fritz Lang's anti-Nazi Hollywood film *Hangmen Also Die* (1943). This is followed by a discussion of several pieces about the Spanish war that Eisler and Ernst H. Meyer composed in the GDR during the late 1950s and early 1960s, in a period marked by significant propagandistic exaltation of the Spanish war in East Berlin. These pieces include Meyer's score for the feature film about the Spanish war *Wo du hin gehst* (*Where You Are Going*, 1957) and the second movement of Eisler's *Bilder aus dem Kriegsfiebel* (*Pictures from Warprimer*, 1957) which denounces the alignment of the Catholic Church with the rebels. The chapter then turns to the propagandistic readings of the *Peasant Cantata* in relation to the Spanish war in the context of the premiere of the *German Symphony* in 1959, in East Berlin. The study ends with a discussion of two songs about the Spanish war that Eisler composed in Berlin shortly before his death: the *Lied der Tankisten* (*Song of the Tank Crewmen*, 1956) after a poem by Erich Weinert, and *Abschied von Spanien* (*Farewell to Spain*, 1961) with lyrics by Busch. The unusual musical setting of the latter song is one of several indicators of Eisler's adverse reaction to the romanticisation of the Spanish war that became commonplace in the GDR after 1956.

The monograph concludes with two appendixes. The first one is a comprehensive list of all the battle songs written by Spanish communist composers during the Republican period for which the complete scores (typically the vocal melody and piano accompaniment) have been preserved. This has been my analytical corpus in examining the influence of Eisler's battle songs in Spain. The second appendix presents a compilation of all writings published by Mayer-Serra in Germany and Spain prior to his exile in Mexico in 1939. I have analysed this collection of articles to assess the extent to which Eisler's critical theories and historiographical narratives influenced Mayer-Serra's thinking and were received in Spain through his writings.

*Hanns Eisler in Republican Spain* thus contributes to the study of the composer's biography and music, while more broadly offering critical tools for understanding the complex entanglements between European musical modernism and the various international communist ideologies and antifascist movements of the 1930s. It situates these entanglements within the politically charged final years of the Spanish Second Republic and, more centrally, the Spanish Civil War. The book seeks to illuminate how interwar communist and antifascist ideologies shaped intellectual discourse on music, and to deepen our understanding of the ways in which antifascist propaganda became closely intertwined with musical modernism during this pivotal moment in twentieth-century European history.

# PART I

# HANNS EISLER AND SPANISH ANTIFASCISM

# Chapter 1

# Barcelona, 1936: The Comintern, the ISCM, and the People's Olympiad

Eisler visited Spain for the first time in 1936 to attend the 14th Festival of the International Society for Contemporary Music (ISCM). The event was held in Barcelona from 16 to 25 April. The decision to host the 1936 Festival in Barcelona had, just months prior, ignited one of the most intense controversies in ISCM history. At the heart of the debate were Eisler, serving as chairman of the Comintern's International Music Bureau (IMB), and the Catalan composer Robert Gerhard, the principal force behind bringing the festival to Barcelona.

Gerhard was one of Eisler's few Spanish acquaintances, having met and formed a friendship with him a decade earlier, in early 1924, when the Catalan had moved to Vienna to study under Schoenberg.[1] After Gerhard finished his studies in 1928 and returned to Spain, Eisler met him again at the ISCM festival in Prague from 1 to 8 September 1935. The festival was initially scheduled to take place in Karlsbad (Karlovy Vary), in western Czechoslovakia, but the city authorities cancelled the event at the last minute. They were under pressure from the Sudeten German Party, which followed the German Nazi party in considering the ISCM a "culturally Bolshevist" and "anti-German" organisation. Delegates from the Czechoslovakian section decided then to relocate the festival to Prague. Facing similar pressures, politicians in the capital were reluctant to give the go-ahead. The secretary of the Czechoslovakian section and communist sympathiser Alois Hába reported this situation to Eisler, who had just been appointed chairman of the IMB.

1 Gerhard was the only Spaniard to study under Schoenberg. He took composition lessons from him from late 1923 to mid-1928, first privately in Mödling, near Vienna, and then as a member of the "Meisterklasse" of composition at the Prussian Academy of the Arts in Berlin. For insights into Gerhard's relationship with Eisler, see Roberto Gerhard, "Hanns Eisler", *Mirador* 101 (8 January 1931): 5. The composer's studies in Vienna and Berlin have been discussed in Leticia Sánchez, *Pasión, desarraigo y literatura. El compositor Roberto Gerhard* (Madrid: Scherzo, 2013), 68–84; Diego Alonso, "Unquestionably decisive: Roberto Gerhard studies with Arnold Schoenberg", in *The Companion to Roberto Gerhard*, ed. Monty Adkins (London: Ashgate Publishing, 2013), 25–49 and *La creación musical de Roberto Gerhard durante el magisterio de Arnold Schoenberg. Neoclasicismo, octatonismo y organización proto-serial (1923–1928)*. PhD diss., Universidad de La Rioja, 2015.

The IMB was the main musical organisation within the Comintern. It consisted of an international network of pro-Soviet communist musicians founded in 1932 in Moscow under the auspices of the Comintern. It had delegations in the USA, Japan, and numerous north and Central European countries, including France, England, Belgium, Hungary, Austria, Lithuania, Czechoslovakia, and the Netherlands. However, it lacked representation in southern European nations, including Spain. The primary objectives of the IMB were to foster connections and collaboration between Soviet composers and left-wing composers in the West, and to promote the international dissemination of pro-Soviet music. By appointing Eisler as its president, Comintern authorities expected him to play a pivotal role in bridging the gap between the Soviet Union and prominent Western left-wing composers. Eisler, in turn, hoped that strengthening ties with the Society would foster greater acceptance of Western contemporary concert music in the Soviet Union, much of which was being branded as "decadent" and "formalist". The vice-president of the IMB was Hermann Reichenbach, a German musicologist and Jewish émigré to the Soviet Union.[2]

After consulting with Soviet authorities, Eisler sent a letter to the ISCM delegates, announcing that, given the challenges in organising the festival in Czechoslovakia, the Soviet Union was ready to host it in Moscow that November. ISCM president Edward J. Dent, who opposed any rapprochement between the ISCM and the Soviet Union, rejected this offer, citing the Society's statutes, which prevented the festival from being held in a country without a represented section. In reality, the ISCM had lacked a Soviet section since the 1932 dissolution of the Moscow-based avant-garde composers' group, the Association for Contemporary Music (ASM), which had previously fulfilled that role. Eventually, Dent and others convinced the politicians in Prague to allow the festival to be held in the capital.[3]

2 For the history of the International Music Bureau, see Inge Lammel, "Die internationale revolutionäre Musikbewegung. Eine Dokumentation (1985/86)", in *Arbeiterlied. Arbeitergesang. Hundert Jahre Arbeitermusikkultur in Deutschland. Aufsätze und Vorträge aus 40 Jahren 1959–1998* (Berlin: Hentrich & Hentrich, 2002), 232–259; and Maria Kiladi, "The International Music Bureau and the Workers Music Olympiad in Strasbourg, 8–10 June 1935", in *Eisler in England: Proceedings of the International Hanns Eisler Conference, London 2010*, ed. Oliver Dahin and Erik Levi (Wiesbaden: Breitkopf & Härtel, 2014), 51–73. The national delegations of the IMB are listed in Lammel, "Die internationale revolutionäre Musikbewegung", 292.

3 Two detailed examinations of this affair are Anton Haefeli, "Hanns Eisler und die Internationale Gesellschaft für Neue Musik", *Beiträge zur Musikwissenschaft* 23, no. 2 (1981): 104–113; and Anne C. Shreffler, "The International Society for Contemporary Music and its political context (Prague, 1935)", in *Music and International History in the Twentieth Century, ed.* Jessica Gienow-Hecht (New York: Berghahn Books, 2015). See also Giles Masters, "Performing Internationalism: The ISCM as a 'Musical League of Nations'", *Journal of the Royal Musical Association* 147/2 (November 2022): 560–571. A detailed study of the history of the Society is Anton Haefeli, *Die Internationale Gesellschaft für Neue Musik (IGNM)* (Zurich: Atlantis, 1982).

## Moscow vs Barcelona

Hába and other members of the Czech organising committee invited the IMB to participate in the official negotiations in Prague regarding future cooperation between the ISCM and the official state organisation of Soviet musicians since 1932, the Union of Soviet Composers (USC).[4] The Central Committee of the CPSU and the Comintern appointed Eisler and Reichenbach, as president and vice-president of the IMB, to represent the USC at these meetings.[5] The Soviet authorities placed significant importance on fostering a rapprochement between the Soviet Union and the ISCM, assigning them a twofold mission: to persuade the delegates that the next edition of the festival should be held in Moscow, and to prepare a confidential report on the political affiliations of the delegates from the national sections present in Prague. This information would enable Soviet politicians to determine whether the USC should become the Soviet section of the ISCM.

Eisler and Reichenbach's attempts to host the 1936 festival in the Soviet Union generated considerable controversy among the delegates present in Prague. The ISCM statutes stipulated that the venue for each festival should be designated by the delegates during a meeting at the previous festival, which meant that it could not be decided more than one year in advance. Consequently, the bid for Barcelona had not yet received official confirmation in Prague. Nevertheless, Dent and other delegates had been *unofficially* confirming Barcelona's bid to host the 1936 festival since 1933. Dent was concurrently also the president of the International Musicological Society (IMS) and sought to hold the 1936 IMS conference simultaneously with the ISCM festival in the same city. Since Barcelona had already been officially designated as the venue for the upcoming IMS conference, it was of paramount importance to Dent that the Prague delegates voted in favour of Barcelona rather than Moscow as the site for the next festival.

Eisler and Reichenbach detailed in the report the strategies they employed to persuade the delegates to hold the next festival in the Soviet Union. Eisler explained to the delegates that Western modernist composers could only overcome the social "isolation" of their music if the festival took place in a socialist country. To this end, the Soviet authorities would organise a scholarly conference as part of the festival, where composers could reflect on and discuss the social functions of modernist music. Furthermore, the selected works would not be premiered in traditional concerts but in "workshops", where modernist

4 On the Union of Soviet Composers see Kiril Tomoff, *Creative Union: The Professional Organization of Soviet Composers, 1939–1953* (Ithaca, NY: Cornell University Press, 2006).

5 Margarete Lode, "Aufgaben und Ergebnisse der Delegation des I.M.B. zum Musikfest der Internationalen Gesellschaft für neue Musik in Prag", Moscow, 7 October 1935, HEA, sig. 4548.

composers could engage with "the masses".[6] Dent and several delegates opposed these proposals. On the third day of the negotiations, Eisler and Reichenbach sent a letter to Piscator and other Soviet authorities reporting that Dent was "decidedly against us. He doesn't want to know anything about the IMB. [...] The situation is difficult. The spectre of division looms large..."[7] The negotiations continued. Eisler asked Gerhard to voluntarily withdraw Barcelona's candidacy, which the Catalan composer refused.[8] The Comintern's plan ultimately failed, and Barcelona was eventually ratified as the venue for the 1936 festival. According to the report, a "gentleman's agreement" [sic] was reached, whereby Moscow would be a candidate for the 1937 festival.

## The Comintern's Music Bureau and Spain

Despite the failure of their mission, Eisler and Reichenbach adopted a rather constructive tone in their report to persuade the Soviet authorities of the desirability of closer collaboration with the ISCM. They envisioned that the Soviet musical organisations could swiftly influence the Society. This would not be overly difficult – they noted – as many delegates concurred that the Soviet Union was indeed the only place where the crisis of modernist music could be resolved and the "calcification" of the Society effectively "liquidated".[9]

The report included an interesting reflection on the delegates of the Spanish and Catalan sections, whom they met in Prague. These delegates were Enrique Fernández-Arbós, Òscar Esplà, Salvador Bacarisse, and Adolfo Salazar, who belonged to the so-called "Madrid section", as well as Joan Lamote de Grignon and Robert Gerhard, who represented the "Catalan" or "Barcelona sub-section" in their capacity as president and secretary, respectively.[10] Eisler and Reichen-

6 Hanns Eisler and Hermann Reichenbach, "Bericht über die Verhandlungen des IRTB mit der Internationalen Gesellschaft für zeitgenössische Musik", in *Hanns Eisler. Gesammelte Schriften 1921–1935*, ed. Tobias Fasshauer and Günter Mayer (Wiesbaden: Breitkopf & Härtel, 2007), 287–306. In order to convince the delegates, Eisler prepared a speech on these ideas, but it is not clear whether he actually delivered it. The text was published shortly afterwards in Prague; see Hanns Eisler, "Zur Avantgarde der Musik", *Die neue Weltbühne* 31, no. 38 (19 September 1935): 1189–1192. The text is reprinted in Eisler, "Einiges über die Lage des Modernene Komponisten II (Anlässlich des 13. Festivals der I. G. N. M.)", [1935], *Hanns Eisler. Gesammelte Schriften 1921–1935*, 315–318.

7 "Der Vorsitzende Dent ist ausgesprochen Gegen uns. Vom IMB will er nichts Wissen. [...] Wir holen heraus, was zu machen ist. Die Situation is schwierig. Das Gespenst der Spaltung droht dauern..." Letter from Eisler and Reichenbach to the IMB (3 September 1935), quoted in Lode, "Aufgaben und Ergebnisse".

8 Eisler and Reichenbach, "Bericht", 298.

9 Eisler and Reichenbach, "Bericht", 297.

10 The names of the Spanish delegates are mentioned in Adolfo Salazar, "La XIV reunión de la Sociedad Internacional de Música Contemporánea en Barcelona, II", *El Sol* (24

bach had most of their conversations with Gerhard, who was a key figure within the ISCM and the principal advocate for hosting the festival in Catalonia. Gerhard was the only Spanish delegate fluent in German and the only one whom Eisler knew personally. "In Spain there are two sections, in Madrid and Barcelona", reported the Soviet envoys,

> The bolder and more progressive one appears to be the one in Barcelona. One of the delegates, the composer Gerhard, openly sympathised with us and is enthusiastic about cooperation with the Soviet Union, from which he expects great support for the ISCM. The IMB does not actually have a significant section in Spain, but in this case it could build up a section with the help of elements such as Gerhard. The Barcelona group does not sympathise with their [central, conservative] government either, but are people with left-wing, liberal political views, who were also personally closely associated with the previous [1931–1933, left-wing, reformist] government, which also granted them the funds for the next music festival in Barcelona in 1936. Gerhard, for example, in responding to Reichenbach's question, as to whether works with political content of our [communist / pro-Soviet] tendency could be performed at the music festival in Barcelona, [i.e.,] works that are in opposition to the political and ecclesiastic conditions in Spain, stated in confidence that this was possible. We believe, however, that this is an extraordinarily naïve view.[11]

Overall, there seems to be a good deal of truth in this report. Unlike Lamote de Grignon, Gerhard was openly left-wing. Although he never formally joined any communist party or organisation, he was sympathetic towards the Soviet Union, or at the very least, not opposed to it. Possessing considerable diplomatic skills,

---

April 1936): 2. The Catalan/Barcelona chapter was established in the early 1930s at Gerhard's instigation; it was generally understood as a sub-section or parallel section to the main Spanish/Madrid section. To date, no studies have been published on these two ISCM sub-sections.

11 "In Spanien gibt es zwei Sektionen, in Madrid und Barcelona. Die kuehnere und fortschrittlichere scheint die in Barcelona zu sein. Einer der Delegierten[,] der Komponist Gerhard[,] sympathisierte offen mit uns und ist begeistert von einer Zusammenarbeit mit der Sowjetunion, von der er sich eine grosse Foerderung der IGNM verspricht. Das IMB hat in Spanien eigentlich keine nennenswerte Sektion, koennte aber in diesem Falle mit Hilfe solcher Elemente wie Gerhard eine Sektion aufbauen. Die Gruppe Barcelona sympathisiert auch nicht mit ihrer Regierung, sondern es sind Leute von linken, liberalen politischen Anschauungen, die auch persoenlich eng mit der vorhergehenden Regierung verbunden waren, die ihnen auch die Mittel fuer das naechste Musikfest in Barcelona 1936 bewilligt hat. Gerhard erklaerte z. B. auf die Anfrage von Reichenbach, ob denn auch Werke politischen Inhaltes unserer Richtung bei dem Musikfest in Barcelona aufgefuehrt werden koennen, die im Gegensatz zu den politischen und kirchlichen Verhaeltnissen Spaniens stehen, vertraulich, dass dies moeglich waere. Wir meinen allerdings, dass dies eine ausserordentlich naive Auffassung ist", Eisler and Reichenbach, "Bericht", 292.

he likely managed to advocate for Barcelona's bid while ambiguously promising some form of future collaboration with Soviet musical associations. While the IMB indeed had no representatives in Spain, it is difficult to envision Gerhard actively participating in the establishment of an IMB delegation in Barcelona.

The favourable opinions about Gerhard articulated in the report almost certainly prompted the Soviet authorities to swiftly pursue a rapprochement with him. Eisler and Reichenbach noted in their report that "the IMB can utilise its monthly radio hour on the Comintern in conjunction with the ISCM to further strengthen the IMB's influence among progressive musicians and to support those musicians we care about artistically and ideologically."[12] This radio programme was broadcast on the first of each month as part of the IMB's activities to promote music by left-wing Western composers to audiences in the Soviet Union and abroad.[13] Eisler and Reichenbach did not specify any particular "progressive musician" they wished to promote. Significantly, Gerhard was one of the first composers whose music the IMB decided to broadcast. In December 1935, Reichenbach informed Gerhard that his "Catalan Songs" for treble voice and piano (1928–1929) would be performed at a live radio concert, which was set to be broadcast internationally on New Year's Day, 1936, as part of the contemporary music programme on the "Komintern" station. This work comprises a collection of modernist harmonisations of Catalan folk songs. Reichenbach also requested that Gerhard notify local periodicals about this Soviet broadcast.[14] Gerhard likely welcomed the IMB's initiative, as he was actively striving to establish himself internationally as a composer.

## The Spectre of Division

Historians of the Society have traditionally maintained that, following the failure of negotiations in Prague and amid the Shostakovich affair of early 1936, Soviet politicians lost interest in establishing a Soviet section within the ISCM. However, documents related to the festival, now housed in the Biblioteca de

12 "Ebenso kann das IMB seine monatliche Radiostunde im Kominternsender in Verbindung mit der IGNM auszunutzen [sic], um den Einfluss des IMB unter den fortschrittlichen Musikern weiter zu verstärken und diejenigen Musiker zu unterstützen, an denen uns künstlerisch und ideologisch gelegen ist." Eisler and Reichenbach, "Bericht", 304.

13 On this radio station and radio programme see Lammel, "Die internationale revolutionäre Musikbewegung", 239

14 Letter from Hermann Reichenbach to Roberto Gerhardt [sic], Moscow, 17 December 1936. Fons Higini Anglès. Catalogue Number M 7085/418. Documentació sobre el Festival de la SIMC. Secció de Música, Biblioteca de Catalunya. The other works performed at this radio concert were Jørgen Bentzon's Trio for flute, clarinet, and fagot, Georges Migot's Suite for solo flute and Sergei Prokofiev's Suite on Hebrew Themes.

Catalunya in Barcelona, reveal that, after reviewing Eisler and Reichenbach's report, the Soviet authorities resolved to persist in their efforts to engage with and influence the ISCM. In mid-December 1935, Reichenbach informed Gerhard that the IMB hoped "that the cooperation we have begun [in Prague] will be further strengthened at the music festival in Barcelona and would very much welcome it if the issue of the membership of the Union of Soviet Composers was brought to a positive conclusion at the delegates' meeting in Barcelona."[15] In the same letter, he provided the Barcelona organising committee with four works by USC composers, from which the jury could select one to include in the festival programme: Jury Kochurov's Cello Sonata, Op. 1 (ca. 1930); Samuil Feinberg's *Chuvash Songs*, Op. 24, for piano (ca. 1935); Aleksander Mosolov's Symphony No. 2, Op. 30 (date unknown); and Tikhon Khrennikov's Symphony No. 1 in B-flat minor, Op. 4 (1933–1935). The jury members of the Barcelona festival included Ernest Ansermet, Joan Lamote de Grignon, Knudåge Riisager, Bolesław Woytowicz, and Anton Webern.

It appears that, at least initially, Gerhard did not dismiss the Soviet works, as they are listed among the numerous compositions submitted by the various national sections for assessment by the jury.[16] This list also includes Eisler's "Sonate in Form von Variationen", Op. 6 (1925), which the composer submitted to Barcelona through the Austrian section.[17] Neither Eisler's Sonata nor any of the four Soviet works were performed at the festival. The reasons for Eisler's piece not being among the four selected by the jury from the nine presented by the Austrian section remain uncertain. Did the jury members deem Eisler's Sonata insufficiently representative of the best Austrian works? Did they consider the piece too dated, given that it had been composed more than a decade earlier? Or did Eisler's role as a Comintern representative in Prague influence its rejection?[18]

15 "Wir hoffen, dass die begonnene Zusammenarbeit bei dem Musikfest in Barcelona weiter gefestigt wird und würden es außerordentlich begrüßen, wenn die Frage der Mitgliedschaft des Bundes der Sowjetkomponisten anlässlich der Delegiertenversammlung in Barcelona zu einem positiven Abschluss gelangte". Letter from Reichenbach to the Catalan section of the ISCM at the music department of the Catalan Library, 15 December 1936 (Fons Higini Anglès Documentació sobre el Festival de la SIMC, cat. no. M 7085/357).

16 Robert Gerhard, Untitled document, Institut d'Estudis Vallencs, cat. no. 13.07.02.

17 Eisler's work is also included in a list titled "Vorschlage der Wiener Sektion" (Proposals of the Vienna Section), which was sent to Gerhard by the section's secretary, Rita Kurzmann, on behalf of the Austrian section, see Fons Higini Anglès, Documentació sobre el Festival de la SIMC, Biblioteca de Catalunya, cat. no. M M 7085/411, pp. 1–2.

18 The selected Austrian works included Mark Brunswick's *Zwei Sätze für Streichquartett*, Ernst Krenek's *Fragmente aus der Oper Karl V*, Egon Wellesz's *Sonette für Sopran und Streichquartett*, and Ludwig Zenk's Piano Sonata. Alban Berg's Violin Concerto and *Three Fragments from Wozzeck* were performed in homage to the recently deceased composer. The Austrian works that were not selected, in addition to Eisler's Sonata,

In the case of the Soviet works, it is unlikely that the jury rejected all four on the grounds that they were not of sufficient quality or not sufficiently modernist as they chose other works to perform that were not particularly avant-garde, for example *Three Symphonic Movements* by Catalan composer Josep María Ruera (the three first movements of his *Empúries*). In terms of novelty and apoliticism, all four Soviet works would have aligned with the Society's expectations, as they were composed in the first half of the 1930s and lacked overtly political content (none had lyrics or were explicitly programmatic). A more plausible explanation is that the works were rejected outright and thus not assessed by the jury because they originated from a country that did not have a section in the ISCM.[19]

At the end of January 1936, the IMB wrote again to Gerhard, inquiring whether the Soviet scores had safely arrived in Barcelona and which Soviet work had been selected for performance at the festival.[20] As discussed below, Gerhard apparently responded with a letter (now lost) stating that no Soviet works would be performed at the festival and inviting a Soviet delegation to attend and discuss the possibility of the USC becoming the Soviet section. This refusal to include the Soviet works in the festival programme occurred just a few days after the publication of "Muddle Instead of Music" and the onset of the intense campaigns against Shostakovich and, more broadly, Western modernism that characterised the year 1936. The Shostakovich affair was the most prominent and consequential example of the debates surrounding musical modernism in the Soviet Union during the Stalin era, marking the first instance in which the rhetoric of political denunciation that preceded the "Great Purge" was directed at an artist.[21] In this context, the Soviet authorities decided, in February, to terminate any further efforts to collaborate with the ISCM.

---

were Paul von Klenau's *Drei Bruchstücke aus der Oper Michael Kohlhaas*, Julius Schloss' *Vorspiel zu einem Tanzmärchen* for orchestra, Alexander von Zemlinsky's *Sinfonietta* for orchestra, and Alexander von Spitzmueller-Harmersbach's *Marschmusik* for wind, piano, and drums. For further details, see Fons Higini Anglès, Documentació sobre el Festival de la SIMC, cat. no. M M 7085/411, pp. 1–2.

19 The Robert Gerhard Archive in Valls holds a notebook (cat. no. 14.01.01) with notes taken by Gerhard on some deliberations of the jury in Barcelona. The question of whether or not to accept the Soviet works is not mentioned in these notes.

20 Letter from the IMB appointing Margaret Lode as secretary to the Catalan section of the ISCM, Moscow, 26 January 1936 (Fons Higini Anglès, Documentació sobre el Festival de la SIMC, cat. no. M 7085/357).

21 The Shostakovich affair has received sustained attention from musicologists; see Sheila Fitzpatrick, "The Lady Macbeth Affair: Shostakovich and the Soviet Puritans", in *The Cultural Front: Power and Culture in Revolutionary Russia* (Ithaca, NY: Cornell University Press, 1992); Royal S. Brown, "The Three Faces of Lady Macbeth", in *Russian and Soviet Music: Essays for Boris Schwartz*, ed. M. H. Brown (Ann Arbor, MI: UMI Research Press, 1984), 245–252; Laurel E. Fay, *Shostakovich and His World* (Princeton, NJ: Princeton University Press, 2004), 84–105.

In an attempt to mitigate the rift, Eisler sought permission to attend the Barcelona festival as a Soviet representative. Around 15 March 1936, he sent a telegram to theatre director and producer Erwin Piscator, who was then the director of the Soviet organisation International Revolutionary Theatre League, to which the IMB was integrated. Eisler explained that his attendance at the Barcelona festival as a representative of the IMB was crucial to avoid a "total estrangement" between Soviet musical organisations and the ISCM. Piscator immediately wrote to the General Secretary of the Comintern, Georgi Dimitrov, requesting that Eisler be permitted to visit the festival in Barcelona on behalf of the Soviet Union. The response was apparently negative, prompting Piscator to take the petition to Klement Gottwald, the secretary of the Comintern's executive committee. Piscator informed him that failing to send a Soviet delegation would undermine the efforts of several pro-Soviet delegates to establish a Soviet section within the Society, ultimately jeopardising their goal of "conquering the entire ISCM from within". He also referred to the newly elected left-wing coalition government of the Popular Front in Spain, which had come to power in February 1936, stating:

> This year's music festival in Barcelona would certainly help to strengthen our wishes and demands given the highly favourable political situation in Spain. It is also worth noting that our music movement in Spain is already in the process of creating a broad united front movement in the realms of music and song, and a delegation from our side could certainly contribute a great deal to the faster realisation of this goal through personal contact with our comrades there.

Piscator went on to allude to the aforementioned (lost) letter from Gerhard to the IMB. In this correspondence, the Catalan composer apparently expressed his support for initiating procedures aimed at forming a Soviet section within the ISCM. Piscator mentioned that "the head of the organising committee for the festival in Barcelona, the well-known composer Robert Gerhard – a copy of whose letter we enclose – is enquiring about our [Soviet] delegation". Gerhard and members of the Czech and Polish sections "are constantly asking us who is coming to Barcelona, when we are leaving, etc., and it is precisely these [pro-Soviet] circles that require our support in Barcelona".[22]

[22] "Wir haben Ihnen schon damals mitgeteilt, dass wir glauben, in der Perspektive die gesamte IGNM von innen heraus für uns erobern zu können [...]. Das diesjährige Musikfest in Barcelona würde durch die äusserst günstige politische Situation in Spanien sicher dazu beitragen, unseren Wünschen und Forderungen Nachdruck zu verleihen. Ausserdem ist zu sagen, dass unsere Musikbewegung in Spanien bereits drauf und dran ist, eine breite Einheitsfrontbewegung auf dem Gebiete der Musik und des Gesanges zu schaffen, und eine Delegation von uns könnte durch persönliche Fühlungnahme mit den dortigen Genossen sicher sehr viel zur schnelleren Verwirklichung dieses Zieles beitragen. Wir möchten noch hiuzufügen, dass nicht nur der Leiter des Organisationskomitees für das Festival in Barcelona, der bekannte

Not only did the Soviet authorities prohibit Eisler from attending the festival as a Soviet representative, but they also grew increasingly suspicious and critical of his long-standing efforts to strengthen ties between the USC and the ISCM. In late February 1936, Aleksandr Shcherbakov, the head of the Cultural-Education Department of the Central Committee of the Communist Party of the Soviet Union, harshly criticised the composer in a memorandum addressed to four highly influential Soviet politicians. According to historian Caroline Brooke, who had the opportunity to review the letter, Shcherbakov labelled Eisler a "Western formalist", asserting that Soviet music had lost its class content under his influence. Both Eisler and Reichenbach faced criticism for allegedly contravening explicit instructions not to attempt to form a "Soviet delegation" during the negotiations in Prague, and for going so far as to invite the ISCM to hold its next festival in Moscow.[23]

At that point, any attempt to bring the USC closer to the ISCM had become futile. Eisler recognised that the Shostakovich affair made mediation between the USC and the ISCM increasingly difficult. On 20 March, he told Hába: "You must be aware that the music debate in the Soviet Union has made these issues [mediation between Soviet and Western music associations] more complicated than they were a year ago. We must assess that".[24]

The question of establishing a Soviet section within the ISCM was definitively removed from both the Soviet and ISCM agendas a few weeks prior to the Barcelona festival. The issue was not addressed at the ISCM delegates' assembly held during the festival.[25] Unlike in Prague, the option of holding the

Komponist Robert Gerhard – dessen Brief wir in Abschrift beilegen – sich nach unserer Delegation erkundigt, sondern dass auch die tschechische und die polnische Sektion der IGNM uns ständig an fragen, wer von uns nach Barcelona kommt, wann wir abfahren usw.[,] und gerade diese Kreise wären es, die in Barcelona unserer Stütze bedürfen." Letter from Erwin Piscator to Klement Gottwald, 31 March 1936; Erwin Piscator, *Briefe*, vol. 1, ed. Peter Diezel (Berlin: Diezel, 2005), 424–426.

23 Letter from Shcherbakov (Kul'tpros) to Kaganovich, Ezhov, and Molotov (copied to Kerzhentsev), 22 February 1936, RGALI f. 962, op. 10s, ed. khr. 14, ll. 87–90; cit. in Caroline Brooke, "Soviet Music in the International Arena, 1932–41", *European History Quarterly* vol. 31 no. 2 (2001): 231–264. The four politicians to whom Shcherbakov sent the memorandum were Lazar Kaganovich, one of Stalin's right-hand men, associated with some of the worst excesses of the Stalinist period; Nikolai Ezhov, the principal overseer of the Great Purges in 1937 and 1938; Vyacheslav Mikhailovich Molotov, member of the Politburo and Chairman of the Council of People's Commissars, and Platon Mikhailovich Kerzhentsev, cultural official and chairman of the Committee for Artistic Affairs.

24 "Es muss Dir klar sein, dass durch die Musikdiskussion in der Sowjetunion diese Fragen komplizierter stehen, wie vor einem Jahr. Das müssen wir einschätzen." Letter from Eisler to Alois Hába, 20 March 1936; *Hanns Eisler, Briefe 1907–1943*, ed. Jürgen Schebera and Maren Köster (Leipzig: Breitkopf & Härtel, 2004), 117 and 372.

25 The matter was not listed on the agenda of the meeting, see Anon., "Assamblee de Barcelona de la SIMC. Ordre du jour", Institut d'Estudis Vallencs, cat. no. 13.07.03.

following year's festival (1937) in Moscow was uncontroversially discarded. The explanation offered to the press was – in the words of Spanish critic and secretary of the Spanish section, Adolfo Salazar – that "the Republic of Soviets has not yet organised its national section in a definitive way".[26]

## Eisler and the "Anti-Hitlerian" Olympic Games

Eisler's failure to prevent the musical isolationism of the Soviet Union did not deter him from attending the Barcelona festival in a personal capacity. His motivations appeared to be maintaining contact with other Western modernist composers gathered in the city and attending the festival's premiere of Alban Berg's Violin Concerto, among other significant works performed there.[27] The festival was held, as planned, alongside the conference of the International Musicological Society. The scholarly event was attended by several German musicologists known personally to Eisler and Mayer-Serra. Among them were Curt Sachs, Otto Mayer's former professor at Berlin University; Manfred Bukofzer, a musicologist and member of Eisler's former Berlin circle; and Hans Engel, who had supervised Otto Mayer's PhD thesis. Notably, Engel was part of the official delegation of six members representing Nazi Germany.[28]

The joint official opening ceremony of the festival and the conference took place on 18 April at the Palace of the Government of Catalonia, located in the city centre. The ceremony featured speeches by politicians, the conference organisers, and several foreign delegates, including the German musicologist Theodor Kroyer, who delivered the speech on behalf of the Nazi delegation. A few months later, Mayer-Serra recalled this event in an article about Eisler that he published at the onset of the civil war:

26 "Como la República de los Soviets no ha organizado todavía su Sección nacional de un modo definitivo, los festivales del año que viene no se celebrarán en Moscú". Adolfo Salazar, "La XIV reunión de la Sociedad Internacional de Música Contemporánea SIMC en Barcelona, III", *El Sol* (28 April 1936): 2.

27 On the particularly high quality of the works presented at the Barcelona festival compared to those at other festivals, as well as a list of these works and their performers, see Haefeli, *Die Internationale Gesellschaft*, 243–250.

28 Pamela M. Potter and María Cáceres-Piñuel have examined the participation of this delegation at the IMS conference; see Pamela M. Potter, *Most German of the Arts: Musicology and Society from the Weimar Republic to the End of Hitler's Reich* (Yale: Yale University Press, 1998); and María Cáceres-Piñuel, *El hombre del rincon: José Subirá y la historia cultural e intelectual de la musicología en España* (Kassel: Reichenberger, 2018). For additional information on the organisation of the conference and its relation to the ISCM festival, see César Calmell, "El III congreso internacional de musicología en Barcelona 1936, a partir de la documentación guardada en el fondo Higni Anglès de la Biblioteca de Catalunya", *Anuario musical* 70 (2015): 161–178.

> While the representatives of German musicology indulged in insolent speeches during the official reception, with none of the musicians present daring to protest, and while the members of the ISCM wasted time on their usual egocentricities and fruitless discussions, we visited several factories in Barcelona with comrade Eisler. We spoke to comrades in [communist] cells, providing him with all the details he needed to understand the social and political issues in Catalonia.[29]

Regardless of whether this claim is true or not, it seems probable that Eisler came into contact with members of the Barcelona workers' movement through Mayer-Serra, and that, through them, he learned about the organising efforts for the People's Olympiad. These alternative Olympic Games were to be held primarily at the Montjuïc Stadium in Barcelona as an act of protest against the official Games in Nazi Germany. The "proletarian" or "anti-Hitlerian" Games, as they were sometimes referred to in the press, were scheduled to take place in the week preceding the opening of the official International Olympic Committee (IOC) Games in Berlin. As emphasised by the Spanish organisers, this collective sporting and multicultural event aimed to promote international proletarianism and antifascist solidarity, rather than individualistic competition or elitist sportsmanship.

The proletarian Games were organised completely independently of the IOC, which had decided on a venue for the 1936 Games in 1931, selecting Berlin (then still under the Weimar-era democratic regime) over Barcelona. Although the Barcelona "proletarian" Games stemmed from workers' associations rather than the Catalan bourgeoisie, holding these Games represented a means of compensating for the earlier loss of that bid. The Catalan and Spanish governments, the Comintern-led Moscow organisation Red Sport International (the "Sportintern"), and the majority of German exiles residing in Barcelona all supported the People's Olympiad. In conservative circles and media outlets, the project was derided as a scheme of international leftism, Bolshevism, and Judaism.[30]

[29] Mentre els representants de la musicologia alemanya es permetien uns discursos insolents en ocasió de la recepció oficial, sense que cap dels músics presents s'atrevís a protestar i els components de la S. I. M. C. perdien el temps amb els seus personalismes i discussions infructuoses de costum, recorrem amb el company Eisler una sèrie de fàbriques barcelonines, parlem amb els companys de les cèl·lules i li facilitem tots els detalls necessaris per a fer-se una idea dels problemes socials i polítics de Catalunya", Otto Mayer, "Hanns Eisler: Un gran músic revolucionari", *Mirador* 400 (24 December 1936): 7.

[30] For a detailed study of the "People's Olympiad", see Xavier Pujadas and Carlos Santacana, *L'altra olimpíada Barcelona'36: Esport, societat i política a Catalunya (1900–1936)* (Badalona: de l'Index, 1990). André Gounot has explored the international dimension of the event in "El proyecto de la Olimpiada Popular de Barcelona (1936), entre comunismo internacional y republicanismo regional", *Cultura, Ciencia y Deporte* 1, no. 3 (2005): 115–123 and "Barcelona gegen Berlin. Das Projekt der Volksolympiade

The newspaper of the Spanish Communist Party, *Mundo Obrero*, first mentioned the proletarian Games on 3 April; however, it was not until mid-April, coinciding with Eisler's stay in the city, that the project truly gained momentum.[31] According to the Press Service of the People's Olympiad, Eisler "promised" in Barcelona to compose a representative song for the Games.[32] He did so a few weeks later, while in London for other work. The score arrived by letter in Barcelona around the end of June.[33] The piece was a marching song for voice and piano. As with most songs of this type, the piano accompaniment was intended as the basis from which arrangements could be made ad hoc for specific ensembles. Stylistically, the piece resembled other *Kampflieder* or battle songs composed by Eisler in the 1930s. The Games' Press Service described the composition as a "short, powerful, joyous" marching song that "will certainly be sung everywhere very soon" and would "put a new rhythm into the ranks of the world's progressively-minded sportsmen".[34] It remains unclear whether Eisler provided a title for the song. The Press Service called it "March of the People's Olympiad", while *Mundo obrero* reported the title as "Himno de la Olimpiada Popular" (Hymn of the People's Olympiad).

The score that Eisler sent to the organisers has not been preserved. It is possible that the document was kept in the archive of the People's Olympiad, which was later hidden at the end of the civil war, but has never been recovered since.[35] The oldest surviving musical source for Eisler's song is a loose-leaf edition made in early July by the Organising Committee. Fig. 1.1 shows the exemplar of this edition preserved at the Eisler archive in Berlin.[36]

---

1936", in *Der deutsche Sport auf dem Weg in die Moderne. Carl Diem und seine Zeit*, ed. Michael Krüger (Berlin: LIT-Verlag, 2009), 119–130; see also Gabriel Colomé, *La Olimpiada Popular de 1936: deporte y política* (Barcelona: Universidad Autónoma de Barcelona, 2008). For more on the "Sportintern" and the "International Committee for the Defence of the Olympic Idea", see André Gounout, *Die Rote Sportinternationale, 1921–1937. Kommunistische Massenpolitik im europäischen Arbeitersport* (Münster, LIT-Verlag, 2002), 213–225.

31 See Gounot, "El Proyecto", 118.

32 Press Service of the Peoples' Olympiad, No. 7 (29 June 1936). This document is available via the Warwick Digital Collections: https://wdc.contentdm.oclc.org/digital/collection/scw/id/2283/rec/5

33 The Spanish press first reported on the composition on 25 June; see Anon., "El himno de la Olimpíada popular", *Mundo obrero* (25 June 1936): page unknown.

34 Press Service of the Peoples' Olympiad, No. 7 (29 June 1936).

35 Pujadas and Santacana, *L'altra*, 181.

36 Hanns Eisler, *Himne per a l'Olimpíada Popular*, HEA, cat. no. 1092.

HIMNE PER A L'OLIMPIADA POPU.

No és per odi, no és per guerra
que venim a lluitar de cada terra:
sota el cel blau
l'únic crit que ens escau,
és un crit d'alegria i de pau.
Fora enveges, fora noses,
afirmem, contra el viure estret,
el nostre dret
a fê un aire més net
i a fê un món més ple de roses.

Cors enlaire! Llum als braços!
Siguin àgils i ardids els nostres passos!
Dem-nos les mans
per sentir-nos germans
sota el verd dels llorers triomfants!

Força i vida, primavera,
ritme, gràcia i esforç i voluntat
tots hem triat
en l'esclat del combat,
perquè ens facin de bandera!

Pel més àgil, pel més destre,
sigui el sol immortal de la palestra.
Sigui aquest sol,
que ens aplega en un vol,
per cremar la mentida i el dol!
Contra els baixos crits innobles
aixequem cap al cel les nostres mans!
Vibrin els cants
perquè es tornin més grans
i més lliures tots els pobles.

JOSEP M.ª DE SAGARRA

Música del mestre HANNS EYSLER

Fig. 1.1. Loose-leaf edition of Eisler and Sagarra's *Himne per a l'Olimpíada Popular*, prepared in early July 1936 by the People's Olympiad's Organising Committee (source: HEA 1092). Published with kind permission..

## La Marianne, the Popular Front, and the Comintern

The vocal melody of Eisler's song is a reworking of the chorus from the French song *La Marianne populaire*. Composed in 1883 by amateur French composer Léon Trafiers (also known as Saint-Ferréol), the song sets lyrics by French anarchist poet Oliver Souêtre, an active participant in the Paris Commune of 1871. The title refers to the figure that emerged during the French Revolution as an allegory of Liberty, Reason, and the new post-revolutionary republican system. In the decades following the Revolution, Marianne was typically portrayed as a seductive, assertive young woman, her hair flowing and one or both breasts exposed to symbolise motherhood and emancipation. She was often shown wearing the French tricolour sash and the red Phrygian cap, a symbol of liberty. One of the most renowned depictions of this allegory is the central figure in Eugène Delacroix's *Liberty Leading the People* (1830). Over the course of the late nineteenth century, the burgeoning French labour movement adopted the figure of the revolutionary Marianne as a symbol of the workers' struggle.[37]

The lyrics of *La Marianne populaire* denounce the misery of the working classes, proclaim hatred for the rich and religion, exalt both reason and violence, and advocate for women's liberation. Fig. 1.2 shows the vocal melody of *La Marianne*, as it was published in the late nineteenth century. The first two stanzas and refrain are provided below.

| | |
|---|---|
| Mon nom, à moi, c'est Marianne, | My name is Marianne, |
| Un nom connu dans l'univers, | A name known in the universe, |
| Car, j'aime à porter, d'un air crâne, | Because I like to wear, and show off, |
| Mon bonnet rouge, de travers | My red cap, askew. |
| Et, du peuple, robuste fille, | And [I am], of the people, a robust daughter, |
| Au jour des fiers enivrements, | In the day of proud enthusiasm, |
| Je veux, au grand soleil qui brille, | I want, under the great sun that shines, |
| Avoir des mâles pour amants! | To have men for lovers! |

[37] The history of the Marianne allegory has been studied extensively by French historian Maurice Agulhon, in: *Marianne au combat: L'imagerie et la symbolique républicaines de 1789 à 1880* (Paris: Flammarion, 1979); *Marianne au pouvoir: L'imagerie et la symbolique républicaines de 1880 à 1914* (Paris: Flammarion, 1989); and *Les Métamorphoses de Marianne: L'imagerie et la symbolique républicaines de 1914 à nos jours* (Paris: Flammarion, 2001).

| | |
|---|---|
| Va, Va, Marianne!<br>Pour en finir avec tes ennemis<br>Sonne, sonne, la diane<br>Aux endormis<br>Aux endormis | Go, go, Marianne!<br>To make an end of your enemies<br>let the reveille sound, let the reveille sound<br>to the sleeping<br>to the sleeping |
| Dur forgeron, batteur sublime,<br>Noir mineur, du jour exilé,<br>Marin, qui passes sur l'abîme,<br>Vieux laboureur, père du blé, | Strong blacksmith, sublime thresher<br>Blackened miner, exile of the day,<br>Sailor, passing over the abyss<br>Old farmer, father of wheat, |
| Des dirigeants la caste avide<br>Vous répète: Croyez au ciel!<br>Dérision! leur ciel est vide,<br>Et votre enfer seul est réel! | To the leaders of the greedy caste<br>Repeat to them: Believe in heaven!<br>Nonsense! Your heaven is empty,<br>only your hell is real. |
| Va, va, Marianne... | Go, go, Marianne! |
| [six additional stanzas follow] | [six additional stanzas follow] |

The covers for most *fin de siècle* editions of *La Marianne populaire* also reflected the revolutionary ideas expressed in the lyrics. Fig. 1.3 shows the cover of an edition from circa 1902.[38]

Sung regularly by the French anarchist singer Fernande d'Erlincourt (1861–1919), *La Marianne populaire* became well known among late nineteenth-century French-speaking workers' circles, especially before the rise in popularity of *The Internationale* after 1899.[39] Once the lyricist Pieter Cornelis de Ruijter (1855–1889) wrote a Dutch version of the lyrics in 1885, *La Marianne* was also sung in Dutch-speaking socialist circles throughout Belgium and the Netherlands. Its popularity, enduring in the Netherlands through the 1930s, led Eisler to include *La Marianne* among the ten "socialist songs" he arranged for jazz band during a brief stay in Hilversum. The recipients of the arrangement were the amateur musicians of the acclaimed workers' dance-band "De Flierefluiters".[40]

38 I thank Frank Lateur for providing me with a copy of this cover. A similar cover for another edition of *La Marianne* from the *fin de siècle* is reproduced in Robert Brécy, *Florilège de la chanson révolutionnaire de 1789 au front Populaire* (Paris: Hier et Demain, 1978), 116.

39 Brécy, *Florilège*, 117.

40 Hanns Eisler, "Mariannelied. Bearbeitung eines holländischen Sozialistenmarsches", VARA archive (SOMMZ-2623), Hilversum (Muziekbibliotheek van de Omroep, No. 194924; http://www.muziekbibliotheekvandeomroep.nl/mco_page/detail/22033.html). Eisler visited this small Dutch city in April 1933 to collaborate with his close friend, the German communist tenor Ernst Busch, who was then living there in exile.

Fig. 1.2. Vocal melody of *La Marianne de 1883.* Source: Oliver Souêtre/Léon Trafiers, *La Marianne populaire de 1883* (Paris: Joly, ca. 1883), 4.

The figure of Marianne was adopted by the short-lived First Spanish Republic (1873–1874) and, nearly six decades later, by the Second Republic (1931–1939). She was endowed with distinctively Spanish symbols. During the Second Republic, the Spanish Marianne became an essential institutional symbol, reproduced

For more on the context surrounding the creation of the arrangement, see Peter Deeg and Oliver Dahin, "Meeting Marianne in Hilversum", in *Eisler Mitteilungen* 42, ed. Peter Schweinhardt et al. (Saarbrücken: Pfau, 2006), 12–15.

Fig. 1.3. Cover for one of the many French editions of Souëtre and Trafiers's *La Marianne* (Paris: Hayard, ca. 1902). Artwork by the French painter Léon Couturier. Source: private archive of Frank Lateur.

Fig. 1.4. Poster showing the figure of Marianne as an allegory for the French Republic (left) and the Spanish Republic (right), ca. 1931, artist unknown. Source: Biblioteca Nacional de España / Biblioteca digital hispánica.

on public buildings, banknotes, and stamps.[41] One poster, created shortly after the proclamation of the Second Spanish Republic in 1931, depicted a fraternal embrace between the French and Spanish Mariannes (Fig. 1.4).

I argue that two primary factors motivated Eisler's decision to rework *La Marianne populaire* in composing his Olympic march. The first concerns the analogous symbolic meanings attributed to the Phrygian cap (Figs. 1.3 and 1.4), mentioned in the opening stanza of the French song, and the barretina, the traditional male headwear of Catalonia. The Phrygian cap, adopted during the French Revolution as an emblem of revolutionary liberty, became a transnational symbol of freedom and republicanism throughout the nineteenth century. The *barretina*, originally worn by Catalan peasants and fishermen, had by the early twentieth century evolved into a potent emblem of Catalan national identity. Eisler's association of these two caps was likely motivated not only by their pronounced similarity in shape, colour, and material, but more importantly by their shared ideological connotations. Within leftist circles, the *barretina* – like Catalanism more broadly – was widely regarded as a symbol of progressive, republican, and antifascist ideals. Eisler had numerous opportunities to observe the barretina during the ceremonial events marking the opening and closing of the ISCM festival and the ISM congress, both of which featured extensive displays of Catalan folk culture, including traditional costume.[42]

More broadly, Eisler may have related the allegory of Marianne not only to the French Republic, but also its Spanish counterpart. More specifically, he may have understood Marianne as representing both of the left-wing coalitions then in power. The Spanish Frente Popular had won the legislative elections two months before Eisler's visit. The French Front Populaire came to power on 3 May 1936, and the figure of Marianne experienced a revival among the French labour movement at that time, just as Eisler was composing the Olympic song.[43] With preparations for war in Germany becoming ever more evident, these left-wing coalitions were regarded by much of the international left as the principal European bastions against international fascism. According to Mayer-Serra's statements later that year, this view was shared by Eisler, who responded with "revolutionary optimism" to the political situation he encountered in Spain during the spring of 1936, namely the government of the Frente Popular coalition.[44] The decision to

41 Marie-Angéle Orobon, "Marianne y España. la identidad nacional en la Primera República Española", *Historia y política. Ideas, procesos y movimientos* 13 (2005): 79–98.

42 On these displays see J. S. [Joan Salvat], "El III Congrés de la Societat Internacional de Musicologia a Barcelona", *Revista musical catalana* 33, no. 389 (May 1936): 185–186.

43 Agulhon, *Les Métamorphoses de Marianne*, 83–93.

44 Mayer-Serra wrote, "A week's stay in Barcelona in April of this year gave Hanns Eisler the certainty that the social tensions in the Iberian lands [Catalonia and Spain] had created an eminently revolutionary situation, and that on his next visit to our country, he would find the political landscape profoundly changed. I allowed myself to doubt. However,

Ex. 1. 1. Comparison of the vocal melody for the refrain from Trafier's *La Marianne populaire* as published in the first edition of 1888 (voice 1) and the vocal melody from Eisler's "March of the People's Olympiad" (voice 2).

rework the refrain from *La Marianne populaire* likely also stemmed from the symbolism of Marianne as an allegory for the values upheld by the left-wing coalitions governing the Spanish and French Republics.[45]

As Ex. 1.1 shows, Eisler adapted the original melody to the style of his interwar battle songs by increasing the number of dotted motifs and accentuating several upbeats, including the added anacrusis. Moreover, he composed a new, slightly more varied piano accompaniment, as well as a new bass line that conforms to what scholars have termed the "Eisler bass" – the typical battle-song

Hanns Eisler's empathy and revolutionary optimism, and above all his analytical strength, proved him absolutely right." ("Una setmana d'estada a Barcelona el mes d'abril d'aquest any donava a Hanns Eisler la certitud que les tensions socials a les terres ibèriques havien creat una situació eminentment revolucionària i que en la seva pròxima visita a la nostra terra ja trobaria el panorama polític profundament canviat. Nosaltres ens permetérem de dubtar. Però l'empenta i l'optimisme revolucionari de Hanns Eisler, i sobretot la seva força analitzadora, li han donat tota la raó."), Mayer, "Hanns Eisler".

45 For more information on Eisler and the Popular Front strategy against fascism, see Albrech Betz, *Hanns Eisler. Musik einer Zeit, die sich eben bildet* (Munich: text + kritik, 1976), 129–142.

Ex. 1.2. Excerpt from the *Comintern Song* (bb. 17–20) that Eisler quoted in his battle song for the Barcelona Games. © by Deutscher Verlag für Musik Leipzig.

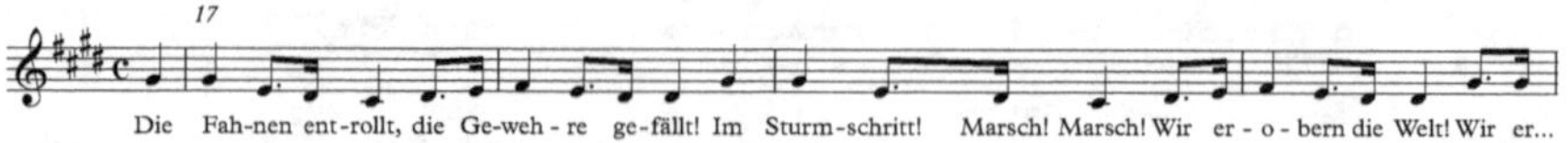


bass melody, consisting of regularly repeated semiquavers moving in steps or small skips (see Ex. 1.1).[46]

One of the most notable changes Eisler made to Trafier's melody is the incorporation, in bars 5 and 13, of a quotation of a motif from his own *Comintern Song*, the anthem of the Communist International (Ex. 1.2). A slightly shorter version of this Comintern motif is restated one tone lower in bars 6 and 14. The song concludes with an incomplete version of the motif in bar 15. These motifs are marked with square brackets in Ex. 1.1. In the original song, the lyrics of this motif read: "The flags unfurled! The rifles ready! With quick steps, march, march! We conquer the world!" ("Die Fahnen entrollt! Die Gewehre gefällt! Zum Sturmschritt! Marsch, marsch! Wir erobern die Welt!") These quotations, absent from the aforementioned 1933 arrangement for jazz band, likely responded to the Comintern's support for the People's Olympiad, and more broadly to Eisler's understanding of international communism and antifascism as two sides of the same coin. A few years later, this quotation would become one of the reasons that led Eisler to reconfigure the melody as an antifascist anthem in the Hollywood anti-Nazi film *Hangmen Also Die*, which I discuss in the epilogue.[47]

## Sagarra's *Himne per a l'Olimpíada Popular*

Since Eisler sent a song without lyrics, the organising committee asked the then-popular Catalan poet Josep María de Sagarra i Castellarnau (1894–1961) to write a poem for the vocal melody of the Olympic march.[48] The choice of Sagarra for that task might seem surprising, as his sophisticated literary style

46 On the "Eisler bass" see Tobias Fasshauer, "Fesche Märsche. Hanns Eisler und die Militärmusik", *Eisler-Mitteilungen* 67 (Saarbrücken: Pfau, 2019), 4–18.

47 The Olympic song is one of several instances in which Eisler quoted excerpts from political anthems and songs in his compositions. For an exploration of the significance of quotation in Eisler's oeuvre, see Frieder Reininghaus, "Über die Kunst zu erben und den Meister des Zitats. Hanns Eisler als Objekt und Subjekt der Rezeptionsgeschichte", *Österreichische Musikzeitschrift* 67, no. 4 (2012): 6–20.

48 Anon., "El Himno de la Olimpiada Popular", *El luchador, diario republicano* 24, no. 8578 (8 July 1936): page unknown. Sagarra is now regarded as one of the classic authors of Catalan literature. For an examination of the significance of his work in 1930s Catalonia, see Narcis Garolera, ed., *Josep M. de Sagarra Obra complete* (Valencia: Eliseu Climent, 1994).

was quite different from the straightforward style of battle-song lyrics at that time. Moreover, as a member of the Catalan petty aristocracy, he lacked any links to the labour movement and was even critical of it on occasion. The commission was most likely prompted by the poet's extensive popularity in Barcelona and his close friendship with Jaume Miravitlles, the main organiser of the People's Olympiad. Sagarra fulfilled the commission at the beginning of July. His lyrics extol the Olympic ideals of pacifism, tolerance, freedom, hospitality, brotherhood among nations, youth, courage, and joy.[49]

*Himne per a l'Olimpíada Popular*

No és per odi, no és per guerra
que venim a lluitar de cada
terra:
sota el cel blau
l'únic crit que ens escau,
és un crit d'alegria i de pau.

Fora enveges, fora noses
afirmem contra el viure
estret,
el nostre dret
a fê un aire més net,
i a fê un món més ple de
roses.

Cors enlaire! Llum als braços!
Sempre àgils i ardits els nostres
passos!
Dem-nos les mans
per sentir-nos germans
sota el verd dels llorers triomfants!

*Hymn for the People's Olympiad*

It is not for hatred, it is not for war
that we come to fight from every
land:
under the blue sky
the only cry that is ours
is a cry of joy and peace.

No more envy, no more difficulties,
Let us assert against narrow-
mindedness
our right
to create a cleaner air,
and to create a world more full of
roses

Hearts lifted high! Light in our arms!
always nimble and brave our
steps!
Let us join hands
so that we may feel brothers
under the green of triumphant laurels!

49 Three slightly different versions of Sagarra's poem exist, featuring subtle variations among them. The earliest was published on 9 July 1936 in the Catalan daily *La humanitat*, the official organ of the party Esquerra Republicana de Catalunya (Republican Left of Catalonia). See Josep María de Sagarra, "Himne per a l'Olimpíada Popular", *La humanitat* (9 July 1936): 9. The version presented above is the one published as part of the score edited by the organisers of the People's Olympiad (Fig. 1.1). Jaume Miravitlles published a third version in his 1972 memoir *Episodis de la guerra civil*, see Jaume Miravitlles, *Episodis de la guerra civil Española* (Barcelona: Portic, 1972), 63. The editor of Sagarra's complete works, Narcís Garolera, explained to me that the *Himne* was not included in this publication due to a simple oversight (Garolera's email to the author, 30 December 2018). See Narcís Garolera, ed., *Josep María de Sagarra. Obra completa* (Valencia: Tres i Quatre, 1996).

| | |
|---|---|
| Força i vida, primavera, | Strength and life, spring, |
| ritme, gràcia i esforç i voluntat | rhythm, grace, and effort, and will |
| tots hem triat | all that we have chosen |
| en l'esclat del combat | in the outbreak of combat |
| perquè ens facin de bandera! | to be our banner! |
| | |
| Pel més àgil, pel més destre, | For the most agile, for the most dextrous, |
| sigui el sol immortal de la palestra. | be the immortal sun of the arena. |
| Sigui aquest sol, | Let this sun |
| que ens aplega en un vol, | that lifts us in flight |
| per cremar la mentida i el dol! | burn the lie and the mourning! |
| | |
| Contra els baixos crits innobles | Against the low ignoble cries |
| aixequem cap al cel les nostres mans! | let us raise our hands to heaven! |
| Vibrin els cants | Let the songs vibrate |
| perquè es tornin més grans | so that all peoples become greater |
| i més lliures tots els pobles. | and freer |

In this commission, Sagarra did not excel as a lyricist. The refined vocabulary, style, and structure of his lyrics are more akin to the artificiality of contemporary "cultured" poetry than to the popular forms prevalent in workers' battle songs, to which Eisler's piece unmistakably belongs. His distinctly erudite stylistic choices encompass the use of nine-syllable lines and a rhyme scheme of aabbb cdddc, both of which are unusual even within more sophisticated forms of Catalan poetry. More importantly, the relationship between his lyrics and the vocal melody appears ineffective on three main levels. Firstly, Sagarra composed ten-line stanzas, each divided into two five-line semi-stanzas, whereby each five-line semi-stanza corresponds to a four-bar phrase. A simpler approach for writing lyrics for eight-bar phrases would involve crafting four-line stanzas. Secondly, the length of the poem's lines is highly diverse, ranging from four to eleven syllables. A particularly surprising feature is the varying lengths of the second and seventh lines in each stanza, which results in the awkward arrangement of these lines, as illustrated in Fig. 1.5. Thirdly, Sagarra failed to account for the octave leap in the antepenultimate bar of the song, as circled in Fig. 1.5. This represents one of the most significant alterations in Eisler's vocal line compared to the original refrain of *La Marianne* (see Ex. 1.1). Eisler marked the upper F as sforzando and marcato; this is the highest pitch in the piece. He clearly aimed to capture the attention of both the singers and the audience with this octave leap. However, Sagarra's assignment of insignificant words to this musical "shout" undermines that intended effect.

I hypothesise that the poet's lack of engagement with the workers' movement led to his decision not to commit seriously to the project, potentially resulting in a failure to grasp the type of lyrics best suited to Eisler's melody.

Fig. 1.5. End of *Hymne per a l'Olimpíada Popular* (final bars).

The inadequacy of Sagarra's poem becomes evident when compared to the lyrics penned for the same melody by the Spanish communist poet José Herrera Petere in 1937, under the wartime circumstances detailed in Chapter 2. Unlike Sagarra, Petere composed eight-line stanzas divided into two quatrains. His setting is strictly syllabic, with a vocabulary that is both popular and simple. Petere's straightforward rhyme scheme (abcb dbeb) closely aligns with the romance, one of the most popular poetic forms in Spanish literature, extensively used for propaganda poems and lyrics on the Republican side during the war. The accentuated leap of an octave is consistently employed to introduce the slogans "For the Fifth Regiment!" and "Long live the Fifth Regiment!" As we shall see in Chapter 4, the wartime versions of Petere's lyrics for this melody, in German, French, and Russian – each by different communist authors – feature comparable, simplified vocabularies and rhyme schemes, and all take care to set similar slogans with the accented octave leap.

## The *Himne* in Radio Advertising

According to information published in June 1936 by the Press Service, the organisers of the Games sent the score of Eisler's song to their "music commission", asking them to arrange the piece so that "it can be played by an orchestra and sung at the opening [of the Games]".[50] The head of the music commission was Enric Morera (1865–1942), who was one of the most popular Catalan composers of the time.[51] A few days later, the newspaper *La Humanitat* reported

50 Anon., "El himno de la Olimpíada popular", *Mundo obrero* (25 June 1936): page unknown; anon., "El famoso compositor H. Eisler dedica una marcha a la Olimpiada Popular", *El diluvio* (26 June 1936), 4.

51 Anon., "El famoso compositor H. Eisler", 4. Morera was a composer of the generation before Eisler. Relatively conservative in style, he specialised in traditional Catalan music.

Fig 1.6. Lewy, Fritz: advertising poster of the People's Olympiad (1936), 71 x 49 cm. Barcelona: Publicitat Coll. Published with kind permission by Biblioteca Pavelló de la República (Col.lecció Cartells del Pavelló de la República (UB); F-593; F-772).

that the *Himne per a l'Olimpíada Popular* premiered on 9 July at 11:30 p.m. on Radio Barcelona, the city's main radio station, and that the radio orchestra participated in that performance. According to the PCE organ *Mundo Obrero*, the *Himne* was broadcast over the radio every evening.[52] It is therefore possible that the arranger of the piece for voice(s) and (radio) orchestra was a radio musician rather than Morera. Eisler's song seems to have primarily served a radio advertising function. The piece would thus constitute the musical parallel to the posters and stamps created to advertise the People's Olympiad by the German-Jewish painter, photographer, and graphic designer Fritz Lewy, who had been exiled in Barcelona since the summer of 1933. Lewy's poster employs a modernist, Bauhaus-influenced graphic design, featuring three masculine, geometric silhouettes that evoke solidarity and brotherhood among different races and peoples – an idea also expressed in Sagarra's lyrics' (Fig. 1.6).[53]

The initial plan to perform a choral and orchestral version of the *Himne* at the Games' opening ceremony had been abandoned by early July at the latest. This decision was largely prompted by the growing prominence of Catalan folk and traditional music within the event's propaganda framework. From late spring onward, the People's Olympiad increasingly came to be viewed as a strategic platform for promoting Catalan national identity on the international stage. As a result, the sporting competitions were complemented by an extensive cultural programme that included art exhibitions, art-music concerts, a literary competition – on whose jury Sagarra served – and, most prominently, performances of folk music and dance, particularly from Catalonia. The event ultimately evolved into a major sporting and cultural celebration under the title *Setmana Popular d'Esport i Folklore* (*Popular Week for Sport and Folklore*), with the People's Olympiad as its central attraction.

The opening ceremony, scheduled for 19 July, was conceived as a grand folkloric spectacle of unprecedented scale. At 4 p.m., approximately 5,000 proletarian athletes from Spain and abroad, together with some 3,000 "folklorists", were to parade through Montjuïc Stadium.[54] Following the parade and the opening

---

For further information on Morera, see Xosé Aviñoa, *Història de la Música Catalana, Valenciana i Balear*, Vol. IV, "Del Modernisme a la Guerra Civil (1900–1939)" (Barcelona: Ed. 62, 1999), and *Enric Morera* (Barcelona: Nou Art Thor, DL, 1985).

52 Anon., "L'Himne de l'Olimpíada Popular serà radiato avui nit", *La humanitat* 5, no. 1364 (9 July 1936): 9; Mariano Perla, "La ciudad de la Olimpíada", *Mundo obrero* (17 July 1936): 6.

53 On Lewy's style and his exile in Barcelona, see Santiago Barjau, "Un cartellista alemany a Catalunya 1933–1938", *Serra d'Or* 432 (December 1995): 75–77; and Michael Matzigkeit and Birgit Bernard, eds., *Fritz Lewy (1893–1950). Ein Leben für die Form* (Düsseldorf: Theatermuseum, Dumont-Lindemann-Archiv, 2002).

54 The parading folklorists included sardanistes (sardana dancers), bastoners (stick-clashing dancers), cercolets (dancers with a bow), moxiganguers (performers of choreographed dances), xiquets de Valls and other groups of castellers (performers of human towers), as well as troupes from the Patum festivities of the Catalan city

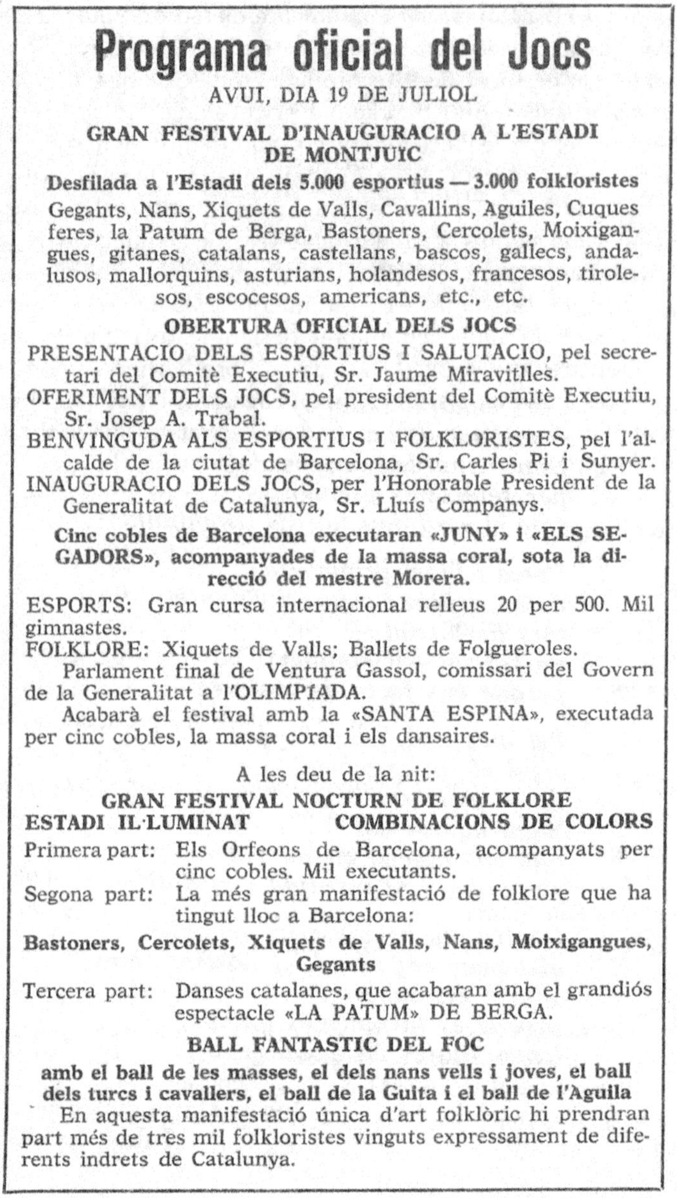

**Programa oficial del Jocs**

AVUI, DIA 19 DE JULIOL

**GRAN FESTIVAL D'INAUGURACIO A L'ESTADI DE MONTJUIC**

**Desfilada a l'Estadi dels 5.000 esportius — 3.000 folkloristes**

Gegants, Nans, Xiquets de Valls, Cavallins, Àguiles, Cuques feres, la Patum de Berga, Bastoners, Cercolets, Moixigangues, gitanes, catalans, castellans, bascos, gallecs, andalusos, mallorquins, asturians, holandesos, francesos, tirolesos, escocesos, americans, etc., etc.

**OBERTURA OFICIAL DELS JOCS**

PRESENTACIO DELS ESPORTIUS I SALUTACIO, pel secretari del Comitè Executiu, Sr. Jaume Miravitlles.

OFERIMENT DELS JOCS, pel president del Comitè Executiu, Sr. Josep A. Trabal.

BENVINGUDA ALS ESPORTIUS I FOLKLORISTES, pel l'alcalde de la ciutat de Barcelona, Sr. Carles Pi i Sunyer.

INAUGURACIO DELS JOCS, per l'Honorable President de la Generalitat de Catalunya, Sr. Lluís Companys.

**Cinc cobles de Barcelona executaran «JUNY» i «ELS SEGADORS», acompanyades de la massa coral, sota la direcció del mestre Morera.**

ESPORTS: Gran cursa internacional relleus 20 per 500. Mil gimnastes.

FOLKLORE: Xiquets de Valls; Ballets de Folgueroles.

Parlament final de Ventura Gassol, comissari del Govern de la Generalitat a l'OLIMPÍADA.

Acabarà el festival amb la «SANTA ESPINA», executada per cinc cobles, la massa coral i els dansaires.

A les deu de la nit:

**GRAN FESTIVAL NOCTURN DE FOLKLORE**

**ESTADI IL·LUMINAT COMBINACIONS DE COLORS**

Primera part: Els Orfeons de Barcelona, acompanyats per cinc cobles. Mil executants.

Segona part: La més gran manifestació de folklore que ha tingut lloc a Barcelona:

**Bastoners, Cercolets, Xiquets de Valls, Nans, Moixigangues, Gegants**

Tercera part: Danses catalanes, que acabaran amb el grandiós espectacle «LA PATUM» DE BERGA.

**BALL FANTASTIC DEL FOC**

**amb el ball de les masses, el dels nans vells i joves, el ball dels turcs i cavallers, el ball de la Guita i el ball de l'Àguila**

En aquesta manifestació única d'art folklòric hi prendran part més de tres mil folkloristes vinguts expressament de diferents indrets de Catalunya.

Fig. 1.7. Programme of the People's Olympiad's opening ceremony, 19 July 1936; reprinted in Miravitlles, *Episodis*, 64.

speeches, a large choir, accompanied by five *cobles*, would perform the popular sardana *Juny* (1921) by the Catalan composer Juli Garreta, along with the then-unofficial Catalan anthem *Els Segadors*. (A *cobla* is an eleven-member ensemble that performs traditional Catalan music.) The musical performances were to be followed by an international relay race, the construction of a *castell* (human tower), and a performance of the *Ballet de Folgueroles*, which involved dancers weaving ribbons around a tall pole. The first half of the event would conclude with a performance of Morera's immensely popular sardana *La Santa Espina*. The second half, scheduled for that evening, was to feature a concert of Catalan choral music and another large-scale folkloric performance – a re-enactment of the *Patum* of Berga.[55] Figure 1.7 reproduces a poster announcing the "official programme" of the "Grand Opening Festival" of the Games, planned for 19 July.

The prominent role of folk and traditional music, particularly from Catalonia, served to emphasise the connections between the Games, the common people, Republicanism, the Popular Front, and Catalanism. This situation reflected the political direction the Olympiad had taken in the weeks following Eisler's visit in April. Since then, the Games had increasingly been conceptualised as an event welcoming participation from all forms of antifascist individuals and organisations, including members of the bourgeoisie and even the petty aristocracy, such as Sagarra. In the spirit of the Popular Front, the organisers celebrated primarily left-wing Catalanism and Republicanism as expressions of antifascism, rather than focusing on political labour movements. In fact, the programme for the opening ceremony did not include any performances of workers' anthems, such as *The Internationale*, the then-popular anarchist anthem *A las barricadas* (the Spanish version of the *Warszawianka*), or Eisler's *Anthem of the Communist International* (the *Comintern Song*). In this context, it is likely that Eisler's Olympic marching song was deemed insufficiently spectacular and at odds with the ceremony's folkloric programme. The poorly defined relationship between the lyrics and the music, coupled with Eisler's relative obscurity in Spain outside very small communist circles, likely contributed to the decision to exclude the piece as well. Contrary to the assertions of several historians, Eisler's Olympic song was not performed at any Games-related event beyond the aforementioned radio broadcasts.[56] The work would

of Berga. As part of the parade, they also showcased a large number of oversized, fantastical animal and human figures traditionally displayed in Catalan festivities, including groups of gegants i capgrossos (human giants and figures with oversized heads), cavallins (dwarf horses), àguiles (eagles), and cuques feres (dragon-tortoises). Traditional regional folk costumes featured prominently.

55 Further context on the cultural programme of the People's Olympiad, including details of its opening ceremony, can be found in Miravitlles, *Episodis*, 53–58 and 64; Pujadas and Santacana, *L'altra*, 202–212; Gounot, "Barcelona gegen Berlin"; Gounot, "El proyecto".

56 Both Ferran Aisa's assertion that Eisler and Sagarra's *Himne* was "rehearsed by several

likely have fallen into oblivion were it not for José Herrera Petere, who wrote new lyrics to the melody during Eisler's stay in Madrid in 1937. As demonstrated in the next chapter, the Olympic anthem subsequently became the *Marcha del Quinto Regimiento*, one of Eisler's most popular battle songs in wartime Spain.

Catalan choirs" in the days prior to the premiere, and Téllez Cenzano's claim that it was meant to premiere in a concert at the Teatre Grec de Montjuïc on July 19, are unsupported by historical sources and appear to be inaccurate. These claims are presented respectively in Ferran Aisa, *Una història de Barcelona. Ateneu Enciclopèdic Popular (1902–1999)* (Barcelona: Virus, 2000), 368; and Enrique Téllez Cenzano, *La música como elemento de representación institucional: el himno de la Segunda República española* (PhD diss., Universidad Complutense de Madrid, 2016), 52.

# Chapter 2

# Eisler in Wartime Spain: A Re-Examination in Light of New Sources

The opening ceremony of the People's Olympiad, meticulously planned for 19 July 1936, never took place. Two days earlier, on 17 July, the military garrisons of the Spanish protectorate of Morocco revolted against the Spanish government. On 18 July, most of the foreign athletes arrived in Barcelona, and a dress rehearsal for the opening ceremony was conducted at the Montjuïc Stadium.[1] The military garrisons of the Canary Islands and Seville revolted that day. In light of the uprising's scale, the organisers decided to cancel the entire People's Olympiad the following morning, the planned opening day. The military rebellion in Barcelona and Madrid was suppressed that same day. The failure of the coup's conspirators to swiftly seize control of the State led to an armed conflict that would endure for nearly three years. Most of the proletarian athletes returned to their home countries after the attempted coup; a few joined the armed struggle as part of the workers' militias that formed immediately afterwards and later enlisted in the International Brigades.[2]

Eisler, who was in London at the outbreak of the Spanish war, appears to have considered travelling to Spain around the time the International Brigades were established in October 1936. In an undated letter from early autumn of that year, he informed the director of the New School for Social Research in New York that he would have to postpone the start of his classes there, having received a letter from Barcelona suggesting he would likely be "needed" in Spain in the near future.[3] From Eisler's only account of his stay in wartime Spain, I infer that it was most likely his friend Ludwig Renn who sent the letter requesting the composer's visit.[4] Renn arrived in Spain in October 1936. He was

1 Xavier Pujadas and Carlos Santacana, *L'altra olimpíada Barcelona'36: Esport, societat i política a Catalunya (1900–1936)* (Badalona: Llibres de l'Index, 1990), 179.

2 On the cancellation of the People's Olympiad see Pujadas and Santacana, *L'altra olimpíada*, 213–226.

3 Hanns Eisler, letter to Alvin Johnson, London, undated (around autumn 1936); in: *Hanns Eisler, Briefe 1907–1943*, 120.

4 Hanns Eisler, "Koncert na frontě", *Illustrovaný časopis*, Prague, (November 1937). A German translation has been published as "Über ein Konzert bei den internationalen Brigaden in Spanien", in *Hanns Eisler. Musik und Politik. Schriften 1924–1948*, ed. Günter Mayer (Leipzig: Deutscher Verlag für Musik, 1973), 395–397.

initially in Barcelona for a period before moving to the front in Madrid. Eisler later recalled that when they met in Spain in January 1937, Renn informed him that he had previously sent the composer several battle-song lyrics, asking him to set them to music and send the scores to the German Brigade.[5] Eisler apparently did not receive that letter, at least not before he departed for Spain.

After delivering several lectures on music and politics, as well as conducting concerts in France, Belgium, and the Netherlands during October and November 1936, Eisler arrived in Paris that December.[6] The French capital was then the centre for German exiles in Western Europe and the primary location for recruiting the International Brigades. On 4 January 1937, he obtained a "salvoconducto" (safe-conduct or letter of safe transit) from the Spanish Embassy in Paris.[7] This document was necessary for Spaniards and foreigners to move from one province to another within each portion of the divided country, in an effort to control the movements of the enemy. The letter of safe transit, signed by Spanish ambassador Luis Araquistán, requested that Spanish authorities apply the necessary stamps for movement between provinces directly on the letter itself, rather than on Eisler's passport. This unusual request for incognito entry documents was likely made at Eisler's suggestion, to prevent future complications when travelling to the United States and elsewhere. In fact, during his 1935 tour of the United States, members of the Phoenix, Arizona police had deemed him an "agitator" and requested that the immigration authorities in Washington initiate his immediate deportation.[8]

Eisler spent twelve days in Spain. He flew from Paris to Barcelona on 6 January, then travelled to Valencia, where he stayed for approximately four days.[9] The city had been the capital of Republican Spain since November 1936. It hosted the government ministries, the offices of the KPD in Spain, and the premises of the secret anti-Nazi broadcasting station "Deutscher Freiheitssender" (German Freedom Radio). This KPD-led station broadcast news and information daily from 10 to 11 p.m. on a short-wave frequency of 29.8 from Madrid to Nazi Germany.[10] The first broadcast of this secret German radio station took place on 10 January 1937, which was most likely during Eisler's stay in

5 Eisler, "Über ein Konzert bei den internationalen Brigaden".

6 See Manfred Grabs, *Hanns Eisler. Kompositionen, Schriften, Literatur. Ein Handbuch* (Leipzig: Deutscher Verlag für Musik, 1984), 20 and 206.

7 "Salvoconducto" for Hanns Eisler (1937); University of South Carolina Library, special collection. Hanns Eisler papers 0207, Box 5, Folder 86, item 41215.

8 Caled Boyd, *They Called me an alien. Hanns Eisler's American Years, 1935–1948* (PhD diss., Arizona State University, 2013), 50.

9 Eisler, "Salvoconducto".

10 On this station see Silvia Schlenstedt, "Exil und antifaschistischer Kampf in Spanien", in *Exil in den Niederlanden und in Spanien*, ed. Klaus Hermsdorf (Leipzig: Reclam, 1981), 243–257.

Valencia.[11] Eisler's brother, Gerhart Eisler, and the German interbrigadist Erich Glückauf served as editors for the station.[12] In addition to them, Eisler met the communist writer Arthur Koestler and the secretary of the KPD's office in Spain, Käthe Dahlem, in Valencia.[13]

From Valencia, Eisler travelled to Madrid. The front line had been situated on the outskirts of the city since October 1936. The absence of stamps from Madrid on Eisler's letter of safe transit suggests that he travelled in an official car. During his three-day stay in the city, he visited the headquarters of the communist-led Quinto Regimiento de Milicias Populares (Fifth Regiment of Popular Militias), located within the former complex of a Catholic church and school in the city centre. There, Eisler met the communist composer Carlos Palacio and the communist poet José Herrera Petere, among others.[14] At that time, Palacio was one of the Spanish composers most involved in communist musical propaganda. Eisler then travelled to the headquarters of the German 11th International Brigade, located in the northern Madrid neighbourhood of Fuencarral. There, he met several German interbrigadists, including his friend Ludwig Renn, the brigade's Chief of Staff Hans Kahle, and the communist activist Norbert Kugler.[15]

After a brief return to Valencia around 15 January, where he met writers Arthur Koestler and Alfred Kantorowicz, Eisler followed Renn and other volunteers from the German Brigade to Murcia.[16] In this small southeastern city, the composer organised a concert for both German and Spanish soldiers. There, he met the German composer Eberhard Schmidt, who had been fighting in Spain as a soldier since 1936, as well as the journalist Gerda Taro.[17] As evidenced by the only known photograph of Eisler with the German interbrigadists, he also met the German writers Kurt Stern and Bodo Uhse (Fig. 2.1).

11 Schlenstedt, "Exil und antifaschistischer Kampf", 243.

12 See Erich Glückauf, *Begegnungen und Signale. Erinnerungen eines Revolutionärs* (Berlin: Neues Leben, 1976), 317–318.

13 Michael Scammell, *Koestler: The Literary and Political Odyssey of a Twentieth-Century Skeptic* (London: Random House, 2009), 131. On Koestler's experiences in Spain see Arthur Koestler, *Ein spanisches Testament* [1938] (Zürich: Europa Verlag, 2012). See also Glückauf, *Begegnungen*, 317–318.

14 For more information on this meeting see Carlos Palacio, *Acordes en el alma* (Alicante: Institut Juan Gil-Albert, 1984), 139–140, and the letter to Manfred Grabs, 8 March 1974 (HEA, cat. no. 7687). For a German translation of this letter see Carlos Palacio, "Erinnerungen an Hanns Eisler in Spanien", in *Hanns Eisler heute*, 67–69.

15 Eberhard Schmidt, *Ein Lied – ein Atemzug. Erinnerungen und Dokumente* (Berlin: Neue Musik, 1987), 60.

16 Alfred Kantorowicz, *Spanisches Kriegstagebuch* (Frankfurt am Main: Fischer, 1982), 112.

17 Schmidt, *Ein Lied–Ein Atemzug*, 61. On Taro's work in wartime Spain see Irme Schaber, *Gerta Taro: Fotoreporterin im spanischen Bürgerkrieg: eine Biografie* (Marburg: Jonas, 1994).

Fig. 2.1. Hanns Eisler in Spain with the German volunteers of the International Brigades Source: HEA 10235.

Years after Eisler's death, his widow, Stephanie Eisler, recalled that a "high official of the International Brigades" invited him to "relax" for two days in the small city of Alicante on the Mediterranean coast, where he was made an honorary citizen.[18] Although no documentary evidence of this honour has surfaced since, Eisler certainly travelled to Alicante, as he flew back to Paris from there on 18 January.[19]

Throughout most of his stay in Spain, Eisler was accompanied by the antifascist émigré from Berlin, Werner Meister, who served as his official German–Spanish interpreter. The Spanish Ministerio de Instrucción Pública and the General Directorate of Security hired Meister for this role at a rate of 15 pesetas a day. Throughout the war, Meister accompanied many other foreigners from northern Europe. Years later, when interrogated by the Gestapo, he explained

[18] Manfred Grabs, "Hanns Eisler. Lebensbild eines unbequemen Komponisten", unpublished typescript (ca. 1984), kept at the HEA (no signature provided), 387. The passage in the original German reads: "Wie später Stephanie Eisler von ihrem Mann erfuhr, sei er von einem hohen Funktionär für zwei Tage zum Ausspannen in die wunderschöne Stadt Alicante am Mittelmeer geleitet worden, wo ihn zum Ehrenbürger ernannt habe."

[19] Eisler, "Salvoconducto".

that he had travelled with Eisler not only to the aforementioned cities but also to Albacete. This small city near Murcia hosted the headquarters of the International Brigades. This is the only document that mentions Eisler's presence in Albacete. If he was indeed there, it was likely only in passing, as no records of any significant activity at the brigade's headquarters have been preserved.[20]

## Eisler and the Communist Fifth Regiment

The Fifth Regiment of Popular Militias was an elite corps of volunteers established at the beginning of the war at the behest of the Spanish Communist Party and the Marxist-Leninist youth organisation Juventudes Socialistas Unificadas (Unified Socialist Youth). It was disbanded in late January 1937. The regiment also functioned as a cultural and educational institution for its predominantly illiterate soldiers, who were mainly peasants. Notable writers, artists, actors, and at least one composer, Rafael Oropesa, collaborated with this regiment.[21] Oropesa conducted the regiment's wind band, which comprised approximately thirty-two musicians who accompanied the military units, often at the front lines. At that time, he was a relatively well-known composer of one-steps, pasodobles, chotis, and other genres of popular music.[22] Unlike other Spanish communist composers of his generation, Oropesa did not compose any surviving communist battle songs before the civil war, and only one during the conflict: the *Himno del 5º cuerpo* (*Hymn of the Fifth Corps*), see Fig. 2.2.[23] No documentary evidence exists to indicate that Eisler met Oropesa in Madrid.

Eisler's collaboration with the Fifth Regiment was primarily limited to his work with the poet José Herrera Petere (1909–1977). After joining the PCE in 1931, Petere wrote mainly novels and poems on political and social topics, adopting a more restrained style than the modernism of his youth. During the civil war, he was engaged in cultural and educational work within the Fifth Regiment

20 I am thankful to Michel Uhl for providing this information, which he derived from the Gestapo's postwar interrogation records of Meister.

21 On the Fifth Regiment see Juan A. Blanco Rodríguez, *El Quinto Regimiento en la política militar del PCE en la guerra civil* (Madrid: UNED, 1993).

22 Oropesa's biography and music have received little scholarly attention. For his work as a conductor after the civil war, see Eva Moreda Rodriguez, "Why do orchestral and band musicians in exile matter? A case study from Spain", *Music and Letters* 101, no. 1 (2019): 71–88; Olga Picún, "La vida musical en el buque Sinaia. Construcciones de sentido en torno a la Banda del Quinto Regimiento de Milicias Populares en el proceso de exilio a México", *Acta Musicologica* 96/1 (2024): 59–80.

23 The *5º Cuerpo*, established in March 1937, was the fifth unit of the Republican army (not to be confused with the Fifth Regiment). Based on its lyrics, the song appears to have been composed during or shortly after the Battle of the Ebro, i.e., in mid- or late 1938; see Carlos Palacio, *Colección de canciones de lucha* (Valencia: Tipografía Moderna, 1939), 106.

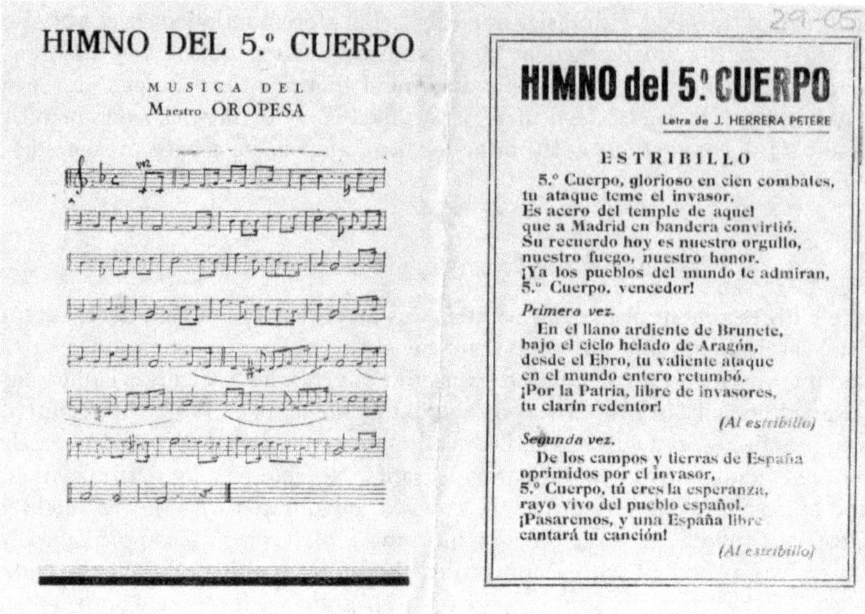


Fig. 2.2. Wartime edition of Oropesa's vocal line and lyrics for the *Himno del 5º Cuerpo* (ca. 1938). Source: Fondo Fotográfico de José Herrera Petere, Centro de la Fotografía y de la Imagen Histórica de Guadalajara. Sección de Archivos, Biblioteca y Fototeca. Diputación Provincial de Guadalajara.

and published numerous novels, plays, and short stories on war-related themes, as well as a significant number of "romances de guerra" (war romances). He authored battle-song lyrics set to music by Eisler and Oropesa, as well as Spanish versions of several foreign battle songs, including *Rote Reiterarmee* by Soviet composers Daniel and Dmitri Pokrass (Petere's title reads *Caballería del Don*), *Das Lied vom Vaterland* by Isaak Dunajewsky (*Canción de la patria socialista*), and Eisler's *Song of the United Front* (*Canción del Frente Popular*).[24]

Petere wrote new lyrics for Eisler's former Olympic march during the composer's stay in Madrid. The new text exalts the Fifth Regiment's courageous, violent, yet optimistic struggle against fascism, advocating for a prosperous future in Spain and worldwide. Petere's references to the "steel heroes" allude to

[24] Recent studies on José Herrera Petere's work during the civil war include Carlos Ramírez Morcillo, *Literatura y compromismo político. Experiencias y contenidos en José Herrera Petere* (PhD diss., Universidad de Castilla La Mancha, 2017); and Guillermo Ginés Ramiro, "Poesía como método de propaganda activa: Guerra viva de José Herrera Petere", in *Métodos de propaganda activa en la guerra civil española,* eds. Emilio Peral and Francisco Sáenz (Madrid: Iberoamericana, 2015), 115–146.

the first combat units established within this regiment, the approximately 250-strong "Compañías de Acero" (Steel Companies). He entitled the song *Marcha del Quinto Regimiento* (*March of the Fifth Regiment*).

| | |
|---|---|
| 1. Adelante batallones,<br>adelante los héroes de acero<br>Rompe el silencio del alba el tronar<br>del fusil, del cañón y el mortero.<br>Adelante, milicianos<br>pecho fuerte y alegres pensamientos:<br>vamos a hacer una España feliz<br>por el Quinto Regimiento. | 1. Forward, battalions,<br>forward heroes of steel!<br>The silence of dawn is broken by the thunder,<br>the rifle, the cannon, and the mortar.<br>Forward, militiamen!<br>Strong chest and happy thoughts:<br>we will make a joyful Spain<br>for the Fifth Regiment! |
| 2. Sangre roja de españoles,<br>brasa viva del Quinto Regimiento,<br>lucha en tus cuadros el viento español<br>por el pan y la paz de los pueblos.<br>Nada importa lo que pase,<br>nuestros nervios van templados al fuego.<br>Ni un paso atrás, adelante a luchar<br>por el Quinto Regimiento.[25] | 2. The red blood of Spaniards,<br>living ember of the Fifth Regiment!<br>The Spanish wind battles in your cadres<br>for the bread and the peace of the people.<br>No matter what happens,<br>our nerves are hardened by fire.<br>Don't step back, onward to fight<br>for the Fifth Regiment! |
| [2 strophes follow] | [2 strophes follow] |

Petere also wrote the lyrics for *No pasarán. Marcha de las Compañías de Acero* (*They Shall Not Pass: March of the Steel Companies*).[26] Eisler set these to music in Spain. Neither the lyrics nor the music of *No pasarán* appear to have been published during the civil war. Eisler's original musical manuscript is lost. The only surviving musical source from the period is a recording made in 1937 or early 1938, featuring an unidentified mixed choir accompanied by a small military wind ensemble. The opening portion of this recording has sur-

25 "La "Marcha del 5.º Regimiento", *Milicia popular* 2, no. 159 (14 January 1937), 2. Translation by the author.

26 This is one of at least four battle songs from the civil war that bear this popular slogan as their title; the others are by Paul Dessau, Paul Arma, and Vadim Kochetov. On these songs see Paul Dessau, "No pasarán" (Paris: Comité internationale d'aide au peuple espagnol, 1937), manuscript at Paul-Dessau-Archiv, Berlin (Cat. No. 1.74.0098); Tobias Widmaier, ed., *Paul Arma. Avantgarde und Arbeiterlied: Autobiographie 1904–1934* (Büdingen: PFAU, 2016), 222 and 271; Palacio, *Colección*, 37. Music and text sources related to this song are kept at Arbeiterlied-Archiv of the AdK, sig. ALA 1802 and 1803.

vived because it was included in the soundtrack of the two-minute government propaganda film *Palabras del Excmo. Sr. Presidente del Consejo, Dr. Negrín* (*Speech by His Excellency the President of the Council, Dr. Negrín*) from early 1938. In the film, Prime Minister Juan Negrín calls for resistance on the home front.[27] Because arrangements for military wind bands were often made ad hoc by their conductors, I infer that the recorded arrangement is not Eisler's. The scores for the arrangement used in this recording have not survived.

The earliest written source that includes the complete lyrics to *No pasarán* is Palacio's book *Colección de canciones de lucha*. This compilation of seventy war-song lyrics was published in Valencia in February 1939, near the end of the war. No scores were included in this book. The lyrics are reproduced below as published in Palacio's book.[28] The allusions to "steel" in Petere's lyrics indicate the song's intended support for the Fifth Regiment. The regular combination of octosyllabic and decasyllabic verses suggests that, unlike the *Marcha del Quinto Regimiento*, these lyrics were not composed for a pre-existing melody by Eisler.

¡No pasarán! ¡no
pasarán!
¡Los de acero firmes están!
Temple duro, roca viva
que al fascismo aplastará, ¡vencerá!
Bomba al cinto, bayonetas,
al combate acero va, ¡pasará!

¡No pasarán! ¡no
pasarán!
Por la tierra y por el pan
vista al frente, pulso firme,
los fusiles apuntad: ¡disparar!
Salte tierra a cañonazos
nada importa, ¡acero va!, ¡pasará![29]

[3 stanzas follow]

They shall not pass! They shall not
pass!
The steel [soldiers] stand firm!
Hardened steel, living rock
that will crush fascism, shall triumph!
Bomb at the ready, bayonets,
steel goes to combat, it shall pass!

They shall not pass! They shall not
pass!
For land and bread
Look ahead, hands steady,
aim your rifles: fire!
The earth jolts from cannon fire,
no matter, steel, go! It shall pass!

[3 stanzas follow]

27 Manuel Villegas López (film director), *Palabras del Excmo. Sr. Presidente del Consejo, Dr. Negrín* (*Speech by His Excellency the President of the Council, Dr. Negrín*), early 1938. See Alfonso del Amo García, ed., *Catálogo General del Cine de la Guerra Civil* (Madrid: Filmoteca Española 1996), 714. The film can be viewed on the Youtube channel of the Spanish Ministry of Education and Culture (song timeframe 0:05–1:34), https://www.youtube.com/watch?v=jiwBbOMUopo [Accessed 20 June 2025].

28 The HEA keeps a small sheet of paper, apparently brought by Eisler from Madrid, which contains the title of the song: "*No pasarán. Marcha de las companías de acero*" and the first stanza of the lyrics. The text of the stanza differs only slightly from that reproduced in Palacio's book. Hanns Eisler, "No pasarán", HEA, Cat. No. 1790.

29 Palacio, *Colección*, 27–28.

Ex. 2.1. *No pasarán* as notated by Palacio in 1974. Analytical markings are mine.

Tempo de Marcha

simile

d minor: VI bVII i iv

F Major: I V vi ii

7

V i bVII i iv V i

V/vi vi V vi ii V/vi vi

The earliest written musical source for Eisler's *No pasarán* is a copy made in 1974 by Spanish composer Carlos Palacio for the GDR music scholar Manfred Grabs.[30] My transcription of this source is provided in Ex. 2.1. The piece displays prominent modal indeterminacy (here between F Major and D minor) as well as the use of the Aeolian mode VII degree (♭VIII) in lieu of a triad built on a leading tone. The song begins with the progression F–$C^7$ but does not include any perfect cadences on F major, featuring only two perfect cadences on D minor (bars 6–8 and 10–12). The $C^7$ chord between them (b. 9) functions as a seventh chord, on the seventh degree of the natural minor scale (or Aeolian mode) of D, rather than as a dominant for F. Because these two features are typical among Eisler's interwar battle songs, I conclude that he was almost certainly the author of *No pasarán*.

## War Elegy

Eisler's primary artistic collaboration in Spain was with Ludwig Renn (1889–1979). Born in Dresden to a family of Saxon nobility, Renn was given the name Arnold Vieth von Golßenau. From 1911, he served as an officer in a prestigious Saxon Guards Regiment. After the First World War, he became a captain in the Dresden security police, a paramilitary force. During the Kapp Putsch in 1920, he refused to open fire on striking workers and subsequently left the police service. Following that life-changing event, he studied law, economics, art history, and Russian philology at university. He then undertook a two-year journey throughout south-

30 Palacio, "Erinnerugen an Hanns Eisler". This version has been recorded and included in *Ana Vega – Canciones de lucha*, Dahiz Produccions, 014 CD, Spain, 2001.

ern Europe and the Near East. In 1928, he joined the KPD, became a member of the KPD-affiliated paramilitary organisation Rotes Frontkämpferbund, and published his first novel, the acclaimed *Krieg* (*War*).[31] Under increasing attacks from the Nazis, he renounced his noble title in 1930, subsequently adopting the name of his novel's main character. His books *Nachkrieg* (*Post-War*, 1930) and *Rußlandfahrten* (*Journeys to Russia*, 1932) garnered relative popularity among German communists during the interwar period. Due to his popularity and rejection of aristocratic privileges, coupled with his discreet approach to his homosexuality, Renn became a prominent communist activist in the early 1930s.[32]

Renn and Eisler met each other in the early 1930s at the Marxistische Arbeiterschule (Marxist Workers' School) in Berlin.[33] Renn lectured there on the history of warfare and military theory, and Eisler on music and dialectical materialism. They remained lifelong friends. Following the burning of the Reichstag, Renn was arrested in January 1934 and sentenced to thirty months' imprisonment, serving eighteen months in the Bautzen penitentiary. He left for Spain shortly after his release in October 1936. After the formation of the 11th International Brigade at the end of that month, Renn took over as Chief of Staff for the brigade in December 1936. He became the most important supporter of Brigade Commander Hans Kahle. This brigade included the Thälmann Battalion, where many of the volunteers were exiled German communists.[34]

Approximately three days before Eisler met Renn in Madrid, the German battalion endured one of its most traumatic experiences when rebel troops annihilated nearly 200 German soldiers – roughly 90% of the battalion – in a matter of moments. This occurred during an intense attack near Madrid, as part of what became known as the Third Battle of the Road to La Coruña. The massacre, which took place on 7 January, was partly the result of human error, as the battalion's trench had not been laid out in a proper serpentine formation for defence.[35] The slaughter was the most dramatic in a series of continuous losses of German interbrigadist lives over the preceding two months. According to Renn, he and the few survivors were profoundly affected by the

31 Ludwig Renn, *Krieg* (Frankfurt am Main: Frankfurter Societäts-Druckerei, 1928). The novel was re-edited by Aufbau Verlag, Berlin in 2014.

32 Manfred Herzer, "Schwule Widerstandskämpfer gegen die Nazis", in *Dokumentation der Vortragsreihe "Homosexualität und Wissenschaft"*, ed. Shwulenreferat im AStA der FU Berlin (Berlin: Rosa Winkel, 1985), 222–226.

33 For an account of how they met, see the transcription of Ludwig Renn's interview with Günter Lippmann and Günter Mayer, preserved at the HEA, cat. no. 7585.

34 Two recent studies of Renn's activities in Spain are Edward Reichel, "Ein Spanienkämpfer ohne Spanienbild: Ludwig Renn", in *Dresden und Spanien: Akten des interdisziplinären Kolloquiums, Dresden, 22.–23. Juni 1998*, ed. Christoph Rodiek (Frankfurt am Main: Vervuet, 2000), 179–189; and Jakob Taube, *Hans Kahle (1899–1947). Der vergessene Kommandeur der "Thälmann-Brigade"* (Leipzig: Leipziger Universitätsverlag, 2017).

35 Taube, *Hans Kahle*, 108–120; and Antony Beevor, *The Battle for Spain. The Spanish Civil War 1936–1939* (New York: Penguin Books, 2006 [1982]), 189–192.

incident on an emotional level.[36] The trauma caused by this massacre affected the German soldiers for several months.[37]

On 16 January, approximately one week after this massacre, the survivors were transferred to a military camp in Murcia in order for the battalions to recuperate and learn new military techniques.[38] Eisler and Renn met in Fuencarral, Madrid, during the interval between the massacre and the transfer to Murcia.[39] Eisler later recalled that Renn proposed organising a concert in Murcia for the survivors of the massacre and that the writer crafted new lyrics from old drafts of his poetry. The composer greatly admired "how calmly he continued working on his poems in between military manoeuvres, discussing individual phrases with me. After two hours of work, I went back to my quarters with four new songs and finished writing the music".[40]

Of those alleged four songs, only the music for *Das Lied vom 7. Januar* (*The Song of 7th January*) has been found. A typewritten copy of the original four-stanza untitled poem, which Renn adapted for the musical setting – possibly in collaboration with Eisler – has been preserved. As with other lyrics for propaganda songs of the time, the vocabulary, structure, metre, and rhyme are all straightforward. The poem makes no explicit mention of the massacre, suggesting that it was written before the disaster and later recontextualised through its title during Eisler's stay in Spain. The following transcription presents Renn's original poem along with the alterations he (or they) made to the text before Eisler set it to music.

36 Two contemporary eyewitness accounts of the massacre are Ludwig Renn, *Der spanische Krieg. Dokumentarischer Bericht* (Berlin: Das Neue Berlin, 2006), 182–190; and Alfred Kantorowicz, *Spanisches Kriegstagebuch* (Frankfurt am Main: Fischer, 1982), 88–110.

37 Nine months later, the soldiers who fell on 7 January were still remembered in the magazine of the 11th Brigade, *Pasaremos*. The periodical noted that one particular Thälmann soldier, Erwin Krath, was "crushed by fascist tanks in the Remisa forest on 7 January. He stayed with his comrades. We have wept and clenched our fists." Such expressions of sadness and weeping were rare in *Pasaremos*. ("Erwin Krath wurde am 7. Januar im Walde von Remisa von faschistischen Tanks zermalmt. Er blieb mit seinen Kameraden. Wir haben geweint und die Fäuste geballt.") Anon., "Ein Jahr XI. Brigade. Erste Internationale Brigade", *Pasaremos. Organ der XI. Brigade* 31 (15 October 1937), 10 (a copy of this issue is kept at the Ernst-Busch-Archiv of the AdK, cat. no. 771).

38 This transfer and the Murcia camp are discussed in Hans Kahle and Franz Dahlem's reports at the Stiftung Archiv der Parteien und Massenorganisationen der DDR-Bundesarchiv (Berlin), with ref. SgY 11 / V 237 / 1 / 6 (Folder I. 1.3).

39 See Eisler's "salvoconducto" and "Über ein Konzert bei den internationalen Brigaden".

40 Eisler wrote: "Renn [...] fing an, aus alten Gedichtentwürfen Liedertexte auszuarbeiten. [...] Ich habe Ludwig Renn sehr bewundert, wie ruhig er zwischen militärischen Dispositionen an seinen Gedichten weiterbastelte und mit mir einzelne Wendungen diskutierte. Nach zwei Stunden Arbeit fuhr ich mit vier neuen Liedern in mein Quartier zurück und schrieb die Musik ins Reine", Eisler, "Über ein Konzert bei den internationalen Brigaden".

~~fern~~ im span'schen land
in dem unterstand
sitzen ~~rauchende~~ unsere genossen.
an dem grabenrand
wo der posten stand
ward ein Kamerad erschossen.

blutig sank er dahin,
doch in unserm sinn ~~g~~
gab und gibt es nie ein
~~schw~~Wanken.
auf die freiheit hin,
auf die freude hin
zielen alle die gedanken

**[from here on: all crossed out]**
freiheit unsrer art,
von des volkes art
ist das ziel, fuer das wir
schiessen.
ist der kampf auch hart,
hier wird nicht gespart,
weil wir endlich siegen muessen.

fern im span'schen land
in dem unterstand
sitzen ~~rauchende~~ unsere genossen.
an dem grabenrand,
wo er [sic] posten stand,
ward ihr bester freund
erschossen.[41]

~~far away,~~ in the Spanish land,
in the dugout
~~smoking~~ our comrades sit
at the edge of the trench
where the sentry stood
a comrade was shot dead.

he collapsed bleeding,
yet in our purpose
there was and is no
faltering
for freedom,
for joy
all [our] thoughts are aimed

**[from here on: all crossed out]**
freedom of our kind
of the people's kind,
is the aim for which we
shoot.
[though] the struggle is hard,
no effort shall be spared
for we must win in the end.

far away, in the Spanish land,
in the dugout
~~smoking~~ our comrades sit
at the edge of the trench
where the sentry stood
their best friend was shot
dead

Renn, possibly alongside Eisler, removed the words "fern" (far away, distant), likely to avoid evoking associations with homesickness, as well as "rauchend" (smoking), perhaps to prevent any implication of carelessness. The decision to eliminate the entire latter half of the lyrics is particularly noteworthy, as most propaganda songs of the time featured three or more stanzas. One reason for this omission may have been the connotations of the term "bester Freund" (best friend), which could have not only overemphasised the soldiers' emotional or personal bonds to their fallen comrades, but also left room for interpretations suggesting homoeroticism.[42] For the final version of the lyrics, see Ex. 2.2 below.

41 "Das Lied vom 7. Januar. Text", typewritten text, HEA, cat. no. 1764.

42 The term "friend", and in particular "best friend", was used in the interwar period to

Ex. 2.2. *Das Lied vom 7. Januar*. Motivic organisation. Source: Ernst Busch, ed., *Canciones de guerra de las Brigadas Internacionales*. © by Deutscher Verlag für Musik Leipzig, p. 83.

According to his own account, Eisler set Renn's lyrics to music in Madrid, shortly before his departure to Murcia. He composed a song for voice and squeezebox – an instrument he employed only rarely throughout his career. This decision, he noted, stemmed from encountering an Austrian interbrigadist who had brought this instrument with him[43] (the interbrigadists, predominantly composed of workers, primarily played bandurrias, guitars, and accordions).[44] Stylistically, the song resembles Eisler's slow political ballads from the late Weimar era, such as *Stempellied* (1929), *Seifenlied* (1929), and *Feldfrüchte* (1930). However, it differs from most of these earlier ballads in its terseness and the absence of ironic or comic elements.

allude to a homosexual male lover. For instance, allusions to "der Freund" can be found in *Der Hirschfeld-Lied*, or "die Freundin" in the number "Wenn die beste Freundin" from the revue *Es liegt in der Luft (etwas Idiotisches)*, created in 1928 by Marcellus Schiffer (libretto) and Mischa Spoliansky (music). The most popular Weimar-era German lesbian magazine was titled *Die Freundin*.

43 Eisler, "Über ein Konzert bei den internationalen Brigaden".

44 Javier Pérez López, *La música en las brigadas internacionales. Las canciones como estrategia de guerra* (PhD diss., Universidad de Castilla-La Mancha, 2014), 64 and 557.

The song structure derives from Renn's lyrics. Each section of the bipartite song comprises a six-bar antecedent and a six-bar consequent, corresponding to the three-line subsections of the stanzas. For each line of lyrics, Eisler composed two bars of music, except for lines 5 and 6, which are set as 1.5 bars and 2.5 bars respectively (bb. 9–12). The strategic use of irregular phrasing to avoid monotony is also a prominent feature of Eisler's other battle songs from the period (e.g., *Solidarity Song*). The song's four main motifs (a, b, c, and d in the score below) strictly follow the poem's rhyme scheme (aab aab ccd ccd).

Two slightly different drafts of the music, both handwritten and signed by Eisler, have survived. I have labelled these A and B. The manuscript of version A is preserved at the Hanns Eisler Archiv in Berlin under catalogue number 743 and has never been published. The original manuscript of version B has not been retained; however, a facsimile copy was first published in November 1937 as part of Eisler's article for the Czech newspaper *Spanelsko*. This version reappeared shortly thereafter in the fourth and fifth editions of Busch's songbook *Kampflieder der Internationalen Brigaden* (published in December 1937 and May 1938, respectively).[45] This songbook, compiled by Ernst Busch for use by the interbrigadists, was issued in five editions, with each subsequent edition containing a slight increase in the number of songs. Small in size and designed to be carried in a rucksack, the book included over fifty songs. The only difference between the music in sources A and B lies in motif c of the vocal melody: in manuscript A, the note in question is a B-natural, whereas in manuscript B, it is a B-flat (see bb. 13, 15, 19, and 21 in Ex. 2.2). Since Eisler published version B towards the end of his life as part of the "complete edition" of his vocal works, it can be considered the composer's preferred version.[46]

Sustained minor seventh chords clearly predominate in this F-Major song (Ex. 2.2. bb. 2–5, 8–10, 17–18, 23–24). To express the pain associated with death, Eisler accompanies the word "Genossen" vertically with an augmented triad – the most dissonant harmony in the piece – as well as horizontally, with a descending melodic semitone, a centuries-old topos for expressing pain or loss (Ex. 2.2, b. 6). Additionally, he introduces a chain of descending appoggiaturas, functioning as a whole-tone "Seufzermotiv", beginning with the word "blutig" (bleeding) (Ex. 2.2, bb. 19–22). Eisler's incorporation of various musical elements traditionally linked to mourning stands in stark contrast to Renn's resolute call to maintain high morale in the struggle. While Renn's lyrics declare that "there will never be any hesitation" in the fight against fascism, Eisler's composition appears to convey a more sombre sentiment. *Das Lied vom 7. Januar* is notable as one of the few songs composed during the war specifically for soldiers, in which grief is musically expressed.

45 *Spanelsko*, Prague, 8 (1 December 1937); Ernst Busch, *Kampflieder der Internationalen Brigaden* (Madrid: Diana (UGT), 1937 (4th ed.), p. 83 / 1938 (5th ed.), p. 35.

46 Hanns Eisler, *Lieder und Kantaten*, vol. 5 (Berlin: Deutsche Akademie der Künste, 1961), 103.

## It's Revolution in Spain

The Hanns Eisler Archive preserves a bundle of papers that Eisler brought back from Spain to Paris, catalogued under the title *Nicht vertonte Texte* (*Texts Not Set to Music*).[47] As most of these documents originally belonged to Renn, I refer to them as "Source R". This nineteen-page source, largely overlooked by scholars until now, contains drafts and clean copies of six poems Renn wrote during the early months of the Spanish Civil War. These poems fall into three categories: two are battle-song lyrics reflecting the German interbrigadists' antifascist struggle in Spain, two are ironic recollections of Renn's life in Nazi prisons, and two are more personal, where Renn conveys his feelings and fears, some of which relate to his homosexuality. These texts illuminate important facets of cultural life within the German Thälmann Battalion, as well as significant aspects of Renn's personal biography.

One of the two lyrics for a battle song in Source R begins with the incipit *In Spanien ist Revolution* (*It's Revolution in Spain*). Source R includes two slightly different handwritten drafts of the poem, as well as a typewritten clean copy, as illustrated in Fig. 2.3. This copy was apparently produced by the battalion's secretary, as noted by Eisler in the sole account he wrote of his experiences in wartime Spain.[48] The pencil marks on the sheet depicted in the figure below are Eisler's. The lyrics celebrate the united antifascist struggle of interbrigadists from various nations and diverse political creeds. My translation of this document is provided below.

In Spain, in Spain it's revolution.
You can see it in the street, you can hear it in its sound.
We came here from every country
it was not difficult for us to come on foot.
Others came by train.
The main point is, we all came to fight for Spain.

From France, there came our strongest stride:
Dutch and Danish, they brought them along.
The language confusion soon became quite great.
Most of [them] knew merely their own language.
The Spaniard got English military units.
Italy gave the German a hand here to fight for Spain.

The Jew, he's truly scorned in Germany,
There he's mocked as a cowardly criminal.
Here he stands on watch with the Swede,
And their guns lash throughout the night.
And beside him the Hungarians, Belgians, Serbs,
They are all ready to die in the field in the fight for Spain.

47 "Nicht vertonte Texte", HEA, cat. no. 4026. I thank Peter Deeg for his help and advice relating to this source.

48 See Eisler, "Über ein Konzert bei den internationalen Brigaden".

We watch and entrench and load our rifles
Bullets come crashing by.
The hand grenade flies with vigour toward the enemy
Antifascists are all united here
The democrat stands with the communist
We like everyone who is a warrior in the fight for Spain.

The second set of lyrics included for a battle song is *Drüben in Deutschland herrscht Not* (*Misery Reigns over in Germany*). Although the poem is not signed by Renn, its literary style closely resembles that of *In Spanien ist Revolution*, and, given that the text is written in Renn's hand, I infer that he also authored this poem. Only an untitled handwritten draft of this text has survived. The poem frames the antifascist struggle in Spain as the initial stage of liberation for Germany and Europe from fascism, representing a significant step forward in the international establishment of communism.

| | |
|---|---|
| Drüben in Deutschland herrscht Not.<br>Dort werden die Menschen gequält und geknechtet,<br>Dort wird, was noch frei ist, völlig entrechtet.<br>Aber Spanien wird frei.<br>Und nach Spanien kommt dann Frankreich,<br>und nach Frankreich kommt wohl Deutschland<br>kommt Italien, Polen, Lettland.<br>Alles, alles wird geeinigt<br>zu dem Riesenstaat der Welt. | Misery reigns over in Germany.<br>There, people are tortured and enslaved,<br>there, what is still free is completely disenfranchised.<br>But Spain will be free.<br>And after Spain will come France,<br>and after France will come Germany, will come Italy, Poland, Latvia.<br>All, all will be united<br>in the [one] giant state of the world. |
| Freilich Genossen, Geduld!<br>Hier ist doch zum Teil erst das Alte vergangen<br>Noch hält der Faschismus Genossen gefangen<br>Schlagt den Drachen erst tot.<br>Und nach… | Oh sure, comrades, patience!<br>Here the old [world] has passed only in part,<br>fascism still holds comrades captive.<br>Slay the dragon, first of all!<br>And after… |
| Immer zum Schüsse bereit!<br>Wir kämpfen für Spanien und werden da siegen<br>und Hitler wird mächtige Prügel bei kriegen.<br>Spanien wird jetzt befreit.<br>Und nach… | Always ready to shoot!<br>We'll fight for Spain and we'll triumph there<br>and Hitler will take a mighty beating.<br>Spain will now be freed.<br>And after… |

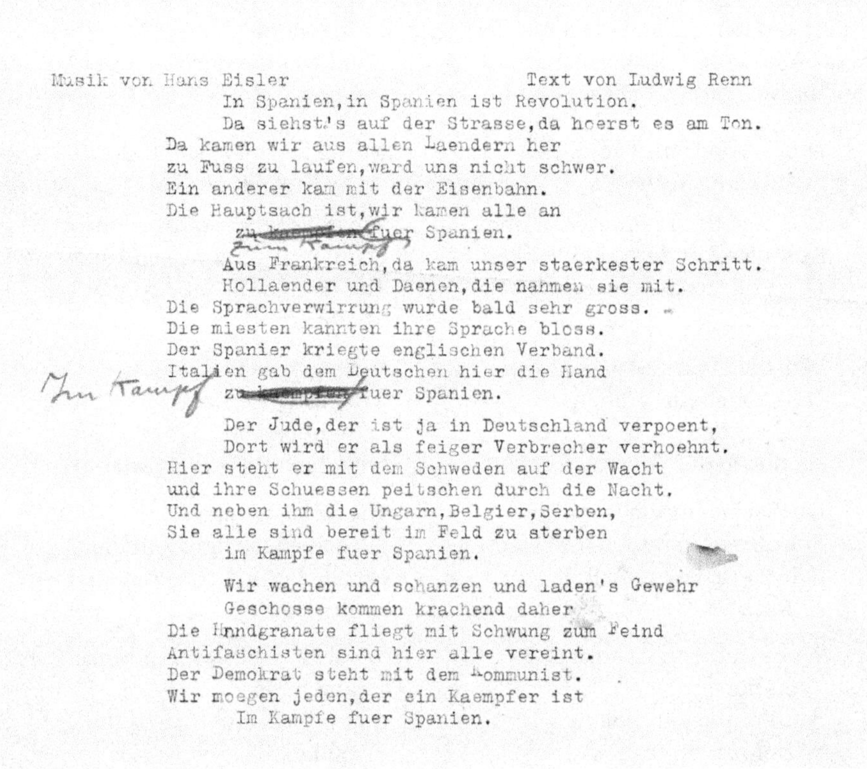

Musik von Hans Eisler Text von Ludwig Renn

In Spanien, in Spanien ist Revolution.
Da siehst's auf der Strasse, da hoerst es am Ton.
Da kamen wir aus allen Laendern her
zu Fuss zu laufen, ward uns nicht schwer.
Ein anderer kam mit der Eisenbahn.
Die Hauptsach ist, wir kamen alle an
~~zu kaempfen~~ fuer Spanien. Zum Kampf

Aus Frankreich, da kam unser staerkester Schritt.
Hollaender und Daenen, die nahmen sie mit.
Die Sprachverwirrung wurde bald sehr gross.
Die miesten kannten ihre Sprache bloss.
Der Spanier kriegte englischen Verband.
Italien gab dem Deutschen hier die Hand
Im Kampf ~~zu kaempfen~~ fuer Spanien.

Der Jude, der ist ja in Deutschland verpoent,
Dort wird er als feiger Verbrecher verhoehnt.
Hier steht er mit dem Schweden auf der Wacht
und ihre Schuessen peitschen durch die Nacht.
Und neben ihm die Ungarn, Belgier, Serben,
Sie alle sind bereit im Feld zu sterben
im Kampfe fuer Spanien.

Wir wachen und schanzen und laden's Gewehr
Geschosse kommen krachend daher
Die Handgranate fliegt mit Schwung zum Feind
Antifaschisten sind hier alle vereint.
Der Demokrat steht mit dem Kommunist.
Wir moegen jeden, der ein Kaempfer ist
Im Kampfe fuer Spanien.

Fig. 2.3. Sheet containing the lyrics of *In Spanien ist Revolution*. The pencil marks are by Eisler. The English translation is provided below. Source: "Nicht vertonte Texte", Hanns-Eisler-Archiv, cat. no. 4026, p. 1 recto.

The Hanns-Eisler-Archiv also holds a sheet containing a clean typewritten copy of an untitled poem attributed to the Jewish journalist and exiled writer Kurt Stern (1907–1989).[49] A member of the German Communist Party since 1927, Stern left Berlin shortly after the Nazis seized power in 1933. He was in Spain from October 1936 to January 1938, serving as the political commissar of the 11th International Brigade. During this time, he also worked as the editor of the brigade's newspaper, *Pasaremos* (1937), as well as the newspaper for all brigades, *Le Volontaire de la Liberté*.

Following the Comintern's preferred line, Stern's lyrics describe the International Brigades as "the Popular Front Army of the World". The opening line may

[49] Kurt Stern, "Wir sind der Freiheit Soldaten", HEA, cat. no. 1937.

allude to the first line of the refrain of *Lied der Moorsoldaten* ("Wir sind die Moorsoldaten / und ziehen mit dem Spaten / ins Moor") from 1933. This song was popular among German interbrigadists and was included in every edition of Busch's *Songbook of the International Brigades.*[50]

| | |
|---|---|
| Música de Hans [sic] Eisler. Texto de Kurt Stern. | Music by Hans [sic] Eisler. Text by Kurt Stern. |
| Wir sind der Freiheit Soldaten<br>Aus allen Ländern und Staaten<br>Die Volksfrontarmee der Welt | We are soldiers of freedom<br>From every country and state<br>The Popular Front Army of the World |
| Wir sind nach Spanien gekommen<br>Und haben die Waffen genommen<br>An denen der Feind zerschellt | We have come to Spain<br>And have taken the weapons<br>On which the enemy shatter |
| Die Sache, für die wir werben<br>Für die wir kämpfen und sterben<br>heißt: Friede, Freiheit und Recht | The cause we promote<br>For which we fight and die<br>Is called peace, freedom, and justice |
| Wer glaubt, daß Tanks und Kanonen,<br>daß Bomben und blaue Bohnen<br>uns schrecken, der kennt uns schlecht. | Whoever believes that tanks and guns,<br>that bombs and blue beans [lead bullets]<br>frighten us, they hardly know us. |
| Der Faschismus wird Spanien nicht kriegen<br>Wir müssen und werden siegen<br>Vorwärts, Genossen, faßt Schritt! | Fascism will not get Spain<br>We must win, and we will<br>Forward, comrades, hold [your] stride! |
| Wir werden Franco verjagen<br>Und unsere Fahnen dann tragen<br>Weit weg, weit weg von Madrid | We will drive out Franco<br>And then carry our flags<br>Far away, far away from Madrid |

The document containing Stern's lyrics is not part of Source R. Nevertheless, as the sheet resembles the one shown in Fig. 2.3, I infer that the copy was made for the concert in Murcia. That concert took place on 15 or 16 January at Murcia's main theatre, Teatro de Romea. *Das Lied vom 7. Januar, In Spanien ist Revolution, Drüben in Deutschland herrscht Not*, and *Wir sind der Freiheit Soldaten* seem to be some of the poems that Eisler and Renn reportedly reworked for this concert. This is evidenced, among other things, by the

50 Schmidt, *Ein Lied – ein Atemzug*, 65.

Fig 2.4. Right: Eisler with a group of interbrigadists, almost certainly in Murcia. Source: Work and War in Spain. Guerra y Trabajo de España. Photographies von Keystone Press, Agency Wide World Photos, Associated Press Photos, Planeta News Ltd. Altavoz del Frente. London, The Press Department of the Spanish Embassy, 1938.

pencil note "18:00 – 15:00. Teatro Romea" on one of the drafts for *In Spanien ist Revolution* (page 15 of Source R). These times could represent the concert and rehearsal timings. The following photograph (Fig. 2.4) shows Eisler at the piano, surrounded by interbrigadists, who appear to hold the hectographed copies reproduced above. The photograph depicts either the concert rehearsal or an improvised "party" organised impromptu at the Hotel Victoria, where Eisler was apparently staying. According to Renn's civil war chronicle, a number of interbrigadists sang battle songs there, accompanied by Eisler at the piano.[51] The seriousness of the photographed soldiers, along with the title of the photo, points to the first option.

Did Eisler actually set these three lyrics for battle songs to music? As no musical sources for songs setting either *In Spanien ist Revolution* or *Drüben in Deutschland herrscht Not* have been found, and no interbrigadist ever mentioned a musical setting for these poems, I infer that he did not. Renn's marginal symbols marking the verses' rhythmic structures in the drafts for *In Spanien ist*

51 On this gathering at the Hotel Victoria see Ludwig Renn, *Der spanische Krieg. Dokumentarischer Bericht* (Berlin: Das Neue Berlin, 2006), 197 and Schmidt, *Ein Lied – ein Atemzug*, 61.

*Revolution* and *Drüben in Deutschland herrscht Not* (Fig. 2.5) suggest that the poems may have been rhythmically declaimed by the German interbrigadists at the Murcia concert. The same is likely true of an undetermined French poem, also now lost. Eisler stated he received it from Jules Dumont, the commander of the French battalion of the XI Brigade, a poem he then "rehearsed with the French comrades".[52]

Rhythmically organised unison declamation of political texts had already become a common performance practice in German communist circles since the early 1920s, particularly among agitprop collectives, at a time when appropriate battle songs were still lacking. The Berlin organisation of the KPD founded a *Sprechchor* (speaking choir) in 1922 for this purpose. A snare drum sometimes accompanied the declamation, providing the metric pulse.[53] Faced with a similar situation in Spain, Eisler and Renn may have resorted to this practice during their improvised concert. According to GDR music historian Inge Lammel, prisoners in Sachsenhausen and other Nazi concentration camps also employed this technique on occasion, having learned it in their youth as members of communist groups.[54] An example of how these speaking choirs may have sounded can be found in Eisler's *Die Maßnahme* (1930), in which he notated some sections where the choir rhythmically declaims the lyrics, accompanied by the constant and regular sound of a snare drum (Ex. 2.3).

A few days after the arrival of the German survivors in Murcia, a new relief of soldiers – apparently consisting mostly of Spaniards – arrived at the military compound to replenish the ranks of the XI Brigade following the massacre in Madrid on 7 January. According to a contemporary report by Franz Dahlem, head of the Central Political Commission of the International Brigades, approximately 200 Spaniards joined the Thälmann Brigade in Murcia.[55] In addition to providing the interbrigadists with recreation and a degree of cultural stimulation, Renn noted that the concert organised in Murcia aimed to foster personal and cultural bonds between the German and Spanish soldiers by introducing "our [German] popular music to the Spaniards and theirs to us."[56]

52 See Eisler, "Über ein Konzert bei den internationalen Brigaden".

53 On the history of the communist *Sprechchöre* see Oliver Bendel, *Das revolutionäre Arbeitertheater der Weimarer Zeit. Theater als Instrument kommunistischer Propaganda* (PhD diss., University Konstanz, 2004), 24–34; Inge Lammel, *Lieder der Agitprop-Truppen vor 1945* (Leipzig: Friedrich Hofmeister, 1959), 16–17; Friedrich Knilli, "Die Arbeiterbewegung und die Medien. Ein Rückblick", *Gewerkschaftliche Monatshefte* 25 (1974), 349–362.

54 Inge Lammel, *Arbeiterlied–Arbeitergesang. Hundert Jahre Arbeitermusikkultur in Deutschland. Aufsätze und Vorträge aus 40 Jahren 1959–1998* (Berlin: Hentrich & Hentrich, 2002), 163.

55 Franz Dahlem's reports at: Stiftung Archiv der Parteien und Massenorganisationen der DDR-Bundesarchiv (Berlin), Ref. SgY 11 / V 237 / 1 / 6 – Folder I. 1. 4.

56 Renn, *Krieg*, 199. "Denn dieses Konzert sollte zuerst die Spanier mit unserer volkstümlichen Musik bekannt machen, dann uns mit ihrer."

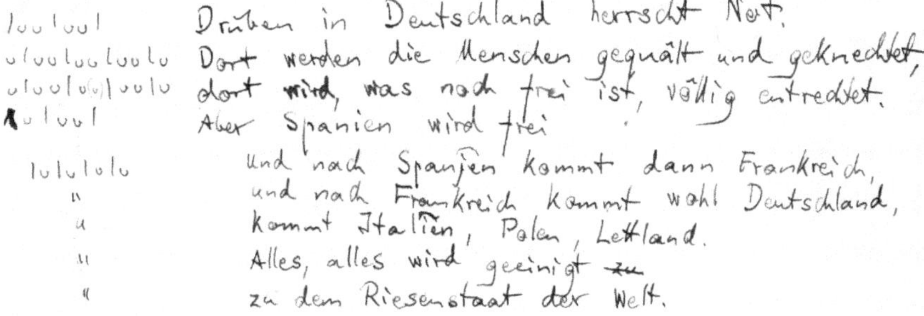


Fig. 2.5. Renn's markings of the lyrics's rhythmic structures in the drafts for *Drüben in Deutschland herrscht Not.* Source: "Nicht vertonte Text", Hanns-Eisler-Archiv, cat. no. 4026, p. 14.

Ex. 2.3. Sprechchor "Wer für den Kommunismus kämpft" (Those who fight for communism), no. 3b from Eisler's *Die Massnahme,* op. 20 (1931). Source: Universal Edition, Vienna, no. 16903 (1977), p. 24.

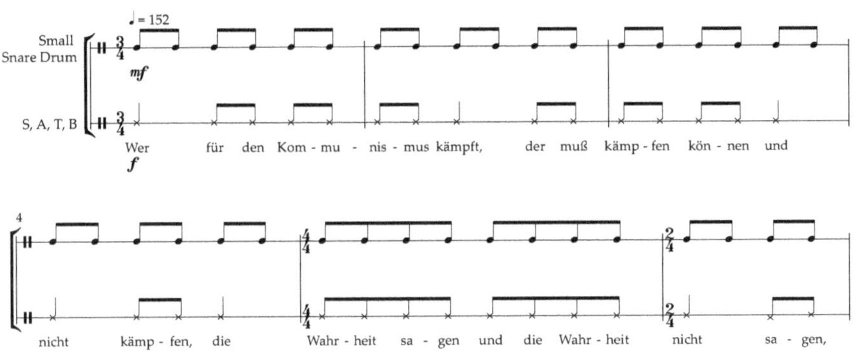


NB. Das Tempo des Sprechchores ist etwa Viertel = 152 gedacht, es ist jedoch auf umbedingte Deutlichkeit der Aussprache Rücksicht zu nehmen (The tempo of the spoken chorus is intended to be around quarter note = 152, but the clarity of pronunciation must be taken into account)

According to Renn's and Eisler's accounts, the first part of the concert featured several German and Spanish battle songs performed by a chorus of interbrigadists. They sang Paul Dessau's *Spaniens Himmel breitet seine Sterne* (*Spain's Sky Spreads Its Stars*), Eisler's *Das Lied vom 7. Januar*, and his *Marcha del Quinto Regimiento,* among others. Eisler also provided accompaniment at the piano for "a group of Jewish volunteers singing some of their wonderful folk songs" and played some unspecified "militant music [kämpferische Musik] without vocal accompaniment". Rhythmic choral recitations of the aforementioned German and French poems were likely included in this first portion of the concert. Eisler wrote an insightful account of the performance by the traumatised German survivors.

> The volunteers sang on the stage. Some of them were wounded and had bandages. Volunteers and Spaniards sat in the auditorium. The wild hunger for a cultural life, even the simplest one, was shocking. You have to understand that correctly. The volunteers had been through enormous hardships and had even greater hardships ahead of them. Having been pulled out of their positions, they felt the need to give expression to all that was difficult and great, to socialise with the other battalions of the various nationalities, to fraternise.
>
> It was a truly moving event. The singing was not beautiful, the voices were hoarse due to the extreme cold in the trenches. But the singing was fresh and enthusiastic. This is how the peasants must have sung their Bundschuhl songs during the peasant wars, this is how the Taborites must have sung, this is how the "Marseillaise" must have sounded for the first time. For me as a composer, it was the most instructive evening, because it showed once again how necessary music is and how important it can be in the great battles for a new world.[57]

Renn wrote in his chronicle of the civil war, *Der spanische Krieg*, that in the second part of the concert, one or several Spaniards sang a number of unspecified flamenco songs accompanied by a guitarist. What Renn referred to as "flamenco" also possibly included contrafacta of popular southern Spanish songs such as *Los cuatro muleros* (*The Four Muleteers*) or perhaps more modern pieces in the popular forms of *copla* or *cuplé*. The soldiers likely provided these songs with new lyrics about the antifascist struggle in Spain. These "flamenco" or "aflamencado" musical genres, which were very popular among the Spanish working classes at the time, offered a model for musical bonding among Spanish leftists that was quite different from the model of battle songs favoured by German leftists. "Our internationals were not enthusiastic about

[57] "Auf der Bühne sangen die Freiwilligen. Ein Teil von ihnen war verwundet und hatte Verbände. Im Zuschauerraum saßen Freiwillige und Spanier. Erschütternd war der wilde Hunger nach einem kulturellen Leben, selbst nach dem einfachsten. Man muß das richtig verstehen. Die Freiwilligen hatten enorme Strapazen hinter sich und noch größere vor sich. Aus der Stellung gezogen, war es für sie ein Bedürfnis, allem Schweren und Großartigen einen Ausdruck zu geben, mit den anderen Bataillonen der verschiedenen Nationalitäten Fühlung zu bekommen, sich zu verbrüdern. Es war eine wirklich ergreifende Veranstaltung. Schön wurde nicht gesungen, die Stimmen waren heiser durch die große Kälte in den Stellungen. Aber es wurde frisch gesungen, und so wurde begeistert gesungen. So müssen die Bauern in den Bauernkriegen ihre Bundschuhlieder, so die Taboriten gesungen haben, so muß die 'Marseillaise' das erste Mal geklungen haben. Für mich als Komponisten war es der lehrreichste Abend, denn er zeigte wieder, wie notwendig die Musik und wie wichtig sie sein kann in den großen Kämpfen um eine neue Welt." Eisler, "Über ein Konzert bei den internationalen Brigaden"; Renn, *Krieg*, 199.

it [the "flamenco" songs]," Renn recounted, because "[t]he musical flourishes and the squeezing of the voice through the nose were too foreign to them. And the Spanish dances also left them cold. The Spaniards, however, raved all the more with joy."[58] Although Renn emphasised that the concert's "political aim" was to strengthen the bonds between the Germans and the Spaniards through a common celebration, his description of the cold reception of flamenco contrasts with usual historiographical accounts of musical performance as a form of universal understanding and brotherhood among the interbrigadists.

## Dark Evenings

Source R also contains two satirical poems authored by Renn, entitled *Gefängnis* (*Prison*) and *Betrachtung* (*Contemplation*). *Gefängnis* reflects his experiences in a Nazi prison between 1934 and 1935. Both poems are written in an ironic tone and do not convey any high literary ambitions.[59] The poems may have been intended for recitation aloud, possibly as part of some entertainment activity within the German brigade, perhaps at the end of the day. According to Kantorowitz, Renn's experiences in Nazi prison were a relatively common topic of conversation among his circle of interbrigadists.[60]

The document also contains two typewritten, non-political texts that are significantly more ambitious in style and form than the battle-song lyrics or the poems about life in prison. These poems explore Renn's inner experiences and feelings during that period. One of them is an untitled love poem dedicated "to H. S."[61] These are most likely the initials of the German antifascist writer and journalist Hans Siemsen (1891–1969), whom Renn presumably admired both as an activist and a writer. Siemsen, who lived in Berlin from 1919 until he went into exile in Paris in 1934, was open about his homosexuality and maintained extensive contacts with other homosexual intellectuals and artists such as Klaus Mann and Alfred Flechtheim. Unlike Renn, he openly addressed homosexual love in his literary work and was politically committed to opposing Paragraph 175, the German law criminalising homosexual acts between men. Renn's poem begins with a "dark evening", an allusion to the secrecy and covertness of homosexual desire. The poetic use of twilight as a symbol for homosexuality was relatively common among homosexual writers of the time.[62]

58 Renn, *Krieg*, 199

59 The poems are reproduced in Diego Alonso, "Kampflieder, Satiere, Homoerotik. Ludwig Renns 'nicht vertonte Texte' aus der Zeit des Spanischen Bürgerkriegs im Hanns Eisler Archiv", *Eisler-Mitteilungen* 72 (February 2022), 7–13.

60 Kantorowicz, *Spanisches Kriegstagebuch*, 81–82.

61 HEA, cat. no. 4026, p. 19.

62 André Tellier's then-popular novel about homosexuality was entitled *Twilight Men* (1931); the Spanish poet Federico García Lorca called his 1935–1936 collection of

| An H. S | To H. S. |
|---|---|
| dunkel der abend. | dark [is] the evening. |
| es klangen die toene | the sounds |
| von deines fluegels | of your wing's [/piano's] |
| klingenden saiten, | resounding strings rang out, |
| und von gruengold | and a tendril of green-gold |
| flocht sich ein rankwerk | woven through |
| mit roter rubine | with red ruby |
| fruechten durchsaeht. | fruits throughout. |
| weit war der raum | the space was wide |
| und der himmel gespannt | and the sky stretched out |
| grenzenlos blauend. | boundlessly blue, |
| da flammte mein herz | my heart flared then |
| in trunkener lohe empor | in a drunken blaze |
| und du trugst mich dahin | and you carried me there |
| im sturme des jauchzens. | in a storm of rejoicing. |

Given the private nature of these poems, the question arises as to why Renn passed them on to Eisler or why Eisler took these documents with him. What seems certain is that Renn did not give them to Eisler with the intention of setting them to music, not only because of the very private content of these texts but also because they represent the kind of sentimental poetry that Eisler generally rejected. Did Eisler inadvertently take not only the two battle-song texts but also other papers from Renn due to the hectic military environment or the general hustle and bustle of concert preparations? Or did Renn want the documents to be kept safe and, therefore, asked Eisler, who was about to return to Paris by plane, to hold onto them until they met again? Did Renn feel a need to remove these documents from the military environment of the International Brigades precisely because of allusions to his homosexuality in these two poems? If that was the case, this concern was probably justified, as just six months after Eisler's visit, Renn's homosexuality became more widely known, and he was effectively expelled from the army by the Soviet colonel and military adviser to the 11th Brigade. He was relieved of his post and forced to leave Spain.[63]

---

poems about homosexual love *Sonetos del amor oscuro* (*Sonnets of Shaded Love*). See "Color Symbolism", in Wayne R. Dynes and Warren Johansson, eds., *Encyclopedia of Homosexuality*, vol. I (London: Routledge, 2016), 250.

63 On Renn's expulsion from the brigade, see Erich Günthart, "Der Tod von Hans Beimler und Louis Schuster in Ludwig Renns 'Der Spanische Krieg'", *Zeitschrift des Forschungsverbundes SED-Staat der Freien Universität Berlin* 43 (2019): 106–130; and Michael Uhl, *Mythos Spanien. Das Erbe der Internationalen Brigaden in der DDR* (Bonn: J. H. W. Dietz, 2004), 165.

## Disillusionment and Confusion

On 15 January, during Eisler's second stay in Valencia, the local press wrote that the composer was in Spain "informing himself" for a series of lectures on the Spanish Civil War that he planned to give soon thereafter in the United States.[64] Although no notes by him on the Spanish conflict have survived, and he never lectured on this topic in the USA or elsewhere, the report could be partly true, as he had given some lectures on music and antifascism during his 1935 tour of the USA, and he may have intended to do so again during his upcoming return there. Nevertheless, his primary reason for visiting Spain was certainly to collaborate as a composer with antifascist groups, most notably the German-speaking volunteers of the International Brigades. As mentioned, it was almost certainly Renn who facilitated Eisler's awareness of the need for his compositional skills in Spain. The privileges Eisler enjoyed in Spain – such as travelling incognito, his exceptional arrival in and departure from the country by plane, having an exclusive interpreter throughout his stay, and even enjoying a short "holiday" in Alicante – all suggest that the Comintern encouraged and supported his trip to the country.

But then, why didn't he stay longer in the country and take a more active role in musical propaganda for the war, as his friend Ernst Busch did shortly after Eisler left the country? The Moscow-based newspaper for the German-speaking section of the Comintern, the *Deutsche Zentral-Zeitung*, attempted to provide a reasonable narrative in a piece of news published on 15 January 1937. After discussing Eisler's stay and compositional activities in Madrid, the anonymous German journalist wrote that "for the time being, Eisler will only be in Spain for a short time. After fulfilling contractual obligations in Amsterdam, he will return to Madrid soon to make himself available to the International Brigades."[65]

As there are no records of any professional obligations for Eisler in Amsterdam or elsewhere in 1937, it is possible that this information was false and simply an excuse to justify the composer's relatively quick departure from the country. I consider it more likely that Eisler left Spain for personal reasons, including his less-than-perfect health, or perhaps psychological condition, or that his wife was waiting for him in Paris. A further reason might have been the composer's disillusionment with practical Soviet communism at the time. He likely did not overlook the repercussions that Comintern-led campaigns against "Trotskyism" entailed for the group of German intellectuals he met in Spain, in particular Arthur Koestler, Alfred Kantorowicz, Bodo Uhse, and Kurt Stern.[66]

64 Anon., "El compositor Hans [sic] Eisler en Valencia", *La voz valenciana* (15 January 1937), 6.

65 Anon., "Hans [sic] Eisler in Spanien", *Deutsche Zentral-Zeitung* 13, no. 12 (15 January 1937). I thank Christof Kugler and Peter Deeg for calling my attention to this source.

66 On these repercussions see Werner Abel, "Die versuchte Neutralisierung der

If Eisler really intended to return to Spain soon – however unlikely – he abandoned the idea quickly. At the end of January, he moved for almost eight months to Svendborg, Denmark, not far from where Brecht was living at the time. It was one of Eisler's longest stays in a single place since the beginning of his exile. The question arises whether his withdrawal from all public activity for such a long period was related, in part, to his (traumatic) experiences in Spain. In retrospect, his brief visit to wartime Spain seems less like the heroic act of a brave antifascist militant, as so often described, and more like a somewhat confused and relatively unproductive attempt to collaborate with the main struggle against fascism at the time. His diminished success there and his growing disillusionment with Soviet politics may have influenced his decision to withdraw from the militant political scene for some time.

The news item in the *Deutsche Zentral-Zeitung* contained other propagandistic half-truths, such as the claim that Eisler had just given "a concert in Madrid that was a great success" and that he intended to form an orchestra with members of the International Brigades. There is no documentary evidence of any concert organised by Eisler in Madrid. It is likely that the journalist was inaccurately referring to the aforementioned concert in Murcia, which took place one day after the report's publication. The claim that Eisler intended to form an orchestra composed of interbrigadists is almost certainly a propagandistic fabrication: the founding of musical ensembles was never a primary concern for Eisler, nor would such an initiative have been feasible in the context of wartime Spain. Amidst these fabrications, the journalist reported that Eisler was "working on a large musical work about the Spanish people's struggle for freedom against the fascist rebels". This statement was not entirely fabricated, as Eisler had indeed just completed a large vocal-symphonic work in response to the Spanish conflict, namely his *Bauernkantate* (*Peasant Cantata*). The following chapter discusses the connections of this composition to the Spanish Civil War.

---

'Münzenberg-Kreise' durch die KPD-Abwehr im republikanischen Spanien", in *Globale Räume für radikale transnationale Solidarität*, ed. Bernhard H. Bayerlein, Kasper Braskén, and Uwe Sonnenberg (Berlin: International Willi Münzenberg Forum, 2018), 467–492.

# Chapter 3

# The *Peasant Cantata* from the *German Symphony:* A Response to the Spanish War

On 4 January 1937, two days before he set out for wartime Spain, Eisler completed in Paris his only vocal-symphonic work of the wartime period inspired by the conflict: the twelve-tone *Bauernkantate* (*Peasant Cantata*) for solo bass, two speakers, choir, and orchestra. He divided the single-movement composition into four parts, titled 1. *Missernte* (*Crop Failure*), 2. *Sicherheit* (*Safety*), 3. *Flüstergespräche. Melodram* (*Whispered Conversations: Melodrama*), and 4. *Bauernliedchen* (*Peasant Ditty*). The figure of the revolutionary peasant-fighter – a common symbol of Spanish antifascism at the time – is key in parts 1, 2, and 4; these parts were scored for solo bass accompanied by choir and orchestra. Part 3 was composed in direct response to the bombing of Madrid by the Nazi Condor Legion; this section is a melodrama for two speakers (actors), also accompanied by choir and orchestra. This chapter analyses these relationships in detail and shows how the cantata belongs to a large corpus of artworks that addressed the Spanish Civil War through the figure of the revolutionary peasant as a transhistorical and supranational subject.[1]

Eisler wrote the text for parts 1–3 based on several excerpts from the novel *Brot und Wein* (*Bread and Wine*, 1936) by the communist politician and writer Ignazio Silone (1900–1978), who is now regarded as one of the most significant Italian novelists of his generation.[2] Silone completed this novel, originally entitled *Pane e vino* (*Bread and Wine*), in 1935 while in exile in Switzerland, fleeing fascist Italy. Set in contemporary Italy, *Brot und Wein* explores the desperate situation of the peasantry in the Abruzzo region. The main character, Pietro Spina, is a socialist hero who secretly returns from exile to his native Abruzzo in 1935, on the eve of the Italo–Abyssinian War. His aim is to restore the lost

1 The date of completion of the cantata is noted on the manuscript, which is now preserved in the HEA in Berlin, under the signature HEA 944, fols. 35–52. For my study of the cantata, I have used this manuscript and the work's partial publication in *Hanns Eisler. Lieder und Kantaten*, vol. 3 (Leipzig: Breitkopf & Härtel, 1958) as musical sources.

2 On Silone's life and work in the 1930s see Deborah Holmes, *Ignazio Silone in Exile: Writing and Antifascism in Switzerland 1929–1944* (Aldershot: Ashgate, 2005); Maria Nicolai Paynter, *Ignazio Silone: Beyond the Tragic Vision* (Toronto: University of Toronto Press, 2000).

sense of brotherhood among the peasants of this region and compel them to resist fascism. In addition to depicting the peasants' misery and the clandestine antifascist resistance in contemporary Italy, key themes in this novel include the Italian expansionist war in Ethiopia, the peasants' religious faith, and the Catholic Church's allegiance to fascism.

The novel was first published in German translation and was soon thereafter translated into several languages, gaining considerable popularity in Europe and the Americas.[3] Eisler, who read it no later than December 1936, shared his appreciation for *Brot und Wein* with a wide array of antifascist intellectuals worldwide, including Stefan Zweig, Arturo Toscanini, Thomas Mann, and Bertolt Brecht.[4]

For the text of parts 1 and 2 of the *Peasant Cantata*, Eisler used excerpts from a single portion of *Brot und Wein*, on pages 99–100, which he modified slightly. In this passage of the novel, an Italian peasant shares his despair with Pietro Spina after a severe storm has extensively damaged the peasants' fields. The original text of the cantata and my English translation are provided below. I have marked Eisler's main additions and changes from Silone's original in italics.[5]

Part 1. *Missernte*

Wenn Gott sich nicht um den Regen kümmert, um was kümmert er sich dann? Wenn er die Macht hat, sich um den Regen zu kümmern, und erlaubt einem Orkan, die Armen zu ruinieren, was ist das für ein Gott? Gibt es denn keine Gerechtigkeit, die er fürchten muss? Ist es denn möglich, dass er niemand Rechenschaft schuldig ist? *Wenn Gott sich nicht um den Regen kümmert, um was kümmert er sich dann?*

Part 1. *Crop Failure*

If God does not care about the rain, what does he care about? If he has the power to take care of the rain and allows a hurricane to ruin the poor, what kind of God is that? Is there then no justice that he must fear? Is it possible that he is not accountable to anyone? *If God does not care about the rain, what does he care about?*

3 Ignazio Silone, *Brot und Wein. Roman*, translated by Adolf Saager (Zürich: Oprecht & Helbling, 1936). On the date of publication, see the advertisement in *Der Bund*, vol. 87, no. 161 (5 April 1936): 6.

4 On the esteem of the novel by these and other authors, see Arturo Larcati, "Stefan Zweigs heimliche Liebe zur italienischen Literatur", in *Am liebsten wäre mir Rom! Stefan Zweig und Italien* (Blaufelden: Königshausen & Neumann, 2019), 31–53; Elisabetta Mazzetti, *Thomas Mann und die Italiener* (Frankfurt am Main: Peter Lang, 2000), 163–184; David Pike, *Deutsche Schriftsteller im sowjetischen Exil. 1933–1945* (Frankfurt am Main: Suhrkamp, 1981), 286.

5 For a more detailed study of Eisler's modifications see Phleps, *Deutsche Sinfonie*, 201–204.

Part 2. *Sicherheit*

Während des ganzen Lebens sucht so ein armer Mann sich ein wenig in Sicherheit zu bringen, aber er kommt nie in Sicherheit, in Sicherheit. Ein armer Mann baut sich ein Haus, kommt ein *Hitzesommer* oder eine Überschwemmung, und er ist ohne Dach. So ist er nie in Sicherheit, in Sicherheit. *So ein armer Mann ist immer in Angst.* Da hat man ein Haus, kommt ein Erdbeben. *Da ist man gesund, kommt eine Krankheit. Man hat ein Stück Land, muß es verkaufen.* Man kommt nie aus der Angst heraus. Man kommt nie aus der Angst heraus. *Wenn Gott sich nicht um die Armen kümmert, um wen kümmert er sich dann? Was ist das für ein Gott?*

Part 2. *Safety*

Throughout life, such a poor man seeks to make himself a little safe, but he never makes it to safety, *to safety*. A poor man builds a house, comes a *hot summer* or a flood, and he is without a roof. Then he is never safe, never safe. *Such a poor man is always in fear.* You have a house, an earthquake hits. *You're healthy, then an illness comes along. You have a piece of land, you have to sell it.* You never escape fear. You never escape fear. *If God does not care about the poor, who does he care about? What kind of God is that?*

The text for part 3 of the cantata is extracted mostly from two related scenes at the end of *Brot und Wein* (pp. 317 and 330). In these scenes of the novel, Pietro Spina is in Rome and talks to the wife and the mother of an antifascist political prisoner. The wife complains about the constant postponement of her husband's trial and mentions the Italian fascist government's efforts to hide the actions of the underground resistance against the imperialist war in Ethiopia. Spina later informs the man, newly released from prison, about the war's development. Slightly modifying Silone's original, Eisler wrote the following dialogue for two male speakers.[6] His main additions to Silone's text are marked in italics; words deleted from the original are in strikethrough.

Part 3. *Flüstergespräche*

– Wenn sie wenigstens den Prozeß den Verhafteten machen würden.
– Alle diese Prozesse werden immer wieder verschoben. Die Regierung will nicht, daß es bekannt wird, daß es Leute gibt, die den Krieg bekämpfen.

Part 3. *Whispered Conversations*

– If they would at least put the arrested on trial.
– All these processes keep getting postponed. The government does not want it to be known that there are people fighting the war.

6 For a detailed comparison of Silone's and Eisler's texts see Phleps, *Deutsche Sinfonie*, 201–205.

| | |
|---|---|
| – Wie steht es mit dem Krieg? | – How goes the war? |
| – Gestern haben sie wieder ein Spital bombardiert. | – They bombed another hospital yesterday. |
| – Wer? | – Who? |
| – Die, die Kultur dorthin bringen wollen. | – Those who want to bring culture there. |
| – Wann beginnt die Regenzeit wieder? | – When does the rainy season start again? |
| – Im Mai. | – In May. |
| – Erst im Mai? ~~Die armen Abessinier!~~ | – Not until May? ~~The poor Abyssinians!~~ |
| [Eisler's addition] | [Eisler's addition] |
| – *Die Generäle sagen, daß sie die Kultur verteidigen wollen!* | – *The generals say they want to defend culture!* |
| – *Was für eine Kultur?* | – *What culture?* |
| – *Die der Generäle.* | – *That of the generals.* |

## The Culture of the Generals

The choice of this particular passage from *Brot und Wein* and the changes that Eisler made to Silone's text strongly suggest that part 3 of the cantata was composed in reaction to the bombing of Madrid by the German Condor Legion in late 1936. Significantly, the chosen passage is the only one in the entire *Brot und Wein* in which fascist bombardments are mentioned. Silone referred to the 30 December 1935 airstrike by the Italian air force on a hospital in Dolo, Ethiopia, which killed around twenty-two to thirty people, if not similar bombardments of Ethiopian hospitals in early January 1936. When Eisler composed the cantata one year later, these figures would have seemed small in comparison with the larger number of people killed by bombs in Spain from mid-November on. Most of these bombs were dropped from German aircraft by soldiers of the Condor Legion under Franco's direction. This unit of the German air force served the rebels during the civil war, where they developed strategic bombing methods that were later used widely throughout the Second World War. The Condor Legion heavily bombed Madrid's main buildings, including numerous libraries, archives, museums, and several hospitals in the city centre. Between the onset of the bombardments and the completion of the cantata in January 1937, several hundred civilians were killed by these bombs, including a significant number of patients admitted to these hospitals.[7]

7 On these bombings see Josep Maria Solé i Sabaé and Joan Villarroya, *España en llamas. La guerra civil desde el aire* (Madrid: Temas de Hoy, 2003).

Compared to the bomb load-outs developed for the Second World War, these bombings were not as intensive; however, as the first of their kind to occur in Europe, they evinced significant psychological effects both in Spain and abroad. From that point on, many other international artists and intellectuals denounced these bombardments in their works. Most of them conveyed a profound sense of outrage akin to that expressed by the Chilean poet Pablo Neruda in *España en el corazón* (*Spain in the Heart*, 1936–1938).

Generales
traidores:
mirad mi casa muerta,
mirad España rota:
pero de cada casa muerta sale
metal ardiendo
en vez de flores,
pero de cada hueco de España
sale España,
pero de cada niño muerto sale un
fusil con ojos,
pero de cada crimen nacen balas
que os hallarán un día el sitio
del corazón.

Preguntaréis ¿por qué su
poesía
no nos habla del sueño, de las hojas,
de los grandes volcanes de su país
natal?

¡Venid a ver la sangre por las
calles,
venid a ver
la sangre por las calles,
venid a ver la sangre
por las calles![8]

Treacherous
generals:
look at my dead house,
look at Spain broken:
from every house, burning metal
comes out
instead of flowers,
but from every crater of Spain
comes Spain
from every dead child comes a
rifle with eyes,
from every crime bullets are born
that will one day find in you the site
of the heart.

You will ask: why doesn't his
[Neruda's] poetry
speak to us of dreams, of leaves,
of the great volcanoes of his
native land?

Come and see the blood in
the streets,
come and see
the blood in the streets,
come and see the blood
in the streets!

I contend that Eisler chose the above-quoted passage from *Brot und Wein* about the bombing of hospitals as a reaction to the contemporary bombing of civilians by the Condor Legion in Madrid. He linked the text more closely to the war events in Spain by deleting Silone's references to the Second Italo–Abyssinian War and including a mention of "the generals". The term "generals", which also opens Neruda's poem, was one of the designations for the rebels, as they were led by a military junta (Francisco Franco had been appointed "General-

8 Neruda, "Generales traidores", in *España en el corazón*, 8

issimo" of the rebel side in September 1936). These links to real events seem to explain why Eisler preferred the directness of the spoken words, which he further enhanced by requesting the speakers to present the dialogue "without expression" ("ohne Ausdruck"). Up until 1937, Eisler had employed melodrama only once, for his 1931–1932 setting of Brecht's *Die Mutter* (*The Mother*), in which he also alluded to non-fictional events.[9]

Eisler related the melodrama's orchestral accompaniment to the notion of war through an ostinato pattern consisting of fivefold repetitions of a single pitch in *pianissimo*. This insistent motif, which evokes a sense of anxious expectation, is consistently played by the strings, except once, immediately before the question: "Wie steht es mit dem Krieg?" (How goes the war?), where it is played by the kettledrum and followed by a roll (see Ex. 3.1, bb. 175–177). The contrasting timbre of the kettledrum and the introduction of the roll draw the listener's attention and link the five-note rhythmic ostinato to this inquiry about war. This motif is almost certainly modelled on the prominent kettledrum ostinato in the "Agnus Dei" of Haydn's *Missa in tempore belli* (*Mass in Times of War*, 1796), also known as the "Paukenmesse" (Timpani Mass) due to the expressive use of timpani[10] (compare Exx. 3.1 and 3.2). In the *Missa solemnis* (1819–1823), Beethoven similarly introduced martial timpani sounds to accompany the "Agnus Dei", pleading for peace and mercy.

Musically, the melodrama is one of the most remarkable aspects of the cantata, as it constitutes a form of musical montage, akin to techniques applied in interwar photography and cinema, that unites multiple disparate and contrasting formal units.[11] The melodrama contrasts sharply with the sections that precede (*Missernte* and *Sicherheit*) and follow it (*Bauernliedchen*) by the almost total absence of motivic elaboration. The dialogue is accompanied by

9 In "Bericht vom 1. Mai 1905" (Report from the 1st of May 1905), the main characters declaim spoken dialogue accompanied by a musical ensemble, detailing the brutal police repression of a workers' demonstration on 1 May 1905 in Russia. This "report" was based on Brecht's own experiences during May 1929 in Berlin when the police shot down many workers demonstrating for better working conditions. See Jan Knopf, *Brecht-Handbuch. Theater, Lyrik, Prosa, Schriften* (Stuttgart: Metzler, 1984), 121.

10 I thank Thomas König for bringing my attention to this connection. On the meanings of this motif in Haydn's Mass, see Howard Chandler Robbin Landon, *Haydn: Chronicle and Works*, vol. 4, *The Years of The Creation* (London: Thames and Hudson, 1994), 175; Thomas Tolley, *Painting the Cannon's Roar: Music, the Visual Arts, and the Rise of an Attentive Public in the Age of Haydn, c.1750 to c.1810* (Aldershot: Ashgate Publishing, 2001), 260.

11 On Eisler's recourse to montage techniques in other works of the 1930s see Albrech Betz, *Hanns Eisler. Musik einer Zeit, die sich eben bildet* (Munich: Edition text + kritik, 1976), 44 and 115; Bernd Sponheuer, "Angewandte Instrumentalmusik Hanns Eislers Kleine Sinfonie op. 29", *Die Musikforschung* 32, no. 3 (July/September 1979), 258–273; Károly Csipák, *Probleme der Volkstümlichkeit bei Hanns Eisler* (Munich: Emil Katzbichler, 1975).

Ex. 3.1. Hanns Eisler, *Peasant Cantata*, bb. 173–189.

15

a tempo

Kl. I (B) II

Pk.

Chor S. A.

1. Sprechst. Wie steht es mit dem Krieg? Wer?

2. Sprechst. Ges-tern ha-ben sie wie-der ein Spi - tal bom-bar-diert.

a tempo

Vl. I Vl. II Va. Vc. Kb.

Fg. I II

Chor S. A.

1. Sprechst. Wann be-ginnt die Re-gen-zeit wie-der? Erst im Mai?

2. Sprechst. Die die Kul-tur dort-hin brin-gen wol-len Im Mai.

Vl. I Vl. II Va. Vc. Kb.

Ex. 3.2. Joseph Haydn, "Agnus Dei" of the *Missa in tempore belli* (1796), bb. 8–12. © by Deutscher Verlag für Musik Leipzig.

long *pianissimo* notes played by the strings and hummed by the choir's women with closed mouth. While the cantata's sections 1, 2, and 4 have ternary, quaternary, and binary structures respectively, the structure of the melodrama is non-repetitive. The free structure, lack of motivic development, and the predominance of sustained sonorities are suggestive of film-music styles. This montage-like character differentiates this melodrama from those featured in *Die Mutter* (1931–1932), in Eisler's later theatre works of the 1940s and 1950s, and in canonical German operas such as Beethoven's *Fidelio* (1805), Carl Maria von Weber's *Der Freischütz* (1821), or Alban Berg's *Wozzeck* (1922).

## Transhistorical Peasant Revolutions

After this montage on militaristic aggression and urban antifascism, the cantata returns in part 4 to the central narrative of peasants' misery and revolution. The composition concludes with an appeal to the peasants, urging them to take up arms against their oppressors.

| | |
|---|---|
| Bauer, steh auf!<br>Nimm deinen Lauf!<br>Laß es dich nicht verdrießen,<br>du wirst doch sterben müssen. | Peasant, rise up!<br>Take your course!<br>Don't let it bother you,<br>you will have to die after all. |
| Bauer, steh auf!<br>Nimm deinen Lauf!<br>Niemand kann Hilf dir geben,<br>mußt selber dich erheben. | Peasant, rise up!<br>Take your course!<br>No one can give you help,<br>you must rise yourself. |
| Bauer, steh auf!<br>Nimm deinen Lauf! | Peasant, rise up!<br>Take your course! |

The text of the cantata's final section, the *Bauernliedchen* (*Peasant Ditty*), is drawn from Brecht and Eisler's *Lied der Sichel* (*Song of the Sickle*). This piece is one of Eisler's thirteen songs composed for Brecht's satirical anti-Nazi theatrical play *Die Rundköpfe und die Spitzköpfe* (*Round Heads and Pointed Heads*, 1934–1936). Brecht sets the story in the fictitious southern country of Yahoo, where most of the inhabitants are impoverished peasants, distinguished by either round or pointed heads. A group of peasants from both sides plan to revolt against their oppressive landlords. The sickle becomes the symbol of their revolution, and the *Sichel* song their anthem. (Eisler composed the songs for Brecht's play in 1934 in the style of his *Kampfmusik* or militant music from the late 1920s and early 1930s.)

The lyrics of *Lied der Sichel* are a textual reworking of the *Bauernlied* (*Peasant Song*) from the opera *Der Bergsee* (*The Mountain Lake*, 1909–1911) by the now largely forgotten Austrian composer Julius Bittner (1874–1939). Like most of Bittner's operas, *Der Bergsee* was composed in a post-Wagnerian style, with a libretto written by Bittner himself. The three-act opera, based on historical events, portrays the violent uprising of Salzburg's peasants in 1525, as they sought to end their suffering under oppressive local rulers. These uprisings were part of the German Peasants' Wars, a topic that deeply interested Eisler throughout his life and one he regarded as a precedent for the fight against fascism in Spain, as we shall later explore. Bittner's lyrics read as follows:

| | |
|---|---|
| Bau'r steh auf!<br>Nimm dein' Lauf!<br>Es darf dich nicht verdrießen,<br>Daß du wirst sterben müssen. | Peasant, rise up!<br>Take your course!<br>Let it not grieve thee<br>that thou must die. |
| Bau'r, wahr dein Recht!<br>Bau'r, sei kein Knecht!<br>Wir woll'n auch unser Leben han,<br>nicht wie ein Stück'l Vieh dastahn! | Peasant, protect your right!<br>Peasant, don't be a slave!<br>We want to have our lives back,<br>not to be like a piece of cattle! |
| Bau'r steh auf!<br>Nimm dein' Lauf! | Peasant, rise up!<br>Take your course! |

Ex. 3.3. *Bauernlied* (*Peasant Song*) in Bittner's *Der Bergsee* (Act II, bb. 7–14, following rehearsal number 13). Source: Julius Bittner, *Der Bergsee* (Berlin: K. Fliegel & co., 1911), p. 151.

In Bittner's opera, the *Bauernlied* serves as the revolutionary anthem of the Salzburg peasants. The melody first appears in the overture (bb. 32–50), before being sung by a group of male peasants at the close of Act I (bb. 7–26, following rehearsal mark 44) and again at the start of Act II (bb. 6–30, following rehearsal mark 13; see Ex. 3.3).

For the *Peasant Cantata*'s final section Eisler maintained Brecht's lyrics for the *Sickle Song* and reworked part of Bittner's original melody. The vocal melody shown in Ex. 3.4 begins with a recognisable quotation of the opening motif from Bittner's *Bauernlied.* The remaining ten pitches are twelve-tone organised and unrelated to Bittner's song. The marching-song character is preserved by the constant pulse in the bass. The triplets in the strings are a reworking of the dotted descending melody that accompanies the vocal melody in Bittner's song (Ex. 3.3).

Ex. 3.4. *Bauernliedchen* (bb. 219–226) (Piano reduction from *Lieder und Kantaten*, p. 100).

[Marschtempo]

Bau - er, steh auf, nimm dei - nen Lauf, laß es dich nicht ver - drie - ßen, du wirst doch ster - ben müs - sen.

Vls, Vla.

Vc. Cb

## The Peasant-Fighter as a Symbol of Spanish Antifascism

Eisler's decision to centre the cantata around the revolutionary peasant-fighter was largely driven by his Marxist worldview, which framed Spain as still deeply entrenched in "feudal" structures. From this perspective, the Spanish war was seen as an extension of historical peasant uprisings from the "feudal" period. Indeed, Spain at the time remained predominantly agrarian, with vast single-crop latifundia dominated by wealthy landowners, while impoverished, landless peasants laboured under harsh conditions. This stood in stark contrast to the situation in Germany, Britain, France, and the Netherlands, where industrial workers constituted a significantly larger proportion of the population, and a greater percentage of peasants owned their own land. The Spanish peasants' persistent demands for land ownership were categorically dismissed by affluent landowners, who received support from both the Spanish monarchy and the Church. Consequently, many peasants turned to revolutionary anarchism from 1870 onwards, with their frequent insurrectionary protests routinely suppressed by the police. Viewed through the lens of early twentieth-century Marxism, the Spanish peasantry were potential revolutionary agents within a pre-industrial "feudal" framework.

When the Spanish monarchy was overthrown in 1931, the vast majority of landowners and the Catholic Church rejected the liberal, social, and secularising political programme of the new Republican government, which included the first serious attempt at land reform in Spain's history. Consequently, the military's effort to overthrow the Second Spanish Republic in 1936 garnered support from most landowners and the Catholic Church, although it faced opposition from the unlanded peasants, who constituted the majority of the population. Throughout the war, the peasants constituted the bulk of the Republican army. Consequently, hundreds of artworks created both in Spain and abroad in support of the Republic featured the figure of the revolutionary peasant-fighter as a central motif. The *Peasant Cantata* belongs to this corpus, sharing its primary subject with key artworks of the same period, in which the Spanish peasantry also symbolised the antifascist struggle within the country.[12]

Figs. 3.1 to 3.3 illustrate three examples of this symbolism in its quintessential form: the poster, a prominent medium of visual propaganda during the conflict. The first poster, created shortly after the war began by the renowned Spanish communist artist Josep Renau, features a snake impaled on a rifle. This imagery represents the "rebel landlord" (*propietario faccioso*), depicted as treacherous for opposing the democratically elected Republican government. In Fig. 3.2, the peasant raises a clenched fist in salute, a widely recognised symbol of support for the Spanish Republic and antifascism. Above his head, the slogan reads, "Peasants. Land is yours". POUM is the acronym for the Partido Obrero de Unificación Marxista, one of the leading Spanish Marxist parties of the time. The stamp and poster, created in 1937 by the renowned Catalan artist Joan Miró for international distribution, features a figure wearing the red Catalan peasant hat (the barretina) and carries the straightforward message, "Help Spain!" (see Fig. 3.3).

The figure of the revolutionary peasant was central to several artworks showcased in the Spanish pavilion at the 1937 Exposition Internationale des Arts et Techniques dans la Vie Moderne in Paris. Notable pieces included Miró's large mural painting *El segador. Pagès català en rebel·lia* (*The Reaper: Revolutionary Catalan Peasant*, 1937) and Renau's mural-sized photomontage *L'Agriculture espagnole reposait sur: Des salaires misérables, Une inique réparation de la terre* (*Spanish Agriculture Was Based On: Miserable Wages, Unjust Compensation for the Land*, 1937). In the right section of the photomontage (see Fig. 3.4), Renau depicts a Spanish peasant ploughing a field. To the left of his mule, a vertical black graph illustrates statistical figures regarding land distribution in pre-Republican Spain, revealing that 1% of the peasants owned 43.72% of the land, while 40% of the peasants owned nothing. The landless peasant and his mule ascend diagonally toward the top of the land distribution graph, representing the wealthiest 1% of landlords. Renau's photomontage shares thematic elements with Eisler's cantata, highlighting peasant misery and the pressing need for (revolutionary) change. The use of the past tense verb

12 A recent study that examines in detail the motif of the peasant-fighter in the Spanish war is Jordana Mendelson, *Documenting Spain. Artists, Exhibition Culture, and the Modern Nation, 1929–1939* (Pennsylvania: The Pennsylvania State University, 2005), 93–184.

Fig. 3.1. José Renau. *Cartel. Decreto 7 octubre 1936* (second half of 1936), 150 x 104.5 cm. Museo Reina Sofía, Madrid. © Fundació Josep Renau – València.

Fig. 3.2. "Siwe", *Campesinos. La tierra es vuestra. P.O.U.M.* (ca. 1936). 99 x 70 cm. Source: Biblioteca Pavelló de la República, Barcelona.

Fig. 3.3. Joan Miró, *Aidez l'Espagne* (1937). 31.5 x 24.5 cm. Source: Museo Reina Sofía. Cat. no.: DE01116. © Successió Miró 2025.

in the message at the top (*reposait*) indicates to viewers that such change was already occurring in Republican Spain.[13]

Among the numerous literary works that address the plight of the Spanish peasantry and their role in the civil war, André Malraux's novel *L'Espoir* (*Hope*, 1937) and Spanish poet Miguel Hernández's *Campesino de España* (*Peasant from Spain*, 1936) stand out. The latter is one of the most well-known Spanish poems about the Civil War, featuring peasant-fighters as protagonists. Hernández composed it during the war for public recitation at events. The refrain "campesino, despierta / español, que no es tarde" (peasant, wake up! / Spaniard, it's not too late!) bears a striking resemblance to the opening of Bittner's and Brecht's peasant revolutionary anthems.[14] Among the propaganda battle songs

13 On Miró's mural for the pavilion see Robin Adèle Greeley, *Surrealism and the Spanish Civil War* (Yale: Yale University Press, 2006). On Renau's photomural see Mendelson, *Documenting Spain*, 125–184; and Javier Ortiz-Echagüe Trujillano, "Una imagen para salvar la República: fotomontajes del pabellón español en la exposición internacional de París 1937", in *La comunicación durante la Segunda República y la Guerra civil*, ed. Antonio Checa Godoy et al. (Madrid: Fragua, 2007), 471–484.

14 Miguel Hernández, "Campesino de España", *Frente Extremeño. Periódico del Altavoz del Frente de Extremadura* (24 June 1937), 2.

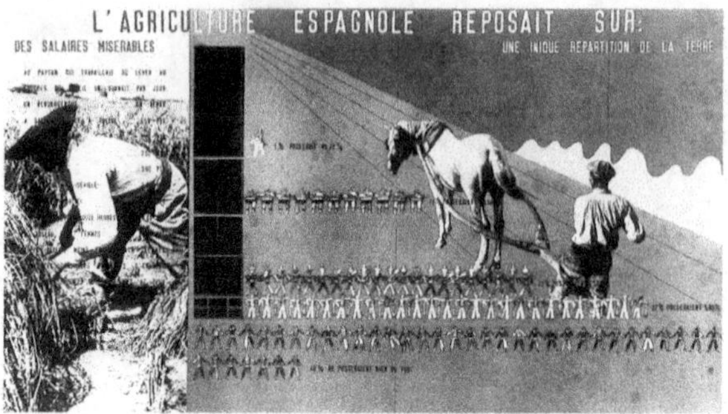


Fig. 3.4. José Renau, photomural *L'Agriculture espagnole reposait sur: Des salaires misérable, Une inique reparation de la terre,* first floor, Spanish Pavilion, 1937 Exposition Internationale des Arts et Techniques dans la vie Moderne, Paris. © Fundació Josep Renau – València. Published with kind permission.

composed during the war, the most explicit call for peasants to rise against fascism was made in Antonio Aparicio and Enrique Casal Chapi's *Los campesinos* (*The Peasants*, 1936), which I discuss in Chapter 5. The figure of the Spanish peasant-fighter also featured prominently in numerous films made in the USA to support the Republic during the Spanish Civil War, notably the documentaries *Spain in Flames* (1936) and *The Spanish Earth* (1937), as well as the Hollywood feature film *Blockade* (1938). Similar representations of peasant-fighters appear in secondary roles in *Heart of Spain* (1937), *Return to Life* (1938), and *The Will of a People* (1938).[15]

In many artworks created during the war in support of the Republic, the Spanish conflict was depicted as the final battle in a centuries-old struggle against oppression, with Spanish peasants portrayed as transhistorical revolutionary figures. This perspective was particularly evident in reinterpretations of Spanish literature from the Siglo de Oro (the sixteenth and seventeenth centuries), notably Lope de Vega's *Fuenteovejuna* (1612–1614). This play recounts the real rebellion of the Andalusian village Fuenteovejuna against the tyranny of the powerful in the fifteenth century. When the play was staged in February 1938 at the Paris Théâtre du Peuple, several French and Spanish critics highlighted the relevance of Lope de Vega's work in the context of the civil war in Spain. For Spanish playwright and literary critic Max Aub,

[15] On US films from the mid-1930s that deal with the Spanish peasantry and the Spanish Civil War, see Sonia García López, *Spain is us. La guerra civil española en el cine del Frente Popular 1936–1939* (Valencia: Universidad de Valencia, 2013).

> Today, *Fuenteovejuna* is the clearest and quickest explanation that can be given of our struggle. Four hundred and fifty years ago, the peasants were also right and had the same reasons to take up arms as they do today. [...] By bringing our problem to the stage, in the heart of Paris, *Fuenteovejuna* makes clear the tradition we [antifascists] defend, the reason and justice of our cause, and the certainty of our victory: never has a perjurer or a clique been able to do anything against an entire people.[16]

On these grounds, *Fuenteovejuna* found significant resonance in the Soviet Union. A ballet based on the play, named after its main female character, *Laurencia* (1939), premiered at the Mariinsky Theatre in Leningrad, featuring music by Soviet composer Alexander Krein and choreography by Vakhtang Chabukiani. The work was touted as a portrayal of the contemporary struggle in Spain. A prime example of realist socialist music, the stylistically conservative score is infused with orientalist, folk-like melodies, evoking the exoticist colour of nineteenth-century Russian compositions about Spain by Mikhail Glinka and Nikolai Rimsky-Korsakov. The music and choreography emphasise the ongoing contrast between the good-natured, brave peasants and their evil rulers.[17]

Eisler's cantata belongs to this corpus of works that addressed the Spanish Civil War through the figure of the revolutionary peasant as a transhistorical and supranational subject. The allusions to the bombing of hospitals and to "the generals" in the central part were sufficiently concrete to be interpreted at the time as an indirect reference to the conflict in Spain, thereby resituating the notions of peasant revolution in relation to contemporary antifascism. The significance of these symbolic elements links the cantata to many other artworks of the era that also incorporated powerful allegories related to the civil war without explicitly referencing the conflict. One of the better-known examples is Picasso's *Guernica* (1937), a large painting that, like the cantata, includes no visual elements

16 "Escuchada hoy Fuenteovejuna, es la explicación más clara y rápida que se puede dar de nuestra lucha. Hace 450 años los campesinos tenían la misma razón y las mismas razones que hoy para empuñar las armas. [...] Al llevar a las tablas, en el corazón de París, nuestro problema, *Fuenteovejuna* hace constar la tradición que defendemos, la razón y la justicia de nuestra causa y la seguridad de nuestra victoria: nada puede ni ha podido nunca un perjuro o una camarilla contra todo un pueblo". Max Aub, "El estreno de Fuenteovejuna en París", *La Vanguardia* 18.2 (1938) : 3. On the context of this theatre production and its reception see Emilio Peral Vega, *Retablos de agitación política. Nuevas aproximaciones al teatro de la Guerra Civil española* (Madrid: Iberoamericana, 2013), 111–164.

17 For this ballet piece and its premiere see Vera Vladimirovna Kuleshova, *Ispaniya i SSSR: kul'turnye svyazi 1917–1939* (*Spain and the USSR: cultural relations 1917–1939*) (Moscow: Nauka, 1975), 176–178; Maria Chiginskaya, "Lope de Vega de puntillas: el estreno del ballet *Laurencia* en Leningrado (1939)", *Anuario Lope de Vega. Texto, literatura, cultura* 22 (2016): 344–354; Veronika Ryjik, "La recepción de *Fuente Ovejuna* en Rusia", in *Fuente Ovejuna (1619–2019). Pervivencia de un mito universal*, ed. Javier Huerta Calvo (New York: IDEA/IGAS, 2019), 255–272.

directly alluding to the Spanish Civil War but features many powerful metaphors of the confrontation. In both cases, these symbolic elements were intended to be understood more broadly as universal condemnations of fascism.

## The *Peasant Cantata* in the *German Symphony*

The *Peasant Cantata* is known today as the eight movement of Eisler's impressive *German Symphony.*[18] Most studies published thus far assume that he conceived the cantata from the outset as a movement of this symphony, which he had been working on since mid-1936.[19] My analysis suggests that Eisler most likely composed the cantata as a stand-alone piece, as both the libretto and the music of the cantata differ significantly from the other movements of the symphony. Unlike all other texted movements of the *German Symphony,* the text of the cantata does not allude to events directly related to German history and includes words by an author other than Brecht. In its recourse to Silone's texts, the *Peasant Cantata* is the direct predecessor to eight twelve-tone chamber cantatas for voice(s) and ensemble that Eisler composed in early summer 1937, drawing from excerpts of Silone's first novel, *Fontamara,* and *Brot und Wein.* Musically, the cantata differs from all other vocal movements in its structure and instrumentation. The structure varies slightly from that of the other vocal movements of the symphony, as the cantata is divided into subsections and includes a substantial spoken section (the melodrama). The instrumentation is also somewhat reduced compared to that of the other movements: it does not require trombones, contrabassoon, or bass tuba, and it includes only two French horns instead of four, as well as two trumpets in B♭ instead of three.[20]

Why did Eisler decide to include this work, composed in response to the Spanish war, as a movement of his symphony about Germany? The first and perhaps most apparent answer lies in the significant number of Germans involved on each side of the Spanish conflict: around 5,000 served in the International Brigades, of whom approximately 2,000 died in Spain, while around 20,000 were part of the Condor Legion, with approximately 315 fatalities in Spain.[21] Accordingly, Eisler may have perceived the Spanish conflict as a

18 On the *German Symphony* see Phleps, *Deutsche Sinfonie,* 51–64; and Erik Levi, "Hanns Eisler's Deutsche Sinfonie", in *Hanns Eisler. A Miscellany,* ed. David Blake (Luxembourg: Harwood, 1995), 181–202.

19 Phleps, *Deutsche Sinfonie*; Rienäcker, "Die 'Bauernkantate'".

20 The cantata was not the only piece originally composed as an independent composition or as part of other works that Eisler later included as movements of his *German Symphony.* This was also the case for the third movement, the *Epilogue,* and, according to Phleps, even the *Prelude.* See Phleps, *Deutsche Sinfonie,* 56.

21 Beevor, *The Battle for Spain,* 468; Stefanie Schüler-Springorum, *Krieg und Fliegen. Die Legion Condor im Spanischen Bürgerkrieg* (Paderborn: Ferdinand Schöningh, 2010).

"small" German civil war. A second reason was the prevailing belief among many German communists that the German interbrigadists fighting fascism in Spain were the successors of the peasants who had fought in the German peasant wars of the sixteenth century. Eisler's perspective on this connection is suggested by his account of the interbrigadists' concert in Murcia, mentioned in Chapter 2. Ten months after his stay in Spain, Eisler reflected on the "fresh and enthusiastic" singing of the German interbrigadists: "This is how the peasants in the Peasants' Wars must have sung their Bundschuh songs, this is how the Taborites must have sung, this is how the 'Marseillaise' must have sounded for the first time."[22] The Bundschuh were a series of peasant rebellions in southwestern Germany from 1493 to 1517, serving as the immediate precedent for the German Peasants' War. The Taborites were a fifteenth-century religious reform sect within the Hussite movement that fought in the Land of the Bohemian Crown against the corruption of the Catholic Church.

This understanding of the German Peasants' Wars as the precursor to the class struggles of their time was primarily influenced by Eisler's reading of Friedrich Engels' *Der deutsche Bauernkrieg* (*The German Peasants' War*, 1850). Engels described the revolutions of his own time as a continuation of the peasant wars of the sixteenth century, stating, "we find already as traitors in 1525, albeit at a lower stage of development, the [same] classes and class factions that betrayed everywhere in 1848 and 1849."[23] At the end of his life, Eisler copied this excerpt from Engels' essay and updated it by adding the annotation, "1914, 1918, 1933, 1939, 1941–1945".[24] Because these notes were most likely made in response to criticisms of his opera project for *Faust* – conceived as an allegory for Germany's past and present – Eisler did not include the dates 1936–1939 as part of this series. However, it seems certain that for him, as for many other Marxist thinkers, Engels' thesis was perfectly applicable to the war against fascism in "feudal" Spain.[25]

22 "... Aber es wurde frisch gesungen, und so wurde begeistert gesungen. So müssen die Bauern in den Bauernkriegen ihre Bundschuhlieder, so die Taboriten gesungen haben, so muß die 'Marseillaise' das erste Mal geklungen haben". Hanns Eisler, "Koncert na fronte", translated into German in Eisler, "Über ein Konzert", 395–397.

23 "... Die Klassen und Klassenfraktionen, die 1848 und 49 überall verraten haben, werden wir schon 1525, wenn auch auf einer niedrigeren Entwicklungsstufe, als Verräter vorfinden", Friedrich Engels, *Der deutsche Bauernkrieg*, in *Karl Marx, Friedrich Engels, Werke*, vol. 7 (Berlin: Dietz Verlag, 1960), 409.

24 Hanns Eisler, [Notizen zur Faustus-Polemik II], in *Hanns Eisler. Musik und Politik. Schriften 1948–1962*, Gesammelte Werke III / 2, ed. Günter Mayer (Leipzig: Deutsche Verlag für Musik, 1985), 283.

25 On Ernst H. Meyer's similar understanding of the peasant wars of the sixteenth century and their musical realisation in the *Mansfelder Oratorio* (1950), see Golan Gur, "Classicism as Anti-Fascist Heritage: Realism and Myth in Ernst Hermann Meyer's Mansfelder Oratorium (1950)", in *Classical Music in the German Democratic Republic: Production and Reception*, eds. Kyle Frackman, Larson Powell (Rochester: Camden House, 2015), 34–57.

The *German Symphony* premiered in 1959 in East Berlin. For several reasons, which I discuss in the Epilogue, Eisler chose that moment to disclose the cantata's connections to the Spanish war. Just over two decades earlier, and shortly after completing the *Peasant Cantata,* he had travelled to Spain for the second and final time. The songs he composed there for the communist Fifth Regiment of Popular Militias, along with the Spanish and Catalan versions of some of his most popular battle songs, became significant propaganda artefacts, not only in Spain but also in the Soviet Union and within several European communist groups controlled by the Comintern. The following chapter recounts the uses of these songs as part of national and international propaganda in support of the Spanish Republic.

# PART II

# RECEPTION AND INFLUENCE

# Chapter 4

# Battle Songs in Times of Peace and War

In Spain, it was a very specific segment of Eisler's output – namely, his most popular battle songs – that began to gain recognition within certain leftist circles, and this only after the early 1930s. This development contrasted sharply with the reception of his atonal concert works in Austria and other Central and northern European countries, where they had begun to gain recognition from the mid-1920s onwards. His Piano Sonata No. 1, op. 1 (1923), the culmination of his studies under Schoenberg, was met with critical acclaim following its premiere and was published the following year by the prestigious Austrian publisher Universal Edition. By the end of 1924, the sonata had been performed in major cities around the world – including Berlin, Paris, New York, and Moscow – though none of these performances took place in Spain.[1] At that time, and throughout the 1930s and 1940s, Eisler's atonal concert works were virtually unknown in Spain.

The Catalan composer Robert Gerhard, who had been acquainted with Eisler since 1924, was the only Spaniard who knew Eisler's music, aesthetics, and political stance relatively well. Gerhard's profound interest in the music of Schoenberg and his school distinguished him from most Spanish modernist composers and critics of the time, who were primarily focused on French neoclassicism, particularly the music of Stravinsky. This lack of interest meant that the atonal works of Arnold Schoenberg, Alban Berg, and Anton Webern were seldom performed in interwar Spain; Eisler's works were not performed at all.

As mentioned in Chapter 1, Gerhard and Eisler met in Vienna shortly after the Catalan moved there to commence his studies with Schoenberg. During his stays in the Austrian capital and in Berlin (1923–1925 and 1926–1928, respectively), Gerhard studied the scores of some of Eisler's concert works and may have also attended several concerts featuring Eisler's music. Furthermore, Gerhard regularly read *Musikblätter des Anbruchs, Die Musik, Melos,* and other major Austrian and German musical journals, in which discussions of Eisler's music occasionally appeared.[2]

1 My sources for this survey of early international performances of Eisler's op. 1 include announcements and other news items in the *Musikblätter des Anbruch*, 1923–1925.

2 Early reviews of Eisler's works in these and other journals include Erwin Ratz, "Hanns Eisler", *Musikblätter des Anbruch* 6, no. 9 (1924): 381–384; Theodor W. Adorno, "Hanns Eisler: Duo für Violine und Violoncello op. 7 Nr. 1", *Musikblätter des Anbruch*

Upon returning to Catalonia, Gerhard authored the first essay about Eisler's music ever published in Spain. In this article, published in 1931 in the renowned weekly *Mirador*, he encouraged Catalan musicians to "dare" to perform Eisler's atonal Piano Sonata and *Piano Pieces*, op. 3 (1923), along with modernist vocal works such as *Palmström* (1924) and *Zeitungsausschnitte* (*Newspaper Clippings*, 1927).[3] Gerhard then discussed Eisler's recent reorientation towards Marxism, describing the Austrian composer as a "rabid anti-individualist" for whom musical composition served society rather than being "a refined but sterile exercise of aesthetes". He praised his friend's recent works as being "absolutely of the present time", noting that their style and subject matter neither looked to the past – likely in reference to French/Spanish neoclassicism – nor to the future, seemingly alluding to Schoenberg and his school's non-tonal works.

> Hanns Eisler plays, indeed, one of the most singular roles in today's musical life. Although he hardly ever appears in "bourgeois" concert programmes, he is one of the young composers whose works receive a high number of performances nowadays in Germany. Coming from the Schoenbergian school and gifted with one of the subtlest [compositional] techniques and the deepest spiritual quality, he has of late evolved towards a style that is of great simplicity and lapidary concentration. His choral works – leaving aside their effectiveness as propaganda, which does not interest me – have impressive musical power. And what is most impressive is that, without ever falsifying the current [modernist] state of his sonic materials, within the atonal evolution, he achieves an extraordinary thematic plasticity and harmonic coherence that reveal his most lucid hearing and immediately convinces you of the ease of assimilation and performance of this music by the popular masses for whom it is intended. The aggressive emphasis of some choral pieces "for singing in the streets" or the satirical tone of some parodies of [traditional] choral lyricism through closed-mouth singing and some bim, bam bell-like effects, are given an intensity of musical expression and a persuasive force that silences all objections. Musically, at any rate, these works absolutely convince you.[4]

---

7, no. 7 (1925): 422–423; Theodor W. Adorno, "Hanns Eisler. *Klavierstücke* op. 3", *Die Musik* 19, no. 10 (July 1927): 749–750; Hans Heinz Stuckenschmidt, "Hanns Eisler", *Musikblätter des Anbruch*, 10, no. 5 (1928): 163–167; Theodor W. Adorno, "Hanns Eisler. Zeitungsausschnitte. Kompositionskritik", *Anbruch* 11, no. 5 (1929): 219–221; Hans F. Redlich, "Neue Probleme der Chorkomposition", *Anbruch* 12, nos. 9 and 10 (1930): 279–280.

3 Robert Gerhard, "Hanns Eisler", *Mirador* 101 (8 January 1931): 5. In this essay Gerhard borrows a number of ideas from Hans Heinz Stuckenschmidt's 1928 article on Hanns Eisler for the *Musikblätter des Anbruch* (see n. 2).

4 "Hanns Eisler juga, en efecte, un paper dels més singulars en la vida musical actual. Sense figurar gairebé mai en els programes de concert 'burgesos', és un dels compositors joves les obres del qual assoleixen major nombre d'audicions avui a Alemanya. Procedent de l'escola schönberguiana i posseïdor d'una tècnica de les més subtils i de més fina qualitat

By "choral pieces for singing in the streets", Gerhard referred to *Auf den Straßen zu singen* (*Demonstrationslied*), op. 15, a 1928 polyphonic choral piece for mixed choir and snare drum. The lyrics of the piece call for workers to revolt, featuring phrases such as "We [workers] want our share of the world's wealth. We march day after day towards that goal. Damn those who do not want to march with us!"[5] The piece premiered at the Staatlichen Hochschule für Musik in Berlin in November 1929.[6] As Gerhard was in Spain at that time, he may have become acquainted with this work through the score published in 1929 by Universal Edition. The "bim, bam bell-like effects" refer to the first piece in *Vier Stücke für gemischten Chor* (*Four Pieces for Mixed Choir*), op. 13 (1928), in which Eisler parodies several evocative extramusical topoi typical of the old-fashioned bourgeois choral repertoire, particularly the vocal imitation of church bells (see Ex. 4.1).

Gerhard described Eisler's polyphonic choral works for workers, as well as the "sort of communist oratorio" *Die Maßnahme* (*The Measures Taken*), as typical examples of modern German "Zweckmusik" [sic] (music for a purpose). He urged the Catalan orfeós (choral societies) to premiere these types of contemporary works in Catalonia.[7] I am not aware of any Spanish performer or ensemble that followed Gerhard's advice to premiere any of Eisler's "atonal" and "proletarian" concert works in 1930s Spain. The only portion of his output that received performances during this period was his most popular battle songs and political ballads, which only emerged during the civil war. One solitary exception was the *Comintern Song*, which became a feature of musical propaganda organised by the Spanish PCE starting in approximately 1933.

espiritual, ha evolucionat darrerament cap a un estil vocal d'una simplicitat i d'una concentració lapidàries. Els seus cors, deixant a banda la seva eficàcia de propaganda, que no m'interessa, tenen una força musical impressionant. I el que fa més impressió és que, sense falsificar mai l'estat actual dels materials sonors, dins de l'evolució atonal, arriba a una extraordinària plasticitat temàtica i a una coherència harmònica que revelen l'audició més lúcida, per part del compositor, i convencen immediatament de la facilitat d'assimilació i d'execució d'aquesta música per part de les masses populars a les quals van destinades. L'empenta agressiva d'alguns chors 'per cantar pels carrers' o el mordent satíric d'alguna parodia del lirisme orfeònic a base d'efectes de boca tancada i de campanetes la bim, bam, estan realitzats amb una intensitat d'expressió musical i una força persuasiva que fan callar totes les objeccions. Musicalment, almenys, us deixen absolutament convençuts", Gerhard, "Eisler". Translation by the present author.

5 "Wir wollen unsern Anteil uns holen am Reichtum der Welt. Wir marschieren Tag um Tag bis ans Ziel. Verdammt, wer nicht mit uns mitmarchieren will!"; see Johannes C. Gall, *Hanns Eisler: A Cappella Choruses 1925–1932*, Hanns Eisler Gesamtausgabe, Serie I: Chormusik, vol. 5 (Wiesbaden: Breitkopf &Härtel, 2018), 46–53.

6 Gall, *Hanns Eisler: A Cappella Choruses*, XIX.

7 Robert Gerhard, "Música Aplicada", *Mirador* 124 (18 June 1931): 5.

Ex. 4.1. Hanns Eisler, *Vier Stücke für gemischten Chor*, op. 13, mov. 1 (bb. 18–22) ["Bim, Bam, Bim, Bam... Hear the church bells ringing..."].

## The Anthem of the Communist International in Spain

Eisler composed the *Comintern Song* in 1929 to commemorate the tenth anniversary of the organisation's founding.[8] The original German lyrics by Karl Jahnke and Maxim Vallentin advocate for the worldwide establishment of (Soviet) communism. The sheet music was first published in 1931 by the Soviet state music publishing house Muzgiz in Moscow. This publication included the original German lyrics and a "Soviet translation" – as Eisler referred to it – by the Russian poet Ilya Frenkel.[9] The Spanish version of the lyrics was written in 1932 or 1933 by the Valencian typographer Salvador Chardí Rusies, about whom little is known today. Born around 1903 and a member of the PCE since 1931, Chardí learned Russian and attended the International Lenin School in Moscow during his youth. This official training school, operated by the Communist International, provided courses on Marxist theory and practical under-

[8] A detailed analysis of Eisler's *Comintern Song* can be found in: Schebera, *Hanns Eisler. Eine Biographie*, 58–59; and Gall, *Hanns Eisler*, xxix, xxxii.

[9] Hanns Eisler, *Коминтерн – Komintern* (Moscow: Muzgiz, 1931). For more on Frenkel and Eisler's collaboration in creating this version, see Yana Alexandrovna Lowry, *From Massenlieder to Massovaia Pesnia – Musical Exchanges between Communists and Socialists of Weimar Germany and the Early Soviet Union* (PhD diss., Duke University, 2014), 253.

ground political techniques. During the civil war, he served as the editor for several important communist periodicals, including *Verdad* (*Truth*), the organ of the youth Marxist-Leninist organisation Juventudes Socialistas Unificadas. He succeeded a well-known communist artist, Josep Renau, in this role.[10]

The Russian lyrics, rather than the original German, served as the source for Chardí's Spanish version. His main deviations from the Russian text include the elimination of references to the Soviet Civil War and the White movement, as well as the inclusion of a call for peasants to "overthrow" capitalism by force of arms. This latter appeal reflects the political tensions in 1930s Spain arising from the poor living and working conditions among the peasantry (see Chapter 3). Chardí's complete lyrics, along with my own translation of them, are provided below:

| **La Comintern** | **The Comintern** |
|---|---|
| Legión proletaria, legión campesina,<br>en filas compactas marchemos al frente.<br>Al hombro el fusil y con ojo avizor,<br>disponte a abatir con enérgico ardor<br>al capitalismo, que es nuestro opresor. | Proletarian legion, peasant legion,<br>in united ranks let us march to the front.<br>With your rifle on your shoulder and with a watchful eye,<br>prepare to strike down, with energetic zeal,<br>capitalism, which is our oppressor. |
| Del paria que sufre prisión o destierro<br>está con nosotros su gesto rebelde,<br>sin miedo al terror del fascismo cruel,<br>lucharemos unidos en haz contra él<br>y al mundo del fraude podremos vencer. | Of the outcast, who suffers imprisonment or exile,<br>his rebellious gesture is with us,<br>without fearing the terror of cruel fascism,<br>we will fight against it united in a bundle<br>and we will defeat the world of fraud. |

10 There are very few sources on Chardí's life or militant political activity in Spain. The details offered above are taken from Antonio Ramírez Navarro, *La fuerza de los débiles. Vida, prisiones y muerte de Vicente Talens Inglá (1892–1940)* (Almería: Instituto de Estudios Almerienses, 2021), 215; and Fernando Arias, *La Valencia de los años 30. Entre el paraíso y el infierno* (Valencia: Ayuntamiento de Valencia, 1996), 29. In regard to the International Lenin School and its links in Spain, see Lisa A. Kirschenbaum, *International Communism and the Spanish Civil War: Solidarity and Suspicion* (Cambridge: Cambridge University Press, 2015).

En filas de acero llevemos delante
la roja bandera del Soviet triunfante.
Nuestro frente rojo no puede volver
del duro camino que ha de recorrer,
siguiendo la línea de la Komintern.

Let us carry in ranks of steel
the red flag of the triumphant Soviet.
Our red front cannot turn back,
it has to travel the hard path
following the line of the Comintern.

La luz leninista alumbra el camino,
de frente al asalto del capitalismo,
dos clases están a la lucha final,
palabra de orden: El Soviet mundial,
en pie, proletarios, con temple a luchar.

The Leninist light shines on the path,
forward to the assault of capitalism,
two classes are at the final struggle,
word of order: The World Soviet,
stand up, proletarians, to fight with courage![11]

The earliest documentary evidence of a performance of *La Comintern* in Spain dates back to 1934. In August of that year, the widely-read illustrated magazine *Crónica* informed readers that the song was part of the repertoire of the Orquesta y Coros Proletarios de Madrid (Proletarian Orchestra and Choirs of Madrid). This orchestra and mixed choir was established in the spring of 1934 under the auspices of the PCE, apparently initiated by composers Joaquín Villatoro and Carlos Palacio, along with other communist musicians in Madrid. Rehearsals were held at the PCE facilities, in the city centre. The relatively small orchestra comprised about thirty musicians, while the mixed choir included approximately fifty members. The instrumentalists and singers were mostly pro-communist amateurs or semi-professional musicians. According to Palacio, prominent communist leaders in Madrid, including Dolores Ibárruri, "La Pasionaria", occasionally sang in the choir. The twenty-three-year-old Ataulfo Argenta conducted the orchestra for a time, before later rising to prominence as one of Spain's leading conductors during the Franco era. Carlos Palacio and Joaquín Villatoro provided the choir members with instruction in reading music and conducted the ensemble on some occasions. Figures 4.1 and 4.2 display images of these ensembles from mid-1934.[12]

Like most amateur or semi-professional Spanish orchestras of the time, the repertoire of the Proletarian Orchestra consisted primarily of popular symphonic pieces, particularly overtures from well-known zarzuelas and operas,

[11] The sources used for this comparative study of the lyrics include Franz Jahnke and Maxim Vallentin, "Kominternlied", *Das Rote Sprachrohr* 1, no. 2 (February 1929): 4–8; Hanns Eisler, *Komintern* (Madrid: Cultura Popular, 1937), HEA cat. no. 1371; Hanns Eisler, *Коминтерн* (Moscow: Musgiz, 1931), HEA, Berlin, sig. 2009. I am grateful to Sophia Belik for providing a translation of the latter Russian text into English.

[12] See Santiago Masferrer y Canto, "La orquesta y los coros proletarios de Madrid", *Crónica* 6, no. 248 (12 August 1934): 28–29; Palacio, *Acordes en el alma*, 119–121 and "Erinnerungen an Hanns Eisler in Spanien", 67–68.

Fig. 4.1. The Proletarian Orchestra and Choirs Rehearsing. Source: Santiago Masferrer y Canto, "La orquesta y los coros proletarios de Madrid", *Crónica* (Madrid), Year VI, Nr. 248 (12 August 1934), 29.

Fig. 4.2. The Proletarian Choir conducted by Ataulfo Argenta. Source: Santiago Masferrer y Canto, "La orquesta y los coros proletarios de Madrid", *Crónica* (Madrid), Year VI, Nr. 248 (12 August 1934), 1.

such as Ruperto Chapí's *La revoltosa* (1897) and Richard Wagner's *Rienzi* (1842). What distinguished this pro-communist orchestra and choir from other amateur ensembles was their regular inclusion of workers' songs, such as *The Internationale, Marcha fúnebre* (a Russian song popular in Germany under the title *Unsterbliche Opfer*),[13] *La joven guardia* (a Spanish version of the 1912 French socialist song *La Jeune Garde*), *Bandera roja* (*The Red Banner*, a pre-revolutionary Russian song), and several "modern" pro-communist songs, including Eisler's *La Comintern*, Joaquín Villatoro's *Himno a Thälmann* (1933), Dmitry Pokrass' *Caballería roja* (*The Red Cavalry*, 1920),[14] various unspecified songs by Isaak Osipovich Dunayevsky, and works by the celebrated composer of battle songs, Alexander Davidenko.[15] Except for Villatoro's piece, which I discuss in Chapter 5, these vocal works belonged to a largely transnational repertoire of propaganda songs, many of which were regularly performed, in translation, by numerous pro-communist choirs and ensembles across Europe, America, and the Soviet Union.[16]

The Orquesta y Coros Proletarios de Madrid performed at proletarian festivals and political events in the Spanish capital. According to Palacio, the choir also sang a cappella at workers' meetings, street demonstrations, and funerals for "fallen comrades". As a result, *La Comintern* was likely well known among the most active communist circles in Spain. Both the orchestra and the choir disbanded at the outset of the civil war, if not earlier.[17] It remains to be determined whether other pro-communist choirs with similar repertoires existed in Spain before the conflict.

## *La Comintern* in Wartime

During the civil war, the anthem of the Communist International was widely disseminated due to the rapid expansion of the PCE and the growing influence

13 For more information on this song see Eckhard John, *Brüder, zur Sonne, zur Freiheit. Die unerhörte Geschichte eines Revolutionsliedes* (Berlin: Ch. Links Verlag, 2018), 45–53.

14 Palacio, *Acordes en el alma*, 121. The score for this song is reproduced in: Amy Nelson, *Music for the Revolution: Musicians and Power in Early Soviet Russia* (Pennsylvania: The Pennsylvania State University Press, 2020), 99.

15 Palacio, *Acordes en el alma*, 121–122.

16 See Robert Brécy, *Florilège de la chanson révolutionnaire de 1789 au front Populaire* (Paris: Hier et Demain, 1978); Maria Cristina Fava, "The Composers' Collective of New York, 1932–1936: Bourgeois Modernism for the Proletariat", *American Music*, vol. 34, no. 3 (Fall 2016): 301–343; Inge Lammel, *Das Arbeiterlied* (Leipzig: Philipp Reclam, 1980).

17 Palacio, "Erinnerungen an Hanns Eisler in Spanien," and *Acordes en el alma*, 119 and 126.

of the Comintern in the Republican zone. The mixed choir of the PCE-controlled propaganda organisation Altavoz del Frente (Loudspeaker of the Front, or AdF) was one of the key ensembles that performed *La Comintern* in live concerts and on the radio throughout the conflict. Conducted by Palacio and others, this choir performed regularly at political-cultural events, known as *actos*, in Madrid and other cities, as well as during radio broadcasts organised by the AdF. An *acto* typically featured political speeches, musical performances, poetry readings, and film screenings or small exhibitions. Fig. 4.3 displays a programme for one such political event held in Murcia, where *La Comintern* was part of a brief recital of five communist propaganda songs that concluded the first part of the event.[18]

*La Comintern* and other pro-Soviet and communist songs were regularly broadcast via AdF radio programmes, aired from Madrid's main radio station, Unión Radio, beginning in mid-September 1936. These broadcasts targeted both Republican civilians and militiamen, as well as the enemy across the front lines. Their content mirrored that of the *actos* and typically included a war newsreel, political speeches, readings of political poems, and live performances of various political songs. Selected songs were occasionally performed by professional operatic and zarzuela singers, alternating with the AdF choir. (Alternating between solo and choral performances was a common practice for these songs in the 1930s.) The singers were accompanied by either a piano or the station's orchestra.[19] Fig. 4.4 shows a photograph of the AdF Choir with the radio ensemble in the Madrid studios of Unión Radio, taken in late 1936.

Several editions of the sheet music for *La Comintern* were produced in Spain during the initial phase of the civil war. One of the earliest was published by Cultura Popular, an organisation closely associated with the PCE. Cultura Popular was founded in April 1936 with the aim of coordinating cultural and propaganda activities organised by the Popular Front, particularly the establishment of *ateneos* (proletarian cultural centres) and libraries.[20] The score for voice and piano was published in the former palace of the Counts of Revilla-

18 This programme was printed in the PCE-linked newspaper *Unidad y lucha, órgano del comité central del PCE* (13 March 1937): 8, and other Murcia periodicals, including: *El Liberal de Murcia* (13 March 1937): 2. For further discussion of the activities organised by the AdF, including theatre performances, art exhibitions, and film screenings, as well as publications of sheet music and periodicals, see Palacio's *Acordes en el alma*, 135–139, 152; and Emilio Peral Vega, "'Altavoz del frente': una experiencia multidisciplinar durante la Guerra Civil Española", *Hispanic Research Journal* 13, no. 3 (2012): 234–249.

19 Palacio, *Acordes en el alma*, 135–136. See also Adolfo Salazar, "Altaveu del Front. Cançó popular i cançó revolucionària", *Mirador* 392 (22 October 1936): 7.

20 The history of the organisation Cultura Popular has not been studied in detail. One of the few studies available is Romà Seguí i Francés, "Teresa Andrés y la organización *Cultura Popular*: una propuesta de coordinación bibliotecaria (1936–1938)", *Métodos de información* 2, no. 3 (2011): 127–154.

**Altavoz del Frente. Murcia**

**Al Servicio del Pueblo en Armas**

**Gran acto inaugural**

Lunes 15, a las seis de la tarde, en el TEATRO CIRCO

Programa

Primera parte

1.º *Presentación del camarada Vicente Arroyo, por el responsable de Altavoz del Frente, Cipriano de Hoyos.*

2.º *El pianista Rafael Casasempere Juan, interpretará:*

*Nocturnas (Tangos populares Mejicanos).*

*Ojos Negros (Canción popular Rusa).*

*Danza Ritual del Fuego. – Falla.*

3.º *Romancero de la Guerra Civil, recitado por Miguel González.*

*Romance de Francisca Solano. – José Antonio Balbontín.*

*El último Duque de Alba. – Rafael Alberti.*

*Los Desheredados. – Arturo Serrano Plaja.*

*Con la Derecha. – Luis de Tapia.*

4.º Coros de Altavoz del Frente. – *Director, Julián Santos.*

*Joven Guardia.*

*Komintern. – Música de Hans Eisler.*

*Compañías de Acero. – Texto de Luis de Tapia y Música de Carlos Palacio.*

*Marcha Fúnebre a los Héroes caídos.*

*La Internacional.*

Segunda parte

*Proyección del Gran Film Soviético, estreno en Murcia:*

**Golpe por golpe**

Somos el Ejército de la Paz, pero estamos dispuestos a devolver

**Golpe por golpe**

*Visitad la magnífica Exposición de Trofeos de Guerra, instalada en el local de* **Altavoz del Frente.**

*Fermín Galán, 63.*

Fig. 4.3. Example of a programme for an *acto* held in Murcia on 15 March 1937. Source: *Unidad y lucha, órgano del comité central del PCE* (13 March 1937), 8.

**ALTAVOZ DEL FRENTE, MURCIA**
**IN THE SERVICE OF THE PEOPLE IN ARMS**
**Grand opening event.**
Monday 15th, at 6 p.m. in the Circo Theatre [Murcia].

Programme
First part

1. Presentation of comrade Vicente Arroyo by the person in charge of the Altavoz del Frente, Cipriano de Royos.
2. The pianist Rafael Casasempere Juan will perform: *Nocturnas* (Mexican folk tangos), *Ojos negros* (Russian folk song), *Danza ritual del fuego*, Falla.
3. "Romancero de la guerra civil" [Civil War ballads], recited by Miguel González. *Romance de Francisca Solano* by José Antonio Balbontín; *El último duque de Alba* by Rafael Alberti; *Los desheredados* by Arturo Serrano Plaje; *Con la derecha* by Luis de Tapia.
4. Altavoz del Frente Choir. Conductor: Julián Santos. [Programme:] *Joven guardia*, *Komintern*, music by Hans [sic] Eisler; *Compañía de Acero*, lyrics by Luis de Tapia and music by Carlos Palacio; *Marcha fúnebre a los caídos* [= *Unsterbliche Opfer*]; *La Internacional.*

Second part
Screening of the Great Soviet Film, premiere in Murcia:

**BLOW FOR BLOW**
We are the Peace Army but we are ready to give back
BLOW FOR BLOW

Visit the magnificent Exhibition of War Trophies installed on the premises of the **Altavoz del Frente**, Fermín Galán Street, 63.

Fig. 4.4. Choir of the Altavoz del Frente in the Madrid studios of Unión Radio, ca. October 1936. Source: excerpt from the cover page of *Crónica*, 1 November 1936, p. 1.

gigedo in Madrid, which had been seized by the workers' militias at the outset of the conflict.

An anonymous wartime edition, arranged for choir and wind band, along with a recording of that same version, provides further evidence that *La Comintern* was regularly performed and broadcast in Spain during the war. The publication of this arrangement underscores the song's significance as a propaganda tool in wartime Spain (arrangements of anthems for military wind bands were typically produced on an ad hoc basis for specific ensembles, normally by their conductor, and were seldom published). The score includes the note that this arrangement was made "in accordance with the official edition of the USSR".[21] This was most likely the aforementioned 1931 Soviet publication for voice and piano. The arranger transposed the music from C-sharp minor to D minor – an easier key for most wind instruments – and added ornamentation, including grace notes in bar 9 and melismas in bars 2 and 4 (Fig. 4.5). This type of arabesque-like melisma was common in the repertoire of Spanish wind bands, for instance within the then-popular genre of the pasodoble.

The published arrangement for choir and wind band was recorded by the Barcelona-based mixed choir Orfeón Gervasiense, from the affluent district of Sant Gervasi, and the military wind band of Barcelona's "Cuartel Carlos Marx" (Karl Marx Headquarters), conducted by the composer and organist Tomás Mancisidor Aquino. The Schweizerisches Sozialarchiv in Zurich preserves the shellac discs of this recording, along with three others of battle songs made by the same performers, likely produced on the same occasion. Although the discs

21 "de acuerdo con la edición oficial de la URSS". Hanns Eisler, *Komintern* (Madrid: Música moderna, ca. 1937). A copy of this publication is kept at the HEA under cat. no. 1371.

Fig. 4.5. Spanish arrangement for wind band of Eisler's *Comintern Song.* Source: Hanns Eisler, *Komintern* (Madrid: Música moderna, ca. 1937); Hans-Eisler-Archiv 1371. Published with kind permission.

appear to have been marketed commercially, they were probably recorded primarily for radio broadcasts and transmission through large public loudspeakers on the front lines and the home front.[22]

22 The recordings are hosted online and can be accessed at: https://www.bild-video-ton.ch/bestand/objekt/Sozarch_F_1020-040b. The other recorded songs include: *Marcha fúnebre a los caídos en la lucha antifascista* (the Spanish version of *Unsterbliche Opfer*), *La joven guardia* (the anthem of the PCE's youth organisation Juventudes Socialistas Unificadas), and *Himno a la juventud universal* (a particularly intriguing song, on which no information or further sources have been found). The shellacs belonged originally to the socialist worker and singer Robert Risler, who was in Spain during the civil war. He was a collector of workers' songs who probably purchased the records in Spain. A more detailed summary of this collection is present on the website of the Schweizerisches Sozialarchiv: https://www.findmittel.ch/archive/archNeu/Ar151.html

## The Songs of the Popular Front

Another widely disseminated Eisler song in wartime Spain was the *Song of the United Front*. Brecht and Eisler created this piece in 1934 as part of the Comintern's propaganda advocating for unity among all democratic parties in a common struggle against fascism.[23] Two different Spanish versions of the lyrics emerged shortly after the onset of the civil war: one by José Herrera Petere and the other by Félix Vicente Ramos. For a discussion of Herrera Petere, see Chapter 2. Ramos, like Chardí, appears to have been a worker with a proclivity for poetry, whose literary production consisted largely of propaganda verse and song lyrics, only a few of which have survived. Hardly any historical sources containing biographical information about Ramos have been preserved.

Both Petere and Ramos translated the term "Einheitsfront" (United Front) as "Frente Popular" (Popular Front). This designation referred to the left-wing coalition that had governed Republican Spain since early 1936 and was formalised as the official terminology for the new international antifascist alliance at the Seventh Comintern Congress in July 1935. The lines "never, ever shall fascism pass!" in Petere's lyrics, and Ramos' rendering that "Spain will be the torch" in which "fascism will burn", suggest that both versions were penned during the civil war. Petere's text is a fairly literal translation from the French or English versions of Brecht's original German lyrics.[24] In contrast, Ramos' lyrics do not translate the German, English, or French versions; rather, they were written anew and exhibit greater literary merit than Petere's.[25] Perhaps the poor literary quality of Petere's version motivated Ramos to create a new Spanish version.

[23] Further context for this song and its date of creation can be found in: Albrecht Dümling, *Lässt euch nicht verführen. Brecht und die Musik* (Munich: Kindler, 1985), 401–407; Hanns-Werner Heister, "Brecht / Eisler. Das Einheitsfrontlied", in *Vom allgemeingültigen Neuen Analysen engagierter Musik: Dessau, Eisler, Ginastera, Hartmann*, eds. Thomas Phleps and Wieland Reich (Saarbrücken: Pfau, 2006), 91–102; Tobias Fasshauer, "Zur Krise der Volkstümlichkeit bei Hanns Eisler", in *Musik in der DDR. Beiträge zu den Musikverhältnissen eines verschwundenen Staates*, ed. Matthias Tischer (Berlin: Ernst Kuhn, 2005), 26–49.

[24] Brecht's original lyrics plus French and English translations, both from 1935, were included in Busch, *Kampflieder der Internationalen Brigaden*, 1st ed., 17 and 47.

[25] The Bertolt Brecht Archive of the Berlin Academy of the Arts holds a third, anonymous Spanish version of the text for Brecht's song, entitled *La canción del frente unido*. This version provides a very faithful translation of Brecht's original, though it appears unsuitable for singing. The translator does not use the term "frente popular" and makes no other reference to Spain. It is uncertain when, where, or why this version was written. See Brecht, "Canción del frente unido", Brecht catalogue number 0398/026.

**José Herrera Petere's Version**

Y como ser humano
el hombre lo que quiere es su pan.
Las habladurías le bastan ya
porque estas nada le dan
Pues: un, dos, tres.
Pues: un, dos, tres.
Compañero, ¡en tu lugar!
Porque eres del pueblo afíliate
ya
en el Frente Popular

El hombre por ser hombre
la libertad anhela conquistar.
No quiere a tiranos obedecer
ni a nadie esclavizar

Pues: un, dos, tres...

Despierto está el fascismo
despierto brilla y sangra su
puñal
¡Atrás la muerte y la
opresión
unidos todos, luchad!

¡Nunca jamás
nunca jamás
el fascismo pasará;
en viva muralla de la libertad
nuestro Frente Popular!
[one further stanza][26]

And as human beings
men want to have bread.
Gossip is enough for them
because that is worthless
And: one, two, three
And: one, two, three
Comrade, in your place!
Because you belong to the
people, join now
the Popular Front!

Man, because he is man
longs to conquer freedom.
He does not want to obey tyrants
nor enslave anyone

And: one, two, three...

Fascism is awake,
its dagger is awake, it shines and
bleeds
Let us drive back death and
oppression,
all united, fight!

Never ever,
never ever,
shall fascism pass;
on the living wall of freedom
our Popular Front!
[one further stanza]

**Felix Vicente Ramos' Version**

En pie esclavos del mundo,
dispuestos al fascismo aniquilar.
Nuestro esfuerzo fecundo es
en la lucha en pro de la paz.
Luchad, luchad,
con gran tesón
por la solidaridad

Stand up, slaves of the world,
ready to annihilate fascism.
Our effort is fruitful
in the struggle for peace.
Fight, fight,
with great tenacity
for solidarity,

26 Ernst Busch, ed., *Kampflieder der Internationalen Brigaden*, 5th ed. (Barcelona: Brigadas Internacionales, 1938), 24.

| | |
|---|---|
| reforzando las filas con<br>ilusión<br>en el Frente Popular | strengthening the ranks<br>with enthusiasm<br>in the Popular Front. |
| Será España la antorcha<br>que al mundo proletario<br>alumbrará.<br>En esas llamas rojas<br>el fascismo se abrasará<br>Luchad, luchad… | Spain will be the torch<br>that will light the proletarian<br>world.<br>In those red flames<br>fascism will burn.<br>Fight, Fight… |
| Uniós, proletarios,<br>pidió a los oprimidos Carlos<br>Marx.<br>Si viviera el apóstol<br>gritaría ¡Unidad!<br>Luchad, luchad…[27] | "Unite, proletarians",<br>Karl Marx asked of the<br>oppressed.<br>If the apostle were alive<br>he would shout, "Unity!"<br>Fight, Fight… |

Both Ramos' and Petere's versions were recorded in Spain around 1937, representing the earliest recordings of the *Song of the United Front* ever produced in any language. Busch recorded a multilingual version of the *Song of the United Front* in December 1937 as a tribute to the International Brigades.[28] He sang the first stanza of Petere's lyrics, followed by one stanza each from the English, French, and German versions. The multilingual nature of this recording symbolised the international dimension of the Popular Fronts and the International Brigades' struggle against fascism in Spain. The inclusion of Petere's lyrics in this recording, along with the fact that these lyrics were only published in Busch's songbook, suggests that the poet may have written his version specifically for the International Brigades.[29]

The Ramos version was recorded by an unidentified male choir accompanied by a military wind band. This recording has survived because it was included as film music in the 1938 propaganda short, *Los trece puntos de la victoria* (*The Thirteen Points of Victory*), a copy of which has been preserved.[30] Originally released in the summer of 1938, the film outlined the thirteen main political objectives, or "points", of Republican President Juan Negrín. The

27 Otto Mayer-Serra, *Cançoner Revolucionari Internacional*, vol. 2 (Barcelona: Comissariat de Propaganda de la Generalitat de Catalunya, 1937), 30–31.

28 Ernst Busch, *Los cuatro generales / Lied der Einheitsfront* (Barcelona: Brigadas Internacionales [Gramola España], 1938), Nr. 6004 (Bri 1/2, Bri I°).

29 Busch, *Kampflieder*, 5th ed., 24

30 I am grateful to Lidia López for drawing my attention to this film. The film can be viewed at: https://www.rtve.es/alacarta/videos/archivo-historico/trece-puntos-victoria/2833191/ [Accessed 20 June 2025]. Additional research on this film can be found in Alfonso del Amo García, ed., *Catálogo General del Cine de la Guerra Civil* (Madrid: Filmoteca Española, 1996), 850–851.

public announcement on 30 April 1938 included a programme featuring the film alongside a series of modernist photomontages by Renau. These propaganda artworks targeted not only the rebel leaders in an attempt to achieve a negotiated peace but also antifascist organisations, both Spanish and foreign, in a bid to convince them to abandon their internal conflicts and unite in the antifascist struggle. The choice of *Canción del frente popular* as film music appears intended to emphasise this latter objective.

## Revolutionary Songbooks

In December 1937, the Comissariat de Propaganda de la Generalitat de Catalunya (Propaganda Agency of the Catalan Government) published the second volume of the *Cançoner Revolucionari Internacional* (*International Revolutionary Songbook*). This volume included the vocal parts and piano accompaniments for several bilingual Catalan/Spanish versions of propaganda songs from Spain and abroad, notably Eisler's *Cançó del Front Popular / Canción del frente popular* and *La Comintern*.[31] The publication of these "revolutionary songbooks" constituted one of the major initiatives of the music department within the Comissariat de Propaganda, which had been under the direction of Otto Mayer-Serra since late 1936.[32]

The Comissariat was established on 3 October 1936 as an autonomous entity within the Catalan government, with its headquarters in Barcelona and satellite offices in Paris, London, Brussels, and Stockholm. The propaganda activities undertaken by the organisation encompassed political speeches, lectures, broadcasts, exhibitions, sports competitions, and concerts. Additionally, the Comissariat published books, manifestos, musical scores, and periodicals, including the international, multilingual illustrated magazine *Nova Iberia*, for which Mayer-Serra contributed a brief article.[33] Moreover, the agency facilitated the creation of posters, films, photographs, and musical works. Approximately 300 individuals, organised into various departments, were employed by the Comissariat.

The project to publish a multi-volume *Revolutionary Songbook* was spearheaded by Mayer-Serra in his role as head of the music department. The book was modelled after similar publications by communist organisations in Europe and the United States, particularly the songbooks issued between 1933 and

31 Mayer, *Cançoner*, vol. 2, 27–31. The Catalan lyrics of the latter song were written by an anonymous poet, based on Chardí's version; those of the *Cançó del Front Popular* were by a certain Lluís Ensenyat, who took Ramos' version as their source.

32 Mayer-Serra's position at the Commissariat is mentioned in a document drafted by his close friend Rodolfo Halffter; see Antonio Iglesias, *Rodolfo Halffter (tema, nueve décadas y final)* (Madrid: Fundación Banco Exterior, 1992), 73.

33 Otto Mayer, "La Catalogne musicale", *Nova Iberia* 1, no. 1 (January 1937): 36.

1935 by the International Music Bureau in Moscow, the Workers Music League in New York, and the Fédération Musicale Populaire in Paris.[34] The two published volumes contained a total of twenty songs, most featuring bilingual Catalan/Spanish lyrics. Mayer-Serra originally intended to publish a third volume, which was to include a bilingual version of the *Solidarity Song*. However, this plan was ultimately abandoned, partly due to the Comissariat's financial difficulties in 1938.[35]

This is one of several clues suggesting that the Spanish version of the *Solidarity Song* might have been performed and perhaps regularly broadcast during the Spanish Civil War. Additional indications include Ludwig Renn's assertion in his fictionalised war chronicle *Der spanische Krieg* that the song was widely sung in Madrid at the war's outset.[36] However, no textual or musical sources containing the Spanish or Catalan versions of the *Solidarity Song* have been discovered. Spanish performers and composers may have relied on copies of various editions published across Europe and the USA, particularly Busch's songbook, which featured the vocal melody with lyrics in German, English, and Dutch.

*Der Rote Wedding* (*The Red* [Berlin district] *Wedding*), one of Eisler's most popular battle songs at the time, was likely sung in Spanish during the war. Busch's songbook, along with two other Spanish collections of "revolutionary songs", included a Spanish version of the lyrics, titled *Links und links. Canción antifascista alemana* (*Left and Left: German Antifascist Song*).[37] The Spanish lyrics call for the unification of all antifascist forces in the class struggle and the fight against fascism. References to "cannons" in the Spanish version suggest that it was possibly created during the civil war. However, it remains unclear how frequently the song was performed, in what contexts, or whether it was ever recorded or broadcast during the war. The author of these lyrics remains unknown.

34 Valentina Iosifovna Ramm, ed, *International Collection of Revolutionary Songs* (Moscow: Moscow State Musical Publishing Office, 1933); Anon., ed., *Workers Songbook 1934*, vol. 1 (New York: Workers Music League, 1934); Anon., ed., *Workers Songbook*, vol. 2 (New York: Workers Music League, 1935); Anon., ed., *Chants révolutionnaires de divers pays*, vol. 3 (Paris: Editions sociales internationales, 1937).

35 Mayer-Serra, *Cançoner*, vol. 2, 33. For the history of these songbooks and a detailed study of the contents in each volume of the publication, see Diego Alonso, "Transnational Networks of Communist Musical Propaganda in the Spanish Civil War", *Journal of War & Culture Studies* 14, no. 4 (2021): 454–478.

36 Ludwig Renn, *Der spanische Krieg* (Berlin: Das neue Berlin, 2006), 196.

37 *Cançons revolucionàries* (Barcelona: Edicions Europa-Amèrica, date unknown (ca. 1936); *Canciones revolucionarias*: place and date unknown (ca. 1936). Copies are held at the Institut d'Estudis Catalans. Both songbooks include the same short note, which translates the terms "links" and "Rote Front". Palacio included the lyrics in his *Colección*, 141–142.

## *Ernst H. Meyer's Song for Spain*

The first volume of Mayer-Serra's *International Revolutionary Songbook* features an intriguing, anonymous battle song entitled *Marxa de l'Exèrcit Popular* (*March of the Popular Army*). According to Carlos Palacio, this piece "dates from the creation of our glorious People's Army", referring to the period shortly after October 1936, when the organisation was established by merging military units loyal to the Republican government with the workers' militias formed at the outset of the war.[38] I have found no evidence that the song was published elsewhere prior to this, making it almost certain that it was composed specifically for use during wartime Spain. Ex. 4.2 illustrates the opening of the piece.

The song's vocal melody was first published in *Treball*, the newspaper of the Catalan Communist Party (PSUC), in late February 1937. The earliest known complete score, with piano accompaniment, followed in *Mirador* in early March.[39] The first volume of the *Revolutionary Songbook* was released a few months later, in the summer of 1937. This timing suggests that the piece was either composed or introduced to Spain in early 1937. Given that the song was first published in *Treball* and *Mirador*, the two main periodicals for which Mayer-Serra worked during the war, and was subsequently included in the *Revolutionary Songbook*, of which he was the principal editor, it is likely that he played a key role in disseminating the piece in Catalonia. It is even possible that he commissioned its composition.

The lyrics were almost certainly composed after the music. According to several Catalan scholars, the author was most likely the Catalan poet Joan Oliver i Sellarès (1899–1986), better known by his pseudonym, Pere Quart.[40] Oliver is now regarded as one of the most outstanding poets and playwrights of twentieth-century Catalan literature. His lyrics read:

38 "Data de la creación de nuestro glorioso Ejército Popular", Carlos Palacio, *Colección de canciones de lucha* (Valencia: Tipografía moderna, 1939), 34.

39 Anon., "Marxa de l'Exèrcit Popular", *Treball* (28 February 1937): 3; anon., "Marxa de l'Exèrcit Popular", *Mirador* 410 (5 March 1937): 7.

40 On Pere Quart's authorship see Rafael Pascuet and Enric Pujol, eds., *La revolució del bon gust. Jaume Miravitlles i el Comissariat de Propaganda de la Generalitat de Catalunya (1936–1939)* (Figueras: Viena Edicions, 2006), 66; José Fernándo Mota Muñoz, "Milicians, reclutes i comissaris a Sant Cugat. El campament militar i l'escola de comissaris de Pins del Vallès (1937–1939)", *Gausac* 48–49 (2016): 63–78.

| | |
|---|---|
| Un dia tràgic la gent més innoble<br>d'aquesta terra desfeia la pau.<br>Els vils feixistes dreçats contra el poble<br>volien fer-lo per a sempre esclau.<br>Vingué la guerra, ferotge i sense treva,<br>al Nord, al Centre, Sud i a Llevant<br>i arreu d'Espanya s'alçà la gran lleva<br>dels voluntaris que lluiten cantant.<br>ENDAVANT! | One tragic day, the most ignoble people<br>of this land sought to dismantle peace.<br>The vile fascists rose up against the people,<br>aiming to enslave them forever.<br>War came, fierce and relentless,<br>in the North, in the Centre, in the South, and in the Levant.<br>And across Spain, the great draft arose<br>of volunteers who fight, singing:<br>FORWARD! |
| *refrain*<br>Amb fúria i disciplina<br>enfonsarà a l'abisme<br>el criminal feixisme<br>l'Exèrcit Popular. | *refrain*<br>With fury and discipline<br>the People's Army will drive<br>criminal fascism<br>into the abyss |
| Però nosaltres a més de la glòria<br>volem la força que dóna la unitat.<br>Per la total i immediata victòria<br>com un sol home marxem al combat.<br>Passa la tropa i el poble l'aclama;<br>rengles de ferro, fussels rutilants:<br>l'esguard enlaire dessota la flama<br>de la bandera que ens fa a tots germans.<br>ENDAVANT! | But we seek not only glory<br>but also the strength of unity.<br>For total and immediate victory,<br>united, we march into battle.<br>The troops pass by, and the people acclaim them;<br>iron ranks, shining rifles:<br>the gaze raised beneath the flame<br>of the flag that unites us all as brothers.<br>FORWARD! |
| Amb fúria i disciplina... | With fury and discipline... |

As no sources exist that attribute the composition of *Marxa de l'Exèrcit Popular* to a specific composer, I believe the author wished to remain anonymous, likely for political and professional reasons. The song's compositional style suggests that Ernst H. Meyer is the most likely candidate. The piece features two characteristics common to other songs by Meyer from the 1930s. One characteristic is the inclusion of a single 2/4 bar within a song predominantly written in a 4/4 time signature; this bar contains an accented semiquaver followed by a rest on the second beat (Exx. 4.2 and 4.3). A very similar configuration

Ex. 4.2. Opening of *Marxa de l'Exèrcit Popular*. Source: Otto Mayer-Serra, *Cançoner Revolucionari Internacional*, vol. 1 (Barcelona: Comissariat de Propaganda de la Generalitat de Catalunya, 1937), p. 11.

appears in his songs *Krieg* (*War*, 1931, b. 1) and *1. Mai* (*1st of May*, 1932).[41] This procedure of momentarily generating metrical irregularity in a marching song through a change of time signature is likely modelled on Eisler's *Solidarity Song* (see Chapter 5). Another piece of evidence pointing to Meyer's authorship is the ending of *Marxa de l'Exèrcit Popular*, which consists of a single accented chord repeated three times in a dotted rhythm at *fortissimo* (Ex. 4.3, final bar). Meyer's *Kampflied gegen Hitler* (1933), *The Refugees* (1939), *Schlaflose Nächte* (1939), *Frau Kraemer* (1941), and *Strike in the West* (1941) all conclude with similarly repeated, accented chords. Compare the closing of *Marxa de l'Exèrcit Popular* (Ex. 4.3) with that of *Kampflied gegen Hitler* (Ex. 4.4). Eisler's battle songs do not exhibit this closing motif, nor do the works of other composers in his circle, such as Paul Arma, Paul Dessau, Karl Rankl, or Karl Vollmer.

The elided attribution also suggests Meyer's authorship. Unlike other composers in Eisler's circle at the time, Meyer preferred not to be identified as the author of overtly political songs and writings during his exile in England. He published most of his political songs under the pseudonym "Peter Baker", including the popular *Labour's Marching Song* and *The Final Struggle*, both from 1936. One of the main reasons for his desire to remain anonymous was to

41 The scores of these songs are kept at the Arbeiter-Lied-Archiv of the Akademie der Künste, under cat. no. 3336 (*1. Mai*) and 3204 (*Krieg*).

Ex. 4.3. Closing of *Marxa de l'Exèrcit Popular*. Source: Otto Mayer-Serra, *Cançoner Revolucionari Internacional*, vol. 1 (Barcelona: Comissariat de Propaganda de la Generalitat de Catalunya, 1937), pp. 12–13.

Ex. 4.4. Final bars of Meyer's *Kampflied gegen Hitler* (1933).

avoid jeopardising his career as a musicologist, which he was developing while in exile. Around the same time, other communist musicologists who were also composers, such as Charles Seeger, similarly chose not to reveal their real names when composing war songs, opting instead to use pseudonyms.

The fact that the song was most likely commissioned by Mayer-Serra further indicates that Meyer authored it. Among the German communist composers in Eisler's former circle, Meyer was by far the closest to Mayer-Serra. Evidence suggests they corresponded during the war, although most of their letters have not been preserved. Additionally, there is proof of another collaboration between the two during this period, with Meyer acting in his capacity as a musicologist: Mayer-Serra published a translation of an article by his friend in the music section of *Mirador*, where he served as editor-in-chief, in mid-1937. Meyer's article was published under the pseudonym Peter Baker.[42]

[42] Peter Baker [Ernst H. Meyer], "Carta de Londres. La vida musical a Anglaterra", *Mirador* 423 (10 June 1937): 10.

Palacio asserted that *Marxa de l'Exèrcit Popular* was "sung frequently" during the war, "especially on the fronts in Catalonia".[43] This appears to be true, considering the frequency with which this song was mentioned in the Catalan wartime press. The earliest documented performances occurred in various Catalan cities and towns throughout March 1937.[44] The Cantors de l'Escola Popular de Guerra (Singers of the People's Wartime School) recorded a version for choir and band, accompanied by the band from the PSUC's Vorotxilov military headquarters in Barcelona. This recording served as the soundtrack for a short documentary film about a military training camp for the Popular Army in Catalonia.[45] I infer that this recording was broadcast on the radio, much like many other recordings of battle songs, and was also played on large loudspeakers in public spaces. The song's enduring popularity in military contexts during the war is further evidenced by the fact that the vocal melody was still remembered in 2005 by Narcís Matas i Sabater, a former Catalan peasant born in 1916 who fought on the Republican side. His rendition of the piece was recently recorded as part of the "Càntut" project, which aims to collect orally transmitted songs from northern Catalonia.[46]

## Eisler's Political Ballads in the Voice of Ernst Busch

During his sixteen-month stay in wartime Spain, from March 1937 to July 1938, the German communist tenor Ernst Busch sang selections of Eisler's most popular political ballads in a large number of live and radio concerts – apparently over a hundred in total, as he reported to the Soviet musicologist Grigori Schneerson.[47] I have found documentary evidence for several of these concerts.

43 "Se canta mucho, muy especialmente en los frentes de Catalunya", Palacio, *Colección*, 34.

44 Muñoz, "Milicians, reclutes i comissaris…"; Lluís Companys, "Míting a la Monumental en ocasió del 'Dia de Madrid', 14 de març del 1937", in *Els discursos inèdits de Lluís Companys*, Booklet of the recording published by the Arxiu Nacional de Catalunya/ Fons Lluís Companys i Jover.

45 The Schweizerisches Sozialarchiv keep a copy of the recording, which can be listened to online. See https://www.bild-video-ton.ch/bestand/objekt/Sozarch_F_1020-041a. For more on that film, entitled *Primer campo de instrucción del Ejército Popular Regular* (*First Training Camp of the People's Army*), see Alfonso del Amo García, ed., *Catálogo General del Cine de la Guerra Civil* (Madrid: Filmoteca Española 1996), 774. An excerpt can be found at: https://www.youtube.com/watch?v=1G_N99GufSY [Accessed 20 June 2025].

46 The recording was digitised and preserved for online access. See the project's website: https://www.cantut.cat/canconer/cancons/item/151-marxa-de-l-exercit-popular [Accessed 15 September 2025].

47 On the number of live and radio concerts, see Ernst Busch, letter to Schneerson, 19 May 1938, Ernst Busch Archiv (AdK), cat. no. 2218. Busch's activities in Spain have

One took place on 21 August 1937 at the Valencia Conservatory in homage to the International Brigades; the concert opened with a short lecture or speech by Carlos Palacio.[48] Another concert took place on 6 February 1938 at the Club Internacional Antifascista in Barcelona, apparently for a predominantly German-speaking audience. This club was led by Karl Mewis, who operated under the alias "Fritz Arndt", and served as the head of the KPD's secret counter-intelligence apparatus in Barcelona. At this event, Erich Weinert recited "antifascist poems", while several others delivered political speeches.[49]

One further concert was organised at the Barcelona communist-controlled organisation, the Casal de la Cultura (House of Culture), on 15 September 1937. The event was likely initiated by Mayer-Serra, who served as the "secretary of propaganda" for the Casal's music department and was a member of the department's executive committee. Established in January 1937, the Casal de la Cultura was modelled after the Parisian Maison de la Culture, which had been founded in 1935 by the French Communist Party. The Casal began its activities shortly after the outbreak of street fighting known as the "May Days of 1937". Its efforts included exhibitions, film screenings, educational courses, book launches, concerts, lectures, and various political events, such as the closing ceremonies of the Second International Congress of Intellectuals of the Alliance for the Defence of Culture.[50]

At the inauguration of the music department in April 1937, Mayer-Serra read aloud one of the Casal's manifestos, in which he emphasised that the organisation's main objective was to eliminate the barriers between (art-) music and the people.[51] To achieve this, the Casal's music department organ-

---

been discussed in Karl Siebig, *"Ich geh' mit dem Jahrhundert mit". Ernst Busch. Eine Dokumentation* (Reibeck bei Hamburg: Rowohlt Taschen, 1980), 155–168; Ludwig Hoffman and Karl Siebig, *Ernst Busch. Eine Biographie in Texten, Bildern und Dokumenten* (Berlin: Das Europäische Buch, 1987), 19–196; Ben Leenders and Bernd Meyer-Rähnitz, *Der Phonographische Ernst Busch. Eine Discographie seiner Sprach- und Gesangsaufnahmen* (Dresden: Ústí nad Labern, 2005); Jochen Voigt, *Er rührte an den Schlaf der Welt. Ernst Busch. Die Biographie* (Berlin: Aufbau, 2010), 139–141.

48 A flyer for the event is held at the Ernst Busch Archive (AdK), cat. no. 766.

49 Anon., "Club Internacioal Antifaxista", *Treball* (4 February 1938): 4. Concerning Busch and the Club Internacional Antifascista, see Voigt, *Er rührte an den Schlaf*, 136.

50 On the Casal de la Cultura see María Campillo, *Escriptors catalans i compromís antifeixista (1936–1939)* (Barcelona: Publications de l'Abadia de Montserrat, 1994), 155–181; Esther Boquera Diago, *La batalla de la persuasió durant la Guerra Civil. El cas del Comissariat de Propaganda de la Generalitat Catalunya (1936–1939)* (PhD diss., Universitat Ramon Llull, 2015); and Rafael Pascuet and Enric Pujol, eds., *La revolució del bon gust (Barcelona:* Viena Edicions, 2006), 66–108.

51 Anon., "La constitució de la Secció 'Música' del Casal de la Cultura", *Mirador* 418 (29 April 1937): 8. On the Casal's music department see Eduard Prieto, "La Secció de Música del Casal de la Cultura", *Mirador* 415 (8 April 1937): 8; César Calmell, "Barcelona, 1938: una ciutat ocupada musicalment", *Recerca Musicològica* XVII–XVIII (2007–2008): 323–344.

ised a series of events for Barcelona's workers, primarily lectures on music and concerts, predominantly featuring chamber works from the Western classical canon, particularly German and French compositions.

Ernst Busch gave at least one concert at the institution, performing a selection of political ballads and battle songs, including several by Eisler. The concert programme, reproduced below, is the only preserved example from Busch's live concerts in Spain (Fig. 4.6). He sang thirteen songs, all with German lyrics, accompanied at the piano by the now-forgotten pianist and composer Max Signer, an alias of Max Schlesinger. Almost every song was by a communist composer, with more than half by Eisler. These included ballads in moderate tempos, such as *Stempellied* (*Stamp Song*, 1929), *Lied vom SA-Mann* (*Song of the SA Man*, 1931), and *Deutsches Lied 1937* (*German Song 1937*, 1936), the cabaret song *The Ballade vom Nigger Jim* (*The Ballad of Nigger Jim*, 1930), as well as the battle songs *Song of the United Front* (1934) and *Der heimliche Aufmarsch* (*The Secret Deployment*, 1930).

The concert was entitled "La nostra època a través de la cançó" (Our Times through Song). This was the Catalan translation of "Das Lied der Zeit", a slogan that Busch and Eisler had been using since 1932 to title concert programmes, which they continued to use regularly in the GDR.[52] Mayer-Serra opened the concert with the lecture "Music as Weapon in the Anti-Fascist Struggle". The slogan "music as weapon" (or, more generally, "culture as weapon") was commonplace among communist intellectuals at that time, both in Europe and the USA. The event was announced in the press as "an insight into a truly revolutionary conception of music", which was "almost unknown in Catalonia".[53] Whether Busch collaborated further with Mayer-Serra or with the Casal de la Cultura remains unclear. Evidence suggests personal disagreements between them dating back to October 1937, likely stemming from the strong personalities of both individuals, as well as potential political reasons.[54]

Several of Busch's "radio recitals" took place at Ràdio Barcelona, the principal radio station in the Catalan city. The surviving sources for these recitals suggest that they were similar in content, duration, and structure to the live concert at the Casal de la Cultura. One of the earliest recitals for which the song list has survived occurred on 24 August 1937 at 22:30 on Ràdio Barcelona. It lasted thirty minutes and included the following songs, in this order: Eisler's *Der Rote Wedding* (1929), *Lied der Moorsoldaten* (1933/1935), *Lied vom SA-Mann* (1931), *Song of the United Front* (1934), Paul Dessau's *Die Thälmann-Kolonne* (also known as *Spaniens Himmel*, 1936), Walter Göhr's *Lied des arbeitslosen*

52 Leenders and Meyer-Rähnitz, *Der phonographische Ernst Busch*, 351.

53 "una modalidad de la canción casi desconocida en Cataluña", "una concepción auténticamente revolucionaria de la música", anon., "Canciones de guerra", *La Vanguardia* (15 September 1937): 2.

54 File of the executive committee of the International Communist, 41 (RGASPI 495-205-2727). I thank Cristoph Kugler for providing me with a copy of this document.

CASAL DE LA CULTURA
SECCIÓ DE MÚSICA

CINQUENA SESSIÓ

La nostra època a través de la cançó
INTERPRETADA PER
ERNST BUSCH
Al piano: M. SINGER
Ambientació: EDUARD PRIETO

LA SESSIÓ SERÀ PRECEDIDA D'UNA
DISSERTACIÓ SOBRE EL TEMA:
La música com a arma en la
lluita antifeixista
LLEGIDA PER
OTTO MAYER

---

DIMECRES, DIA 15 DE SETEMBRE DEL 1937,
A UN QUART DE VUIT DE LA TARDA

Fig 4.6. Programme for Busch's concert on 15 September 1937 in Barcelona's Casal de la Cultura, from the present author's archive.

*Bergmannes* (also known as *Kumpellied*, ca., 1932), and Carlos Palacio's *Las compañías de acero* (1937).[55] The programmes for two additional radio recitals on 13 September and 25 November included just one Eisler song each: the ballads *Deutsches Lied 1937* (1936) and *Die Baumwollpflücker*, op. 22, no. 1

[55] Guions de Ràdio Barcelona, file for August 1937, 27 (Dipòsit Digital de Documents de la UAB: https://ddd.uab.cat/record/33210 [Accessed 15 September 2025]). On Walter Göhr's *Kumpellied*, see Inge Lammel, *Und weil ein Mensch ein Mensch ist* (Leipzig: Deutscher Verlag für Musik, 1986), 174.

(1929), respectively.[56] Given the political nature of these songs, the lyrics might have been read aloud beforehand in either Catalan or Spanish translation.

## Eisler's Songs for Spain

The three songs that Eisler composed in 1936 and 1937 specifically to support Spanish antifascism – the Olympic song (reconfigured as *Marcha del Quinto Regimiento*), *No pasarán*, and *Das Lied vom 7. Januar* – found diverse uses and achieved various degrees of dissemination in Spain and abroad. Carlos Palacio's claims that *Marcha* was one of the most popular battle songs in wartime Spain while *No pasarán* remained barely known appear largely accurate.[57] Both *Marcha* and *No pasarán* were sung somewhat regularly by the choir of the Altavoz del Frente and broadcast during the war.[58]

The lyrics for the *Marcha* were published in 1937 via the official print organ of the Fifth Regiment, *Milicia popular*. Several other military units' periodicals subsequently followed suit.[59] Busch's *Kampflieder der Internationalen Brigaden* included the vocal melody for the *Marcha* starting in its second edition. His omission of any French, English, or German lyrics suggests that, contrary to previous assertions,[60] the song may not have been especially popular among interbrigadists. The *Marcha* saw its first publication in December 1937 as an entry in the second volume of Otto Mayer-Serra's *International Revolutionary Songbook*. Unlike Busch's songbook for soldiers, this edition included Eisler's piano accompaniment. This version also features a four-bar instrumental introduction to help amateur singers pitch the first note of the song correctly (Fig. 4.7). This introduction, absent in the 1936 edition of the Olympic march, is almost certainly not by Eisler.[61]

Outside Spain, the *Marcha del Quinto Regimiento* played a significant role in Comintern-controlled propaganda concerning the Spanish Civil War. French

56 Guions de Ràdio Barcelona, file for September 1937, 13 (Dipòsit Digital de Documents de la UAB: https://ddd.uab.cat/record/33210 [Accessed 15 September 2025]); Guions de Ràdio Barcelona, file for November 1937, 29 (Dipòsit Digital de Documents de la UAB: https://ddd.uab.cat/record/33210)

57 Palacio, *Acordes en el alma*, 140.

58 Anon., "La marcha del 5º Regimiento", *ABC Madrid* (16 January 1937), 6.

59 Anon., "La 'Marcha del 5.º Regimiento'", *Milicia popular* 2, no. 159 (14 January 1937): 2. The lyrics were also published in: *Hierro*, no. 15 (2 February 1937): 7; *Al Ataque*, no. 7 (20 February 1937): 1; *Frente Sur, Jaén*, no. 148 (15 April 1937): 4. See also Ramírez Morcillo, *Literatura*, 217.

60 Schebera, *Hanns Eisler. Eine Biographie*, 146.

61 Otto Mayer-Serra, ed., *Cançoner revolutionari international*, vol. 2 (Barcelona: Comissariat de Propaganda, 1937), 8. A recent recording of this version is included on the album *Ana Vega: Canciones de lucha*, Dahiz Prouccions, 014 CD, Spain, 2001.

Fig. 4.7. *Marcha del Quinto Regimiento,* as published in the *International Revolutionary Songbook* edited by Mayer-Serra for the Propaganda Agency of the Catalan Government. Source: Otto Mayer-Serra, ed., *Cançoner revolutionari international,* vol. 2. (Barcelona: Comissariat de Propaganda, 1937), 8.

publishers affiliated with the Comintern promptly distributed the French version of the lyrics, penned by Georges Bénichou, a journalist for the communist paper *L'Humanité.* As the *Marche du 5e Régiment de l'armée républicaine espagnole,* this French version was published in 1937 as both a loose leaflet and in the aforementioned songbook *Chants révolutionnaires de divers pays* (*Revolutionary Songs from Various Countries*). This book was the third volume in an International Songbooks series, edited and published by the pro-communist French publishing house Editions Sociales Internationales.[62]

A leaflet copy of the *Marche du 5e Régiment* held by the HEA in Berlin includes a handwritten Russian translation of the song's title and lyrics. Fig. 4.8 shows the first page.[63] An unidentified hand indicates that the authors are the Soviet writers Samuil Borisovich Bolotin and Tatiana Sergeevna Sikorskaia.

62 Hanns Eisler, *Marche du 5e Regiment de l'armée républicaine espagnole* (Paris: Editions Sociales Internationales, 1937); see also *Chants révolutionnaires de divers pays* (Paris: Editions Sociales Internationales, 1937). A copy of the score is kept at the HEA in Berlin under cat. no. 1073. For more information on this songbook and on the Editions Sociales Internationales more generally, see Christopher Lee Moore, *Music in France and the Popular Front (1934–1938): Politics, Aesthetics and Reception* (PhD diss., McGill University, 2006), esp. 136–171.

63 Hanns Eisler, *Marche du 5e Regiment de l'armée républicaine espagnole* (Paris: Editions Sociales Internationales, 1937). HEA, cat. no. 1073.

Fig. 4.8. Edition of the French version of Eisler's *Marcha del Quinto Regimiento,* published by Editions Sociales Internationales as a loose leaflet in Paris (1937). Source: HEA cat. no. 1073. Published with kind permission.

Bolotin and Sikorskaia provided the Russian lyrics for several civil war battle songs, either independently or in tandem, including Kochetov's *No pasarán* and Szabó's *Marcha de las Brigadas Internacionales.*

The score for the Russian version of the *Marcha* was included in the Soviet songbook *My pojom. We sing. Nous chantons. Wir singen* (1938). This book was published in Moscow by the Soviet state music publishing house for international distribution. It also included German and English versions of the lyrics, by Erich Weinert and Ben Blake, respectively. Blake was the American representative of the Comintern's International Union of Revolutionary Theatre.[64] The French, Russian, and English versions included the following explicit calls to join the fight in Spain: "Notre Espagne vous appelle / La milice vous appelle"; "Spain is calling, Spain is calling / Join the fighters for your freedom"; "За свободный край испанский / В бой зовёт нас народ республиканский" ("For the free land of Spain / The republican people call us to battle"). Judging by these appeals, absent from Petere's original lyrics, these versions of Eisler's *Marcha* could have been used in international volunteer recruitment campaigns for the International Brigades led by the Comintern.

A recording of the Russian version, performed by Soviet baritone Wladimir Sacharow, was made in Moscow in 1938, likely intended for broadcast within the Soviet Union as part of domestic propaganda supporting intervention on behalf of the Republic.[65] Another recording of the *Marcha,* sung a cappella in Spanish by a group of men, was made during the war. An excerpt of this recording was included in the soundtrack for the 1939 Soviet documentary film *Ispaniya* (*Spain*) by Esfir Shub. The recording accompanies footage of soldiers conducting military exercises. This field recording was likely made in wartime Spain by the two Russian war correspondents who documented most of the visual material for the film.[66]

The wider dissemination of the *Marcha* stood in contrast to the limited use of *No pasarán* for propaganda, both in Spain and internationally. For reasons that remain unclear, neither the lyrics nor the music of *No pasarán* were included in any songbook published in Spain or in the allied countries during the war. It is possible that Spanish propagandists deemed the song to be of inadequate quality or insufficiently effective for their purposes.

The case of *Das Lied vom 7. Januar* was quite different. As a lament or elegy, rather than a battle song, it was less suited for use as propaganda. As noted

64 C.f. Erich Weinert, *Camaradas. Ein Spanienbuch* (Berlin: Volk und Welt, 1956), 26.

65 Wladimir Sacharow, *Марш Пятого полка*, Gramplasttrest 7354; a recording of the song can be found at: http://www.russian-records.com/details.php?image_id=16889. See also Deeg and Schebera, "Hanns Eisler auf Schallplatte", 5.

66 Esfir Shub, *Ispaniya* (Mosfilm: Soviet Union, 1939), timestamp 24' 30". On this film see Wolfgang Martín-Hamdorf, "Del testigo presencial a la transformación poética. *Ispanija-España*: poesía, narrativa y propaganda", *Secuencias*: *Revista de historia del cine* 3 (1995): 60–77.

in Chapter 2, its musical setting appeared in the final two editions of Busch's songbook *Kampflieder der Internationalen Brigaden*. Only the lyrics were published in a 1937 special edition of *Der deutsche Schriftsteller*, dedicated to Republican Spain. This journal was produced in Paris by the Schutzverband deutscher Schriftsteller im Ausland (Protective Association for German Writers Abroad). In October 1943, during the Second World War, the lyrics were reprinted in *Freie Deutsche Kultur* (*Free German Culture*), a German-language monthly literary journal published in London by the Free German Cultural League, an organisation of German exiles.[67]

## Songs for the Illiterate

In conclusion, apart from Busch's regular performances of Eisler's political ballads, only the Spanish and Catalan versions of Eisler's most popular battle songs – particularly *La Comintern*, *Canción del Frente Popular*, and *Marcha del Quinto Regimiento* – were performed with notable frequency in wartime Spain. These songs comprise the portion of his vocal output that was especially easy for the largely illiterate soldiers to sing and remember. As the soundscape of war propaganda was shaped not only through live performances but also by broadcasts in domestic and public settings, it is likely that these songs reached a wide audience via the new technologies of radio and large-scale sound systems.

Unlike in Germany, Austria, Denmark, England, the United States, and the Soviet Union, none of the choral compositions written for performance by trained workers' choruses – such as the aforementioned op. 13, or the pro-communist modernist music-theatre plays of the Weimar period, such as *Die Maßnahme* – were performed in 1930s Spain. This absence can be attributed to the relative weakness of the communist movement in Spain prior to the civil war and the lack of prominent Spanish composers or ensembles invested in this kind of repertoire. By contrast, in England and the United States, figures such as Alan Bush and Marc Blitzstein actively championed several of Eisler's concert works for workers.[68] The Orquesta y Coros Proletarios de Madrid

67 Elke Bleider-Staudt, *Die deutschsprachige Lyrik des spanischen Bürgerkriegs. Eine Untersuchung der Lebensform und lyrischen Sprache* (PhD diss., University of Tübingen, 1983), Appendix (Quellenanhang), 13.

68 For the reception of these choral and theatre works outside Spain see Erik Levi, "A Composer under Surveillance: Hanns Eisler and England, 1925–1962", in *Eisler in England: Proceedings of the International Hanns Eisler Conference, London 2010*, ed. Oliver Dahin and Erik Levi (Wiesbaden: Breitkopf & Härtel, 2014), 9–31; Maria Kiladi, *The London Labour Choral Union, 1924–1940: A Musical Institution of the Left* (PhD diss., Royal Holloway, University of London, 2016); Michael Fjeldsoe, "Hanns Eisler und seine Bedeutung für die linkskulturelle Szene in Dänemark in den 1920er und 1930er Jahren", in *Hanns Eisler und die Nachwelt*, ed. Peter Schweinhardt (Berlin: Bärenreiter, 2018), 81–99; Gall, *Hanns Eisler*, xxxix; see also Grabs, *Eisler*, 66.

might have been one of the few Spanish ensembles interested in performing these works for ideological reasons. However, it appears that most of its members were conservative regarding repertoire and, more importantly, lacked the musical competence to perform pieces of such complexity. As for the Catalan bourgeois choirs, it would have been inconceivable for them to engage with Eisler's proletarian choral music, despite Gerhard's recommendation. These compositions openly satirised the evocative and sentimental repertoire favoured by the politically conservative *orfeós*, while their lyrics explicitly called upon both performers and audiences to engage in the class struggle.

The limited influence of communist ideology in prewar Spain also helps explain why Eisler's "proletarian" modernist choral and stage works – those we particularly value today – had little impact on the music of Spanish left-wing composers. The only work by Eisler to exert notable compositional influence in Republican Spain was the *Solidarity Song* (1931). The following chapter examines how and why this piece became a key model for the composition of propaganda songs that sought to convey antifascist ideology not only through their lyrics but also through their musical style.

# Chapter 5

# Musical and Political Progressivism: Emulating the *Solidarity Song*

As one of Eisler's most accomplished and innovative battle songs, the *Solidarity Song* exerted a significant compositional influence in Republican Spain. It served as a key model for at least seven Spanish propaganda songs analysed in this chapter. These case studies include some of the most important propaganda songs written by Spanish communist composers both before and, more prominently, during the civil war. Their authors range from established composers to lesser-known figures. As noted in the Introduction, the influence of this battle song can be attributed above all to the association, among communist composers, of its "modernist" features with political progressivism. This link was rooted in a view of both political history and musical style as teleological processes defined by continuous progress.

The *Solidarity Song* was created in 1931 by Bertolt Brecht, Hanns Eisler, and Ernst Busch for Slatan Dudow's film *Kuhle Wampe oder: Wem gehört die Welt?* (*Kuhle Wampe or: Who Owns the World?*). Unlike in Germany, the film did not play a major role in disseminating the song in Spain (its Spanish premiere in mid-1933 was a failure, with screenings limited to just two cinemas, one in Madrid and one in Barcelona). As noted in the previous chapter, the complete score, including the piano accompaniment, was never published in Spain during the 1930s. It is likely that Spanish composers accessed the song through printed or handwritten copies of one of the various foreign editions circulating in the country before and during the civil war. These may have included the 1932 edition published by Universal Edition, or the second volume of the *Workers Songbook*, published in 1934 by the Workers Music League in New York, which featured the English-language version of the piece.[1]

Brecht's original lyrics call for unity and mutual support among employed and unemployed workers in their shared struggle against capitalist exploitation. This theme forms the central focus of *Kuhle Wampe*, which portrays the devastating social consequences of the 1929 Wall Street Crash in Germany. The song begins with a refrain, followed by seven stanzas, each interspersed

1 I use the Universal Edition score as the source for my analysis; see Hanns Eisler, *Das Solidaritätslied*, Sonntagslied der freien Jugend, op. 27/1 (UE 10.073), reduced for piano by Erwin Ratz (Vienna: Universal Edition, 1932).

with a repetition of the refrain. A slight variation of the refrain concludes the song. The main and closing refrains are provided below.[2]

| *Main Refrain* | *Main Refrain* |
|---|---|
| Vorwärts und nicht vergessen, | Forward, and without forgetting |
| worin unsere Stärke besteht! | what our strength is! |
| Beim Hungern und beim Essen, | Whether starving or eating, |
| vorwärts und nie vergessen: | forward, and never forgetting: |
| die Solidarität! | solidarity! |
| | |
| [seven stanzas follow, with refrain] | [seven stanzas follow, with refrain] |
| | |
| *Closing Refrain* | *Closing Refrain* |
| Vorwärts und nicht vergessen | Forward, and without forgetting |
| unsere Straße und unsere Feld | our street and our field |
| Vorwärts und nicht vergessen: | Forward, and without forgetting: |
| Wessen Straße ist die Straße? | Whose street is the street? |
| Wessen Welt ist die Welt? | Whose world is the world? |

Several innovative features distinguish the *Solidarity Song* musically from most workers' songs and political anthems of the time.[3] One of the most conspicuous – and most often imitated by Spanish composers – is Eisler's irregular metrical organisation, introduced through changes in time signature. In the chorus sections (A and A'), the primary 4/4 time signature shifts to 2/4 at three distinct points (in bars 6, 10, and 26). The first two metrical changes are illustrated in Ex. 5.1 (bars 6 and 10). Since these changes each last for one bar, they can also be understood as the elimination of the second half of a four-beat bar, causing the subsequent bar to begin half a bar earlier than anticipated. The result is a form of metrical anticipation, or forward push, which Eisler scholar Christian Glanz describes as a type of rhythmic "intensification".[4] Some scholars interpret these metrical shifts as a strategy to generate critical distance

2 For further analysis of the subject matter and structure in Brecht's lyrics, see Albrecht Dümling, *Lässt euch nicht verführen. Brecht und die Musik* (Munich: Kindler, 1985), 323–335; Ibid., "Solidaritätslied", in *Brecht Handbuch*, vol. 2, eds. Jan Knopf and Joachim Lucchesi (Stuttgart: Metzler, 2001), 196–201.

3 The original compositional features of Eisler's battle songs – *Das Solidaritätslied* in particular – have been the subject of extensive analytical scholarship. Some of the most relevant studies include Reinhold Brinkmann, "Kompositorische Maßnahmen Eislers", in *Über Musik und Politik*, ed. Rudolf Stephan (Mainz: Schott, 1971), 9–22; Jürgen Elsner, *Zur vokalsolistischer Vortragsweise der Kampfmusik Hanns Eislers* (Leipzig: Deutscher Verlag für Musik, 1971), 49–50, 58–59, and 125–126; Christian Glanz, *Hanns Eisler, Werk und Leben* (Vienna: Steinbauer, 2008), 76–80; see also Tobias Fasshauer, "Fesche Märsche. Hanns Eisler und die Militärmusik", *Eisler-Mitteilungen* 67 (Saarbrücken: Pfau, 2019), 4–18.

4 Glanz, *Hanns Eisler*, 78.

Ex. 5.1. *Solidarity Song*, section A (setting of the main refrain), as published by Universal Edition, bb. 1–10. © C. F. Peters GmbH & Co. KG, Leipzig und Deutscher Verlag für Musik Leipzig.

between the *Solidarity Song* and more traditional marching songs for soldiers. Nonetheless, Eisler's piece is suitable for marching, as evidenced by its use in the final scene of *Kuhle Wampe*, where a group of working-class sportsmen walk to the rhythm of the song.

Another original feature of the *Solidarity Song* is the absence of traditional harmonic closure at the end of the piece, along with the related ambiguity in certain sections regarding whether the referential collection is D minor or A Phrygian. As Albrecht Dümling has demonstrated, Eisler and Brecht initially composed the verses (section B) in D minor, which corresponds to the notated key signature (see Ex. 5.2, bb. 11–22).[5] The dominant chords in this section omit the third scale degree, thereby maintaining ambiguity concerning their major or minor quality (see Ex. 5.2, bb. 13, 16, 19, 22). The lack of leading-tone resolutions (C-sharp to D) weakens the tonal definition. The prevailing mode is not the conventional minor, but rather an Aeolian mode, or natural minor.

In the chorus sections A and A', Eisler alternates the use of the leading tone (C-sharp) and the subtonic (C). This feature also characterises other interwar battle songs by Eisler, including the *Comintern Song*. Sections A and A' contrast harmonically with the verse section B in their ambiguity regarding whether the diatonic collection refers to D minor or A Phrygian. Both sections A and A' conclude with the same progression: D minor seventh–E major–G minor–A major.

5 Dümling, *Lässt euch nicht verführen*, 323.

Ex. 5.2. *Solidarity Song*, section B, verse (bb. 11–22) followed by the final chorus, A' (bb. 23–31). © C. F. Peters GmbH & Co. KG, Leipzig und Deutscher Verlag für Musik Leipzig.

In the transition from section A to section B, the A major chord resolves to the D minor tonic (see Ex. 5.2, b. 11), representing a dominant function. At the end of the song, however, the A major chord remains unresolved (see Ex. 5.2, b. 31). The song concludes with a Phrygian cadence, or iv6–V half cadence in a minor key (here D minor), which includes semitonal descending motion in the bass line (here B-flat to A). This type of imperfect cadence was frequently used in the Baroque period, typically at the ends of slow movements or introductory sections that would be followed by a faster movement or section in the same key.

The decision to conclude the *Solidarity Song* with a half cadence rather than an authentic one has been interpreted as a musical analogy to the final rhetorical questions posed in the lyrics, which implicitly denounce the unjust capitalist system: "Whose street is the street? Whose world is the world?"[6] In this interpretation, Brecht and Eisler intended for the film's viewers and the song's performers to reflect on these unanswered questions. It should be noted, however, that this is not the only Eisler song that does not end on the tonic; many of his chansons and ballads from that period conclude with weak or ambiguous progressions regarding tonal functionality.

In part because Eisler composed the *Solidarity Song* as film music – an uncommon context for battle songs of the period – he introduced what Eisler scholar Tobias Fasshauer terms "shimmy-anapaest". This term refers to pairs of repeated demisemiquavers on accented beats, typical of contemporary "light" popular dance or "jazz", primarily from the USA (see Ex. 5.1., bb. 1–8). Eisler incorporated shimmy-anapaest figurations in other works from the interwar period, including his 1933 arrangement of *La Marianne Populaire* (see Chapter 1). In 1932, he explained that these "energetic" rhythmic configurations were the only elements of "jazz" suitable for composing "revolutionary militant music". In contrast, the melodic and harmonic features of "bourgeois Schlager" represented a "thoroughly corrupt, inactive musical attitude" and should not be adopted for militant music.[7]

One additional noteworthy aspect of the *Solidarity Song* is the marked differentiation between the chorus and verse sections in the lengths of their phrases and melodic profiles. In the chorus sections A and A', the phrases are four bars long, and the vocal melody is angular, characterised by many leaps (Exx. 5.1 and 5.2). In contrast, the verse section B features phrases that are six bars long, with the vocal contour primarily moving by stepwise motion (Ex. 5.2). The bass line of the chorus exemplifies what several Eisler scholars have termed the "Eisler bass", consisting of regular semiquavers that move in steps or thirds.[8]

6 Brinkmann, "Kompositorische Maßnahmen", 14–15. See also Dümling, *Lässt euch nicht verführen*, 325–326.

7 Hanns Eisler, "Neue Methoden der Kampfmusik" (1932), in *Hanns Eisler. Gesammelte Schriften 1921–1935*, ed. Tobias Fasshauer and Günter Mayer (Wiesbaden: Breitkopf & Härtel, 2007), 156.

8 The "Eisler bass" is discussed in Fasshauer, "Fesche Märsche", 6 and 9.

## *Himno a Thaelmann* (*Hymn to Thaelmann*, 1933 or 1934)

*Himno a Thaelmann* is the earliest Spanish battle song influenced by the *Solidarity Song* and, according to communist composer Carlos Palacio, one of the first "social" (that is, communist) songs ever created in Spain.[9] Its author, Joaquín Villatoro (1911–1987), trained as a composer at the Madrid Conservatory under Spanish composer Conrado del Campo. He then studied from 1932 to 1934 at the École Normale de Musique in Paris under Paul Dukas and Alfred Cortot. After completing these studies, he became a prominent communist activist in Madrid.[10] The lyrics for *Himno a Thaelmann* were written in late 1933 by the communist Rafael Alberti, who had already gained recognition as a poet. They consist of two parts, each comprising two stanzas. His prominent use of quatrains with eight-syllable lines corresponds to a popular format commonly found in political poems and song lyrics during the war.[11]

| *Part I* | *Part I* |
|---|---|
| 1. ¡Camaradas, hombro con hombro!<br>¡Camaradas, más firme el paso!<br>¡Para libertar a Thelman [sic]<br>hoces y puños en alto! [x2]<br>¡Norte, Sur, Este, y Oeste! | Comrades, shoulder to shoulder!<br>Comrades, maintain the pace!<br>To free Thaelmann,<br>sickles and fists raised! [x2]<br>North, South, East, and West! |
| 2. Ya las hachas retroceden,<br>Tiemblan los nazis sangrando,<br>rueda por tierra el fascismo,<br>¡Muera!<br>al pie del proletariado. | The axes are already retreating,<br>the Nazis are trembling and bleeding.<br>Fascism falls to the ground.<br>Death to fascism!<br>At the foot of the proletariat. |

9 Carlos Palacio, *Colección*, 150.

10 On Villatoro's career as a composer, see Pilar Serrano Betored, "La influencia silenciada: Paul Dukas y la música española de la Edad de Plata" (PhD diss., Universidad Complutense de Madrid, 2019), 529. See also Francisco Cañaveras Garrido, *Joaquín Villatoro. Vida y Obra* (Córdoba: Ayuntamiento de Castro del Río, 1998); and Sara Cuevas, *La actividad musical de Joaquín Villatoro Medina* (Seville: Junta de Andalucía, 2015). Villatoro's political activism has yet to receive significant scholarly attention; a brief discussion can be found in Palacio, *Acordes en el alma*, 115.

11 The lyrics were first published in Rafael Alberti, *Poemas de Alberti* (Mexico City: Ediciones de la L.E.A.R., 1935) and then Palacio, *Colección* (1939), 149–150. These versions differ slightly from the lyrics that Villatoro set to music, provided below. For more on Alberti's lyrics, see Eladio Mateos, "Rafael Alberti y la música" (PhD diss., Universidad de Granada, 2003), 158–162.

| *Part II* | *Part II* |
|---|---|
| 3. ¡Camaradas, hombro con hombro!<br>¡Camaradas, más firme el paso!<br>¡Para marchar en cadena<br>una cadena tejamos! [x2]<br>¡Norte, Sur, Este, y Oeste! | Comrades, shoulder to shoulder!<br>Comrades, keep up the pace!<br>To march [united] in a chain<br>let's weave a chain! [x2]<br>North, South, East, and West! |
| 4. Unidos vienen cantando<br>los proletarios avanzan,<br>ya avanza el proletariado.<br>¡Viva!<br>Thelman [sic] será libertado. | United they come singing,<br>the proletarians advance,<br>the proletariat is advancing!<br>Long live!<br>Thelman [sic] will be liberated. |

Villatoro's composition is one of the earliest among many international artefacts of cultural propaganda created to protest the imprisonment of Ernst Thälmann, the leader of the German Communist Party, by the Gestapo in March 1933.[12] The earliest documented performance of *Himno a Thaelmann* was a concert held in June 1934 by the Orquesta y Coros Proletarios in Madrid, possibly conducted by Villatoro himself.[13] The concert was part of a "Proletarian Festival" at the María Guerrero Theatre, which also featured several "proletarian theatre plays" by the communist playwrights Alberti and Rafael Dieste. The press described the performance of *Himno a Thaelmann* as the festival's "most moving part", noting that the "enthusiastic audience" called for an encore of the song, after which they "rose to their feet, saluted with raised fists, and cheered the authors and performers, shouting '¡Viva Thaelmann!'"[14]

12 Other battle songs created by communist composers for similar purposes included Paul Arma's *Thälmannlied* (*Thälmann Song*, early 1934), Charles Koechlin's *Libérons Thaelmann* (*Let's Free Thaelmann*, 1934), Ferenc Szabó's *Ernst Thälmann* (1934) and Viktor Tomilin's *Pesnja o Telmane* (*Song about Thälmann*, 1935). On Paul Arma's *Thälmannlied*, see Tobias Widmaier, ed., *Paul Arma, Avantgarde und Arbeiterlied: Autobiographie 1904–1934* (Büdingen: PFAU, 2016), 222 and 271. A recording from the mid-1930s can be heard at: http://sovmusic.ru/m32/pesnotel.mp3. Charles Koechlin's *Libérons Thaelmann* is reproduced in Robert Brécy, *Florilège de la chanson révolutionnaire de 1789 au front populaire* (Paris: Hier et Demain, 1978), 276; Ferenc Szabó's *Ernst Thälmann* (1934) was published in 1934 in Moscow by the Soviet State Music Publishing House (a copy is held at the Arbeiter-Lied-Archiv of the AdK, cat. no. 189); Tomilin's *Pesnja o Telmane* was published in 1935 in Leningrad by Triton Publishing House. A contemporary recording of the song is hosted at: https://www.russian-records.com/details.php?image_id=13411

13 Anon., "Cines y teatros. Teatro María Guerrero. Presentación del Guiñol Octubre", *El Socialista* (1 July 1934): 5; quoted in Mateos, "Rafael Alberti y la música", 163.

14 "...siendo clamorosamente ovacionados los artistas y obligados a bisar. El público, entusiasmado, se puso en pie y saludando con el puño en alto vitoreó a autores y ejecutantes y se dieron vivas a Thaelmann". Anon., "Fiesta Proletaria", *El Heraldo de Madrid* (2 July 1934): 5.

Two undated, unpublished versions of Villatoro's composition have been preserved: one scored for a one-part choir and piano, and the other for a wind band.[15] I focus here on the version for choir and piano, which is almost certainly the earliest. The song features an ABC structure, comprising a twenty-bar introduction (section A, bb. 1–20), followed by the setting of the first stanza (section B, bb. 21–34) and the second stanza (section C, bb. 35–48) of each part. Each formal section employs a different time signature. Ex. 5.3 shows the complete section C. The unorthodox phrasing of this section is modelled after the *Solidarity Song*. Unlike the regular two-bar and four-bar phrases of sections A and B, the phrases in section C are three and a half bars long. Although there are no metrical changes on the page, the perceived effect for both singers and listeners is that the succeeding phrase begins half a bar earlier than expected. These passages could have been notated using metrical changes, as demonstrated in Ex. 5. 4. With this unconventional phrasing, Villatoro effected a form of metrical anticipation similar to Eisler's through alternative notational means.

The influence of the *Solidarity Song* is also evident in the Aeolian avoidance of the leading tone throughout the entire A section of Villatoro's song. Notably, the relative prominence of minor dominant and subtonic chords is present in the opening, as illustrated in Ex. 5.5. Like Eisler, Villatoro combines vocal melodies with contrasting profiles in each section: leaps predominate in sections A and B, while stepwise motion characterises section C. Furthermore, the opening repeated motif in Villatoro's vocal melody is likely modelled on the motif that opens the *Solidarity Song*. Ex. 5. 6. compares the opening motifs of each song.

The singing in Villatoro's song is interrupted three times, each time by shouts of "Muera", "Viva" (Ex. 5.3, b. 45), and the four cardinal directions (Ex. 5.7, bb. 32–33). These interjections are followed by rests. Similar shouts are prominent in Eisler's *Der rote Wedding* (1929), which features the repeated phrase "Links, links, links, links" (Left, left, left, left). Villatoro's inclusion of these shouted interjections does not draw directly from *Der rote Wedding*; rather, it reflects a common interwar performance practice in agitprop songs, whereby participants interrupted the singing of political songs by shouting pithy slogans.[16]

15 The version for choir and piano is kept at the Fundación Juan March, Legado Joaquín Villatoro, cat. nos. M. 677 and 678. The version for wind band is reproduced in Mateos, "Rafael Alberti y la música", 393–399. The version for voice and piano has been recently recorded; see Ana Vega et al., *Canciones de lucha*. Dahiz Produccions, 014 CD, Spain, 2001.

16 Further details regarding this performance practice can be found in Lammel, *Das Arbeiterlied*, 64–65.

Ex. 5.3. Villatoro, *Himno a Thaelmann*, section C, bb. 35–48.

Ex. 5.4. Alternative notation for the first phrases of section C.

Ex. 5.5. Opening of *Himno a Thaelmann* (bb. 1–12).

Ex. 5.6. Leaps of a perfect fourth in the openings to the *Solidarity Song* and the *Himno a Thaelmann*.

Solidaritätslied
1
Himno a Thaelmann
1

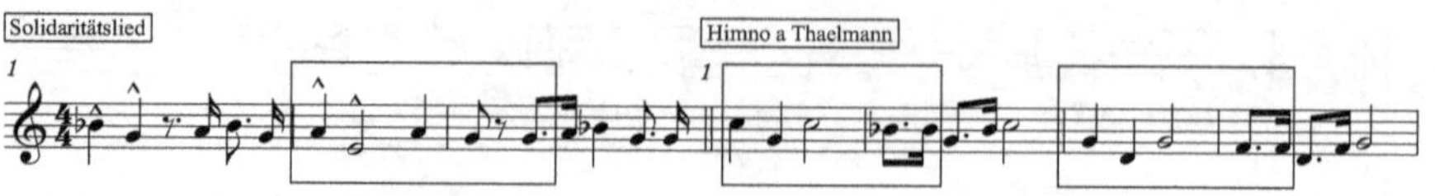

Ex. 5.7. Villatoro, *Himno a Thaelmann*, section B, bb. 19–33.

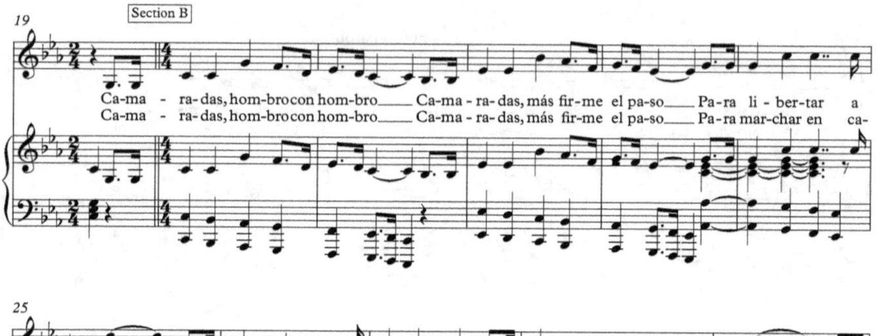
19
Section B
Ca-ma - ra-das, hom-bro con hom-bro Ca-ma - ra-das, más fir-me el pa-so Pa-ra li - ber-tar a
Ca-ma - ra-das, hom-bro con hom-bro Ca-ma - ra-das, más fir-me el pa-so Pa-ra mar-char en ca-
25
Thel-man ho-ces y pu-ños en al - to Pa-ra li - ber-tar a Thel-man ho-ces
de - na u-na ca - de - na te - ja - mos Pa-ra mar-char en ca - de - na u-na
30
[shouted]
section C
y pu-ños en al - to ¡Nor-te, Sur, Es-te y O-es-te! Ya las ha-chas re - tro
ca-de-na te - ja - mos ¡Nor-te, Sur, Es-te y O-es-te! U - ni-dos vie- nen can

## *Canto a la Marina* (*Hymn for the Navy*, 1936)

*Canto a la Marina* by Salvador Bacarisse (1898–1963) presents another compelling case study regarding the influence of the *Solidarity Song*. Bacarisse also studied composition under Conrado del Campo at the Madrid Conservatory. A member of the PCE since the early 1930s, he became a leading figure in the "Grupo de los Ocho" (This "group of eight" Spanish neoclassical composers was founded in 1930 to combat musical conservatism, much in the spirit of the French "Les Six"). Bacarisse's compositions garnered significant respect in Spain, leading to his appointment as vice president of the newly established Consejo Central de la Música (Central Music Council) in 1937.[17]

*Canto a la Marina* was composed in early autumn 1936 at the request of the PCE, which asked several composers in Madrid to write new battle songs using lyrics from the Madrid poet Luis de Tapia's popular "coplas" (couplets) about the civil war. These are some of the earliest battle songs composed by Spanish musicians during the civil war.[18] Beginning in September 1936, radio programmes from the propaganda organisation Altavoz del Frente (AdF) regularly broadcast *Canto a la Marina*. However, according to Palacio, the song did not gain significant popularity.[19] The score was published by the AdF in 1936. The cover featured a drawing by the esteemed Spanish painter Francisco Mateos González (Fig. 5.1). Tomás Mancisidor, the director of the Barcelona Carlos Marx Wind Band, arranged the piece for wind band shortly after the war began, with Catalan lyrics supplied by an unknown author.[20]

Bacarisse set the copla *Marinero* (*Marine*) to music. Tapia had written this poem shortly after the beginning of the war, most likely in August 1936, as an

17 See Christiane Heine, "Salvador Bacarisse (1898–1963) en el centenario de su nacimiento", *Cuadernos de música iberoamericana* 5 (1998): 43–75; and Enrique Casal Chapí, "Salvador Bacarisse", *Música* 1, no. 2 (1938): 27–53.

18 Other songs that emerged from this commission include Rafael Espinosa's *Miliciano popular* (*Popular Militiaman*), Palacio's *Las compañías de acero* (*Steel Companies*), Rodolfo Halffter's *En los Frentes* (*On the Frontlines*), José Moreno Gans' *Canto a Valencia* (*Song to Valencia*), and José Castro Escudero's *Dolores*. Only the musical scores for Palacio's, Bacarisse's, and Espinosa's songs have survived. These likely drew their lyrics from the compilation produced by the International Red Aid: Luís de Tapia, *30 coplas del día* (Madrid: Socorro rojo, 1936). On this commission see Palacio, *Acordes en el alma*, 134–135.

19 Palacio, *Acordes en el alma*, 136. The first documented broadcast by Altavoz del Frente was on 25 September 1936; see anon., "Altavoz del frente. Programa para hoy", *El Liberal* (25 September 1936): 7.

20 A copy of the score published by the AdF in 1936 is currently held at the Academia de Bellas Artes de San Fernando; cat. no. 1Q-191. The Military History Museum of Castelló retains a copy of the arrangement for wind band; see anon., "Partitura", in *Gaceta del Aula. Noticiario del Aula Militar Bermúdez de Castro* 41 (March 2005): 4.

Fig. 5.1. Title page to the wartime edition of Tapia and Bacarisse's *Canto a la marina* by Francisco Mateos. Source: Academia de Bellas Artes de San Fernando (1Q-191). Published with kind permission.

homage to the Republican naval artillery.[21] The phrase "sons of the Potemkin" alludes to the Spanish Republican battleships, while the lines "Sailor from Algeciras" and "no more Moors will arrive [to Spain]" refer to Republican efforts to block the arrival of fascist reinforcements, specifically colonial troops from the Protectorate of Morocco, crossing the Strait of Gibraltar.

[21] The earliest documented publication of the poem is: *La Libertad* (9 August 1936): 1.

| | |
|---|---|
| 1. Marinero sube al palo<br>y dile a la patria hispana,<br>que se ha cubierto de gloria<br>la escuadra republicana,<br>los hijos del Potemkin. | 1. Sailor, climb the mast<br>and tell the Hispanic fatherland<br>that it has covered itself in glory<br>the Republican squadron,<br>the sons of the Potemkin. |
| 2. Marinero del estrecho,<br>marinero capitán,<br>los cañones de tu barco<br>retumban: «No pasarán»,<br>retumban: «No pasarán». | 2. Sailor of the strait,<br>sailor captain,<br>the cannons of your ship<br>thunder: "They shall not pass",<br>thunder: "They shall not pass". |
| 3. [=1] | 3. [=1] |
| 4. Marinero de Algeciras<br>estando tu barco allí,<br>ya no llegarán más moros<br>de la costa marroquí,<br>de la costa marroquí. | 4. Sailor from Algeciras<br>when your ship is there,<br>no more Moors shall arrive<br>from the Moroccan coast,<br>from the Moroccan coast. |
| 5. Marinero que en la noche,<br>te orientas al navegar;<br>la estrella de cinco puntas<br>será tu estrella polar,<br>será tu estrella polar. | 5. Sailor in the night,<br>orient your navigation;<br>the [communist] five-pointed star<br>shall be your pole star,<br>shall be your pole star. |

Bacarisse scored this song for soloist, two-part choir, and piano. The piece opens with an instrumental introduction, followed by the vocal setting of the five stanzas. Material from the introduction is varied for each stanza, creating six parts that are similar yet distinct. The two-part choir performs stanzas 1, 3, and 5, while the soloist takes on stanzas 2 and 4. This alternation between soloist and chorus was a common practice at the time in the singing of one-part anthems and battle songs.

The harmonic progression and voice-leading in the song's closing section (Ex. 5.8) are modelled on the final bars of the *Solidarity Song*. Like Eisler's song, *Canto a la Marina* ends on the dominant. Bacarisse finishes the G minor piece with the major dominant (D major) preceded by its dominant seventh (bb. 116–119). This pair of chords is preceded by a perfect cadence on the minor dominant (d minor). This combined use of the subtonic (F) and the leading tone (F-sharp), along with the resulting alternation of the minor dominant and the major dominant, recurs throughout the song (e.g., bb. 1 and 11–16 of the introduction, not shown in Ex. 5.8).

Bacarisse's piece does not conclude with a Phrygian half cadence; instead, it features semitonal descending motion in the bass, created by the pitch E-flat

Ex. 5.8. Final bars of Bacarisse's *Canto a la Marina* (bb. 112–119).

Ex. 5.9. Modal mixture for setting an allusion to the Soviet Union, *Canto a la Marina*, bb. 72–79.

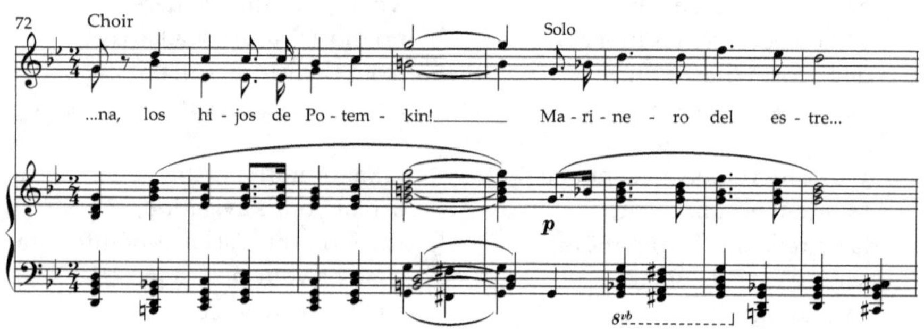


(the sixth scale degree in G minor, b. 115) and the root of the dominant chords on D that precede and follow it (bb. 115–117). These pitches are circled in Ex. 5.8. Bacarisse's inclusion of this gesture is almost certainly modelled on the descending semitone in the bass line at the end of the *Solidarity Song*, where B-flat and A represent the sixth and fifth scale degrees in D minor.

The *Canto a la Marina* is one of the very few civil war battle songs in which the composer engaged in tone painting. Bacarisse employs a centuries-old major-to-minor semantic gesture to symbolise the contrast between darkness and light by harmonising the reference to the Soviet Union ("los hijos de Potemkin"; Ex. 5.9, bb. 75–76) with the tonic triad of G major. This choice was likely inspired by a similar harmonic trajectory from A minor to A major/Phrygian in the outer sections of the *Solidarity Song*, which Eisler scholar Christian Glanz has described as a form of "dark-light" symbolism.[22]

22 Glanz, *Hanns Eisler*, 80.

## *Los campesinos* (*The Peasants*, 1937)

*Los campesinos* is the only battle song by Enrique Casal Chapí (1909–1977) that has survived. Casal Chapí was the grandson of the well-known zarzuela composer Ruperto Chapí. Like many other Spanish composers born in the early 1900s, he studied composition under Conrado del Campo at the National Conservatory in Madrid. Shortly after completing his studies in 1936, he won first prize for composition at the Conservatory with a now-forgotten symphonic work. During the war, he set to music poems such as *Romance del mulo Mola* (*Romance of the Mule* [Fascist General Emilio] *Mola*) and *El Quinto Regimiento* (*The Fifth Regiment*) by the communist poets José Bergamín and Rafael Alberti respectively[23] (both compositions are apparently lost). As a committed communist at the time, he visited the Soviet Union in 1937.[24]

Casal Chapí composed *Los campesinos* for voice and piano in Madrid in 1937.[25] The score was later included in the second volume of Mayer-Serra's *International Revolutionary Songbook* and in the fifth edition of Busch's *Kampflieder der Internationalen Brigaden*. Busch, Mayer-Serra, and Ernst H. Meyer regarded it as a particularly accomplished battle song.[26] The lyricist Antonio Aparicio was a prominent figure in Spanish communist circles. As commissioner for culture and propaganda in the Fifth Regiment, he wrote numerous poems and theatrical pieces intended for performance at the front. *Los campesinos* stands out within the corpus of Spanish battle songs for its focus on peasants as central protagonists. The first part of the lyrics reads as follows:

23 Anon., "Programa del Altavoz del Frente del día 25-9-1936", *El Liberal* (25 September 1936): 7.

24 Alberto González Lapuente, "En el Centenario de Enrique Casal Chapí", *Scherzo* 24(245) (2009): 150–151.

25 Palacio, *Colección*, 56.

26 See the letter from Mayer-Serra to Ernst H. Meyer, 1 August 1938, Ernst-Hermann-Meyer-Archive (AdK), no cat. no. Busch included the vocal line in the fifth edition of *Kampflieder der Internationalen Brigaden*. A decade later, in 1947, he included the lyrics in a songbook he published in Berlin, titled *Spanien 1936–39: So sangen die Kameraden der XI. Internationalen Brigade* (*Spain 1936–39: This is How the Comrades of the XI International Brigade Sang*). Despite the title, no German version of the lyrics appears to have existed that could have been sung by German interbrigadists. The earliest surviving recording of the song also dates from 1947 and was produced by Busch in Berlin – though it features the Spanish lyrics; see Ernst Busch, *Spanien. 1936–39. So sangen die Kameraden der XI. Internationalen Brigade* (Berlin: Lied der Zeit, 1947), 6; and Ernst Busch, *Adelante campesinos*. Lied der Zeit 588 (1947). For a recent recording of the original version for choir and piano, see Ana Vega, *Canciones de lucha*, Dahiz Produccions, 014 CD, Spain, 2001. As noted in the Epilogue, two decades later, Meyer would incorporate a symphonic arrangement of *Los campesinos* into his film score for the GDR film *Wo du hin gehst* (1957).

| | |
|---|---|
| 1. Los campos heridos de tanta metralla, | 1. The fields [are] wounded from so much shrapnel, |
| Los pueblos sangrantes de tanto dolor | the villages [are] bleeding from so much pain |
| Y los campesinos sobre la batalla | and the peasants [are] on the battlefield |
| Para destrozar al fascismo traidor | to smash the traitor fascism. |
| | |
| Dejando el arado tirado en la tierra | Leaving the plough lying on the ground, |
| tomando el fusil para pelear | taking up the rifle to fight |
| marchamos alegres hacia las trincheras | we march joyfully to the trenches |
| para que en España haya libertad | so that in Spain there may be freedom. |
| | |
| *Refrain* | *Refrain* |
| Somos los campesinos, | We are the peasants |
| hoy somos los soldados | Today we are the soldiers |
| ¡Adelante! | Forward! |
| Gritan nuestros fusiles | our rifles cry out |
| gritan nuestros arados | our ploughs cry out |
| ¡Adelante! | Forward! |
| ¡Adelante! | Forward! |
| ¡Adelante! | Forward! |
| | |
| [second stanza and refrain follow] | [second stanza and refrain follow] |

In 1937, Casal Chapí praised Kochetov's *No pasarán* as one of the finest contemporary battle songs and urged Spanish composers to take it as a model.[27] However, it was not this piece but the *Solidarity Song* that served as the primary model for *Los campesinos* – likely because Casal Chapí composed it before becoming familiar with Kochetov's work. Like the *Solidarity Song*, *Los campesinos* is set in D minor and 4/4 time, featuring a short introduction (bb. 1–5), verse (bb. 6–29), and chorus (bb. 30–44). In the verse section, Casal Chapí incorporated both the major and minor dominants, as well as dominant chords that omit the third or leading tones. Following Eisler's approach, he contrasted three-bar phrases in the verse section with two-bar phrases in the

[27] Enrique Casal Chapí, "Cancionero Revolucionario Internacional", *Hora de España* 9 (1937): 72–76. On this review see my "Transnational Networks of Communist Musical Propaganda in the Spanish Civil War", *Journal of War & Culture Studies* 14, no. 4 (2021): 1–25.

Ex. 5.10. Opening of *Los campesinos.*

Ex. 5.11. Closing bars of *Los campesinos.*

chorus section. Ex. 5.10 presents the introduction followed by the first phrase of the verse (bb. 5–7).

In the introduction and closing bars, Casal Chapí briefly shifts the time signature to 2/4, transforming the prevailing quadruple metre into a duple metre. As shown in Ex. 5.11, these changes accompany the word *Adelante* (Spanish for "forward"), possibly reflecting the German *Vorwärts*, which both opens and closes the *Solidarity Song*. The inclusion of this term was likely influenced by Brecht's lyrics.

## *Venguemos a los caídos* (*Avenge the Fallen!*, ca. 1937)

To address the shortage of propaganda battle songs in Republican Spain, the Ministry of Public Instruction and Fine Arts organised a composition contest in

July 1937 to award a prize for the best *canciones de guerra* (war songs). Given that the Minister of Public Instruction and Fine Arts was one of the leading figures of the PCE, it is almost certain that the Communist Party was behind the organisation of this contest. As stipulated by Wenceslao Roces, the General Director of Fine Arts, in the *Gaceta de la República* (*State Gazette*), the compositions submitted for the contest had to be new, unpublished works, scored for either choir alone or choir accompanied by piano or wind band; prize-winning songs would "be intensively disseminated among the combatants and the antifascist People, [...] by means of the radio, the military bands of our Brigades, etc."[28]

According to Palacio, 117 songs were submitted to this contest.[29] This figure warrants further investigation, as I have yet to find additional information about the remaining songs that did not receive any prizes. It is possible that this number was a typo and the actual total was merely seventeen, or perhaps Palacio was exaggerating for the sake of propaganda. A Commission from the Central Music Council awarded five songs with prizes, each worth 1,000 pesetas. Two of these award-winning songs, namely *Venguemos a los caídos* (lyrics by Félix V. Ramos and music by Carlos Palacio) and *Canto nocturno en las trincheras* (by José Miguel Ripoll and Leopoldo Cardona), incorporate several features from the *Solidarity Song*.[30]

Carlos Palacio (1911–1997) also studied composition under Conrado del Campo at the Madrid Conservatory. He wrote at least fifteen battle songs during the war, with musical sources for about half of them preserved.[31] As mentioned in Chapter 4, the lyricist Félix Vicente Ramos was likely a communist worker from Madrid with literary inclinations but limited output beyond a few battle-song lyrics. His *Venguemos a los caídos* (1937) serves as an appeal to Spanish youth to join the "Red Front" and avenge the deaths of antifascist soldiers who fell during the civil war.

28 "Estas obras seleccionadas serán intensamente difundidas entre los combatientes y el pueblo antifascista, [...] por medio de la Radio, Bandas militares de nuestras Brigadas, etc." Anon., "Órdenes", *Gaceta de la República* 204 (23 July 1937): 321–322.

29 This figure is provided in Palacio, *Colección*, 68. Palacio also commented on this contest in *Acordes en el alma*, 159.

30 The other three songs that were awarded prizes are: *Unión de Hermanos Proletarios* (Alberto Alcantarilla Carbó and Francisco Merenciano Bosm); *Canto a la flota republicana* (Félix V. Ramos and Rafael Casasempere), and *Himno* (Carlos Ordóñez); see anon., "El concurso de canciones de guerra", *La Libertad* 19, no. 5469 (28 September 1937).

31 A study of the composer's compositional career can be found in the form of Àngel Lluís Ferrando Morales, *Carlos Palacio. Vivencia y pervivencia. Una aproximación a la figura y la obra de Carlos Palacio en el centenario de su nacimiento (1911–2011)* (Alcoy: Ayuntamiento de Alcoy, 2014).

| | |
|---|---|
| 1. En los campos que duermen y en las llanuras | 1. In the sleeping fields and on the plains |
| vuestros cuerpos se queman de cara al sol. | your bodies burn, facing the sun. |
| En la lucha caídos, sois los mejores | In the struggle fallen, you are the best |
| que la patria amada templó y forjó. | that the beloved homeland tempered and forged. |
| *Refrain* | *Refrain* |
| Con valor a luchar para asi vengar | With courage to fight, to avenge |
| a los que cayeron por la libertad | those who fell for freedom. |
| Juventud, por tu amor y tu corazón | Youth, for your love and your heart |
| para que la patria vibre de pasión | so that the homeland vibrates with passion. |
| [three additional stanzas follow] | [three additional stanzas follow] |

The song, scored for two-part choir and piano, has an instrumental introduction (bb. 1–8), verse section (bb. 9–32), chorus section (bb. 32–49), and instrumental coda (bb. 50–54). Influenced by the *Solidarity Song,* Palacio contrasted six-bar phrases for the verses with four-bar phrases in the introduction and chorus sections. Ex. 5.12 shows the beginning of the verse section.[32]

At the end of the song, a sense of resolution is denied, akin to the *Solidarity Song*. The four-bar closing section, illustrated in Ex. 5.13 (bb. 49–52), repeats the first half of the six-bar opening phrase from the verse; notably, the three-bar consequent of the opening phrase is absent in the closing (compare Ex. 5.12 and Ex. 5.13). Furthermore, the song concludes with an augmented triad instead of a major chord on the tonic (G; bb. 53–54). I posit that this unconventional ending of the song may have been influenced by the half cadence that closes the *Solidarity Song*. While this sense of unfinishedness in Eisler's piece might be motivated and justified by its final rhetorical questions, in *Venguemos a los caídos,* the musical setting appears to contradict the lyrics' resolute call to avenge fallen comrades.

32 For a recent recording of this song, see Ana Vega, *Canciones de lucha*, Dahiz Produccions, 014 CD, Spain, 2001.

Ex. 5.12. Beginning of the verse section, *Venguemos a los caídos* (bb. 9–16).

Ex. 5.13. Closing of Palacio's *Venguemos a los caídos.*

## *Canto nocturno en las trincheras* (*Night Song in the Trenches*, ca. 1937)

*Canto nocturno en las trincheras*, subtitled *Canción guerrera para cuarteto vocal* (*War Song for Vocal Quartet*), was also awarded a prize by the aforementioned Commission. The left-wing freemason Leopoldo Cardona (1911–1982) composed this particularly elaborate propaganda song. He was one of the most recognised and promising young pianists in Republican Spain. *Canto nocturno en las trincheras* appears to be the only propaganda song he created and, to my knowledge, the sole song featuring lyrics by José Miguel Ripoll. (No historical records have been found on Ripoll, suggesting that he was a worker with little literary output.) Both the lyrics and music were likely crafted in the first half of 1937. No recording of the song from the war era has survived.[33]

33 With the exception of one essay by Belén Pérez Castillo, there are no detailed studies on Cardona's career as a musician, nor on his political activism during the war. See

| | |
|---|---|
| Al ronco vibrar del raudo<br>cañón,<br>se van las milicias que el pueblo<br>forjó<br>forjando su fe con esta canción.<br>La muerte no importa,<br>la vida es muy corta;<br>si esclavo he de ser,<br>prefiero caer. | To the hoarse vibration of the<br>raucous cannon,<br>march the militia that the<br>people forged,<br>forging their faith with this song.<br>Death does not matter,<br>life is too short;<br>if I must be a slave,<br>I'd rather fall. |
| Sangre joven que se vierte<br>con raudales de pasión,<br>tu semilla es pura y fuerte,<br>pan de sangre y de dolor. | Young blood that pours<br>with streams of passion,<br>your seed is pure and strong,<br>bread of blood and pain. |
| El sol ya se fue, el canto<br>cesó,<br>centinela, alerta, vigila avizor<br>por la libertad y un mundo mejor,<br>centinela, alerta, vigila avizor.[34] | The sun is gone, the singing has<br>ceased;<br>sentinel, [be] alert, keep watch,<br>for freedom and a better world,<br>sentinel, [be] alert, keep watch. |

Cardona's piece is composed for a vocal quartet with optional piano, or for a soloist singing the upper voice with piano accompaniment. This work is not a marching song but rather a concert piece, featuring "gradations ranging from the nostalgic to the vigorous" (*con gradaciones que van del nostálgico al vigoroso*), as stated in the score. The influence of the *Solidarity Song* is particularly evident in the harmonic organisation. Cardona's song is in G minor. The final harmonic progressions in the outer sections A and A' of Cardona's G minor song closely resemble those that conclude the corresponding sections of the Eisler song. When analysed functionally in A-Phrygian, the penultimate cadential chord in both cases rests on the subtonic, resulting in a lack of leading-tone resolution. The table below compares the final progressions in both songs. The closing bars of Cardona's song are reproduced in Ex. 5.14.

---

Belén Pérez Castillo, "La transformación de un músico en el exilio: Leopoldo Cardona", in *Huellas y rostros: exilios y migraciones en la construcción de la memoria musical de Latinoamérica*, ed. Consuelo Carredano and Olga Picún (Mexico: Universidad Autónoma de Méxiko, 2017), 337–354. Busch recorded a German version of Cardona's song in 1963, arranged for voice and instrumental ensemble; see Ernst Busch, *Canciones de las Brigadas Internacionales*, Aurora No. 5 80 002, 1963. A recent recording of the original version for choir and piano is Ana Vega, *Canciones de lucha*, Dahiz Produccions, 014 CD, Spain, 2001.

34 *Seis canciones de guerra* (Barcelona: Consejo Central de la Música, 1937).

Ex. 5.14. End of *Canto nocturno en las trincheras*, bb. 35–42.

| | | | | |
|---|---|---|---|---|
| **Solidarity Song** Final progression, in A-Phrygian (Ex. 5.1, bb. 27–32) | **Subdominant** (D minor) | Dominant (on E) | minor chord on the **subtonic** G | **Tonic** (A major) |
| **Canto nocturno** Final progression, in G minor (Ex. 5.14, bb. 41–43) | **Subdominant** (C minor) | | Major-minor seventh chord on the **subtonic** F | **Tonic** (G minor) |

The song features an ABA' form, with section A concluding with a harmonic progression similar to that shown in Ex. 5.14. However, in this instance, the cadential chord is a minor-minor seventh chord on the subtonic, F (Ex. 5.15, b. 18, boxed), which resolves to the tonic, G minor. Villatoro introduced the lowered second degree (A-flat) in the cadential chord and voiced that chord in the second inversion, as in the *Solidarity Song*. However, in this instance, the cadential chord is a minor-minor seventh chord on the subtonic. This approach generates a semitonal descending motion (A-flat–G) in the bass voice, mirroring the closing of the Eisler song. Additionally, the lowered second degree, A-flat, appears in the vocal melody (b. 18) as the lowest note, suggesting a madrigalism for "falling", or dying. Harmonically, the influence of the *Solidarity Song* is also manifest in the alternation between passages in which the seventh degree is natural (the subtonic) or raised (the leading tone). This results in the use of both the minor and the major dominant, alongside the prominent use of chords built on the subtonic.

The metrical organisation in section A (bb. 1–20), characterised by constant changes in tempo and time signature, is unconventional for propaganda songs of the time. The song opens with an eight-bar phrase (bb. 1–8) that is repeated with subtle variations in bb. 9–19. Example 5.15. shows the conclusion of this second phrase. Cardona alters the time signature twice, changing from 2/4 to 3/4 (Ex. 5.15, bb. 14 and 16). These changes function in the opposite manner

Ex. 5.15. End of section A (bb. 13–19) of *Canto nocturno en las trincheras*, "Death does not matter, life is too short; if I must be a slave, I'd rather fall".

to the similar device in the *Solidarity Song*. In Eisler's piece, the change from quadruple to duple metre *anticipates* the beginning of the next phrase, creating a sense of rhythmic propulsion; conversely, Cardona's shift from duple to triple metre delays the onset of the subsequent sub-phrase by one beat. Notably, this delay occurs when death is first mentioned.

## *Himno a "La Gloriosa"* (*Hymn to the Glorious One*, ca. 1938)

*Himno a "La Gloriosa"* is the only battle song by the Navarrese composer Jesús García Leoz (1904–1953), who joined the PCE and collaborated on several antifascist cultural projects during the war.[35] The song's lyrics, written by Rafael Alberti, celebrate the Republican Air Force, popularly known as "La Gloriosa" (The Glorious One) during the conflict. The first stanza and the refrain read as follows:

| | |
|---|---|
| Somos la nueva juventud que un día<br>soñó con tener alas y volar.<br>El viento es nuestra sola compañía,<br>el cielo azul de España nuestro hogar. | We are the new youth who once<br>dreamt of having wings and flying.<br>The wind is our only company,<br>the blue sky of Spain our home. |
| Nuestras dos alas son la confianza<br>de la mujer y el niño en la ciudad.<br>En nuestro vuelo vuela la esperanza,<br>en nuestro canto la fraternidad. | Our two wings are the confidence<br>of the woman and the child in the city.<br>In our flight flies hope,<br>in our song, fraternity. |

35 Laura Celaya Álvarez, *Jesús García Leoz, un legado interrumpido (1904–1953)* (Pamplona: Gobierno de Navarra. Fondo de Publicaciones, 2018).

| *Refrain* | |
|---|---|
| Que siempre victoriosa,<br>viva en el aire la<br>Gloriosa!<br>que siempre victoriosa,<br>baje del aire la<br>Gloriosa! | May it always be victorious,<br>may it live in the air, the Glorious<br>One!<br>May it always be victorious,<br>may it live in the air, the Glorious<br>One! |
| [one additional stanza and<br>refrain follow][36] | [one additional stanza and refrain<br>follow] |

Alberti and Leoz created *Himno a "La Gloriosa"* early in 1938. According to Palacio, the song was premiered by some "Coros confederales" (Confederate choir) at the Palacio de la Música in Madrid during the closing of an exhibition in homage to the Republican Air Force.[37] I have yet to locate any sources that report what sort of ensemble this choir was. The exhibition, organised by the PCE youth organisation Juventudes Socialistas Unificadas (Unified Socialist Youth), displayed models and photographs of Republican aircraft.[38] Fig. 5.2 presents a picture from the exhibition.

It remains uncertain whether *Himno a "La Gloriosa"* was recorded or broadcast during the war. However, the score was certainly published in that period. A 1938 poster by the renowned communist artist Josep Renau was reproduced on the title page (Fig. 5.3). No institutional archive seems to hold a copy of this edition. The only copy of this publication of which I am aware was privately owned by an anonymous seller who sold it recently through an internet portal to an anonymous buyer. The seller posted a photograph of the title page and of the last page of the score (which includes the final seventeen bars of the song, bb. 30–47). My sources consist of this photograph and an unfinished draft manuscript of the song, which contains the first thirty-three bars. Fig. 5.4 shows the first page of the draft, held by the Archive of Music and Performing Arts of Navarre.[39]

The song has an instrumental introduction (bb. 1–6) followed by three different sections for voice and piano (A, bb. 7–20; B, bb. 21–36; C, bb. 37–47). The first two sections correspond to each quatrain of the verse stanzas, while the third sets the refrain. Irregular metrical organisation for several phrases indicate the influence of the *Solidarity Song*. As the draft manuscript shows, García Leoz initially intended to compose a piece with a 2/4 time signature throughout. The opening vocal part (bb. 7–20) initially comprised two eight-

36 Palacio, *Colección*, 59–60.

37 Palacio, *Colección*, 60.

38 See anon., "En la exposición homenaje a la 'Gloriosa'", *Ahora. Diario gráfico* 376 (4 March 1938): 3.

39 Jesús García Leoz, boceto del *Himno a "La Gloriosa"*, Archivo Real y General de Navarra – Archivo de la música y de las artes escénicas, folder 03.03.

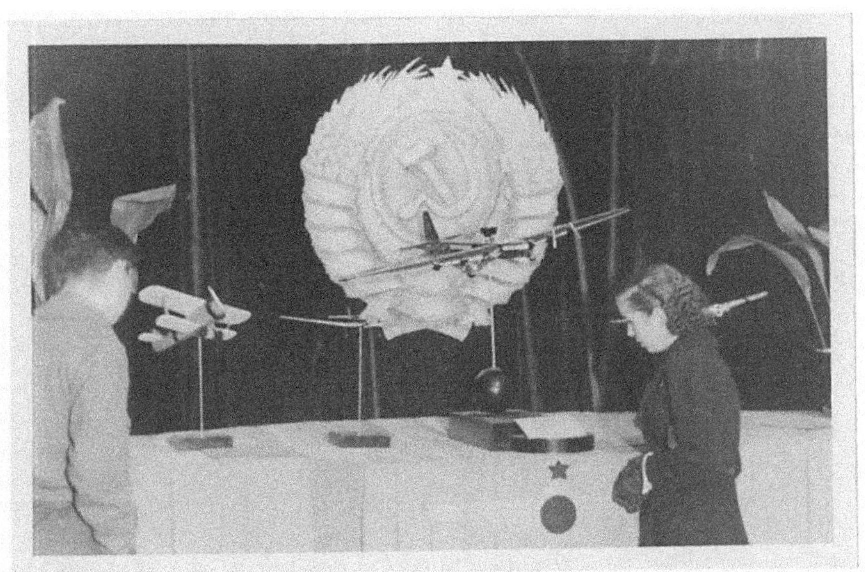

Fig. 5.2. Manuel Albero, *Interior of the "Exposición homenaje a la aviación" (Exhibition in homage to aviation)*, photography, Madrid, January 1938. Source: Archivo Fotográfico de la Delegación de Propaganda de Madrid durante la guerra civil, cat no. AGA,01,PLA,00142,20 (http://pares.mcu.es/ArchFotograficoDelegacionPropaganda/lanzarVisor.do?idImagen=32699463)

Fig. 5.3. Josep Renau, poster *Hoy más que nunca, Victoria* (*Today more than ever, Victoria*, ca. 1936), 99.5 x 138.5 cm. Private collection on deposit to the Museu National d'Art de Catalunya, 2014, cat. no. 250443-000. Published with kind permission of the Renau State.

Fig. 5.4. Jesús García Leoz's manuscript draft for *Himno a "La Gloriosa".* Source: Archivo Real y General de Navarra – Archivo de la música y de las artes escénicas, folder 03.03. Published with kind permission.

bar phrases in 2/4 time (Fig. 5.4). After composing nearly half of the song, he chose to reorganise the metre of several phrases less regularly. The first of these changes is shown in Fig. 5.4, bb. 13–14. García Leoz eliminated the first beat of bar 14 and incorporated the remaining off-beat into the preceding bar (b. 13), thereby transforming it into a 3/4 bar. In doing so, Leoz achieved a metrical anticipation comparable to the effect created in the *Solidarity Song.* In fact, García Leoz could have notated this metrical transformation by adding a single 1/4 bar for the remaining off-beat, which would have visually resembled Eisler's reduction of 4/4 into 2/4. García Leoz also introduces similarly irregular metrical structures with 3/4 bars at five additional points in the song.

Although it does not specify a key signature, García Leoz's piece is clearly in G major. The beginning of the second section (bb. 21–36) is centred on the mediant B minor, the parallel minor of the dominant. In this passage, García Leoz introduces minor instead of major dominant chords and avoids the leading tone (A-sharp) in the Aeolian vocal melody.

As Ex. 5.17 shows, the song ends with a G major tonic chord preceded by a five-tone chord which can be read as the G minor tonic with two added tones: the flattened second degree (A-flat) and the sixth degree (E-natural). The inclusion of the flattened second degree and the final descending semitone in the bass from A-flat to the tonic G was likely inspired by the Phrygian inflection that closes the *Solidarity Song.*

Ex. 5.16. *Himno a "La Gloriosa",* bb. 7–23.

Ex. 5.17. Closing of *Himno a "La Gloriosa",* bb. 42–47.

## *Juventudes proletarias* (*Proletarian Youth*, ca. 1937)

The Madrid-based composer Rafael Espinosa wrote *Juventudes proletarias* to lyrics by one Carlos Caballero. Historical records concerning both figures are exceedingly scarce. What little is known includes the fact that Caballero authored the lyrics for at least two other battle songs (see Appendix 1), and that Espinosa collaborated with Palacio on various musical projects of the Altavoz del Frente, accompanied Busch on piano in at least one concert in Valencia,[40] and composed no fewer

[40] Palacio, *Acordes en el alma*, 135, 151, and 157; see also Carola Schramm and Jürgen Elsner, eds., *Ernst Busch. Schauspieler und Sänger* (Berlin: Paulick, 2003), 81.

than six battle songs.These included *Alianza proletaria: Himno de las trincheras de Mieres* (*Proletarian Alliance: Hymn for the Trenches of Mieres*), written in 1934 during the so-called "Asturias Revolution", and the *Himno a Carlos Prestes* (1934; in collaboration with Palacio).[41] With new lyrics by Erich Weinert, this latter song was transformed into the *Anthem of the International Brigades.* Of Espinosa's known output, only the scores for the *Anthem* and *Juventudes proletarias* have survived.

*Juventudes proletarias* is one of the most compelling battle songs written by a Spanish composer during the civil war, rendering the virtually non-existent information about Espinosa even more intriguing. An anonymous note in Russian among the working materials for the publication of *Pasaremos* asserts that the song was composed in 1937 and was "widely popular among the Spanish youth".[42] The veracity of this statement remains questionable. To my knowledge, the song was neither recorded in Spain nor in the Soviet Union; the complete score of *Juventudes proletarias* with full piano accompaniment was included solely in the Soviet songbook *Pasaremos*, published in Moscow in 1938.[43]

Caballero's lyrics, consisting of two stanzas with a refrain, call on young Spanish proletarians to join the antifascist struggle for world peace and freedom:

| | |
|---|---|
| 1. Juventudes proletarias,<br>defensoras de la libertad:<br>la reaccionaria bestia del fascio<br>mundial<br>debéis unidas, aplastar. | 1. Proletarian youth,<br>defenders of freedom:<br>united, you must crush<br>the reactionary beast of world<br>fascism. |
| *Refrain*<br>Unidos todos, combatamos<br>contra el bárbaro invasor<br>y para siempre consigamos<br>enterrar a la reacción. | *Refrain*<br>All united, let us fight<br>against the barbaric invader<br>and let us bury<br>the reaction forever. |
| 2. Juventudes, ¡adelante!<br>¡A lograr la paz universal!<br>Que vuestra sangre selle con<br>fraternidad<br>El triunfo de la libertad. | 2. Youth, forward!<br>To achieve universal peace!<br>May your blood seal with<br>fraternity<br>the triumph of freedom! |
| Unidos todos, combatamos... | All united, let us fight... |

41 See Palacio, *Colección*, 83–84, 135, 151–154.

42 "широко популярна в ореде испанской молодежи", working materials for the publication of the songbook *Pasaremos*, Archivo de la Memoria Histórica, Salamanca (Incorporados 1918), 7.

43 Grigori Schneerson, ed., *Pasaremos! Canciones de guerra. Испанские революционные песни* (Moscow, Art State Publishing House, 1938), 13–15.

Ex. 5.18. Closing of *Juventudes proletarias* (bb. 33–40).

Ex. 5.19. Similar motifs open the verse section of the *Solidarity Song* (bb. 11–13) and *Juventudes proletarias* (bb. 9–13).

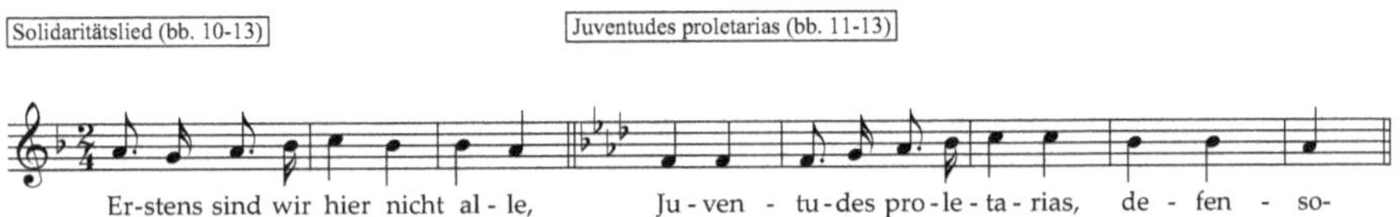


The anonymous note in the working materials for *Pasaremos* states that the song "undoubtedly bears the traces of the best traditions in Soviet songs for the masses". Several features, however, are clearly modelled on the *Solidarity Song*. The most conspicuous features are the closing of this F minor song on the dominant – the minor dominant, not the major, as in Eisler's *Solidarity Song* – and the inclusion of a Phrygian inflection preceding the final chord. The penultimate cadential chord is a major triad on D-flat (Ex. 5.18, b. 39). This chord can be interpreted as the submediant in F minor as well as, more appropriately, the flattened second degree (bII) of the closing tonal centre, C minor. Note the D-flat–C semitonal descending motion in the bass line that closes this song, also in much the same way as in the *Solidarity Song*.

The piece exhibits other similarities with the *Solidarity Song*. Like Eisler, Espinosa also generated contrasting melodic profiles for each section: the vocal melody in the verse section (bb. 9–24) predominantly features stepwise motion, while the vocal melody in the chorus section (bb. 24–40) largely consists of small leaps. Furthermore, as illustrated in Ex. 5.19, the opening motifs of the verse sections in both songs are strikingly similar.

## International Proletarian Avant-garde

The influence of the *Solidarity Song* on these seven Spanish songs can be summarised as follows: everyone except Bacarisse and Espinosa emulated Eisler's irregular metrical organisation, some through time signature changes, while others composed phrases of differing lengths. All composers, except Palacio, imitated Eisler's combined use of the leading tone and the subtonic, occasionally introducing the minor dominant and the subtonic chord. Some short motifs in Villatoro's and Espinosa's songs were modelled on motifs from the *Solidarity Song*. Espinosa, Bacarisse, and Palacio avoided traditional closure on the tonic; the first two ended their pieces, like Eisler, on the dominant.

It is particularly significant that Bacarisse, Cardona, García Leoz, and Espinosa each re-interpreted the semitonal motion ♭II–I that closes the *Solidarity Song* in different ways. This semitonal motion defines the Phrygian diatonic collection as well as the Andalusian cadence (two well-known musical topoi for Spain and Spanishness since the early nineteenth century). This was probably one of the reasons why these four composers followed Eisler's example by including Phrygian configurations in their songs. However, none of these composers chose to combine these Phrygian elements with orientalist topoi in common use since the early nineteenth century to suggest Spanishness, such as *floreos* (upper mordents), flamenco-like melismas, or hemiolias. Nothing in these propaganda songs alludes musically to Spain. This choice was surely motivated by the composers' understanding of the civil war as part of the international proletarian movement: they had neither the need nor the interest in expressing their national identity in these propaganda songs, let alone musically defining Spain as an exoticised Other. Regarding this lack of topoi of Spanishness, these works thus stand in contrast to a number of concert works composed in the 1930s by these and other young Spanish composers of their generation, which featured prominent musical elements that ostensibly referred to Spain, for instance Salvador Bacarisse's ballet *Corrida de feria* (*Festive bullfight*, 1930), and Julián Bautista's *Tres ciudades* (*Three cities*, 1937).

The fact that all the songs analysed in this chapter, except for the one by Palacio, are composed in minor mode is attributable not only to the influence of the *Solidarity Song*, but also to a broader international trend in which Soviet and European composers extensively employed this mode for interwar leftist battle songs. The choice of minor mode by communist composers was one of several strategies to musically differentiate their songs from the anthems of more conservative political factions and the military music of their time. In fact, the prevalence of the minor mode is a defining characteristic that sets apart the corpus of battle songs composed by Spanish antifascist composers during the war. While all of the marching songs composed by rebel composers in the analytical corpus of this study are in major mode, almost half of the Republican songs (ten of the twenty-three) are in minor keys.

The only innovative feature of the *Solidarity Song* that no Spanish composers emulated was the inclusion of the shimmy-anapaest, or any other elements derived from "light" popular music genres. This was primarily because these young Spanish composers, adhering to traditional communist theory, rejected the incorporation of "bourgeois" commercial music in the composition of antifascist battle songs. (There is considerable evidence of this rejection. Casal Chapí, for instance, urged Spanish composers to differentiate their propaganda songs as much as possible from the "vulgar little tunes" in vogue in the cities. Palacio similarly stated that Spanish battle songs ought to be "popular" while also retaining their "musical dignity".)[44]

In light of these results, three questions arise: Why did this relatively large number of Spanish composers take the *Solidarity Song* as a model rather than other "revolutionary songs" that were much more popular among urban workers, such as the *Internationale, La Marseillaise*, or *A las barricadas*? Why did they pursue harmonically daring styles for these songs when their target audiences were neither music lovers nor regular concertgoers, but rather "the working masses"? And why did composers associated with the rebels avoid seeking similarly original styles for the propaganda songs they created for comparable purposes during the civil war?

Behind all these creative decisions was an understanding of modernism as an aesthetic closely linked to leftist politics and antifascism. Specific evidence of this connection between modernism and antifascism in the battle-song genre can be found in the commentary that accompanied the wartime publication of Eisler's *La Comintern* by the communist organisation *Cultura Popular* (see Chapter 4). The anonymous commentator explained that Eisler's song superbly expressed "the full force of the antifascist spirit" through its "great harmonic richness", particularly in the first eight bars of the piece. They were most likely referring to either the minor dominant in bar 5 or the augmented triad in bar 7 that precedes the dominant chord.[45]

Further evidence of the pairing of aesthetic and political progressivism within the genre includes Mayer-Serra's particular praise for Rodolfo Halffter's

44 Casals Chapí, "Cancionero revolucionario internacional" (1937); Palacio, *Colección* (1939), 68.

45 The commentary in full reads: "It [the song] condenses all the firmness of the antifascist fighting spirit. It is difficult to express this meaning in such a short work, and yet Hans [sic] Eisler has done it in a masterly manner, the first eight bars of his work being enough. [...] The learned musician will be able to see the great harmonic richness with which Hans Eisler has endowed his work, in which, even though it is so short, all those who love freedom must see a monument, socially and artistically speaking." ("[la canción] condensa toda la firmeza del espíritu de lucha antifascista. Es dificil expresar en una obra tan corta este significado y sin embargo Hans [sic] Eisler lo ha realizado de manera magistral, bastándole paro ello los ocho primeros compases de su obra. [...] El músico estudioso podrá comprobar lo gran riqueza armónica con que ha revestido Hans Eisler su obra, en la cual, aun siendo tan corta, todos los que amen la libertad deben ver un monumento social y artísticamente hablando.") Hanns Eisler, *Komintern* (Madrid: Cultura Popular, 1937), 4.

battle song *Alerta*. This piece was one of the most harmonically unconventional battle songs composed by either Spanish or foreign composers during the civil war. It was commissioned as an anthem for the Escuelas Alerta, a communist institution for pre-military youth training. This piece shows no significant influences from Eisler's battle songs, choosing instead to repurpose the octatonic modernism of early twentieth-century Franco-Spanish art music for the genre of propaganda songs. Ex. 5.20 shows the final bars of the piece. The added boxes enclose subsets of the octatonic collection. Note how the final cadence consists of a ninth chord over C followed by the tonic F-sharp minor. The roots of these chords are separated by a tritone, a structurally significant interval in octatonic music, as it bisects the collection into two equal parts. Throughout the song, Halffter frequently employs the tritone as a fundamental interval.[46]

The idea that modernism and leftism were inextricably linked was embraced in the 1930s by other communist composers outside Spain. Most members of the Composers' Collective of New York were exponents of this international trend, which some scholars have called "proletarian avant-garde".[47] This group emerged during the Great Depression, following the organisation in 1932 of a seminar led by Charles Seeger and Henry Cowell on the "Historical and Theoretical Factors in the Composing of Workers' Songs".[48] Marc Blitzstein and Lan Adomian were also members of the Collective, while George Antheil, Aaron Copland, Ruth Crawford Seeger, and Eisler (during his time in the United States) were unofficial participants. The group's primary aim was to contribute from the USA to the international movement of "proletarian revolutionary music", a movement that had largely developed in Europe, particularly through the work of Eisler and other composers in his circle. The Collective remained active until 1936.[49]

46 The sheet music was included in the second volume of Mayer-Serra's *International Revolutionary Songbook* (pp. 14–17) and in the aforementioned Soviet songbook *Pasaremos* (pp. 33–36).

47 Michael Denning, *Cultural Front: The Laboring of American Culture in the Twentieth Century* (London: Verso, 1997), 64–67; Elizabeth B. Crist, *Music for the Common Man. Aaron Copland during the Depression and War* (Oxford: Oxford University Press, 2005), 27–34.

48 "Notes on the Work of the Composers' Collective", 3, folder 6, box 7, Blitzstein Papers; cited in Maria Cristina Fava, "The Composers' Collective of New York, 1932–1936. Bourgeois Modernism for the Proletariat", *American Music* 34, no. 3 (Fall 2016): 318.

49 Studies on the Composers' Collective include Carol J. Oja, "Marc Blitzstein's 'The Cradle Will Rock' and Mass-Song Style of the 1930s", *The Musical Quarterly* 73, no. 4 (1989): 445–475; Ann M. Pescatello, *Charles Seeger: A Life in American Music* (Pittsburgh: University of Pittsburgh Press, 1992); Maria Cristina Fava, "The Composers' Collective of New York, 1932–1936. Bourgeois Modernism for the Proletariat", *American Music* 34, no. 3 (Fall 2016): 301–343; Daniel Opler, "Music from the Vanguard. The Songs of the Composers Collective of New York, 1933–1936", *Journal for the Study of Radicalism*

Ex. 5.20. Closing section of *Alerta* (bb. 42–59). The boxes enclose subsets of the octatonic collection. Source: Otto Mayer, *Cançoner Revolucionari Internacional,* vol. 2 (Barcelona: Comissariat de Propaganda, 1937), 16.

Seeger extensively theorised on the necessity of setting pro-communist battle-song lyrics to music that was equally "forward-looking".[50] He lamented that the German fascists had written counter-revolutionary contrafacta of Eisler's *Comintern Song, Roter Wedding,* and other contemporary antifascist songs. To prevent such re-appropriation from occurring again, he urged composers to write songs in a musical style that listeners would associate exclusively with proletarian ideals. "We must strive for the utmost unification of form and content", he urged, "so that the style and general character of the song should fully ensue from and define itself by its ideological content". This would "hamper and sometimes even make it impossible for the Fascists to use our songs with their words, because colossal contradictions will arise between the music and the text, which will ruthlessly destroy the artistic features of the songs".[51] Seeger

10, no. 2 (Fall 2016): 123–152; Abigail Chaplin-Kyzer, *Searching for Songs of the People: the Ideology of the Composers' Collective and its Musical Implications* (Master Thesis, University of North Texas, 2018).

50 Charles Seeger, "On Proletarian Music", *Modern Music* 11, no. 3 (March/April 1934): 126; Carl Sands (Charles Seeger), "Proletarian Music is a Historic Necessity", *Daily Worker* (6 March 1934).

51 Carl Sands, "The International Collection of Revolutionary Songs", *Daily Worker* (31 January 1934). On Seeger's writings on this topic see Robert Grimes, "Form, Content, and Value: Seeger and Criticism to 1940", in *Understanding Charles Seeger, Pioneer in*

Ex. 5.21. Carl Sands (Charles Seeger), *Mount The Barricades.* Source: *Workers' Songbook*, vol. 1. New York: Workers Music Leaguer, 1934, 4.

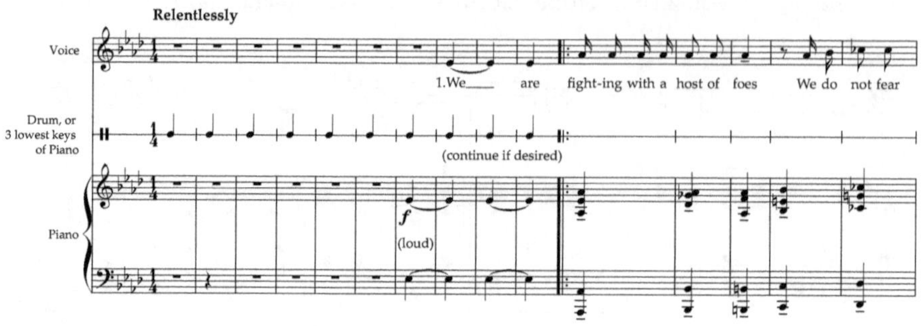


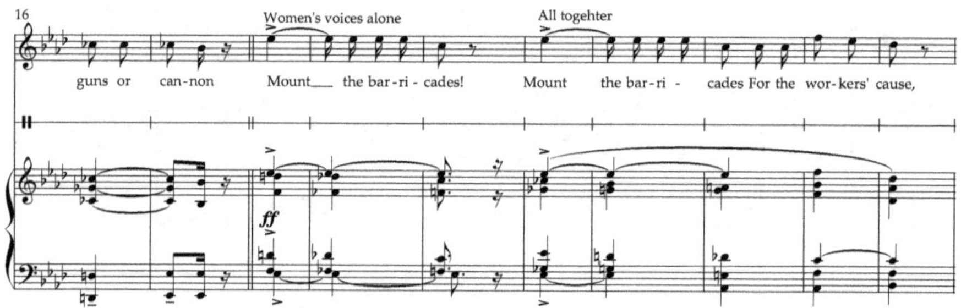


put these ideas into practice in several battle songs. His *Mount the Barricades* (1933) particularly exemplifies the innovative idioms that most Collective composers advocated for the new proletarian songs.[52] Copland singled out *Mount the Barricades* and other Seeger songs as examples of the dialectic between modernist compositional styles and leftist political content.[53]

Copland's *Into the Streets May First!* (1934) was the battle song most extolled as a model by the members of the Collective and other New York communist organisations.[54] Most commentators praised the fact that, despite

*American Musicology*, eds. Bell Yung and Helen Rees (Urbana and Chicago: University of Illinois Press, 1999), 66.

52 The score of the song was published (under the pseudonym "Carl Sands") in the first volume of the *Workers Songbook*, the first modern communist songbook created in the United States. Carl Sands, "Mount the Barricades", *Workers Songbook*, vol. 1 (New York: Workers Music League, 1934), 4.

53 323See his review of the first volume of the *Workers Songbook* in Aaron Copland, "Workers Sing!", *New Masses* (5 June 1934): 28.

54 The song won a competition sponsored by the communist organ *New Masses*. The score was published, among others, in the 1 May issue of *New Masses*, and in the second volume of the *Workers Songbook*. See Aaron Copland, "Into the Streets May First!", *New Masses* 11 (May 1934): 16–17.

Ex. 5.22. Aaron Copland, *Into The Streets May First! Workers Songbook*, vol. 2, pp. 6–7.

its unexpected modulations and piercing harmonies, the song could be sung by amateur performers without too much difficulty. In spite of this success in US communist circles, I have no record that *Into the Streets May First!* or any other battle songs composed by members of the Collective in 1933–1934 were known in Republican Spain.

At the end of his life, Seeger recalled that the lack of national battle songs led many Collective composers to take Eisler's *Kampflieder* as one of their main compositional references.[55] Something similar occurred in the United Kingdom. The leading British communist composer of the period, Alan Bush, devised a style for proletarian songs that was greatly influenced by Eisler's battle songs and markedly distinct from the existing English repertoire of choral and unison workers' songs. The impact of Eisler's battle-song style is particularly noticeable in the structure, bass-line configuration, and harmonic organisation of *Make Your Meaning Clear* (1939).[56] The song's opening is shown in Ex. 5.23.

Although detailed studies are lacking, something similar can be said about the production of Soviet battle songs in the 1930s. At the end of his life, Schneerson recalled the influence of Eisler's battle songs on some interwar propaganda songs by Viktor Bely, Boris Schechter, Nikolai Tschemberdshi, and

55 David K. Dunaway, "Charles Seeger and Carl Sands: The Composers' Collective Years", *Ethnomusicology* 24, no. 2 (May 1980):164; on Eisler's influence on the output and thought of the Collective composers see also Chaplin-Kyzer, *Searching for Songs*, 27; and Opler, "Music from the Vanguard".

56 On the influence of Eisler's music and thought on Bush's theoretical and creative output see Joanna Bullivant, *Alan Bush, Modern Music, and the Cold War. The Cultural Left in Britain and the Communist Bloc* (Cambridge: Cambridge University Press, 2017); Maria Kiladi, *The London Labour Choral Union, 1924–1940: A Musical Institution of the Left* (PhD Thesis, Royal Holloway, University of London, 2016); Emer Bailey, *The Music and Politics of Alan Bush with Reference to the Application of his Socialist Principles to his Workers' Choral Music and Songs between 1926 and 1939* (MA Thesis, Waterford Institute of Technology, 2013).

Ex. 5.23. Alan Bush, *Make your meaning clear!* (1939). Source: London: The Workers' Music Association, 1939.

Matwej Blanter.[57] Recent research has also pointed to the influence of Eisler's pieces on some of Kochetov's songs.[58] The emulation of the modernist language of Eisler's battle songs by Spanish communist composers was, therefore, not a phenomenon confined to Spain or to the wartime context, but was part of an international trend during the 1930s.

## Degenerate Modernism

The idea of a dialectic between the political orientation of a propaganda song and its compositional style also influenced the work of Spanish composers who supported the rebel side with musical propaganda pieces. The style of all propaganda marching songs composed for the rebels was decidedly more conservative and less original than that of most Republican battle songs. To a certain extent, this was because most composers of propaganda songs on that

57 Grigori Michailowiisch Schneerson, "Erinnerungsbericht" (memory report), 1980, cited in Inge Lammel, *Arbeiterlied. Arbeitergesang. Hundert Jahre Arbeitermusikkultur in Deutschland. Aufsätze und Vorträge aus 40 Jahren 1959–1998 (Berlin: Hentrich & Hentrich, 2002)*, 237.

58 See Konstantin Vershinin, Andrej Tereshchuk, and Yuri Ignashov, "Algunos rasgos característicos de las canciones soviéticas sobre la Guerra Civil Española", *Mundo eslavo: revista de cultura y estudios eslavos* 18 (2019): 126–135.

side were from an older generation than the Republican composers discussed above. However, this was not always the case. Fernando Moraleda's *Canción del falangista*, also known as *Falangista soy* (*Song of the Falangist*; a.k.a., *I am a Falangist*), offers an example of a wartime propaganda song created by a rebel composer of the same generation as the Spanish communist composers discussed above. In fact, Moraleda was exactly the same age as Villatoro, Palacio, and Cardona; all were born in 1911.

Moraleda also authored the lyrics to *Falangista soy*. A "falangista", or Falangist, referred to a member of Falange española, the predominant fascist party in Spain at that time. The yoke and arrows mentioned in the poem were the main political symbols of Falange, while the blue shirt was part of the Falangists' uniform. The first stanza reads:

| | |
|---|---|
| Falangista soy, | I am a Falangist, |
| falangista hasta morir o vencer. | a Falangist until death or victory. |
| Y por eso estoy | And for that I am |
| al servicio de España con placer. | at the service of Spain, with pleasure. |
| Alistado voy con la juventud | I go with the youth, enlisted, |
| a la lid de nuestra fe. | to the fight for our faith. |
| Mi camisa azul y el escudo | My blue shirt and the shield |
| con el yugo y el haz | with the yoke and beam [of arrows] |
| garantía son | are a guarantee |
| en la España inmortal que triunfará.[59] | of the immortal Spain that shall triumph. |
| | |
| [Two additional stanzas follow] | [Two additional stanzas follow] |

Moraleda's song does not contain any modernist elements, such as irregular phrase structures, unconventional closures, unresolved dissonances, modal elements, pentatonic clusters, or octatonic configurations. The song's major mode, its fanfare-like melodic motifs (Ex. 5.24. bb. 1–9) and the inclusion of a contrasting central section in the subdominant, all draw connections to the genres of the military marches and the martial pasodoble. (The pasodoble was originally a form of military march. Both a modern Spanish dance and a genre of instrumental music, commonly performed during bullfights and other festivities, derive from it.) In this way, Moraleda's song conveyed unity, discipline, order, and militarisation to most contemporary listeners.

Manuel de Falla, the leading modernist composer in Spain at the time, was commissioned to create a propaganda song during the war. Notably, he chose not to compose a new piece but to arrange a very old one: the choral work *Canto de los Almogávares* (*Song of the Almogávares*) from the opera *Los Pirineos* (1902). The new lyrics, penned by the monarchist writer José María

59 Fernando Moraleda, *Falangista soy*, 3rd ed. (Salamanca: Casa de Bernardi, date unknown).

Ex. 5.24. Beginning of Francisco Moraleda's *Canción del falangista* (ca. 1936).

Pemán, appeal for the defence of the Homeland with God's help against the "red clouds" that, coming from the east, "have covered the sun" of Spain.[60] Falla's arrangement, for voice, piano, and drums, was entitled *Himno marcial* (*Martial Hymn*). The post-Wagnerian epic opera *Los Pirineos* had been composed by the Spanish composer Felipe Pedrell (1841–1922) more than three decades earlier. The style of the *Himno marcial* was thus markedly different from the modernist idioms of Falla's own works from the twenties and thirties, such as *El retablo de Maese Pedro* (1923) or the Harpsichord Concerto (1923–1926). It was also decidedly more conservative than the style of the propaganda songs composed around the same time by most antifascist composers in Spain and abroad. Fig. 5.5 shows the opening of the arrangement as notated by Falla.[61]

In conclusion, the influence of the *Solidarity Song* in Spain was not a coincidence, nor was it attributable to the song's particular popularity in the country. In fact, it appears that the piece was not especially well known in Spain at the time. Spanish communist composers emulated the song because they understood its original musical features as progressive and therefore particularly aligned with communism and antifascism. This was part of an international trend that regarded musical modernism as implicitly expressive of an equally "progressive" political stance. Such an association between modernism and leftism largely resulted from a generalised teleological understanding of the histories of both politics and music.

With respect to their modernism and internationalism, as well as their influences from German models, the Spanish songs analysed above can be

[60] The lyrics are reprinted in Lucas Molina Franco and José María Manrique, "Música en la Guerra Civil: Las canciones de marcha de los 'Provisionales'", in *Treinta y seis relatos de la guerra del 36*, ed. Lucas Molina Franco (Madrid: AF Editores, 2006), 211–224.

[61] Falla adapted Pedrell's music so that it could be sung by a choir accompanied by a wind band or other large ensemble. Sketches found at Archivo Manuel de Falla include a band arrangement for the band of Ricardo Dorado Janeiro, Director of Music of the Regiment. Inf. San Marcial no. 22 with date of 15 January 1938 in Burgos. Spain.

Fig. 5.5. Opening of Falla's *Himno marcial.* Source: Archivo Manuel de Falla, cat. no. LXXXV A1. Published with kind permission of the Archivo Manuel de Falla, Granada.

Fig. 5.6. Republican Propaganda train being painted with the antifascist slogan "All against Fascism". Photo: Antoni Campañá, reproduced courtesy of the Campañá family. Antoni Campañà, *Ferrocarriles del Norte. Pintando los trenes con propaganda antifascista*, 1936–1937. Museu Nacional d'Art de Catalunya, depósito de la Generalitat de Catalunya. Colección Nacional de Arte, 2021. Foto: Museu Nacional d'Art de Catalunya, Barcelona; © *Arxiu Campañà.*

interpreted as musical equivalents to various forms of modernist antifascist visual propaganda used during the war in Spain, most notably posters, painted murals, and photomontages. Indeed, in some appeals made to Spanish composers to contribute artistically to the war effort, the "revolutionary songs" were specifically compared to "the great political and social propaganda posters or paintings of revolutionary scenes on the trains that carry our glorious forces to the front".[62]. One of such modernist train murals is shown in Fig. 5.6.

62 A few days after the beginning of the civil war, an anonymous commentator (possibly Mayer-Serra) exhorted in the communist newspaper *Treball*: "Mentre els uns es dediquen a crear una espècie de nou art mural, dibuixant els grans cartells de propaganda política i social o pintant escenes revolucionàries en els trens que porten les nostres forces glorioses al front, els altres, els músics, creen la nova cançó revolucionària i es posen davant de les Bandes militars. [...] Músics! [...] Creeu les cançons revolucionàries que necessiten els nostres lluitadors!" ("While some devote themselves to creating a kind of new mural art, drawing the great posters of political and social propaganda or painting revolutionary scenes on the trains that carry our

Fig. 5.7. Josep Renau, *Industria de guerra, potente palanca de la victoria* (*Military Industry, Powerful Lever of Victory*), 1937 (98.5 x 66 cm). Source: Museo Reina Sofía, Madrid. Published with kind permission of the Renau State.

Photomontage developed as an avant-garde technique in the interwar period, most notably by the German communist artists John Heartfield and George Grosz. In wartime Spain, visual propaganda material was supplied by the exiled Heartfield and other leading figures of the European avant-garde. Their works were emulated by several Spanish visual artists, notably Josep Renau, a prominent communist artist of the period. Fig. 5.7 shows a modernist photomontage by Renau, contemporary to most of the battle songs analysed above.

As civil war scholar Helen Graham explains, photomontage remained one technique that Francoist propaganda could not incorporate, specifically

glorious forces to the front, the others, the musicians, create the new revolutionary song and put themselves before the military bands. [...] Musicians! [...] Create the revolutionary songs our fighters need!") Anon. [most likely Otto Mayer], "Una gran lliçó per als nostres músics", *Treball* (1 September 1936): 6.

because of its deeply modernist, internationalist, and cosmopolitan connotations: “The brash contrasts in photomontage broke the rules of formal composition, and made a virtue of immediacy and contingency. [...] This was exactly what the right had in mind when it spoke of ‘degeneracy’ and ‘cultural bolshevism.’”[63] Significantly, Nazi German discourse applied these terms and related vocabularies specifically to the *Solidarity Song*. A copy of the score from Universal Edition was displayed on a posterboard as part of the 1938 “Degenerate Music” exhibition in Düsseldorf, organised with Josef Goebbels’ support during the Reich Music Days.[64] The *Solidarity Song* was the only battle song on display there. According to Albrecht Dümling, this work was selected for the exhibition primarily because of the music’s “unruly rebelliousness” (*Widerborstigkeit*).[65] It was these “rebellious” modernist and internationalist features, which clashed so strongly with the chauvinism, conservatism, and militarism promoted by the fascists, that attracted communist composers in Spain and abroad.

63 Helen Graham, *The Spanish Civil War: A Very Short Introduction* (Oxford: Oxford University Press, 2005), 58–60.

64 Albrecht Dümling and Peter Gierth, eds., *Entartete Musik. Eine kommentierte Rekonstruktion* (Düsseldorf: Kleinherne, 1988), 18.

65 Albrecht Dümling, “Solidaritätslied”, in *Brecht Handbuch*, vol. 2, ed. Jan Knopf (Stuttgart: J. B. Metzler, 2001), 200; see also Dümling, *Lässt euch nicht verführen*, 333.

# Chapter 6

# Critical Theories of Music and Historiographical Narratives

The critical theories of music developed in Berlin by Eisler and his circle in the early 1930s were introduced to Spain through a corpus of articles published by Otto Mayer-Serra in several renowned Catalan and Spanish periodicals, particularly *Mirador*, *Musicografía*, *Treball*, and *Música*. In these essays, Mayer-Serra followed a paradigm of historical-materialist historiography that linked the socialist Self to notions of (neo)classicism, rationality, and socio-political commitment, while associating the bourgeois-capitalist Other with "Romantic" values such as individualism, elitism, apoliticism, escapism, idealism, and irrationality.[1] One of his most extensive articles discussing music from Marxist perspectives was "En torno de una sociología de la música" (On music sociology). The essay was published in the second year of the civil war in the reputed journal of the wartime governmental organisation Consejo Central de la Música (Central Music Council). The influence of Eisler is particularly evident in this study. Mayer-Serra argued that the ultimate causes of historical transformations in musical practices, repertoires, styles, tastes, and institutions did not stem from independent evolutions in aesthetic or intellectual ideas but, rather, from historical changes in the prevailing modes of economic production. The article categorically rejects the notion of art's autonomy and defines Western "bourgeois" music as merely another commodity for sale and purchase in capitalist society:

> Music, like all the arts, does not exist "for its own sake" or in an "absolute" manner, rather it is addressed to people and only in its relationship with

1 The main publications in which he laid out the foundations of the theoretical and historiographical principles of Eisler's circle are: "Música i economia", *Mirador* 260 (25 January 1934): 8; "L'artista i el public: Temes de sociologia musical", *Mirador* 334 (11 July 1935): 8, also published in a Spanish translation in *Musicografía* 31 (1935): 235–237; "Sectors de la vida musical", *Mirador* 340 (22 August 1935): 8, also published in a Spanish translation in *Musicografía* 34 (1936): 19–21; anon. [Otto Mayer], "Música viva i música 'museal' I", *Treball* (15 September 1936): 9; "Música viva y música 'museal' i II", *Treball* 1, no. 49 (16 September 1936): 5; Otto Mayer, "Què és música revolucionària?", *Mirador* 391 (15 October 1936): 7;"L'apoliticisme del músic", *Mirador* 394 (12 November 1936): 7; "Què és música 'selecta'?", *Mirador* 404 (21 January 1937): 7; "El crític musical en la societat capitalista", *Mirador* 416 (15 April 1937): 9; and "En torno de una sociología de la música", *Música* 1, no. 3 (March 1938): 30–38.

> people, those who know how to perceive it, or, to put it more generally, who know how to *consume* it, is its aesthetic and social necessity justified. [...] Today, most performers are not aware, for example, that one of their highest ambitions, that of winning over the "audiences" through the aesthetic value of a symphonic work or the virtuoso performance of a sonata, is a typical pretence of a commercialised [capitalist] era[,] and that in another era, with essentially different [socio-economic] characteristics, whether in the past or in the future, this would not be one of the main aims of artistic endeavour. Our understanding of music does not admit fixed or eternal rules.[2]

As most Marxist theoreticians, Mayer-Serra classified music in three main categories: primitive, feudal, and bourgeois.[3] Like Eisler's, his main scholarly interest was the music of the bourgeois era in capitalist society, particularly the period after the fall of the *Ancien Régime*. He set the beginning of the bourgeois era in the sixteenth century, resulting from the gradual emergence of capitalism as the economic order in certain European regions, which in turn led to the empowerment of the bourgeoisie as the new ruling class. In the following centuries, so he argued, the bourgeoisie's strong desire for intellectual and social affirmation gradually transformed music into a commodity. As a result, new phenomena emerged and developed, including the concepts of "select music"

2 "La música, como todas las artes, no existe 'por sí misma' o sea de una manera 'absoluta', sino que se dirige a los hombres y solo en su relación con el hombre, que es quien sabe percibirla o, dicho de manera más general, quien sabe *consumirla*, queda justificada su necesidad estética y social. [...] El músico de hoy, en la mayoría de los casos, no sospecha que, por ejemplo, una de sus máximas aspiraciones, la de conquistar el 'público' por el valor estético de una obra sinfónica o la interpretación virtuosista de una sonata, es una pretensión típica de una época comercializada y que en otra época, de características [socioeconómicas] esencialmente diferentes, sea del pasado o del porvenir, ello no constituiría una de las finalidades principales del esfuerzo artístico. Nuestro concepto en materia musical no admite normas fijas ni eternas." Mayer, "En torno", 30. Emphasis Mayer-Serra's. Significantly, the article opens with a translated excerpt from a 1936 research article on Baroque music by Mayer-Serra's friend Ernst H. Meyer, who was then one of the most active Marxist musicologists from Eisler's former Berlin circle. Mayer-Serra probably received a copy of this issue from Meyer himself, who was then in exile in London. The quoted text states that the historical "evolution" of music is related to the evolution of society and depends on the respective social function of music in each historical period. The quotation is from Ernst H. Meyer, "Die Vorherrschaft der Instrumentalmusik im niederländischen Barock. Eine unbekannte Blütezeit niederländischen Musik", *Tijdschrift der Vereeniging voor Noord-Nederlands Muziekgeschiedenis* 15, no. 1 (1936): 5.

3 Mayer, "En torno", 31. Eisler espoused the same categories for the periodisation of music in "Die Kunst als Lehrmeisterin im Klassenkampf", in *Hanns Eisler. Gesammelte Schriften 1921–1935*, ed. Tobias Fasshauer and Günter Mayer (Wiesbaden: Breitkopf & Härtel, 2007), 123–131; and "[Rundfunkmusik]", in *Hanns Eisler. Gesammelte Schriften 1921–1935*, 99.

(elitist classical music) and "audience" (members of the wealthy classes who could afford to "buy their right to attend a concert" of select music). The concert hall was established in the bourgeois era as a venue for the sale and purchase of elitist music. During this time, the figure of the virtuoso also emerged as a new type of highly specialised performer who could no longer compose due to the division of labour under capitalism.[4]

With Eisler's influence clearly evident, Mayer-Serra argued that compositional styles and techniques changed rapidly in the eighteenth century because composers had to adapt quickly to the tastes of the new ruling class: the bourgeoisie. The mounting individualism among the bourgeoisie and their increasing demands for entertainment led composers to introduce ever more varied structural, dynamic, instrumental, and harmonic contrasts. The emergence of sonata form – with its two contrasting themes continually elaborated upon in the central section – was a consequence of bourgeois demands for greater variation and entertainment.[5]

In the nineteenth century, the symphony emerged as the "representative genre" and "aesthetic symbol" of the bourgeoisie. The disciplines of aesthetics and music criticism emerged in this century, when musical works and their performances became commodified, and thus, valued in purely aesthetic terms, rather than for their practical functions in people's everyday lives. Since then, the role of music critics had been, and still was, to assess the affluent yet ignorant bourgeois audiences before they invested their money in concert tickets.[6] These specialists were expected to judge the style, aesthetics, and performance of a composition, but were never to question the musical institutions of capitalism. Like Eisler, Mayer-Serra argued that the judgments of contemporary music critics were seldom honest, as their opinions were often moulded by individuals in positions of power.[7]

4 Mayer, "Sectors".

5 Mayer, "En torno", 34. Eisler had presented strikingly similar ideas in his groundbreaking essay *Die Erbauer einer neuen Musikkultur* (1931). This study stated that the function of the eighteenth-century sonata and symphony genres was to entertain the bourgeois audience through ever-increasing structural, dynamic, instrumental, and harmonic contrast. Such music was best suited to express capitalist individualism; it was "in fact the music of entrepreneurship, the music of the citizen, and it will – in practice – always stabilise capitalist methods of production on its own" ("Diese Musik ist in Wahrheit die Musik des Unternehmertums, die Musik des Bürgers und sie wird – in der Praxis angewandt – immer von sich aus die kapitalistischen Produktionsmethoden stabilisieren."). Hanns Eisler, "Die Erbauer einer neuen Musikkultur", in *Hanns Eisler. Gesammelte Schriften 1921–1935*, 142; see also Eisler, "Die Kunst", 123–31.

6 Mayer, "En torno," 31–32, 35–38.

7 Mayer, "El crític musical". Eisler had made a very similar argument in the article "Zeitungskritik", published in *Melos. Zeitschrift für Musik* 8, no. 3 (March 1929): 111–116. The text is reprinted in *Hanns Eisler. Gesammelte Schriften 1921–1935*, 92–97. See also "Einiges über das Verhalten der Arbeiter-Sänger und -Musiker in Deutschland"

## The Socialist Self vs the Romantic Other

At the heart of Mayer-Serra's account of music history in the bourgeois era lies his interpretation of "Romantic music" as a product of nineteenth-century European bourgeois industrial capitalism and imperialism – conditions that, in his view, ultimately gave rise to fascism.[8] He claimed that Romanticism in music began after Beethoven, with the works of Schumann, Berlioz, Liszt, and other composers of their generation. What he classified as Romantic music also included late Romanticism, expressionism, and other early twentieth-century musical styles that still embodied the bourgeois values of transcendence, inwardness, idealism, overly emotional expression, elitism, and apoliticism.

Similarly to Eisler and his circle, Mayer-Serra argued that the function of Romantic music was "to distract us from everyday problems and create a refuge from crude reality".[9] Common adjectives he used to describe Romantic music included individualistic, idealised, narcotic, escapist, mystical, metaphysical, antirealist, decadent, and passive. In his earliest surviving writings from his Berlin period, he had already argued that Romantic music was composed for the "artistic delight of a highly cultivated bourgeoisie". Such music offered a kind of "sanctuary, to which only those who have unreservedly granted their emotional experience a quasi-religious cult, can enter". Consequently, "today there will be very little understanding found [among workers] for the romantic idea of salvation through 'escape from everyday life'".[10] In Spain, he argued that the conception of music as the epitome of *Kunstreligion* was responsible for the insufficient political engagement of most contemporary composers and performers in class-based struggles, including the fight against fascism during the civil war. Musicians, he lamented, tended to view themselves as artists rather than as salaried workers.[11]

Paradigmatic examples of Romantic escapism included Wagner's operas, which Mayer-Serra – like Eisler – regarded as expressions of "the intense Schopenhauerian pessimism" prevalent among the nineteenth-century bourgeoisie.[12] The pernicious ideals of Romanticism reached their paroxysm in the decades leading up to the First World War. The imperialist ambitions of the

---

[1935], in *Hanns Eisler. Gesammelte Schriften 1921–1935*, 214–233.

8 Mayer, "En torno", 35–38; see also Mayer, "Sectores de la vida artística".

9 "L'art romàntic és un art antirealista, que vol distreure'ns dels problemes de cada dia i crear-nos un refugi fora de la realitat crua", anon. [Otto Mayer], "Música viva I", 9.

10 Otto Mayer, "Musik und Musikpflege im Rundfunk", *Arbeiterfunk* 5, no. 2 (1930): 18.

11 Mayer, "L'apoliticisme del músic", 7.

12 Mayer, "Música viva I". Eisler similarly considered the music of the early Romantic composers "the expression of the depressed, the dissatisfied [nineteenth-century] middle-class man" and a way to "escape" from their problems. He also linked Wagner's "overestimated" operas to Schopenhauer's pessimism, and warned of the "fascist effect" accomplished by these compositions on contemporary audiences. See Eisler, "Einiges über das Verhalten", 217.

German bourgeoisie fostered a taste for "the colossal and the façade",[13] which resulted in the "hopeless, metaphysical" symphonic works composed for huge orchestras by Gustav Mahler, Richard Strauss, and other German composers.[14] Strauss' "bloodthirsty excitements" and "morbid eroticism" – likely alluding to the operas *Salome* (1905) and *Elektra* (1909) – reflected the bourgeoisie's spiritual decadence in the early twentieth century.[15]

Schoenberg's expressionism, for Mayer-Serra, embodied the values of Romanticism in their most decadent forms. Building on Eisler's positions, and more generally, the prevailing historiographic principles of evolution and progress in the arts, he regarded atonal modernism as the last evolutionary stage for German Romantic music, both a continuation and a "liquidation" of Wagner's style.[16] Like Eisler, he considered Schoenberg an exceptional teacher and a revolutionary in the realm of compositional technique.[17] At the same time, he condemned Schoenberg's "individualistic isolation", "selfish intellectualism", lack of "social responsibility", and the "sterility" and "epigonic quality" of his music.[18] On the same grounds, he disapproved of Anton Webern's music, and condemned Schoenberg's excessive influence on the music of Robert Gerhard.[19] Like Eisler, Mayer-Serra never endorsed Theodor W. Adorno's reading of the music of the Schoenberg school as a form of political radicalism. Ador-

13 Mayer, "Música viva I"; "Música viva II"; "Música i economia".

14 Otto Mayer, "Un septuagenari: Richard Strauss", *Mirador* 278 (31 May 1934): 8.

15 Mayer, "Un septuagenari". Eisler also described the music of late Romantic composers such as Mahler and Strauss as sentimental, dishonest, neurotic, hysterical; see his "Einiges über die Lage des Modernene Komponisten I", in *Hanns Eisler. Gesammelte Schriften 1921–1935*, 249; see also Hanns Eisler, "Lectures on the Social History of Music" [1938/39], HEA, folders 2452 and 2727 (unpublished), quoted from Tobias Fasshauer's (unpublished) edition for the Hanns Eisler Gesamtausgabe, 34–36.

16 Otto Mayer, "La vida musical en Barcelona", *Mirador* 259 (18 January 1934): 8; Otto Mayer, "Apunts sobre Alban Berg", *Revista musical catalana* 23, no. 388 (April 1936): 154–157; Otto Mayer, "Igor Stravinsky", *Mirador* 250 (16 November 1933): 8.

17 Otto Mayer, "A propòsit de Wozzek [sic]", *Mirador* 279 (7 June 1934): 8.

18 Mayer, "La vida musical en Barcelona": 12; Otto Mayer, "Paul Hindemith", *Mirador* 274 (3 May 1934): 8. Eisler similarly condemned Schoenberg's "escape into mysticism" and criticised his individualism, lack of class solidarity, and self-conception as an isolated artist; see Hanns Eisler, "Über moderne Musik", *Hanns Eisler. Gesammelte Schriften 1921–1935*, 48; and "Einiges über das Verhalten", 227. On Eisler's relationship to Schoenberg in the interwar period, see Albrecht Dümling, "Schönberg und sein Schüler Hanns Eisler: Ein dokumentarischer Abriß", *Die Musikforschung* 29, no. 4 (1976): 431–461.

19 Mayer, "A propòsit de Wozzek [sic]". See Otto Mayer, "La situació de la jove generació", *Mirador* 329 (6 June 1935): 8; "Tableau de la música moderne a Barcelone", *La Revue Musicale* 17, no. 163 (February 1936): 141–143; letter from Mayer-Serra to Josep Valls, undated [ca. May 1936], Biblioteca de Catalunya, Fons Josep Valls, folder JvA 125.

no's influence on Mayer-Serra's thought was minimal or non-existent in the interwar period.

Mayer-Serra's rejection of Schoenberg's modernism contrasts with his consistent support for Berg's oeuvre, particularly *Wozzeck* (1925) and the *Lyric Suite* (1926), both of which he regarded as masterpieces of the preceding decade. Taking *Wozzeck* as his primary reference point, he concluded that the principal themes of Berg's music were the inhumanity of the contemporary capitalist and militarist world, as well as the "dignification of misery".[20] His positive appraisal of *Wozzeck* was seemingly prompted by the libretto's implicit social critique. In contrast, his appreciation for the *Lyric Suite* appears more paradoxical, as few other compositions from the interwar period so neatly embody the notions of individualism, elitism, and apolitical intellectualism that he harshly criticised.

For Mayer-Serra, the history of music entered a new phase once anti-Romantic tendencies emerged following the First World War. He praised works that aimed at the "edification" of the masses in left-wing values by addressing the most topical political issues – those that one could read about in the newspapers. He cited Eisler's *a cappella* choral pieces for workers, Weill's *Die Dreigroschenoper* (1928), and several pieces of functional modernist music (*Gebrauchsmusik*) by Paul Hindemith as examples of unabashedly politically committed music; Hindemith represented for him one of the most prominent contemporary figures. Mayer-Serra wrote more extensively and knowledgeably than any other critic in Spain about German Neue Sachlichkeit in general and Hindemith in particular.[21]

## Reinterpreting the Canon: Beethoven, the Antifascist

Mayer-Serra did not advocate the abolition of the "bourgeois" musical canon of the eighteenth and nineteenth centuries, which he referred to as "museum music". Like Eisler and his circle, he believed it was essential for workers to understand how earlier music had served the interests of the ruling classes: "Only when the masses understand the impact of the great French Revolution

20 Otto Mayer, "Alban Berg: Suite Lírica", *Mirador* 304 (8 December 1934): 8. See also Otto Mayer, "'Lulu', la nova òpera d'Alban Berg", *Mirador* 313 (14 February 1935): 8; Otto Mayer, "Alban Berg", *Revista Ford* 5, no. 39 (February 1936): 60; Mayer, "Apunts sobre Alban Berg", 154–157.

21 See Mayer, "Paul Hindemith", 8; Otto Mayer, "Nous camins de la pedagogia musical", *Mirador* 264 (22 February 1934): 8; Otto Mayer, "Reflexions sobre el disc", *Mirador* 267 (22 March 1934): 8; Otto Mayer, "La Simfonia 'Mathis el Pintor', de Paul Hindemith", *Revista Musical Catalana* 377 (May 1935), 194–198; Otto Mayer, "Bibliografia. Noves obres de musica moderna", *Revista musical catalana* 390 (June 1936): 260–261; Otto Mayer, "'Mathis el pintor', simfonia de Hindemith. La nostra discoteca", *Mirador* 330 (13 June 1935): 8.

on Mozart and Beethoven, the July Revolution of 1830 on Chopin and Liszt, or the imperialism of the Reich on Wagner, will the value of these masters' art, as museum pieces, take on a real, living value."[22] During the civil war, Mayer-Serra argued that a new narrative of music history was essential to the construction of the classless society envisioned in Republican Spain. In this new society, the primary tasks of music critics and scholars would be to revise bourgeois historiography and to combat musical illiteracy among the working class.[23]

One of Mayer-Serra's main challenges to "bourgeois" accounts of music history was his portrayal of Beethoven as the primary historical precedent to the antifascist citizen and socialist composer. These ideas are already contained in his earliest essay on the composer, published in the reputed Catalan weekly *Mirador* in July 1934. This essay was a denunciation of how institutional musicology in Nazi Germany utilised Beethoven's music for fascist propaganda. Its title, "Beethoven en camisa bruna" (Beethoven in a brown shirt), alluded to the uniform of the Nazi paramilitary Sturmabteilung or SA, and by extension to Nazism in general.[24]

The article was one of many scholarly responses – both in Nazi Germany and abroad – to an essay by the German musicologist Arnold Schering (1866–1941), "Zur Sinndeutung der 4. und 5. Symphonie von Beethoven" (On the Interpretation of Beethoven's Fourth and Fifth Symphonies). This study had recently been published in the journal of the German Society of Musicology.[25] Schering was then a professor of musicology at Berlin University (where Mayer-Serra had studied musicology years earlier). He held important institutional positions in Nazi Germany, including the presidency of the German Society

22 "Només des del moment, que les masses comprendran la repercussió de la gran Revolució francesa en Mozart i Beethoven, de la revolució de juliol de l'any 1830 en Chopin i Liszt o de l'imperialisme del Reich en Wagner, el valor museal de l'art d'aquests mestres es convertirà en un valor viu i real", Mayer, "Música viva, II".

23 Mayer, "Problemas". He expressed similar ideas in: Mayer, "El crític", "En torno", and "Què es musica 'selecta'?" Eisler also pointed out in the same period to this need to create new historiographical narratives and "liquidate" workers' ignorance in musical matters. He wrote in 1935 that the proletariat "must conquer Mozart and Beethoven just as it must conquer a healthy home, a good meal, a meaningful profession, a good education for its children and a secure old age", in Eisler, "Einiges über das Verhalten", 215. He put forward similar ideas in Eisler, "Einiges über die Krise der kapitalistischen Musik und über den Aufbau der sozialistischen Musikkultur", in *Hanns Eisler. Gesammelte Schriften 1921–1935*, 281; and "Einiges über die Lage des modernen Komponisten II", in *Hanns Eisler. Gesammelte Schriften 1921–1935*, 317.

24 Otto Mayer, "Beethoven en camisa bruna", *Mirador* 285 (19 July 1934): 8. This essay was Mayer-Serra's only prewar publication in which he openly denounced the Nazi regime that had expelled him from his country

25 Arnold Schering, "Zur Sinndeutung der 4. und 5. Symphonie von Beethoven", *Zeitschrift für Musikwissenschaft* 16, no 2 (1934): 65–83.

of Musicology.[26] One of his primary scholarly interests was the hermeneutic analysis of the German musical canon through "Symboltheorie" (the theory of symbols). Initially, Schering focused on determining composers' uses of musical symbols to convey abstract intellectual or emotional ideas; however, in the 1930s, he sought to "reveal" more specific extramusical narratives within several canonical German works.[27]

His article "On the Interpretation of Beethoven's Fourth and Fifth Symphonies" followed this approach, interpreting the Fourth Symphony as a musical representation of three poems by Schiller and the Fifth as expressing the German people's yearning for a guide (Führer) to lead and redeem the nation. Mayer-Serra's article was written in response to this interpretation of the Fifth. Schering claimed that Beethoven's Fifth was a programmatic work featuring symbolic content that the composer had chosen not to reveal, unlike his explicit programme for the Sixth. He argued that the first movement displayed two primary symbolic musical motifs: the "tyrant motif" (bb. 1–5 and 22–24) and the "motif of the people's struggle" against this tyrant (bb. 6ff). Beethoven pitted these motifs against each other throughout the movement until the tyrant motif "rises triumphantly" at the movement's end. In the second movement, the (German) *Volk* gather in a church or temple to "pray in childlike humility to God, asking Him to send them a saviour, a guide [to lead them] out of shame and misery".[28] Schering went so far as to invent lyrics for the opening melody, presenting the *Volk*'s pleading prayer: "We lie before Thee, Almighty, in the dust, and beseech protection at Thy throne; hear us! Hear us: incline, incline Thine ear towards us! Send, O Lord, the hero full of strength, who leads us out of distress and anguish to salvation and victory!"[29] (Fig. 6.1).

In the third movement Beethoven expressed the (German) people's "fear" (bb. 1–4), their timid question "Who will be our saviour?" (bb. 5–8), and the invocation of a prophet who would herald the arrival of the Hero (bb. 19–26). In the symphony's final movement, "[t]he hero and saviour appears in the full glory of the great man and politician, cheered and embraced by the masses who

26 For additional context concerning Schering's links to Nazism, see Potter, *Most German of the Arts*, 84–98, 125; and Stanley Glenn, "Arnold Schering: ein Nazi-Musikologe? Dokumentation und Analyse", *Archiv für Musikwissenschaft* 70, no 2 (2013): 119–133.

27 In 1934, for instance, he attempted a highly speculative demonstration of how selected string quartets and piano sonatas by Beethoven drew their inspiration from specific dramas by Shakespeare or Schiller; see Arnold Schering, *Beethoven in neuer Deutung* (Leipzig: C. F. Kahnt, 1934).

28 "Das Volk hat sich zusammengefunden und betet in kindlicher Demut zu Gott, daß er ihm einen Retter, einen Führer aus Schmach und Elend sende". Schering, "Zur Sinndeutung", 78.

29 "Wir liegen vor dir, Allmächtiger, im Staube, und flehe um Schutz zu deinem Thron, erhör uns! Erhör uns: Neige, neige zu uns dein Ohr! Erhör uns, erhör uns Fundneige dein Ohr, dein Ohr, dein Ohr! Ach sende, o Herr, den Helden voll Kraft, der aus Not und Qual uns führ hin zu Heil und Sieg!" Schering, "Zur Sinndeutung", 79–80.

Fig. 6.1. Beginning of the lyrics invented by Schering for the second movement of Beethoven's Fifth Symphony. Source: Arnold Schering, "Zur Sinndeutung der 4. und 5. Symphonie von Beethoven", *Zeitschrift für Musikwissenschaft* 16, no. 2 (1934): 79.

longed for him. Horns that sound like 'Hail to the mighty Lord!' (bb. 26 ff.)".[30] Ultimately, Schering read Beethoven's Fifth as a "Symphony of the National Uprising", one that expressed the "existential struggle of a Volk seeking and eventually finding a leader [Führer]", a "symbol that [even] in full daylight shines upon us Germans of the present day".[31]

This study, like others by Schering, received a negative reception even within Nazi Germany, as his interpretations lacked any sound methodological underpinning.[32] Eisler was among the many who adopted a critical stance towards the essay.[33] Mayer-Serra was apparently the only scholar in Spain to write about

30 "Der Held und Retter erscheint im vollen Glanze des großen Menschen und Politikers, umjubelt und umspielt von den Tausenden, die ihn ersehnten. Hörnerrufe, die wie 'Heil dem mächt'gen Herrn!' klingen (26ff.)". Schering, "Zur Sinndeutung", 82.

31 "des Existenzkampfes eines Volkes, das einen Führer sucht und endlich findet, sich in ein Sinnbild verwandeln, das gerade uns Deutschen der Gegenwart in voller Tageshelle entgegenleuchtet". Schering, "Zur Sinndeutung", 83.

32 On the negative reception of Schering's theories see Bernd Sponheuer, "Anmerkungen zu der Kontroverse über Scherings Beethoven-Deutung in den 30er-Jahren", *Die Musikforschung* 58, no. 4 (2005): 341–352. Recent studies of Schering's hermeneutics include Arno Forcert, "Scherings Beethovendeutung und ihre methodischen Voraussetzungen", in *Beitrage zur musikalischen Hermeneutik*, ed. Carl Dahlhaus (Regensburg: Bosse, 1975), 41–52; and Helmut Loos, "Arnold Schering und seine Beethoven-Analysen", in *Beethoven. Studien und Interpretationen 4*, ed. Mieczysław Tomaszewsky and Magdalena Chrenkoff (Kraków: Akademia Muzczna, 2009), 239–255.

33 Eisler denounced this appropriation of Beethoven in a 1935 article on music and politics in fascist Germany: "...the heroes of the classical music era are turned [in Germany] into the fathers of National Socialism, this is how Beethoven becomes Hitler's forerunner, his Fifth Symphony the decoration of the Nazi Party Congress

Schering's work. He expressed his "painful and disappointed surprise" that one of the world's leading musicologists showed such an "adaptation" and "allegiance" to Nazism in a major musicological journal: just "one year after the establishment of the Third Reich, [Schering] has renounced the perhaps dangerous benefits of reason, and is fully immersed in political sentimentality in order to explain the mysteries of the great masters of classical music to the new generation".[34] With such displays of subservience to political power, Schering and other musicologists in Nazi Germany were ruining the reputation of German musicology.

Mayer-Serra concluded his article by emphasising Beethoven's endorsement of the French Revolution and recalling that Soviet musicians regarded the composer as "the most characteristic exponent of revolutionary ideology in music". As he depicted them, Soviet musicians would never "concretise this analogy" by asserting that the first part of the symphony represented the "revolutionary bourgeois chaos" or that the final part symbolised "the coming of the Bolshevik saviour, Lenin!"[35]

Mayer-Serra further developed the concept of Beethoven as a proto-socialist figure in subsequent writings spanning from 1935 to 1937. He characterised Beethoven's symphonic works, particularly the Ninth Symphony, as a form of "humanistic", "universal", "popular", and "active" music, representing the pinnacle of Enlightened libertarian values from the French Revolutionary era, and thus being particularly connected to class struggles and socialism. The Ninth was "the last document of the universality of musical language, now lost forever",[36] "a marvellous synthesis of the *classical* spirit in music" and absolutely *not* a forerunner to the Wagnerian drama, as Wagner and his followers would have it.[37] This reading of the Ninth contradicts the dominant interpretations, both then and now, of the symphony as a romantic declaration of creative independence and musical genius. Unlike Beethoven's late sonatas and, especially, his late string quartets, which he viewed as forerunners of musical Romanticism,

---

and –according to Arnold Schering – the 'image of National Socialism'". Hanns Eisler, "Musik und Musikpolitik im faschistischen Deutschland" (ca. October 1935), in *Hanns Eisler. Musik und Politik. Schriften 1924–1948*, vol. 1, ed. Günter Mayer (Leipzig: Deutscher Verlag für Musik, 1973), 342.

34 "Un any després de la instauració del Tercer Reich, el mateix home ha renunciat als beneficis potser perillosos de la *ratio* i es troba submergit en ple sentimentalisme polític, per explicar a la nova generació els misteris dels grans mestres de la música clàssica". Mayer, "Beethoven en camisa bruna".

35 "l'exponent més característic de la ideologia revolucionària en la música [...] admiren en aquesta obra simfònica un sentiment molt general d'alliberació revolucionari. [...] Mai no han volgut concretar aquesta analogia i han arribat a explicar, potser (suprem horror!), el primer temps de la simfonia com el 'caos burgès pre-revolucionari' i el darrer temps com l'aparició del salvador bolxevista, de Lenin!" Mayer, "Beethoven en camisa bruna".

36 Mayer, "L'artista i el públic', 5.

37 "síntesi meravellosa de l'esperit clàssic en la música", Otto Mayer "Reflexions herètiques sobre la 'Novena'", *Mirador* 315 (1935): 5. Emphasis mine.

the significance of the Ninth, for Mayer-Serra, lay in the message of universal "brotherhood and humanity" that the work conveyed to aúdiences worldwide. Adopting a markedly pessimistic tone in 1935, Mayer-Serra argued that this message had been "disqualified by the European peoples" during a century of struggles, serving as a prelude to the "bloody events of our time".[38]

> [The Ninth] brings us a deep joy and inner satisfaction, from which, however, in the depths of our conscience, we feel excluded, excluded and alienated by the very malaise of our contemporary age. This brings to my mind the prophetic words that Nietzsche wrote half a century ago (*Obres pòstumes*, II, 1931[39]), which seem to anticipate the evolution of historical developments: "Religious forces might still be strong enough to be able to create an atheistic religion, *in the manner of Buddha*, which would eliminate the differences of confession. Science would have nothing with which to oppose this new ideal, but this would never be *human brotherhood*! A new type of human race must appear. I am very far from them and I do not wish for it at all".[40]

Friedrich Nietzsche's "prophetic words" are recorded in a brief note from 1880, in which he predicted the triumph of a new form of atheist religion in the twentieth century.[41] Mayer-Serra related this prophecy to the triumph of Nazism and the regime's messianic overtones, as well as their racialised conceptualisation of the Aryan People (or *Herrenvolk*) as a form of social alliance that, as he implied, stood in stark opposition to the universal brotherhood celebrated in Beethoven's final symphony. The title of this article, "Heretical Reflections on the 'Ninth'", seemingly alludes to Mayer-Serra's pessimism regarding the ease with which Nazis and their followers appropriated the universalist and egalitarian values conveyed by the symphony's music.[42]

38 Mayer, "Reflexions herètiques".

39 I.e., August Messer, ed., *Werke in 2 Bänden. Friedrich Nietzsche*, vol. 2 (Leipzig: Kröner, 1931).

40 "…ens procura una profunda joia i una satisfacció interior, però de la qual, al fons de la nostra consciència, ens sentim exclosos, exclosos i allunyats pel malestar mateix de l'època que vivim i dels nostres contemporanis. Això ens fa pensar en els mots profètics que Nietzsche escrivia, fa mig segle (Obres pòstumes, II, 1931) i que semblen com una anticipació de l'evolució dels esdeveniments històrics: 'Les forces religioses podrien ésser encara prou fortes, per ésser capaces de la creació d'una religió ateista [sic], *a la manera de Budha*, que eliminaria les diferències de la confessió. La ciència no tindrà res a oposar a un nou ideal. Però això no serà mai *fraternité humana!* Un nou tipus de gènere humà ha d'aparèixer. Jo en soc ben lluny i no el desitjo pas." Mayer, "Reflexions herètiques". Emphasis Mayer-Serra's.

41 Giorgio Colli, ed., *Friedrich Nietzsche: Sämtliche Werke: kritische Studienausgabe*, vol. 9 (Munich: Deutsche Taschenbuch, 1980), 341.

42 On Mayer-Serra's pessimism regarding the international political situation, see his letter to Ernst Hermann Meyer, 22 August 1933 (Ernst-Hermann-Meyer Archiv (AdK), no cat. no.).

This pessimism largely dissipated during the civil war, as the defeat of fascism and the establishment of a classless society in Spain seemed closer than ever. During the conflict, Mayer-Serra regarded Beethoven as one of the most significant predecessors of the model antifascist citizen. In his 1937 article commemorating the 110th anniversary of Beethoven's death, Mayer-Serra linked the composer's music to key milestones in the history of the workers' struggle for a more humane and just organisation of society, including the revolutions of 1848, the Paris Commune, the Russian Revolution, "the great socialist edification of the USSR", and "our own revolutionary [civil war] experience".[43] In his review of a concert given by the Pau Casals Orchestra of Barcelona at the beginning of the war, Mayer-Serra praised the inclusion of the *Egmont* overture and Beethoven's Third Symphony in their programme, as the plots and revolutionary impulses of these works perfectly aligned with the collective antifascist sentiment in Republican Spain.[44]

Mayer-Serra divided the historical reception of Beethoven's music into three phases. During his lifetime, Beethoven was primarily appreciated as a "brilliant virtuoso" and "unsurpassed pedagogue". Following his death, bourgeois audiences – "which are still partly the audiences of today" – valued the pathos of his symphonies and surrendered "to vague and romantic associations of ideas", discovering in Beethoven's music "the expression of their own unbridled and uncontrolled individualism".[45] In the present, Mayer-Serra and other Marxist thinkers valued Beethoven's music primarily as a dialectical process:

> Beethoven is for us [Marxists] the Hegel of music, the first genius within the fine arts who has reached a perfect totalitarian realisation of his thought, by means of a dialectical method of aesthetic construction. What is his favourite form, the sonata, if not the complete schema of a dialectical process, with its first theme (=thesis), and the second (=antithesis), which form the "exposition", the "development" (which corresponds to the phase of "evolution" of the philosophical idea) and the "reprise" (=synthesis, that is, according to a Hegelian notion, the "transposition of an object to a higher phase of truth")? [...]

43 "una organització més humana i més justa de la societat, des del assaigs generals de les revolucionés del 48, de la Commune, del gloriós any 1905, fins a la grandiosa obra d'edificació socialista de la U. R. S. S. i la nostra pròpia experiència revolucionària". Otto Mayer, "Beethoven (1827–1937)", *Mirador* 414 (1 April 1937): 4.

44 "els seus arguments, i més encara per la seva empenta revolucionària, s'han adaptar meravellosament a un sentit col.lectiu, latent en cadascú dels que pogueren assistir a aquesta sessió memorable", anon. [Otto Mayer], "El concert de Pau Casals", *Treball* 1, no. 48 (15 September 1936): 5.

45 "el públic de l'època romàntica – que en gran part és encara el públic d'avi dia", "associacions d'idees, tan vagues com romàntiques, per a descobrir en l'èmfasi beethoveniana l'expressió del seu propi individualisme desfrenat i 'incontrolat'", Mayer, "Beethoven 1827–1937".

> The immense popularity of a large part of Beethoven's work is essentially based on this dialectical character of his musical technique, which is always something alive, which never stops in its dynamism. This dialectical character is a great driving force in Beethoven's music and tends towards action. His music always lacks "second ideas", which cannot be said, for example, of Wagner's or Debussy's. This means that it [Beethoven's music] is always comprehensible on its own and enables even the least-musically trained audience to follow the development of the musical ideas. In Beethoven's music there are neither aphorisms nor hidden ideologies. His inspiration has nothing mystical about it, but is rooted in the general notions of humanity and freedom which, for a century, have remained the same for the masses of the people. (This is one reason why Beethoven will always be considered a good educator of the free man and will always be more popular among the masses than, for example, Bach.)[46]

This linkage between sonata form in Beethoven's music and the dialectics of Georg Wilhelm Friedrich Hegel was not new. Hugo Riemann, writing in 1913, was one of the first theorists to discuss the "dialectics of sonata form" concerning Beethoven's music.[47] His interpretation drew on Adolf Bernhard Marx's definition of sonata form, which gained universal acceptance during Riemann's time: a tripartite structure in which two opposing or contrasting themes, termed "masculine" and "feminine", evolve from a state of "rest" (exposition) to one of "movement" (development), and then return to "rest" (recapit-

46 "Beethoven és per a nosaltres l'Hegel de la música, el primer geni dintre de les belles arts que ha arribat a una perfecta realització totalitària del seu pensament, per mitjà d'un mètode dialèctic de construcció estètica. Què és la seva forma predilecta, la *Sonata*, sinó el pla complet d'un procés dialèctic, amb el seu primer tema (=tesi), i el segon (=antítesi), que formen "l'exposició", el "desenrotllament" (que correspon a la fase d'evolució de la idea filosòfica) i la "reprise" (=síntesi, és a dir, segons una noció hegeliana, la "transposició d'un objecte a una fase superior de veracitat")? [...] La immensa popularitat d'una part considerable de l'obra de Beethoven es basa essencialment en aquest caràcter dialèctic de la seva tècnica musical, que és sempre una cosa viva i no s'atura mai en el seu dinamisme. Aquest caràcter dialèctic de la música beethoveniana és d'una gran força motriu i tendeix cap a l'acció: la música és sempre sense "segones idees" – el que no podríem dir, per exemple, de la de Wagner o de Debussy – això vol dir que és comprensible sempre per si mateix i possibilita, àdhuc el públic menys preparat musicalment, a seguir el desplegament de les idees musicals. En la música de Beethoven no hi ha ni aforismes, ni ideologies amagades. La seva inspiració no té res de místic, sinó que radica en les idees generals d'humanitat i de llibertat que, des d'un segle, han quedat les mateixes per a les masses populars (Heus ací una raó per la qual Beethoven serà sempre considerat com un bon mestre educador de l'home alliberat i serà sempre més popular entre les masses populars que, per exemple, Bach)." Mayer, "Beethoven 1827–1937".

47 Hugo Riemann, *Große Kompositionslehre*, vol. 3 (Berlin/Stuttgart: W. Spemann, 1913), 171.

ulation).[48] In the following decades, several theorists, most of whom were not personally acquainted with one another, began to connect this interpretation with Hegel's epistemic model of thesis-antithesis-synthesis. These included the Soviet composer and musicologist Boris Asaf'ev, the German conductor and musicologist Ernst Nobbe (later a close ally of the Nazi Party and its ideology), as well as a number of German Marxist theorists, including Theodor W. Adorno, Hanns Eisler, Ernst H. Meyer – following Eisler's influence – and Otto Mayer-Serra, among others.[49]

As mentioned in the Introduction, Mayer-Serra remembered Eisler as an exceptional analyst of Beethoven's sonatas. This suggests that his understanding of Beethoven's music as a dialectical process was shaped mainly by his former contacts with Eisler and his circle. As his friend Meyer neared the end of his life, he recalled similarly how one of Eisler's main teachings in the Weimar period had been the connection of the Marxist conception of history with a dialectical understanding of sonata form, in which the "conflicting" materials of the exposition were presented in the recapitulation as though they were transformed, reconciled, and elevated to a higher level.[50]

## Antifascist Modernism

During the civil war, Mayer-Serra articulated a strong link between the historical necessity of socialism and that of modernism. Consequently, he urged Spanish composers not to forget that the pieces they created about the socialist revolution in wartime Spain had to adhere to the "fundamental law of artis-

48 Adolph Bernhard Marx, *Die Lehre von der musikalischen Komposition*, vol. 3 (Leipzig: Breitkopf & Härtel, 1845), 213, 218, and 273.

49 See Boris Vladimirovič Asaf'ev, *Muzykal' naja forma kak prozess* (*Musical Form as a Process*), vol. 1 (Leningrad: Muzyka, 1930); Ernst Nobbe, *Die thematische Entwicklung der Sonatenform im Sinne der Hegel'schen Philosophie betrachtet* (Würzburg: Triltsch, 1941); Theodor W. Adorno, *Beethoven. Philosophie der Musik. Fragmente und Texte*, ed. Rolf Tiedemann (Frankfurt am Main: Suhrkampf, 1993). A comprehensive study of Asaf'ev's thought can be found in Arturo García Gómez, *Teoría de la entonación: Sobre el proceso de formación de la música en la via y obra de Boris V. Asaf'ev (1884–1949)* (PhD diss., Universidad Autónoma de Madrid, 2007). On Adorno's thoughts about Beethoven, see Rose Rosengard Subotnik, "Adorno's Diagnosis of Beethoven's Late Style: Early Symptom of a Fatal Condition", *Journal of the American Musicological Society* 29, no. 2 (1976), 242–275.

50 Ernst Hermann Meyer, *Kontraste, Konflikte: Erinnerungen, Gespräche, Kommentare*, ed. Dietrich Brennecke and Mathias Hansen (Berlin: Verlag Neue Musik, 1979), 56–57. For a historical survey of Hegelian interpretations of Beethoven's music, see Janet Schmalfeldt, "The Beethoven-Hegelian Tradition and the 'Tempest' Sonata" [1995], in *In the Process of Becoming: Analytic and Philosophical Perspectives on Form in Early Nineteenth-Century Music* (Oxford: Oxford University Press, 2011), 23–58.

tic evolution" to be effective propagandistically. This required, in his view, the "infiltration" of the styles of "bourgeois" modernist composers – such as Schoenberg, Hindemith, Bartók, and Falla – with "new stylistic elements" more closely aligned with socialist ideals. However, Mayer-Serra left these elements largely undefined.[51] The full "purification" of music from "the rotten elements of decadent bourgeois music" would only be possible after the complete socialist restructuring of Spanish society in the postwar period.[52]

Seemingly due to these considerations of revolutionary music as something yet to be accomplished, he provided very few specific examples of such music. The only concert work he positively reviewed during the war was *Para la tumba de Lenin. Variaciones elegiacas para piano* (*For Lenin's Tomb, Elegiac Variations for Piano*) by the Madrid communist composer Rodolfo Halffter.[53] The piece was commissioned by the music division of the Comissariat de Propaganda – essentially, by Mayer-Serra himself – to commemorate the twentieth anniversary of the Soviet Revolution. Halffter composed this seven-movement piano work in Valencia in October 1937. The propaganda agency promptly published a limited edition of the score. It is uncertain whether the piece was premiered in wartime Spain.[54] The work consists of six variations on an opening theme modelled after the recurring "Promenade" melody from Modest Mussorgsky's *Pictures at an Exhibition* (1874). The first movement is a double canon on the theme, presented in the low register as a topos of darkness and death. The third and fifth movements feature contrapuntal neo-Baroque treatments of the theme, reminiscent of the emulations of Domenico Scarlatti's music by Manuel de Falla and other Spanish neoclassical composers in the

51 Mayer, "Música viva, II,"; Mayer, "L'apoliticisme del músic", 7; Otto Mayer, "Què és música revolucionària?", *Mirador* 391 (15 October 1936): 7. See also Mayer, "El fracas de la SIMC: Vicisitudes de la música moderna", *Mirador* 396 (26 November 1936): 6.

52 "Aquest nou estil, purificat dels elements podrits de la música decadent burgesa i portat per la nova emoció del nou ordre social, donarà un dia a les masses populars els símbols sonors de la seva victòria revolucionària i de les seves aspiracions d'una nova societat més humana i més justa", Mayer, "Què és música revolucionària?" With respect to these "prospects", see also anon. [most probably Otto Mayer], "Cap a la liquidació de la universitat burguesa: El problema universitari", *Treball* (25 September 1936): 5; and Otto Mayer, "La renovació de la vida musical", *Mirador* 402 (7 January 1937): 7.

53 Otto Mayer, "A propósito de dos nuevas composiciones de Rodolfo Halffter", *Hora de España* 2, no 1 (1938): 89–92; see also Otto Mayer, "Una composició de Rodolf [sic] Halffter en honor de la U.R.S.S.", *Treball* (21 December 1937): 2.

54 Rodolfo Halffter, *Para la tumba de Lenin* (Barcelona: Comissariat de Propaganda. Sección de música, 1937). For more on this piece and its compositional context, see Antonio Iglesias, *Rodolfo Halffter: Su obra para piano* (Madrid: Alpuerto, 1979), 317–327; and especially Martin Kranz, "Wem die Stunde schlägt. Die Madrider 'Generation der Republick' im spanischen Bürgerkrieg am Bespiel von Rodolfo Halffter", in *"Form follows function": zwischen Musik, Form und Funktion*, ed. Till Knipper, Martin Kranz, Thomas Kühnrich, and Carsten Neubauer (Hamburg: Bockel, 2003), 217–243.

Fig. 6.2. Theme and first variation from Rodolfo Halffter's *Para la tumba de Lenin* (1937), as published in 1937 by the Comissariat de Propaganda.

early 1920s. All the other variations exclude references to eighteenth-century music, instead opting for an early twentieth-century non-tonal idiom. Fig. 6.2 shows the theme (I) and first variation (II).

Mayer-Serra congratulated Halffter for "dialectically" expressing Lenin's death, not as a crisis or drama, but rather in a virile, affirmative, and emotionally restrained manner, thereby reflecting the promising outlook for a socialist future.[55] Somewhat paradoxically, he lauded the avant-gardism of the work, yet cautioned that the piece's aesthetic elitism should remain exceptional. "Without taking into account *for this time* the musical knowledge and listening skills of the great mass of listeners, and not worrying too much about whether it [the work] might be 'liked' or not [by the masses], Halffter shows himself in this small commemorative work eager to discover new regions of aesthetic expression."[56] This remark exemplifies the tensions that emerged in his wartime writ-

55 "de afirmación viril", "revolucionaria", characterised by "un tono de elevación y de optimismo definitivo hacia un porvenir lleno de perspectivas", Mayer, "A propósito", 91.

56 "Sin contar, por esta vez, con la preparación musical y las facultades auditivas de la gran masa de los oyentes y sin preocuparse mucho de lo que pueda 'gustar', Halffter se muestra en esta pequeña obra conmemorativa anheloso de descubrir nuevas regiones de la expresión estética", Mayer, "A propósito", 92. Emphasis mine.

ings as he advocated for the democratisation, or "proletarianisation", of musical modernism – specifically, for new musical styles that were original while also appealing to the masses. Many European and American communist composers grappled with similar tensions during the mid-1930s, among them Alan Bush, Silvestre Revueltas, and several members of the New York Composers' Collective. Hanns Eisler articulated these contradictions most clearly in a 1937 essay co-authored with the Marxist philosopher Ernst Bloch, *Avantgarde-Kunst und Volksfront* (*Avant-Garde Art and the Popular Front*).[57]

These tensions were particularly evident in Mayer-Serra's writings on contemporary Soviet music. Like Eisler and other European communist musicians, Mayer-Serra shared with contemporary theorists of Soviet socialist realism a disdain for the concept of art for art's sake, arguing that music should promote human emancipation by providing an optimistic and affirmative vision of revolutionary society. However, the conservative aesthetic agenda then espoused in the Soviet Union conflicted with his assertion that revolutionary music must be innovative and aesthetically "progressive". In relation to Soviet aesthetics, Mayer-Serra's (and Eisler's) understanding of "revolutionary music" aligned more closely with the principles advocated by the Association for Contemporary Music (ASM) during the Lenin period than with the musical conservatism that emerged in the Soviet Union in the mid-1930s. (The ASM promoted Soviet and European musical modernism, often explicitly linking it to a radical socialist agenda. It coexisted with the more radical and left-wing Russian Association of Proletarian Musicians. The Soviet leadership liquidated both associations in 1932, replacing them with the Union of Soviet Composers, or USC.)[58]

During the war, Mayer-Serra, who was proficient in Russian, kept abreast of Soviet debates on music aesthetics by reading *Sovetskaya Muzyka*, the USC journal, as well as other foreign publications. The scarcity of Mayer-Serra's writings on Soviet music reflects the extent of his problematic relationship with official Soviet positions. In the earlier of his only two articles on Soviet music, significantly entitled "What is revolutionary music?", he established European musical modernism as the basis for the new revolutionary style. He argued that "the attempts of the post-revolutionary Soviet composers, who have indulged for some time in writing large symphonic poems à la Wagner and à la Strauss, using popular and revolutionary melodies" were not examples of revolutionary music.[59] He was likely alluding to the highly chromatic, neo-Romantic, epic

57 The essay was first published in *Die neue Weltbühne*, then the leading antifascist and anti-militarist newspaper, and later reprinted in Eisler, *Musik und Politik: Schritten, 1924–1948*, ed. Günter Mayer (Leipzig: VEB Deutscher Verlag für Musik, 1985), 397–405.

58 On the ASM see Nelson, *Music for the Revolution*; as well as Neil Edmunds, *The Soviet Proletarian Musical Movement* (Bern: Peter Lang, 2000), 79–84.

59 "Els assaigs dels compositors soviètics post-revolucionaris que, durant una certa època, s'han plagut en escriure grans poemes simfònics a la Wagner i a la Strauss,

idiom of symphonic works by composers such as Yuri Shaporin or Nikolai Myaskovsky. The choral finale of the latter's then-popular Sixth Symphony, from 1923, fits Mayer-Serra's description particularly well, as it relies on the contrast between an old Russian sacred chant and two songs from the French Revolution. Mayer-Serra may have heard this and other post-Romantic works by Soviet composers on the radio.[60]

Mayer-Serra's ambiguous stance on the Shostakovich affair in 1936 reflects his ambivalence toward the Soviet aesthetic agenda. Central to the controversy were the modernist elements of the opera *Lady Macbeth of Mtsensk* (1934), which Shostakovich had largely modelled on Berg's *Wozzeck*, one of Mayer-Serra's favourite contemporary operas. In that same article from October 1936, Mayer-Serra sought to align with the official Soviet stance on Shostakovich's style without abandoning his own modernist agenda. He criticised the eclecticism of the "very gifted" Shostakovich, characterising the composer's style as a blend of "Debussy's sensibility, Strauss's pathos, and the rhythmic orgies of Stravinsky". He argued that this eclectic style had been discredited in the Soviet Union.[61] This claim distorted the actual facts of the case, as the concept or even the term "eclecticism" was seldom used in polemics concerning *Lady Macbeth*, let alone Shostakovich's music in general.

Mayer-Serra wrote his second article on Soviet music in early 1938, at a time when the political influence of the Soviet Union had grown even more significant on the Republican side. After praising the Union of Soviet Composers, as well as the high standards of Soviet conservatories, instrumentalists, music journals, and publishers, he shifted focus to commentary on the *Lady Macbeth* affair:

> After having been on stage [in the Soviet Union] for a year or more, the opera disappears from the repertoire as a result of this public discussion, it is no longer performed for the moment. Certain reactionary foreign journals immediately sounded the alarm bell: Here is how the dictatorship of the proletariat harms individual freedom! Nothing could be more unjust than this perfidious calumny by the longstanding enemies of the working class. It is not difficult to refute this false position with solid arguments. In which country of the world – we ask – would it be possible to imagine this kind of permanent testing [assaig] of an opera? Which theatre in the world could afford the luxury of performing a dramatic work fifty, sixty, one hundred, and two hundred times, and subjecting

amb melodies populars i revolucionàries, han fracassat fins ara", Mayer, "Què és música revolucionària?"

60 For more on Myaskovsky's Sixth Symphony, see Boris Schwarz, *Music and Musical Life in Soviet Russia* (Bloomington: Indiana University Press, 1983), 77–79.

61 "L'eclecticisme d'un Schostakovitx, jove compositor molt dotat, que vacil·la entre una sensibilitat debussyana, un patetisme straussià i l'orgiasme rítmic d'un Stravinski, ha estat desacreditat últimament a la U. R. S. S.", Mayer, "Què és música revolucionària?"

> it to a public discussion in which the workers from all the factories and offices of a large metropolis like Moscow, delegations of the army, of the cooperatives, the intellectuals, the professionals of music and theatre, etc. – in short, the sincere people – take part?[62]

There was neither such a "testing" of the opera, which remained banned in the Soviet Union for twenty-five years (from 1936 to 1961), nor was there anything akin to a public debate, as the only viable stance was one of unconditional support for official censorship. In this instance, Mayer-Serra echoed and even amplified the official reports emerging from the Soviet Union, which he may have increasingly come to believe as the war progressed. The quoted excerpt is an especially stark example of the distortions used for propaganda purposes that characterised some of Mayer-Serra's wartime writings, particularly those published in *Treball,* the organ of the Catalan communist party, PSUC. These occasional ideological exaggerations set his wartime articles apart from Eisler's writings on music from the 1930s, which were generally more nuanced and better substantiated.

## Influences and Continuities

Mayer-Serra developed his critical theories on music history and music sociology in some of the most prestigious Spanish and Catalan periodicals of the Republican era. Prior to the war, the dissemination of his Marxist perspectives remained limited, as only a small fraction of his more than one hundred prewar writings addressed what he referred to as "issues" or "themes of music sociology". Most of these early studies appeared in two languages: in Catalan in the influential weekly *Mirador,* and in Spanish in the music journal *Musicografía.* At the time, *Mirador* was among the most prominent periodicals in Catalonia, written in Catalan and primarily read by the middle and upper classes of Barcelona. *Musicografía,* meanwhile, was a Valencian music journal that attracted

62 "Després d'haver passat per l'escena durant un any o més, l'òpera desapareix del repertori com a resultat d'aquesta discussió pública, ja no és representada momentàniament. Certes revistes estrangeres reaccionàries han donat immediatament el crit d'alarma: Heus ací com la dictadura del proletariat lesiona la llibertat individual! / Res de més injust que aquesta calúmnia pèrfida dels enemics de sempre de la classe treballadora. No ens costa gaire de rebutjar aquesta posició falsa amb arguments sòlids. ¿A quin país del món – demanem forà possible imaginar-se aquesta mena d'assaig permanent d'una opera? ¿Quin teatre del món es podria permetre el luxe de representar una obra dramàtica cinquanta, seixanta cent i dues-centes vegades i sotmetre-la a una discussió pública a la qual participen els treballadors de totes les fabriques i oficines d'una gran metròpolis com Moscou, delegacions de l'Exèrcit, de les cooperatives, els intel·lectuals, els professionals de la música i del teatre, etc., en una paraula; el poble sencer?", Otto Mayer, "La formidable tasca creadora dels musics soviètics", *Treball* 3, no. 480 (1 February 1938): 3.

contributions from leading scholars of Spanish music.[63] Mayer-Serra occasionally addressed topics at the intersection of music, economics, and society in a series of lectures delivered in 1935 at the Ateneum Polytechnicum, most notably in a talk entitled *Social Concerns Through Music*. These lectures were attended by several young composers from Barcelona.[64]

The tone and degree of political commitment in these prewar writings and conferences were remarkably restrained, likely aimed at safeguarding his position at *Mirador* and his prospects for employment in other Catalan "bourgeois" institutions. Nevertheless, he regarded these articles, in which Eisler's influence is most evident, as his most important work. This is evidenced by the fact that when the editors of the Valencian monthly music journal *Musicografía* invited him to collaborate in 1935, he chose to publish translations into Spanish of some of the few articles on the social functions of music that he had previously published in *Mirador*.[65]

In the openly pro-communist political landscape of the civil war, Mayer-Serra was able to address issues related to Marxist historiography and communism with greater freedom and assertiveness. Most of his writings during this period focused on the role of music in society – past, present, and future. His Marxist historiographical perspectives took centre stage, and the tone of his work became markedly more politically incisive. In the first three months of the war, he published the majority of his articles in the cultural section of *Treball. Diari dels treballadors de la ciutat i del camp* (*Work: Daily Paper of the Urban and Rural Workers*), the official publication of the influential Catalan communist party, the PSUC. This newspaper was one of the most widely circulated periodicals in Barcelona during the war.[66] From October 1936 onwards, Mayer-Serra contributed regularly to the "new" *Mirador*, which had become a pro-Soviet communist periodical under the firm control of the PSUC.[67] Fol-

63 On the history and significance of *Mirador* see Josep M. Huertas and Carles Geli, *'Mirador,' la Catalunya impossible* (Barcelona: Proa, 2000); and Carles Singla i Casellas, *'Mirador' (1929–1937): un periòdic al servei d'una idea de país* (Barcelona: Institut d'Estudis Catalans, 2006).

64 On these lectures see anon., "Cursillo musical", *La Vanguardia* (24 February 1935): 12; anon., "Las conferencias del Dr. Mayer", *La Vanguardia* (5 April 1935): 21; anon., "Notas varias". *La Vanguardia* (28 March 1935): 9; anon., "Ateneu Polytechnicum: El Jazz en la música moderna i l'Opera de Quat'Sous", *La Publicitat* (4 April 1935): 7. The attendance by young composers is mentioned in Ricard Lamote de Grignon's open letter about Mayer-Serra, in "Dues cartes obertes", *Mirador* 331 (1935): 8.

65 See footnote 1.

66 The early history of the PSUC is discussed in Josep Puigsech Farràs, *Nosaltres, els comunistes catalans. El PSUC i la Internacional Comunista durant la Guerra Civil* (Vic: Eumo, 1999). On *Treball*, see Josep M. Figueres, *Periodisme en la Guerra Civil (1936–39)* (Barcelona: Publications de l'Abadia de Montserrat, 2010).

67 A few months before the beginning of the war, Mayer-Serra had been dismissed from his post at *Mirador* due to personal, professional, and perhaps political differences

lowing the definitive cessation of *Mirador*'s publication in the summer of 1937, Mayer-Serra's output as a music writer became limited to occasional contributions to several prominent Spanish cultural journals, including *Hora de España* and *Música*. These periodicals were widely read by antifascist intellectuals during the war. Given that the wartime readership was largely politicised and receptive to Marxist theories, future studies could examine how his ideas influenced the intellectual development of Spanish antifascists, many of whom continued their work in exile after the civil war.

This was also the case for Mayer-Serra himself. Like thousands of other civilians, he fled Barcelona just days before the city's fall at the war's end. He likely crossed into France shortly after 5 February 1939, when the French government opened the border to all Spanish citizens. Five days later, Francoist troops reached the French border. After a few weeks in France – possibly interned briefly at the refugee camp in Argelès-sur-Mer – he relocated to New York in April 1939.[68] There, he apparently met Hanns Eisler on the 23rd of that month.[69] As Mayer-Serra was not permitted to remain in the United States, he moved immediately to Mexico City, where he began working as a music journalist and historian. He and Eisler maintained close contact during the composer's stay in Ciudad de México from April to September 1939. It seems that Eisler even resided at Mayer-Serra's house for some time – if not for the entirety of his stay in the city.[70] Significantly, one of the earliest articles

with the journal's editors and part of the Barcelona music establishment. At the onset of the conflict, the PSUC restructured the editorial board, transforming *Mirador* into a pro-communist publication under party control. Mayer-Serra was reinstated as head of the music section. In this role, he published a brief pseudonymous article by Ernst H. Meyer, which examined England's "bourgeois" musical institutions from a sociological perspective. Peter Baker [Ernst H. Meyer], "Carta de Londres", 10. On *Mirador* in the wartime period see Campillo, *Escriptors catalans i compromís antifeixista*; and Singla i Casellas, *'Mirador'*.

68 At the end of his life, Rodolfo Halffter told Spanish music scholar Emilio Casares that Mayer-Serra was interned in the French refugee camp of Argelès-sur-Mer until 1940. (This narrative appears in the entry "Mayer-Serra" of the *Diccionario de la Música Española e Hispanoamericana*.) This date is incorrect, as Mayer-Serra moved to New York in April 1939. If he was interned in that camp, then it would have been only for a few months.

69 Letter from Otto Mayer to Manuel Serra i Moret, 23 April 1939, Biblioteca del Pavelló de la República de la Universitat de Barcelona, Fons FP: Subsèrie Manuel Serra i Moret, sig. XV.

70 I infer this arrangement on the basis of two documents: a letter from Eisler to Joachim and Sylvia Schumacher, Mexico City, 4 May 1939, c.f. *Hanns Eisler, Briefe 1907–1943*, 146; and a notebook retained by the HEA that lists several addresses, including the following: "Otto Mayer Eliseo, 37 / Tel. 35274" (no cat. no.). I thank Peter Deeg for calling my attention to the latter source.

Mayer-Serra wrote in Mexico was devoted to reporting on Eisler's activities in the country.[71]

The theories on music history and sociology that Mayer-Serra developed in Germany and Spain provided a crucial foundation for many of his early studies on the history of Mexican music, particularly his 1941 monograph *Panorama de la música mexicana desde la independencia hasta la actualidad* (*Overview of Mexican Music from Independence to the Present Day*).[72] This influential book is now regarded as one of the foundational works of modern Mexican music historiography. In his only surviving letter to Eisler, dated July 1940, Mayer-Serra explained that he was adopting a "sociological approach" in his research for *Panorama*. He was thus undertaking an intensive study of Mexico's political and economic history.[73] In his foreword to the published monograph, he similarly explained that the findings he presented were "sociological in nature" and therefore "open to debate", as theories of musical nationalism and music sociology remained in an incipient, "experimental" stage.[74] Mexican music scholar Leonora Saavedra, who has examined the narratives in *Panorama*, affirms this tendency in his writings, in which he rationalises certain aspects of Mexican music history as the "result of the social infrastructure and the labour market". This approach influenced several later Mexican music scholars, who regarded this monograph as one of their primary references.[75]

71 Odón Mayer-Serra, "Hanns Eisler", *El Nacional* (18 June 1939): 7.

72 Otto Mayer-Serra, *Panorama de la música mexicana desde la Independencia hasta la actualidad* (Mexico: El Colegio de México, 1941 (facsimile edition: Mexico: CENIDIM, 1996).

73 "...die Ganze Sache soziologisch aufziehen. Studire [sic] also viel Geschichte (politische und oekonomische [sic])". Letter from Otto Mayer-Serra to Hanns Eisler, 4 July 1940, HEA, cat. no. 4145. It seems that the last contact between the musicologist and the composer was this letter and another (now lost) that Mayer-Serra sent to Eisler shortly before. Apparently, Eisler did not respond to any of these letters.

74 Mayer-Serra, *Panorama*, 10.

75 Saavedra explains that Mayer-Serra's historiographical narrative "does not present a concatenation of genres, works and personalities" but "appeals to an interpretation of musical creation as a result of the social infrastructure and the labour market." This approach "had a decisive impact on the way in which Mexican historiography has privileged in its narrative the lack or existence of musical infrastructures in Mexico." ("... no presenta una concatenación de géneros, obras y personalidades, sino que, de nuevo, apela a una interpretación de la creación musical como resultado de la infraestructura social y del mercado de trabajo. Por esta razón entre muchas otras, digámoslo de paso, *Panorama* ha tenido un impacto decisivo en la manera en la que la historiografía mexicana ha privilegiado en su narrativa la carencia o existencia de infraestructuras musicales en México.") Leonora Saavedra, "La sociología de la música de Otto Mayer-Serra", in *De Nueva España a México. El universo musical mexicano entre centenarios (1517–1917)*, ed. Javier Marín-López (Seville: Universidad Internacional de Andalucía, 2020), pp. 208–209.

Seen from a broader historical perspective, Mayer-Serra's writings of the 1930s, alongside the essays on music history by Eisler, Meyer, and other Marxist scholars from their interwar circle, constitute the first accounts of German Marxist music historiography. The corpus of writings produced by these authors provides one of the primary antecedents to the prevailing discourse on music among leading musicologists in the early GDR. Scholars in the early GDR also identified Romanticism as the locus of individualism, imperialism, and irrationality that had led to fascism. The new state was positioned as the second German Enlightenment, with socialism presented as the culmination of a legacy stemming from humanist and rationalist traditions dating back to the French Revolution.[76] A similar heritage, grounded in the classical realism that originated with Beethoven, was heralded as the precedent to socialist realism. The aforementioned understanding of Beethoven's sonata form as a dialectical process developed into a widespread topos for GDR musicology in the 1950s.[77] Such trends in interwar writings on music by German Marxists anticipated a series of calls made by an increasing number of "new" musicologists starting in the 1980s, urging scholars to reconsider musical compositions as human activities rather than as autonomous artworks detached from economies, societies, and politics.[78] Although Eisler, Meyer, Mayer-Serra, and other members of their interwar circle largely set aside issues central to contemporary musicology –such as gender, sexuality, and race – their efforts to understand music as something closely linked to economic, class-based, and social hierarchies are proving increasingly relevant for today's musicologists.

76 On the main historical narratives prevalent in the early GDR, see Elaine Kelly, *Composing the Canon in the German Democratic Republic: Narratives of Nineteenth-Century Music* (Oxford: Oxford University Press, 2014), especially chapters 1–4; and Nina Noeske and Matthias Tischer, eds., *Musikwissenschaft und Kalter Krieg: Das Beispiel DDR* (Cologne: Böhlau, 2010).

77 One of the main proponents of these ideas was Ernst H. Meyer, who took up the newly created Chair of Music Sociology at Humboldt University, Berlin's leading university, in 1949. Mayer-Serra had studied there twenty years earlier. See Ernst Hermann Meyer, *Musik im Zeitgeschehen* (Berlin: Deutschen Akademie der Künste, 1952), especially 70–71. GDR music scholar Georg Knepler exposed related ideas in "Zur Frage der Widerspiegelung der Wirklichkeit in Beethovens Musik", *Musik und Gesellschaft* 2, no 3 (1952): 66–71.

78 See Anne C. Shreffler, "Berlin Walls: Dahlhaus, Knepler, and Ideologies of Music History", *The Journal of Musicology* 20, no. 4 (Fall 2003): 498–525; and Nina Noeske and Matthias Tischer, eds., *Musikwissenschaft und Kalter Krieg: Das Beispiel DDR*, KlangZeiten: Musik, Politik, Gesellschaft 7 (Cologne: Böhlau, 2010).

# Epilogue
# Memorialisation of the Spanish War

The Spanish Civil War continued to shape the creative output of Eisler and other German musicians from his circle for decades after the conflict. Both during his exile and, especially, after his resettlement in the GDR in 1949, Eisler contributed music to the historical commemoration of the war as a defining moment in the history of transnational antifascism. He almost always did so in collaboration with other communist artists – primarily poets, filmmakers, and singers. Among them were Bertolt Brecht and Ernst Busch, who, like Eisler and Ernst H. Meyer, became some of the most highly regarded figures in East Germany within their respective artistic fields. In the GDR, the composition of such works took place in a cultural context marked by the increasing romanticisation of the Spanish war, particularly following the 1956 celebrations of the twentieth anniversary of the beginning of the "struggle for the freedom of the Spanish people" (a phrase that largely replaced the term "civil war" in East German discourse). This commemoration was celebrated with considerable fanfare in East Berlin but not in West Germany. As noted in the Introduction, the official festivities included the awarding of the Hans Beimler Medal to Eisler in recognition of his "outstanding services" during the war. In the wake of this celebration, numerous filmic, literary, artistic, and musical works were produced and promoted in the GDR that idealised the Spanish conflict as one of the last great international antifascist causes and as a direct precursor to the defeat of fascism in the Second World War. Eisler responded to this growing tendency to glorify the war with a measure of critical distance and, at times, seemingly even with a subtle touch of irony.

## After Guernica

The first piece that Eisler composed about the civil war after his final stay in Spain was *Spanisches Liedchen 1937* (*Spanish Ditty 1937*) for voice and piano. This twelve-tone art song, written in a marching style, is based on Brecht's poem *Mein Bruder, der Flieger* (*My Brother, the Pilot*, 1937). The poem is one of several by Brecht that depict German soldiers as both executioners and victims, specifically referring to the soldiers of the Condor Legion. Brecht wrote the poem shortly after the partial destruction of the Basque town of Guernica by German aerial bombardment in April 1937, and Eisler set it to music soon thereafter, likely around mid-1937.[1] The bombing of Guernica – often invoked *pars pro toto* as a symbol of foreign fascist aggression in Spain – was widely condemned by writers and artists across the world. Prominent responses include Pablo Picasso's monumental painting *Guernica* (1937), created for the Paris International Exhibition that same year; Paul Dessau's twelve-tone piano piece *Guernica* (1938); René Magritte's *Le Drapeau Noir* (*The Black Flag*, 1937); and W. H. Auden's poem *Spain 1937* (1937).[2]

The first stanza of Brecht's poem ironically reflects on how the soldiers of the Condor Legion were covertly transported to German airbases, disguised as tourists on holiday under the auspices of the *Kraft durch Freude* programme. Brecht then unveils the soldiers' true intentions in the second stanza, followed by the tragic consequences of his actions in the third. Thematically, the piece is connected to *Flüstergespräche*, the melodrama about fascist bombings in the *Peasant Cantata* that Eisler had completed earlier that year.

| | |
|---|---|
| Mein Bruder war ein Flieger.<br>Eines Tags erhielt er eine Kart',<br>Er hat seinen Koffer eingepackt<br>Und südwärts ging die Fahrt. | My brother was a pilot<br>One day, he received a card,<br>He has packed his suitcase<br>And the journey went south. |
| Mein Bruder ist ein Eroberer.<br>Unserm Volke fehlt's an Raum,<br>Und Grund und Boden zu<br>kriegen, ist<br>Bei uns ein alter Traum. | My brother is a conqueror.<br>Our people lack space,<br>And gaining land and<br>property, is<br>an old dream for us. |
| Der Raum, den mein Bruder<br>eroberte,<br>Liegt am Quadramamassiv;<br>Er ist einen Meter achtzig<br>lang<br>Und einen Meter fünfzig tief.[3] | The space that my brother<br>conquered,<br>Lies on the Quadrama massif<br>[Sierra de Guadarrama];<br>It is one metre eighty long<br>And one metre fifty deep. |

1 Brecht's poem was published for the first time on 17 October 1937 in the Sunday supplement of the *Pariser Tageszeitung* (see Bertolt Brecht: *Mein Bruder, der Flieger*, *Pariser Tageszeitung* year 2, no. 491, p. 3 [Sonntagsbeilage]). On this poem see Edgar Bazing, *Internationale Lyrik zum Spanischen Bürgerkrieg (1936–39)* (St. Ingbert: Roehrig, 2001), 28–33; and Filippomaria Pontani. "Eteokles in Spain? On Brecht's *Mein Bruder war ein Flieger*", *Neophilologus* 101/4 (2017), 575–583.

2 On the thematisation of the bombing of Guernica in contemporary international literature see Rüdiger Reinecke, *Gernika und der Luftkrieg gegen die spanische Republik (1936–1939) in der zeitgenössischen internationalen Literatur* (Bielefeld: Aisthesis, 2020).

3 Hanns Eisler, *Spanisches Liedchen 1937*, in *Lieder und Kantaten*, vol. 2 (Leipzig: Breitkopf & Haertel, 1957), 117–118. For reasons that remain unclear – whether due to a mistake or an artistic decision – Eisler wrote "Quadrama-massiv" instead of "Guadarrama-massiv", as it appears in Brecht's original. The Guadarrama mountain

*Spanisches Liedchen 1937* is part of a series of compositions from the latter half of the 1930s in which Eisler experimented with melodies that were twelve-tone organised but still easily singable. He intensified the dire and dramatic character of the poem by having the instrumental accompaniment foreshadow the soldier's fate before it is explicitly mentioned by the singer. To achieve this, he incorporated a quotation of the thirteenth-century *Dies irae* (*Days of Wrath*) in the piano accompaniment between the first and second stanzas (Ex. 7.1, bb. 10–13). This motif, a well-established symbol of impending death, has been used since the Romantic period. The bass further intensifies the quotation with a series of descending semitones – an age-old topos of grief, loss, and sadness.

The prominence of these musical elements imbued with extramusical meanings related to death and loss stands in stark contrast to the absence of any musical topoi referencing Spain. Like the *Peasant Cantata* and other Eisler compositions addressing the Spanish war, *Spanisches Liedchen 1937* incorporates none of the familiar Orientalist topoi that have been used since the Romantic period to portray Spain as an exotic Other. These topoi include Phrygian motifs, hemiola rhythmic patterns, floreos (upper mordents), flamenco-like melismas, and imitations of popular guitar idioms. Aside from his general rejection of exoticism, Eisler's primary reason for avoiding such topoi in this or any other composition concerning the Spanish conflict appears to stem from his perception of the Civil War as not merely a local struggle but as part of an international antifascist and proletarian movement. As noted in Chapter 5, this was similarly true for all antifascist battle songs composed by musicians from Spain and abroad during the civil war, which also lacked any overtly "Spanish" musical elements. In this context, Eisler's song stands in contrast to Paul Dessau's 1949 setting of the same poem for voice and guitar. In addition to the use of the Spanish guitar as an accompanying instrument, this piece incorporates two elements that unmistakably evoke Spain as an exotic Other: the ostinato bolero rhythm in the accompaniment and the harmonic interplay between E minor and E Phrygian (see, for example, the two settings of the word "südwarts" (south or southward) in Ex. 7.2, bb. 8 and 10).

---

range, located in central Spain, was the site of significant battles during the civil war. For further discussion on the differences between Brecht's poem and Eisler's lyrics, see Thomas Phleps, "Der müde Soldat: Hanns Eisler und der Erste Weltkrieg", in *Musik bezieht Stellung. Funktionalisierungen der Musik im Ersten Weltkrieg*, eds. Stefan Hanheide, Dietrich Helms, Claudia Glunz, and Thomas F. Schneider (Göttingen: V&R unipress, 2013), 403–428.

Ex. 7.1. Hanns Eisler, topoi of death and sadness in *Spanisches Liedchen 1937* (bb. 5–13). © by Deutscher Verlag für Musik Leipzig.

Ex. 7.2. Paul Dessau, *Mein Bruder war ein Flieger* for voice and guitar (from *5 Kinderlieder*, 1949), bb. 1–11. Source: Paul Dessau/Bertolt Brecht: *5 Kinderlieder.* Thüringer Volksverlag, Erfurt 1950.

## Singing European Resistance

During the Second World War, Eisler repurposed the vocal melody of the *Marcha del Quinto Regimiento* to symbolise the communist resistance against fascism occurring in Central Europe at that time. This Spanish melody served as the chorus for a fictional antifascist battle song that he composed in 1943 as part of his film score for Fritz Lang's anti-Nazi film noir *Hangmen Also Die* (1943). Eisler created the score in Hollywood, where he had settled shortly before to pursue a career as a film composer. The film emerged as one of the most successful and critically acclaimed anti-Nazi films produced during the Second World War, earning him an Oscar nomination for Best Score at the 1943 Academy Awards.[4]

*Hangmen Also Die* is a fictionalised account of the 1942 assassination of Nazi protector Reinhard Heydrich in German-occupied Prague. The script was written shortly after the incident by John Wexley, based on a story by Bertolt Brecht and Fritz Lang. The film's hero – the killer – is a member of the Czech antifascist resistance with ties to the Communist Party. It narrates his escape, the assistance he receives from the Czech antifascist resistance, and the reprisals imposed by the Nazi occupiers to compel the assassin's surrender. A key point of interest in the script is the fictional battle song that members of the Czech resistance create during their imprisonment and sing when they are about to be executed by the Nazis (1h52m02s). The filmmakers entitled the piece *Song of the Hostages.* The complete song is reproduced in Ex. 7.3.

In the early stages of the film's production, Brecht wrote German lyrics for this filmic battle song that fit the melody of Eisler's *Comintern Song.* The poet intended to include this version in the film to emphasise the links between the antifascist resistance and communism. However, this plan was eventually abandoned, apparently because Lang wanted to avoid linking the film too overtly to communism and the Soviet Union. The director subsequently commissioned the successful songwriter Sam Coslow to write catchy English lyrics based on Brecht's German text. Coslow's version no longer fits the melody of the Comintern anthem. His lyrics serve as a call for antifascist resistance and include lines such as "Die if you must / for a cause that is just" and "...this war is not won / till the last battle's done." Many battle-song lyrics written in Republican Spain during the civil war contain very similar verses. The complete lyrics are provided in the example below.

Knowing of Brecht's original intention to musically relate the battle song to the Comintern, Eisler then decided to set Coslow's lyrics to a melody that is largely a reworking of the Barcelona Olympic anthem / *Marcha del Quinto*

4 On Eisler's score for *Hangmen Also Die* see Johannes C. Gall, *Eisler goes Hollywood: das Buch Komposition für den Film und die Filmmusik zu Hangmen Also Die* (Wiesbaden: Breitkopf & Härtel, 2015), 166–176; and Sally Blick, "A Double Life in Hollywood: Hanns Eisler's Score for the Film Hangmen Also Die and the Covert Expressions of a Marxist Composer", *The Musical Quarterly* 93, no. 1 (2010): 90–143.

Ex. 7.3. *Song of the Hostages* from *Hangmen Also Die.*

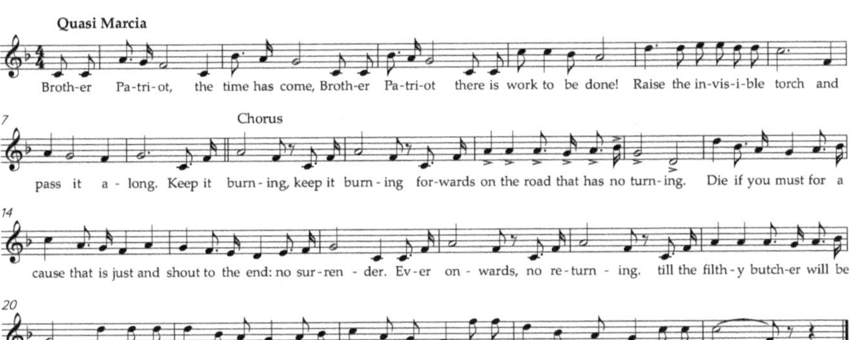


*Regimiento* (Ex. 7.3, bb. 9–24). The reasons for this choice seem to be that the Spanish song was much less well known internationally, yet it maintained a clear link to the Comintern. As explained in Chapter 1, the Spanish melody incorporates several quotations from the *Comintern Song.* Moreover, the Comintern played a fundamental role in both the organisation of the People's Olympiad, for which the song was composed, and later in the Spanish war, during which the new version – the *Marcha del Quinto Regimiento* – was created. Eisler's use of Spanish song in relation to the Czech resistance against Nazism was underpinned by his conception of antifascism as an emphatically supranational movement that transcended national borders. For him and many others, there was no contradiction in using a battle song from the Spanish Civil War to represent Czech antifascism in the film.

The film concludes with the murder of Czech hostages by the Nazis. The closing titles are accompanied by an apotheotic vocal-symphonic arrangement of the *Song of the Hostages* for mixed choir and symphony orchestra. On screen, the words "NOT The End" appear, referencing the necessity to continue the fight against fascism in the context of the Second World War (the film premiered in the United States in 1943). Years later, Eisler recycled this closing cue in the final movement of his cantata, *Mitte des Jahrhunderts* (*Midcentury*), which he composed in 1950 for the Third Political Convention of the Sozialistische Einheitspartei Deutschlands (SED), the sole legal party in the GDR. Writer and SED politician Johannes R. Becher provided an enthusiastic hymn in praise of the party as lyrics for this movement.[5] It is unlikely that either he or the rest of the party were aware that the piece was recycled from a Hollywood film.

5 See Christian Grüneis, "Die Kantate Mitte des Jahrhunderts", in *Hanns Eisler zwischen Systemkonformität und musikalischem Anspruch*, eds. Christian Glanz and Annegret Huber (Vienna: Mille Tre, 2015), 13–114.

## The Spanish War in GDR Film Music

As mentioned, the Spanish Civil War played a central role in the cultures of memory of both the GDR and, more generally, the Eastern Bloc during the Cold War. In East Germany, the conflict was celebrated as a major milestone in a tradition of antifascism that culminated in the formation of the new state. The commemoration of the exploits of the International Brigades was often promoted within the framework of official pro-communist discourses as a strategy for legitimising the SED.[6] The German veterans of the Brigades were hailed as the seed of the "National People's Army", and several former interbrigadists, including Erich Mielke and Walter Ulbricht, attained important political positions in the new state. Following the celebration of the twentieth anniversary of the beginning of the Spanish Civil War, dozens of musical compositions, novels, poetry books, memoirs, paintings, sculptures, theatre plays, and films about the International Brigades were created and officially promoted.[7] Among the films about the Spanish Civil War produced in the GDR during this period are the feature films *Mich dürstet* (*I Thirst*, 1956), *Wo Du hin gehst* (*Where You Are Going*, 1957), and *Fünf Patronenhülsen* (*Five Bullet Casings*, 1960), as well as the documentary *Unbändiges Spanien* (*Untamed Spain*, 1962), in which Eisler was directly involved. The poster for *Unbändiges Spanien* was designed by the exiled Spanish communist artist Josep Renau, whose modernist propaganda work has previously been examined in connection with Eisler's music.

*Unbändiges Spanien* was directed by the couple Jeanne and Kurt Stern, who, like Eisler, had travelled to wartime Spain and actively participated in the cultural propaganda of the International Brigades. The tripartite film is a peculiar example of filmic transtextuality. The central part consists of the German version of Joris Ivens' 1937 documentary about the civil war, *The Spanish Earth*, for which Ernest Hemingway wrote the script. This older documentary is framed by a prologue and epilogue created by the Sterns in the early 1960s. The prologue describes the history of Spain as marked by continuous repression and exploitation of the common people by a caste of landowners, aristocrats,

6 On the roles and meanings of the Spanish war and the International Brigades in the processes of historical memory of the GDR see Wolfgang Asholt, Rüdiger Reinecke, and Susanne Schlünder, eds., *Der spanische Bürgerkrieg in der DDR. Strategien intermedialer Erinnerungsbildung* (Frankfurt am Main: Vervuert, 2009); Michael Uhl, *Mythos Spanien. Das Erbe der Internationalen Brigaden in der DDR* (Bonn: Dietz, 2004); Josie McLellan, *Anti-Fascism and Memory in East Germany: Remembering the International Brigades, 1945–1989* (Oxford: Oxford University Press, 2004); Patrik von Zur Mühlen, *Spanien war ihre Hoffnung. Die deutsche Linke im Spanischen Bürgerkrieg 1936 bis 1939* (Berlin: Dietz, 1985).

7 See Peter H. Feist, "Der Spanische Bürgerkrieg in der bildenden Kunst der DDR", in Asholt et al., *Der spanische Bürgerkrieg in der DDR*, 207–217; and Peter H. Feist, "Der Spanische Bürgerkrieg in der Kunst der DDR", *Der Spanische Bürgerkrieg und die bildenden Künste*, ed. Jutta Helfd (Hamburg: Argument, 1989), 211–226.

churchmen, military officials, and kings. The epilogue denounces Francisco Franco's repression after the civil war and the complicity of the USA, West Germany, and other Western democracies with the Spanish dictator.[8]

The music of the prologue and epilogue consists of several short cues for orchestra alongside a somewhat unoriginal collection of pre-existing recordings of a few German *Kampflieder* sung by Busch and others (the *Solidarity Song* among them), as well as many traditional folk pieces from different Spanish regions, including the well-known *Los cuatro muleros, Ay Carmela,* several flamenco instrumental pieces, and a number of Catalan *sardanas* and Basque folk songs. These pieces correspond to the type of music that had been used as film music in *The Spanish Earth* and other propagandistic documentaries filmed about Spain during the civil war.

Eisler is credited in the film for the music of the sections produced in the GDR. The contract he signed with the state-owned film studio DEFA stipulated that he was to provide the studio "with compositions for the film" and to work "as a musical consultant" for the filmmakers.[9] However, the extent of Eisler's involvement in the project remains uncertain, as the production of *Unbändiges Spanien* occurred just a few weeks before his death, when he was suffering from severe health problems. The most likely scenario is that he did not compose new music for the film but instead recycled pre-existing cues from other, unspecified projects. None of these instrumental cues has musical elements that refer to Spain or to any specific element in the film. What is virtually certain is that Eisler did not serve as a musical consultant in selecting the traditional Spanish pieces heard in the prologue and epilogue. Not only is it improbable that he was familiar with or had access to recordings of most of these Spanish pieces, but more significantly, he deliberately avoided, as noted earlier, the use of national folklore or traditional music to portray wartime Spain as an exoticist Other. I assume that the pre-existing Spanish pieces were most likely selected by the directors, with Eisler having minimal involvement in the project. This was likely not a significant concern for the Sterns or for DEFA, as one of their main motivations in hiring Eisler may have been the promotional and propagandistic value of associating the film with one of the few recognised GDR composers who had actively supported the International Brigades in Spain. In fact, in a promotional article for the film, Jeanne Stern

8 The political dimension and narrative strategies of *Unbändiges Spanien* are analysed in Clara López Rubio and Wolfgang Martin-Hamdorf, "El lacayo de Berlín, Bonn y Washington. La imagen de Franco en el cine documental alemán: el caso de *Unbändiges Spanien* (España Indómita)", *Archivos de la filmoteca* 42/43 (October 2002–February 2003), 100–117.

9 Contract between the DEFA and Hanns Eisler, signed on 2 August 1962, Berlin (HEA, cat. no. 3168).

emphasised Eisler's "experiences" in the Spanish war and noted that the conflict had "remained unforgettable for him".[10]

*Wo du hin gehst* (1957), which premiered five years before *Unbändiges Spanien*, features a more original film score. The music was composed by Ernst H. Meyer, who returned to East Germany in 1948 following his exile in England. His commission to compose the score underscores the significance of the production, as Meyer was one of the most respected figures in GDR cultural circles at the time. (He was Professor of Musicology at Berlin University and held influential positions, including the leadership of the official professional organisation of musicians in the GDR.)[11] The film was directed by German actor, director, and writer Martin Hellberg. Its protagonist, Jakob, is a German anti-Nazi resistance fighter operating clandestinely in Berlin during the 1936 Olympic Games. He receives support from Thea, a Swiss doctor who falls in love with him. Hoping to protect him from the Gestapo, which is actively pursuing him, Thea tries to bring him to Switzerland. Jakob, however, refuses and decides instead to join the International Brigades in Spain. Some time later, Thea follows him there and serves as a doctor for the Brigades. After the war, their paths cross again briefly in an internment camp: he remains imprisoned, while she is deported to Switzerland.

In his musical portrayal of Spain, Meyer notably diverged from the cinematic conventions of the period. This is particularly evident in the scene where Jakob departs for Spain by train (0h29m07s). Rather than grounding the action geographically through the familiar Orientalist topoi traditionally associated with Spain, Meyer composed an epic, neo-Romantic symphonic arrangement of the wartime Spanish battle song *Los campesinos* (*The Peasants*). As discussed in Chapter 5, this song was written in 1937 by the Madrid-based composer Enrique Casal Chapí. Meyer became acquainted with the piece in 1938, when Mayer-Serra sent him a copy of the score from Barcelona to London, where Meyer was living in exile. He expressed his admiration for the song in correspondence

10 Jeanne Stern, "Zu unserem Film 'Unbändiges Spanien'", *Die Frau von Heute, Berlin* (27 October 1962), p. 18.

11 On Meyer's roles in GDR culture see Mathias Hansen, *Ernst Hermann Meyer. Das kompositorische und theoretische Werk* (Leipzig: EB Deutscher Verlag für Musik, 1976); and Dietrich Brennecke and Mathias Hansen, eds., *Ernst Hermann Meyer – Kontraste. Konflikte. Erinnerungen. Gespräche. Kommentare* (Berlin: Neue Musik, 1979). A recent study addressing Meyer's creative output in the GDR is Golan Gur, "Classicism as Anti-Fascist Heritage, Realism and Myth in Ernst Hermann Meyer's Mansfelder Oratorium (1950)", in *Classical Music in the German Democratic Republic*, eds. Kyle Frackman and Larson Powell (Rochester: Camden House, 2015), 34–57.

Ex. 7.4. Ernst H. Meyer, third cue of the film score for *Wo du hin gehst*. Ernst-Hermann-Meyer-Archive 1016.

with Mayer-Serra that same year.[12] It is also likely that the composer had listened to Busch's 1947 recording of the song before working on the film score.[13]

Example 7.4 presents the opening of Meyer's symphonic arrangement of *Los campesinos*. The introduction (bb. 1–6) offers a variation on the opening motif of Casal Chapí's original song, with loud fanfare motifs in the brass (bb. 3–5) standing out as a heroic topos. This is followed by an almost literal quotation of Casal Chapí's vocal melody, first played by the woodwinds (bb. 7–11), and later by the strings (not shown in the example). The theme is accompanied by brief, repetitive motifs in the strings and brass. Notably, Meyer's arrangement of the

12 Meyer's letters to Mayer-Serra are lost. However, the letters Mayer-Serra sent to Meyer are now preserved at the AdK archive in Berlin. In a brief postcard dated 1 August 1938, Mayer-Serra wrote to Meyer: "I'm delighted that you like 'Los Campesinos'. Enrique Casal is, next to the Catalan J. [Josep] Valls, the best [Spanish] composer." ("Je suis heureux que 'Los Campesinos' vous plaise. Enrique Casal est, à côté du catalan J. [Josep] Valls, le meilleur compositeur.") Postcard from Otto Mayer-Serra to Ernst H. Meyer, 1 August 1938. (Ernst-Hermann-Meyer-Archive (AdK), no cat. no.).

13 Ernst Busch, *Adelante campesinos*. Lied der Zeit 588 (1947).

Spanish battle song lacks any recognisable "Spanish" exoticist elements, such as Phrygian melodies, castanets, or hemiolas. The Spain that Jakob journeys to is not the sensual, mysterious southern region portrayed by the Romantics (and Hollywood), but rather one of the major historical battlegrounds in the international struggle against fascism.

## God Is One of Them

In the year of the premiere of *Wo du hin gehst*, Eisler composed one of his most memorable pieces about the Spanish Civil War: the first movement of his *Bilder aus dem Kriegsfibel* (*Pictures from the War Primer*, 1957) for male choir and chamber ensemble. *Bilder aus dem Kriegsfibel* comprises fifteen brief musical settings of selected poems from Bertolt Brecht's book *Kriegsfibel* (*War Primer*, 1955).[14] This book is a collection of sixty-nine images depicting the horrors of the Second World War. The poet assembled them between 1938 and 1945 from newspaper cutouts. Each image is accompanied by a corresponding anti-militarist four-line poem. Brecht referred to this type of montage of a newspaper photograph and a poem as a "Fotoepigramm" (photoepigramme).[15] He included two photoepigrams about the Spanish war at the beginning of the book to indicate that the Second World War did not begin with the invasion of Poland in 1939, but three years earlier in Spain.

Eisler selected less than a quarter of the published photoepigrams (fifteen out of sixty-nine) and set them to music in 1957, shortly after Brecht's death. The selected photoepigrams echoed many of the ideas on war and fascism he had already articulated in the *German Symphony*. Like Brecht's four-line poems, the musical settings are short and aphoristic. Eisler intended for the corresponding photoepigram to be projected as a visual

14 Bertolt Brecth, *Kriegsfibel* (Berlin: Eulenspiegel Verlag, 1955). On Eisler's work see Gerd Rienäcker, "Fibel-Musik? Anmerkungen zu Hanns Eislers und Paul Dessaus Vertonungen der Kriegsfibel", in *Fokus "Deutsches Miserere" von Paul Dessau und Bertolt Brecht, Festschrift Peter Petersen zum 65. Geburtstag*, eds. Nina Ermlich Lehmann, Sophie Fetthauer, Mathias Lehmann, Jörg Rothkamm, Silke Wenzel, and Kristina Wille, Hrsg. (Hamburg: von Bockel Verlag, 2005), S. 87–110; and Arnold Pistiak, "Übersehen oder verbannt? Hanns Eislers Bilder aus der Kriegsfibel", in *The Brecht Yearbook / Das Brecht-Jahrbuch 40*, ed. Theodore F. Rippey (Boydell Press, 2016), 100–124.

15 On this technique and on Brecht's *Kriegsfibel* see Anya Feddersen, "Kriegsfibel", in *Brecht Handbuch*, vol. 2, ed. Jan Knopf (Stuttgart and Weimar: J. B. Metzler, 2001), 382–397.

accompaniment to each movement in the performance of his *Bilder aus dem Kriegsfibel.*[16]

Like Brecht, Eisler also chose to open his work with a reference to the Spanish Civil War. The photoepigram reproduced in Fig. 7.1 corresponds to the first movement following the introduction. The image selected by Brecht depicts hundreds of rebels kneeling in an open-air Catholic thanksgiving mass in Barcelona after the city was captured in early 1939, shortly before the end of the civil war. In the foreground is "the conqueror", Juan Yagüe, one of the most violent right-wing generals of the civil war.[17] Brecht's poem is intended as a song of the Spanish rebels, who praise God for having made their victory possible. He is one of us, they sing:

| | |
|---|---|
| Die Glocken läuten und die Salven krachen. | The bells are pealing and the guns saluting. |
| Nun danket Gott als Mörder und als Christ! | Now thank God as a murderer and as a Christian! |
| Er gab uns Feuer, Feuer anzufachen. | He gave us fire, fire for kindling. |
| Wißt: Volk ist Pöbel, Gott ist ein Faschist. | Know this: the people are the rabble. God is a fascist. |

In his setting, Eisler imitated the sound of bells and machine-gun salvos through resolute *fortissimo* kettledrum motifs. To musically express the idea of the Catholic Church as both archaic and belligerent, he introduced typical gestures from Catholic contrapuntal sacred music of the Counter Reformation period. Particularly characteristic are the suspensions and lower neighbour notes in the voices preceding the final chord's third (Ex. 7.5, b. 27, alto and tenor). In its condemnation of the Spanish Church as an ally of anti-democratic forces, the piece is related to the *Peasant Cantata*. The poem's last line about the Church's connivance with the oppressors – "God is a fascist" – can be viewed as a response to the question that the bass singer poses to himself twice in the *Peasant Cantata* after witnessing the peasants' misfortunes: "What kind of God is this?"

16 Pistiak, "Übersehen oder verbannt?", 112.

17 The whole caption reads: "The conqueror, General Juan Yagüe, kneels before his throne-chair at an open-air mass in Barcelona's Plaza de Catalunya. In the background is the Hotel Colon, whose tower is seen again in the picture below, at lower right. Behind Yagüe are Generals Martín Alonso, Barrón, Vega. Yagüe and Solchaga moved off to chase Loyalists [to the democratically-elected Republic] to the border."

Fig. 7.1. Brecht's Fotoepigrame about the Spanish Civil War. Source: Bertolt Brecht, *Kriegsfibel* (Berlin: Eulenspiegel, 1955), p. 5. Source: Hanns-Eisler-Archiv no. 10549. Published with kind permission of the Hanns Eisler Archive.

Ex. 7.5. Hanns Eisler, *Bilder aus der Kriegsfibel*, second movement, bb. 19–28 (piano reduction from *Lieder und Kantaten*, vol. 10, p. 38). © by Deutscher Verlag für Musik Leipzig.

## (Mis)Readings of the *Peasant Cantata* in the GDR

As explained in Chapter 3, the *Peasant Cantata* became the eighth movement of Eisler's impressive *German Symphony*. He composed most of this "antifascist symphony" in the 1930s; however, due to various reasons – including the vicissitudes of exile and the political context in the early GDR – the work was not premiered until April 1959 at East Berlin's State Opera.[18] On that occasion, the Opera's concert dramaturgist, Horst Richter, noted in the programme notes that the *Peasant Cantata* "was manifestly written under the impression of the struggle for freedom in Spain. Eisler related the texts [...] to the uprising of Spanish peasants and workers against the feudalistic conditions in Spain."[19] This

18 On the chronology of the composition see Phleps, *Hanns Eislers Deutsche Sinfonie*, 63.

19 "Diese Kantate wurde [...] sichtlich unter dem Eindruck des Freiheitskampfes in Spanien geschrieben. Die Texte [...] bezog Eisler auf die Erhebung spanischer Bauern und Arbeiter gegen die feudalistischen Zustände in Spanien." Horst Richter, "Die 'Deutsche Sinfonie. Berlin, IV. Sonderkonzert'", in *Programmheft Deutsche Staatsoper der Staatskapelle, 24.4.1959* (Berlin: Staatsoper, 1959), 2. In Germany, a concert dramaturge (Konzertdramaturg) is the person in charge, among other tasks, of writing

information almost certainly came from Eisler, with whom Richter most likely had an interview before the concert. Significantly, the *Peasant Cantata* was the only movement in the entire *German Symphony* whose political meaning received attention in Richter's programme notes; for the other movements, he penned only a few words about purely formal features, such as the number of sections, the number of themes, or the musical form. As discussed in Chapter 3, Eisler composed this cantata inspired by the war in Spain; however, he did not intend the work to be interpreted exclusively in relation to that conflict, but rather from a more universal perspective as a broad denunciation of fascism and oppression. Why did he and Richter then decide to "unveil" the meaning of the cantata's symbolic elements in relation to the Spanish war and to foreground the work's connections to that conflict?

There were two main reasons for this decision. Firstly, linking the cantata to the civil war was part of the official narratives and propagandistic discourses about "the struggle for freedom in Spain" that were commonplace, as mentioned, in the post-1956 period. Secondly, and more importantly, this approach aimed to dissuade the audience from interpreting the *Peasant Cantata* as related to the GDR's contemporary political crisis concerning the collectivisation of agriculture. A few years earlier, in 1952, the GDR authorities had decided at the Second Party Conference of the SED to "lay the foundations of socialism" in the new state. For agriculture, this meant the transition to collectivisation based on the Soviet model. The farms, most of which were still private, were to join together "voluntarily" to form agricultural production cooperatives, known as LPGs. The vast majority of farmers opposed these measures. Until 1957, collectivisation focused on the expropriation of large private properties for distribution as small parcels to unlanded "new" peasants, and the creation of LPGs. That year, however, the SED agreed on new measures to enforce the mass entry of all peasants – including smallholders – into these cooperatives. Just months before the premiere of the *German Symphony*, these processes of agricultural collectivisation entered a stricter phase. These measures culminated in the passage of a new law two months after the premiere of the *German Symphony*. Enforcement of the law included massive intimidation campaigns against dissenting landowners, many of whom decided to flee to West Germany or resisted by burning their estates, allowing their cattle to die, or even committing suicide.[20] Even though the concert notes made it clear that the *Peasant Cantata* had been composed in the 1930s, the remark on how to interpret its libretto was most likely aimed at avoiding any reading that might relate Silone's and especially Brecht's lyrics – "Peasant, rise up! Take your course!" – to this serious political crisis in the GDR.

---

the notes for concerts played at a given institution.

20 A good summary of this crisis is Jens Schöne, *Die Landwirtschaft der DDR 1945–1990* (Erfurt: Landeszentrale für politische Bildung Thüringen, 2005), 24–36.

## Farewells to Spain

Immediately after the twentieth anniversary of the beginning of the war, Erich Weinert's German version of the *Marcha del Quinto Regimiento* was included in the official songbook of the GDR's National People's Army (Fig. 7.2) and in the songbook of the SED's official youth organisation, Freie Deutsche Jugend (FDJ, or Free German Youth).[21] Both books included additional battle songs about the Spanish Fifth Regiment and the International Brigades by communist composers Carlos Palacio, Paul Dessau, Grigori Schneerson, Nikolai Tschemberdschi, and others. The *Marsch des 5. Regiments* was recorded several times in the GDR. Eisler scholar Manfred Grabs arranged it for choir and wind chamber ensemble as late as the early 1980s.[22] The case of *No pasarán*, the other song that Eisler composed for the Spanish Fifth Regiment, is quite different, as it was not included in any GDR songbook. The reasons for this omission are unclear. Did Eisler, or the GDR authorities, not consider the work to possess sufficient artistic merit, thereby actively preventing its use in the GDR? Or did the composer simply forget about this song more than a decade after its composition?

As has been recently demonstrated, the dogmatism of the GDR's institutional discourses regarding the civil war frequently generated tensions and contradictions with the individual memories of former participants in that conflict.[23] This tension appears to have also characterised Eisler's later life, coinciding with a notable increase in institutional propaganda after 1956. Although the Spanish Civil War was a prominent feature of the GDR's official propaganda during this period, Eisler rarely discussed his participation in that conflict and never in heroic or nostalgic terms. This stands in stark contrast to the narratives of most former interbrigadists living in the GDR, including Eisler's friend Ernst Busch, whose accounts of the war were often imbued with a sense of the epic, sentimentality, and nostalgia.

Eisler's limited interest in glorifying the Spanish Civil War is evident in the two songs he composed about the conflict towards the end of his life. He

21 "Marsch des Fünften Regiments", in *Soldaten singen. Liederbuch der Nationalen Volksarmee* (Berlin: Verlag des Ministeriums für nationale Verteidigung, 1957), 80–81; *Liederbuch der deutschen Jugend. Leben Singen Kämpfen*, eds. Alexander Ott, Siegfried Stolte, Fritz Bachmann, Manfred Grüttner, Wille Hennig, and Heinz Knott (Berlin: Neues Leben, 1958), 113.

22 Grabs, *Hanns Eisler*, 118–119; and Hanns Eisler and Erich Weinert, *Marsch des 5. Regiments.* Arranged for choir and ensemble by Manfred Grabs (Leipzig: Deutsche Verlag für Musik, 1984). Grabs scored the arrangement for voice(s) and an ensemble comprising flute, two B-flat clarinets, one E-flat clarinet, bassoon, two tenor saxophones, horn, two trumpets, trombone, contrabass, and percussion. He based his arrangement on the version published in Mayer-Serra's *Revolutionary International Songbook* (1937), which includes an introductory passage likely not composed by Eisler (see Chapter 4).

23 See Asholt et al., *Der spanische Bürgerkrieg*, particularly the preface.

Marsch des Fünften Regiments

Fig. 7.2. Hanns Eisler, *Marsch des Fünften Regiments, in Soldaten singen. Liederbuch der Nationalen Volksarmee* (Berlin: Verlag des Ministeriums für nationale Verteidigung, 1957), 80–81.

did not write these pieces of his own volition but was commissioned to do so. The earliest of these was requested in 1956 by the GDR's Ministry of National Defence to commemorate the twentieth anniversary of the war's commencement. Eisler was tasked with composing a marching song that would be "not too difficult" for the tank crews of the National People's Army, and he was instructed to use the lyrics of Weinert's *Lied der Tankisten* (*Song of the Tank Crewmen*).[24] This poem is a call to the tankmen of the International Brigades to

24 A certain "Klötzner" from the "Polit-Verwaltung" of the Ministry of National Defence wrote to Eisler in early 1956 (the exact date is unknown): "Dear Comrade Eisler. We have the following wishes: 1) a melody for the text by Erich Weinert 'Lied der

fight with all their might against fascism and for the sake of freedom. Weinert had written it in 1937 while in Spain.

| | |
|---|---|
| Auf, zum Angriff, Tankbrigaden,<br>Da uns ruft der Freiheit Krieg!<br>In die Schlachtfront, Kameraden!<br>Spaniens Sieg ist unser Sieg. | Go, attack, tank brigades,<br>as freedom calls us to war!<br>To the battlefront, comrades!<br>Spain's victory is our victory. |
| Kamen wir aus vielen Ländern,<br>Eint uns doch der Zeit Gebot.<br>Unsere Kraft nur wird sie ändern.<br>Freiheit heißt – Faschistentod! | We came from many countries,<br>but we are united by the needs of our time.<br>Only our strength will bring change.<br>Freedom means: death to the fascists! |
| Mögen ihre Bomber kreisen,<br>Mögen die Granaten schrein –<br>Unsere Fäuste sind von Eisen,<br>Unser Herz wird mutvoll sein. | Their bombers may surround us,<br>their grenades may shriek –<br>Our fists are made of iron,<br>Our hearts will be brave. |
| Durch die Schanzen der Faschisten<br>Bricht der Stoß der Eisentanks.<br>Ans Gewehr! Gebt Gas, Tankisten!<br>Malmt die feindliche Phalanx! | Through the trenches of the fascists<br>break the thrust of the iron tanks.<br>To arms! Faster, tankmen!<br>Smash the enemy's phalanx! |
| [three additional stanzas follow] | [three additional stanzas follow] |

Despite the resolute and aggressive tone of the lyrics, and the fact that the song was primarily addressed to GDR soldiers, Eisler's minor-mode composition does not display either the menacing character found in some of his interwar battle songs – most notably the *Comintern Song* – or the celebratory quality of his *Kampfmusik*-styled works from the 1950s, such as the *Linker Marsch*. The song opens with a sequenced quotation of the initial motif from the *Song of the United Front* (Ex. 7.6, bb. 7–8), likely referencing the Popular Front's antifascist strategy as well as the French and Spanish governments of the mid-1930s. *Lied der Tankisten* was apparently premiered on 18 July 1956 in East Berlin, coincid-

Tankisten'. We believe that it could make a good marching song for the tankmen of the National People's Army. So please don't make it too difficult. Please include a piano part." ("Werter Genosse Eisler. Wir haben folgende Wünsche: 1) zu dem Text von Erich Weinert "Lied der Tankisten" eine Melodie. Wir glauben, daßdaraus ein gutes Marschlied f[ür] d[ie] Panzerleute der Nationalen Volksarmee werden könnte. Also bitte nicht zu schwierig setzen. Bitte mit Klavierauszug.") "Lied der Tankisten" (1956), HEA, cat. no. 5700, and Zusatz (supplementary material therein).

Ex. 7.6. Hanns Eisler, *Lied der Tankisten*, 1956 (bb. 5–10).
© by Deutscher Verlag für Musik Leipzig.

ing with the day on which Eisler, along with many others, was awarded the Hans Beimler Medal. The song's use extended well beyond this commemorative context, as its vocal line was later included in the aforementioned songbooks for the National People's Army and the FDJ.

Eisler's final composition concerning the Spanish war was a commission from his close friend Ernst Busch. In 1961, just a few months before Eisler's death, Busch requested that he set one of his own lyrics to music for inclusion on an upcoming album, *Canciones de las Brigadas Internacionales* (*Songs of the International Brigades*). Busch's lyrics, entitled *Abschied von Spanien* (*Farewell to Spain*), idealise the Spanish war in a sentimental and nostalgic manner characteristic of much of the official GDR propaganda of the time.

| *Spanien* (also known as *Abschied von Spanien*) | *Spain* (also known as *Farewell to Spain*) |
|---|---|
| Wie könnten wir je vergessen das Land<br>darin wir unsre Besten gelassen.<br>Das Land, das uns alle vereinigt fand<br>im Kämpfen, im Lieben und Hassen | How could we ever forget the land<br>where we left our best?<br>The land that united us all<br>in fighting, in loving, and in hating? |
| Denn Länder, in den man sorglos gelebt<br>verläßt man ohne Betrüben<br>Doch das Land, mit dem ~~wir~~ man gehofft und gebebt<br>Das werden wir ewig lieben.[25] | For those countries where we lived carefree,<br>we leave without sorrow,<br>but the land with which ~~we~~ one hoped and trembled,<br>that [land] we shall love forever. |

25 Ernst Busch, "Spanien", Ernst-Busch-Archiv, cat. no. 527, AdK, Berlin.

There are two pieces of evidence that suggest Eisler attempted to distance himself, as much as possible, from such idealisation. The first is the small yet significant change Eisler made to Busch's original lyrics, as noted above. The composer altered the word "*wir*" (we) to "*man*" (one) in the penultimate line of the text. More importantly, the final bars of his music setting convey the ironic distance with which Eisler positioned himself in relation to Busch's romanticisation of the conflict.

The composer set the opening line, which reflects nostalgic memories of the war, to a motif resembling the beginning of his 1953 concert song *Und ich werde nicht mehr sehen das Land* (*And I Will No Longer See the Land*), a piece whose lyrics evoke the German exiles' longing for their homeland. While this musical choice might appear to suggest that Eisler shared Busch's nostalgic idealisation of the conflict, the coda unmistakably conveys a sense of unease, which can only be related to the message conveyed by the lyrics. The unconventional dissonant closing section, following the final words "ewig lieben" (love forever) in reference to wartime Spain, stands out as the most striking feature of *Spanien*. The dominant chord on C for the third beat of bar 16 resolves through a progression of two dissonant augmented triads on C and F followed by a minor plagal cadence to a final major-to-minor tonic sonority, including a very explicit descending semitone (A–A-flat). Eisler instructs performers to play this coda "without ritardando", and thus, unsentimentally (Ex. 7.7). I interpret this unconventional closing, along with the small yet significant change Eisler made to the lyrics, as indicative of his objections near the end of his life to the romanticisation of the Spanish war in GDR propaganda, in which Busch played a prominent role.

For the recording of *Spanien* for the aforementioned album, Busch asked his arrangers to replace Eisler's weird closing bars – the final augmented triads and major-to-minor sonority – with a more harmonically conventional ending. Ex. 7.8 shows how the arrangers modified the final bars of Eisler's *Spanien*. This amendment of Eisler's music was a remarkable move considering the composer's very recent death.

Further evidence of Eisler's discontent with the propagandistic idealisation of the Spanish war can be seen in the editorial choices he made when publishing *Das Lied vom 7. Januar* as part of the fifth volume of his vocal works collection, *Lieder und Kantate* (*Songs and Cantatas*).[26] In this 1961 edition of the piece, Eisler made only one alteration to the 1937 original: the addition of a *piano* dynamic marking for the entire song. This marking was absent from the version Busch had published during the civil war in the soldiers' songbook *Kampflieder der Internationalen Brigaden*. By adding this *piano* marking, Eisler seemingly aimed to prevent any overly emphatic or "heroic" interpretation of the song, which, as discussed in Chapter 2, he composed as an elegy for the massacre of dozens of German interbrigadists during his time in Spain.

26 Hanns Eisler, *Lieder und Kantaten*, vol. 5 (Berlin: Deutsche Akademie der Künste, 1961), 103.

Ex. 7.7. Eisler's *Spanien*, closing section. (Source: Ernst-Busch-Archiv (AdK), Berlin, sig. 527). © by Deutscher Verlag für Musik Leipzig.

Ex. 7.8. Closing bars of the version of *Spanien* recorded by Busch, as arranged by Andre Asriel and Hans Hauska (Source: Ernst-Busch-Archiv (AdK), Berlin, sig. 474, 475). © by Deutscher Verlag für Musik Leipzig.

However, this subtle adjustment did not stop Busch from recording the song a few months later in a markedly epic style, in line with the GDR's preferred narrative of the Spanish war. Busch included this rendition in the aforementioned album *Canciones de las Brigadas Internacionales*, which became one of his most popular records.[27] In addition to Eisler's instruction not to sing *Das Lied vom 7. Januar* too loudly, his silence towards the end of his life regarding

[27] Ernst Busch, *Canciones de las Brigadas Internacionales*, Aurora, 1963 (Au 5 80 001/002), VEB Deutsche Schallplatten Berlin. The album was reissued in 1964, 1968, 1974, 1976.

the civil war, along with the dissonant conclusion of *Abschied von Spanien*, all point to a growing unease with the glorification of the Spanish war, which became more prevalent in the GDR after 1956. While refusing the Hans Beimler Medal would have been difficult for him, the lost war against fascism in Spain seems to have remained a less romanticised memory for Eisler than for most *Spanienkämpfer* in the GDR.

# Appendix 1
## Battle Songs by Spanish Communist Composers

The table below presents all the battle songs composed by Spanish communist composers during the Republican period (1931–1939) for which the complete score (typically the vocal melody and piano accompaniment) has been preserved. This genre of propaganda song was referred to by various names in wartime Spain, including *himnos* (anthems), *canciones de lucha* (songs of struggle), *canciones revolucionarias* (revolutionary songs), or *canciones de guerra* (songs of war). These terms were generally used synonymously. I have translated all these terms as "battle song", as this is the term most commonly employed in English during the 1930s. The songs are listed in chronological order and divided into two blocks: those composed before the war and those created during the conflict. The compositions included in this table constitute the analytical corpus of my study on the influence of Eisler's *Kampflieder* in Republican Spain.

*Songs Composed Before the Civil War*

| Title | Lyrics | Music | Date | Sources / Commentaries |
| --- | --- | --- | --- | --- |
| *Himno de las bibliotecas proletarias* (*Hymn of the Proletarian Libraries*) | Rafael Alberti | Vicente Salas Viu | 1933 | This is the earliest battle song by a Spanish communist composer for which I have located sources. The vocal melody was published in the communist literary magazine *Octubre*.[1] It seems that the song was intended to be performed *a cappella*, lacking a piano accompaniment. |
| *Himno a Thaelmann* (*[Ernst] Thaelmann Hymn*) | Rafael Alberti | Joaquín Villatoro | Late 1933 or early 1934 | This song and the *Himno a Luis Carlos Prestes* (see below) concern then-imprisoned foreign communist leaders as part of the personality cults within the communist movement. On sources for this song see Chapter 5.[2] |
| *Bandera roja* (*Red Banner*) | Pedro Galeote | Manuel Ramos | c.a 1935 or 1936? | Ramos was a self-taught composer. He sent this song to the Soviet Union in 1935. The piece is included in the Soviet songbook *Pasaremos! Canciones de guerra* (1938).[3] |

1 Vicente Salas Viu, *Himno de las bibliotecas proletarias*, *Octubre* 3 (August–September 1933): 12–13.

2 Joaquín Villatoro composed *A los mártires de Asturias. Octubre 1934* (*To the Martyrs of Asturias. October 1934*) in 1935. This song is not included in the table because it is not a marching battle song, but rather a slow song of mourning to commemorate the fallen in the strike that took place in Asturias in 1934. A leaflet with the song is preserved in the Archivo de la memoria histórica (Salamanca), catalogued as "Panfletos-566-567-580-581".

3 Grigori Schneerson, ed., *Pasaremos! Canciones de guerra. Испанские революционные песни* (Moscow: Art State Publishing House, 1938).

| Title | Lyrics | Music | Date | Sources / Commentaries |
|---|---|---|---|---|
| *Himno a Luis Carlos Prestes* (*Hymn to* [Brazilian communist leader] *Luis Carlos Prestes*) | Armand Guerra | Carlos Palacio & Rafael Espinosa | early 1936. | *Das Lied der Internationalen Brigaden* is a contrafacta of this song by Erich Weinert. Apparently, it became rather popular during the war among the interbrigadists. A copy of the score of this song is kept at the Centro de Documentación de la Música Española Contemporánea (F. Juan March). |
| | | *Songs Composed During the Civil War* | | |
| *Las Compañías de Acero* (*The Steel Companies*) | Luis de Tapia | Carlos Palacio | Early autumn 1936 | These are the only songs whose score seems to have survived of the six composed in the autumn of 1936 at the request of the PCE (see Chapter 5). |
| *Canto a la Marina* (*Hymn to the Navy*) | Luis de Tapia | Salvador Bacarisse | | |
| *Miliciano popular* (*Popular militiaman*) | Luis de Tapia? | Rafael Espinosa | | |

| Title | Lyrics | Music | Date | Sources / Commentaries |
|---|---|---|---|---|
| *Venguemos a los caídos* (*Avenge the fallen*) | Félix V. Ramos | Carlos Palacio | 1937 | These six songs were published in 1937 in the songbook *Seis canciones de guerra* (*Six War Songs*). These first five were awarded in the competition organised by the Ministry of Public Instruction and Fine Arts. The last one, by Fernández Blanco, had not been submitted for that contest but was also included in the book because of "its artistic merit".[1] All of them exemplify modernist battle songs, composed in an innovative style for the genre. |
| *Canto nocturno en las trincheras* (*Night song in the trenches*) | José Miguel Ripoll | Leopoldo Cardona | | |
| *U.H.P.* (*Unión de Hermanos Proletarios*) – (UHP Proletarian Brothers' Union) | Alberto Alcantarilla Carbó | Francisco Merenciano Bosch | | |
| *Canto a la flota republicana* (*Ode to the Republican Navy*) | Félix V. Ramos | Rafael Casasempere | | |
| *Himno* (*Hymn*) | Carlos Ordóñez | Carlos Ordóñez | | |
| *Nueva Humanidad* (*New Humanity*) | Carlos Caballero | Evaristo Fernandez Blanco | | |

1 *Seis canciones de guerra* (Barcelona: Consejo Central de la Música, 1937).

| Title | Lyrics | Music | Date | Sources / Commentaries |
|---|---|---|---|---|
| *Los campesinos* (*The Peasants*) | Antonio Aparicio | Enrique Casal Chapí | 1937 | On the compositional context and the sources for these songs see Chapter 5. |
| *Alerta* (*Alert*) | Felix Vicente Ramos | Rodolfo Halffter | 1937 | |
| *Himno de la Sexta División* (*Anthem of the Sixth Division*) | Pedro Garfías | Carlos Palacio | ca. 1937 | A copy of the score of this song is kept at the Centro de Documentación de la Música Española Contemporánea (F. Juan March). |
| *Juventudes proletarias* (*Proletarian Youth*) | Carlos Caballero | Rafael Espinosa | ca. 1937 | To my knowledge, the above-mentioned Soviet songbook *Pasaremos* (1938) is the only surviving musical source of this song. |
| *Marxa del Exèrcit Popular* (*March of the Popular Army*). | Joan Oliver i Sallarès | Anon. (Ernst H. Meyer) | Undated, ca. 1936 | On this song see Chapter 4. |
| *U. H. P* (*Unión de Hermanos Proletarios*) | P.[?] Gallote (Pedro Galeote?) | Manuel Ramos | Before 1938 | The song was included in the above-mentioned Soviet songbook *Pasaremos* (1938). This is seemingly the only surviving source of this piece. |
| *Peleamos, peleamos* (*We fight, we fight*) | Pedro Garfías | Carlos Palacio | ca. 1938 | The score is included in the Soviet Songbook *антифашистские песни* (*Antifascist Songs*), published in Moscow in 1939.[1] |

1 Grigori Schneerson, ed., *антифашистские песни* (Moscow: State Music Publishing House, 1939), 2–5.

| Title | Lyrics | Music | Date | Sources / Commentaries |
|---|---|---|---|---|
| *Himno a La Gloriosa* (*Anthem of La Gloriosa*) | Jesús García Leoz | Rafael Alberti | ca. late 1937 | This is the only battle song by García Leoz (or the only one that has survived). On the compositional context and the sources of this song see Chapter 5. |
| *Himno del Quinto cuerpo* (*Anthem of the Fifth Corps*). | José Herrera Petere | Rafael Oropesa | 1938 | This is seemingly the only battle song by communist composer Oropesa. One of the leaflets published during the war that include the vocal melody of the song is kept at the Fondo Fotográfico de José Herrera Petere, at Centro de la Fotografía y de la Imagen Histórica de Guadalajara. |

# Appendix 2
# Otto Mayer-Serra's Writings in Germany and Spain

Mayer-Serra began his career as a music writer in 1930 in Berlin. His articles for two periodicals associated with the German communist movement are particularly significant from this period: the magazine for proletarian radio amateurs *Arbeiterfunk* (*Workers' Radio*) and the renowned yet short-lived journal *Musik und Gesellschaft. Arbeitsblätter für soziale Musikpflege und Musikpolitik.* (*Music and Society: Worksheets for Social Musical Culture and Musical Politics*).[1] In 1932, he recounted his experiences as a sound technician in an article for the prestigious music journal *Die Musik*. He had acquired this experience as a member of a four-man research team led by the Berlin Marxist conductor Hermann Scherchen. This team conducted experiments on recording and broadcasting techniques in the Berlin radio studios of the Reichs-Rundfunk-Gesellschaft (German Broadcasting Corporation) and at the Rundfunkversuchsstelle (Broadcasting Experimentation Centre) of the Berlin Conservatory.[2]

His career as a music journalist prospered in Spain, where his training as a musicologist was much more exceptional than it had been in Germany. This expertise was promptly acknowledged by the Barcelona musical establishment. During the nearly six years he spent in the city, Mayer-Serra published approximately two hundred articles, primarily in Catalan, with a few in Spanish and other European languages. In November 1933, he was appointed head of the

1 The complete run of *Musik und Gesellschaft* from 1930 to 1931 was reprinted in a single volume in 1978. The editor, Dorothea Kolland, examines the historical significance of the journal in the preface to this reprint; see Dorothea Kolland, ed., *Musik und Gesellschaft* (Berlin: Das europäische Buch, 1978), VII–XXX. For further insight into the historical importance of the journal, see Peter Sühring, "Musik als sozialer Akt und die Grenzen der Gemeinschaft: Eine Einführung in die Zeitschrift Musik und Gesellschaft, 1930/31", *Forum Musikbibliothek* (2020): 36–44.

2 The Hermann-Scherchen-Archiv (AdK) retains a substantial corpus of documents relating to this team (c.f., folders 332, 339, 340, 342, 345, 358, 362). On Scherchen's activities promoting acoustic experimentation in the 1930s, see Martha Brech, "Der lange Weg zum natürlichen Klangbild. Die Beiträge Hermann Scherchens und seiner Mitarbeiter zur Verbesserung der Musikübertragung im Rundfunk der Weimarer Republik", in *Impulse und Antworten. Festschrift für Manfred Krause*, ed. Bernhard Feiten (Berlin: Wissenschaft & Technik, 1999), 25–34.

musical section of *Mirador*, which was then one of the most esteemed Catalan periodicals. Between that date and October 1935, he contributed the majority of his articles to this journal. In the prewar period, he also occasionally published in prestigious Spanish and European music journals such as *Revista musical catalana*, *Musicografía*, *Anbruch*, *La Revue Musicale*, and *The Musical Times*. Mayer-Serra was dismissed from his position at *Mirador* in October 1935, primarily due to personal and professional disagreements with the journal's owners. He subsequently began working as a music journalist for the magazine published by the Ford Company. This opulent magazine targeted an upper-class readership, reflecting the company's potential clientele. For reasons that remain unclear, he ceased working for the magazine in February 1936, coinciding – perhaps significantly – with the electoral victory of the left-wing coalition Frente Popular.

During the civil war, Mayer-Serra published his articles mainly in the PSUC newspaper *Treball* and the new, PSUC-controlled *Mirador*. Almost all the articles he published in *Treball* appear unsigned. (He only signed his articles for this periodical twice, once as "Otto Mayer" and once with the initials "O. M.".) These unsigned features bear the hallmarks of Mayer-Serra's writing style, preferred topics, and vocabulary, suggesting his authorship. Following the final cessation of publication for *Mirador* in June 1937 due to the war's effects, Mayer-Serra's writing activity diminished to sporadic contributions to several esteemed Spanish cultural journals, including the journal of the Consejo Central de la Música. His last work in Spain – a critical review of the zarzuela *Las golondrinas* – was published in April 1938 in the organ of the Front intellectual antifeixista (Antifascist Intellectual Front), *Meridià*.

The table below presents the journals in which Mayer-Serra published his writings prior to his exile in Mexico in 1939. Included are complete references to all his works for which I have documentary evidence, encompassing both those with confirmed authorship (as he signed them) and those published anonymously in *Treball*, but whose style, vocabulary, and subject matter strongly indicate that they were almost certainly authored by Mayer-Serra.

| *Year(s)* | *Title* | *Issues* | *Amount* |
|---|---|---|---|
| **BERLIN** | | | |
| 1930 | *Arbeiterfunk* | 2, 12, 31 | 3 |
| 1930 | *Musik und Gesellschaft* | 1 | 1 |
| 1931 | *Die Musikpflege* | 8 | 1 |
| 1932 | *Die Musik* | 2 | 1 |
| **SPAIN / PREWAR PERIOD** | | | |
| 1933–1935 | *Mirador* | 249–252, 255–264, 266–285, 287–291, 293, 296–298, 300–315, 319–323, 325–331, 333–335, 337–342, 344–346 | 101 |
| 1933–1934 | *Anbruch* | 1933, issue 9/10; 1934, issue 4 | 2 |
| 1934–1936 | *Revista musical catalana* | 362, 364, 372, 377, 383, 388, 390 | 7 |
| 1934, 1936 | *La Revue Musical* | 149, 163 | 2 |
| 1934, 1936 | *Schweizerische Musikzeitung und Sängerblatt* | 74, no. 14/15 and 16/17; 76, no. 1 | 3 |
| 1935–1936 | *Musicografía* | 31, 34, 37 | 3 |
| 1935–1936 | *Revista Ford* | 36–39 | 4 |
| 1935 | *The Musical Times* | 76, no. 1107 | 1 |
| 1936 | *Revista brasileira de música* | 3, no 2 and 3–4 | 2 |
| **SPAIN / WARTIME** | | | |
| 1936 | *Treball* | Uncertain (several dozen articles, almost all of them unsigned) | |
| 1936–1937 | *Mirador* | 390, 391, 394, 396, 400, 402–405, 407, 414, 416–418, 420 | 15 |
| 1937 | *Nova Iberia* | 1 | 1 |
| 1938 | *Hora de España* | 13 | 1 |
| 1938 | *Meridià* | 10, 12 | 2 |
| 1938 | *Música* | 3 | 1 |

## Music Sources in Chronological Order of Publication

### *Germany*

"Musik und Musikpflege im Rundfunk." *Arbeiterfunk* 5, no. 2 (10 January 1930): 17–18.

"Funkische Musikpflege." *Arbeiterfunk* 5, no. 12 (21 March 1930): 152.

"Neue Musik Berlin 1930." *Arbeiterfunk* 5, no. 31 (1 August 1930): 337.

"'Musik und Fabrikarbeit' als Gegenstand einer historischen Theorie." *Musik und Gesellschaft* 1, no. 5 (October 1930): 144–145.

"Berliner städtische Musikpflege." *Die Musikpflege* 2, no. 8 (August 1931): 215–224.

"Der Tonmeister in Rundfunk." *Die Musik* 24, no. 11 (August 1932): 805–808.

### *Spain (before the Civil War)*

"Musik in Katalonien." *Anbruch* 15, no. 9/10 (November/December 1933): 154–156.

"Mossèn Higini Anglès. Un gran musicòleg català." *Mirador* 249 (9 November 1933): 8.

"Igor Stravinsky." *Mirador* 250 (16 November 1933): 8.

"Manuel de Falla. Obertura al Liceu." *Mirador* 251 (23 November 1933): 251.

"El 'mixer' dels sons. Una nova professió creada per la tècnica." *Mirador* 252 (30 November 1933): 8.

"'El arte de dirigir la orquesta', de Hermann Scherchen." *Mirador* 255 (21 December 1933): 11.

"'Oedipus Rex' al Liceu. Un oratori de Stravinsky." *Mirador* 256 (28 December 1933): 8.

"'Història de la música', de J. Wolf and 'Wandlungen der Oper' de P. Bekker." *Mirador* 257 (4 January 1934): 8.

"Arthur Honeger." *Mirador* 258 (11 January 1934): 8.

"La vida musical a Barcelona." *Mirador* 258 (11 January 1934): 8.

"La vida musical a Barcelona." *Mirador* 259 (18 January 1934): 8.

"La crisi de la vida musical. Música i economia." *Mirador* 260 (25 January 1934): 8.

"La vida musical a Barcelona." *Mirador* 260 (25 January 1934): 8.

"Bibliografia musical: Manuel Borgunyó: 'La música, el cant i l'escola.'" *Mirador* 261 (1 February 1934): 8.

"La crisi de la vida musical. La reorganització del Liceu." *Mirador* 261 (1 February 1934): 8.

"La vida musical a Barcelona." *Mirador* 262 (8 February 1934): 12.

"Les edicions de música. J. S. Bach. Inventionen und Sinfonien." *Mirador* 262 8 February 1934): 12.

"Perfils de la música espanyola. Un processat il·lustre [José Subirá]." *Mirador* 263 (15 February 1934): 8.

"Nous camins de la pedagogia musical." *Mirador* 264 (22 February 1934): 8.

"'La Història Mundial de la Dansa', de Curt Sachs." *Revista musical catalana* 362 (February 1934): 47–51.

"La vida musical a Barcelona." *Mirador* 265 (1 March 1934): 8.

"Una nova òpera d'E. Krenek." *Mirador* 266 (8 March 1934): 8.

"Música i tècnica. Reflexions sobre el disc." *Mirador* 267 (15 March 1934): 8.

"La vida musical a Barcelona." *Mirador* 268 (22 March 1934): 8.

"Curt Sachs a Barcelona." *Mirador* 268 (22 March 1934): 8.

"La vida musical a Barcelona." *Mirador* 269 (29 March 1934): 8.

"La vida musical a Barcelona." *Mirador* 270 (5 April 1934): 8.

"La vida musical a Barcelona." *Mirador* 271 (12 April 1934): 8.

"El BBC Year Book." *Mirador* 271 (12 April 1934): 8.

"La nostra discoteca. Les 'Tonadillas' de Granados." *Mirador* 272 (19 April 1934): 8.

"La vida musical a Barcelona. L'opera Amaia al Liceu." *Mirador* 272 (19 April 1934): 8.

"La vida musical a Barcelona. Casals dirigint la 'Simfonia dels Psalms'." *Mirador* 273 (26 April 1934): 8.

"Revista de Revistes." *Revista musical catalana* 364 (April 1934):142–143.

"Die Opersaison in Barcelona." *Anbruch* 16, no. 4 (April 1934): 85–86.

"Perfils de la música contemporània. Paul Hindemith." *Mirador* 274 (3 May 1934): 8.

"La vida musical a Barcelona." *Mirador* 274 (3 May 1934): 8.

"Una conferencia de Higini Anglès." *Mirador* 275 (10 May 1934): 8.

"Perfils de la música contemporània. La música hongaresa des d'ací." *Mirador* 276 (17 May 1934): 8.

"La vida musical a Barcelona. Balls Russos – Kreisler i Cortot." *Mirador* 277 (24 May 1934): 8.

"Perfils de la música contemporània. Un septuagenari: Richard Strauss." *Mirador* 278 (31 May 1934): 8.

"A propòsit de Wozzek [sic]." *Mirador* 279 (7 June 1934): 8.

"La nostra discoteca." *Mirador* 279 (7 June 1934): 8.

"Els antagonismes polítics en la música txeca." *Mirador* 280 (14 June 1934): 8.

"La vida musical a Barcelona. Dos homenatges: Arbós i Casals." *Mirador* 281 (21 June 1934): 8.

"Bibliografia musical: S. Nadel, 'Ferruccio Busonni (1866–1924). Records d'Eisenach del temps de Sebastià Bach." *Mirador* 282 (28 June 1934): 8.

"La nostra discoteca. El triomf del virtuosisme: Paul Whiteman." *Mirador* 283 (5 July 1934): 8.

"Cròniques de la música catalana. Joan Lamote de Grignon i la Banda Municipal." *Mirador* 284 (12 July 1934): 8.

"Beethoven en camisa bruna." *Mirador* 285 (19 July 1934): 8.

"Bibliografia. Nou manual dels diversos instruments." *Mirador* 285 (19 July 1934): 8.
"Chorwesen in Katalonien I." *Schweizerische Musikzeitung und Sängerblatt* 74, no. 14/15 (1 August 1934): 513–517.
"Fi de temporada. 'Catalunya renaixent', de K. Mengelberg." *Mirador* 287 (2 August 1934): 8.
"Perfils de la música contemporània. 'La Dona Serpent'." *Mirador* 288 (9 August 1934): 8.
"Una carta de Romain Rolland. Sobre un art musical soviètic." *Mirador* 289 (16 August 1934): 289.
"Perfils de la música contemporània. Elgar, Holst i Delius." *Mirador* 290 (23 August 1934): 8.
"Vida musical barcelonina. Un quartet inacabat de Schubert." *Mirador* 290 (23 August 1934): 8.
"Bibliografia musical." *Mirador* 291 (30 August 1934): 8.
"Chorwesen in Katalonien II." *Schweizerische Musikzeitung und Sängerblatt* 74, no. 16/17 (1 September 1934): 545–553.
"Cròniques de la música catalana. El mestre Francesc Pujol, compositor, pedagog i folklorista." *Mirador* 293 (13 September 1934): 8.
"Un reportatge de la Illa Daurada. Impressions musicals de Mallorca." *Mirador* 296 (4 October 1934): 8.
"La vida musical a Barcelona." *Mirador* 297 (18 October 1934): 8.
"Noves revistes musicals." *Mirador* 297 (18 October 1934): 8.
"La musique en Catalogne." *La Revue Musicale* 15, no. 149 (September–October 1934): 218–221.
"Crònica musical." *Mirador* 298 (25 October 1934): 8.
"Crònica musical." *Mirador* 300 (10 November 1934): 8.
"La vida musical a Barcelona." *Mirador* 301 (17 November 1934): 8.
"La vida musical a Barcelona." *Mirador* 302 (24 November 1934): 8.
"Crònica de la vida musical: 'El cavaller de la rosa', Hindemith desqualificat, Els mestres del llaüt." *Mirador* 303 (1 December 1934): 8.
"Audicions intimes. Alban Berg: 'Suite lírica'." *Mirador* 304 (8 December 1934): 8.
"Crònica musical. El cas Furtwaengler." *Mirador* 305 (15 December 1934): 8.
"La vida musical a Barcelona. Perspectives confortables." *Mirador* 306 (22 December 1934): 8.
"La nostra discoteca. Diversions nadalenques." *Mirador* 307 (29 December 1934): 8.
"Revista de Revistes." *Revista musical catalana* 372 (December 1934): 365–368.
"Noves perspectives. La música elèctrica." *Mirador* 308 (10 January 1935): 8.
"Crònica musical. La vida musical a Barcelona." *Mirador* 309 (17 January 1935): 8.
"Bibliografia musical." *Mirador* 310 (24 January 1935): 8.
"Crònica musical. Pau Casals a l'Obrera de Concerts." *Mirador* 311 (31 January 1935): 8.

"La vida musical. Els nostres estudiants de música." *Mirador* 312 (7 February 1935): 8.

"Perfils de la música moderna. 'Lulu', la nova òpera d'Alban Berg." *Mirador* 313 (14 February 1935): 8.

"La nostra discoteca." *Mirador* 214 (21 February 1935): 8.

"La vida musical. Reflexions herètiques sobre la 'Novena'." *Mirador* 315 (28 February 1935): 8.

"Sinopsi biogràfica." *Mirador* 319 (28 March 1935): 8.

"Cròniques de la música catalana. Baltasar Samper, il·lustrador de films." *Mirador* 320 (4 April 1935): 8.

"La vida musical a Barcelona." *Mirador* 321 (11 April 1935): 8.

"Otto Klemperer a Barcelona." *Mirador* 322 (18 April 1935): 8.

"Robert Gerhard, premiat." *Mirador* 322 (18 April 1935): 8.

"La nostra discoteca. Un grandiós homenatge a Bach." *Mirador* 323 (25 April 1935): 8.

"La Simfonia 'Mathis el Pintor', de Paul Hindemith." *Revista Musical Catalana* 377 (May 1935): 194–198.

"Musical Life in Catalonia." *The Musical Times* 76, no. 1107 (May 1935), 415–416.

"Sinopsi biogràfica." *Mirador* 324 (2 May 1935): 8.

"BBC Annual 1935." *Mirador* 325 (9 May 1935): 8.

"Perfils de la música contemporània. La 'Història del soldat'." *Mirador* 326 (16 May 1935): 8.

"La vida musical a Barcelona. Una ocasió perduda." *Mirador* 326 (16 May 1935): 8.

"La gran missa de Bach." *Mirador* 327 (23 May 1935): 8.

"La vida musical a Barcelona. L'Orfeó Català canta la 'Missa en si menor'." *Mirador* 328 (30 May 1935): 8.

"Crònica de l'actualitat. Una ocasió perduda?" *Mirador* 328 (30 May 1935): 8.

"Cròniques de la música catalana. La situació de la jove generació." *Mirador* 329 (6 June 1935): 8.

"La nostra discoteca. 'Mathis el pintor', simfonia de Hindemith." *Mirador* 330 (13 June 1935): 8.

"La vida musical de Barcelona. Fi de temporada." *Mirador* 330 (13 June 1935): 8.

"Des de Mallorca. Festivals Chopin." *Mirador* 331 (20 June 1935): 8.

"La nostra discoteca." *Mirador* 333 (4 July 1935): 8.

"Temes de sociologia musical. L'artista i el públic." *Mirador* 334 (11 July 1935): 8 (published in Spanish translation in *Musicografía* 31 (1935): 235–237).

"Bibliografia musical. 'Cravistas portuguezes'." *Mirador* 335 (18 July 1935): 8.

"La nostra discoteca." *Mirador* 337 (1 August 1935): 8.

"Bibliografia musical basca. 'Los esclavos felices'." *Mirador* 338 (8 August 1935): 8.

"La música. A propòsit de Paul Dukas." *Mirador* 339 (15 August 1935): 8.

"Temes de sociologia musical. Sectors de la vida musical." *Mirador* 340 (22 August 1935): 8 (published in Spanish translation in *Musicografía* 34 (1936): 19–21).

"La nostra discoteca. Apunts sobre l'estil de Haydn." *Mirador* 341 (29 August 1935): 8.

"Igor Stravinsky. 'Crónicas de mi vida'; La actualidad musical; Nuestra discoteca." *Ford* 4, no. 36 (September 1936): 312–313.

"La XII reunió de la SIMC." *Mirador* 342 (5 September 1935): 8.

"Sobre regionalisme musical." *Mirador* 342 (5 September 1935): 8.

"Praga 1935–Barcelona 1936. Una conversa interessantíssima." *Mirador* 344 (19 September 1935): 8.

"La nostra discoteca." *Mirador* 345 (26 September 1935): 8.

"Carta oberta. L'orquestra Pau Casals i la Banda Municipal." *Mirador* 346 (3 October 1935): 8.

"Joan Manén: 'Neró i Actea'." *Mirador* 346 (3 October 1935): 8.

"Mittenwald, el pueblo de los violines." *Ford* 4, no. 37 (October 1935): 336–338.

"Assaig sobre el valor actual de Riemann." *Revista musical catalana* 383 (November 1935): 455–456.

"El arte de dirigir la orquesta; E. Halffter; Noticias." *Ford* 4, no. 38 (December 1935): 428 and 472.

Review of "Adolfo Salazar's *La música actual en Europa y sus problemes*." *Schweizerische Musikzeitung und Sängerblatt* 76, no. 1 (January 1936): 60.

"Tableau de la música moderne à Barcelone." *La Revue Musicale* 17, no. 163 (February1936): 141–143.

"Bibliografía; Órganos modernos; Alban Berg; Revista de revistes." *Ford* 5, no. 39 (February 1936): 27 and 58–61.

"Apunts sobre Alban Berg." *Revista musical catalana* 388 (April 1936), 154–157 (published in Spanish translation in *Musicografía* 37 (May 1936): 67–69).

"Bibliografia. Noves obres de musica moderna." *Revista musical catalana* 390 (June 1936): 260–261.

"Notas bibliographicas. Bibliographia musical hespanhola em 1935." *Revista brasileira de Musica* 3, no. 2 (1936): 44–49.

"O XIV Festival da SIMC em Barcelona." *Revista brasileira de Musica* 3, no. 3–4 (1936): 504–512.

## *Spain (During the Civil War)*

Anon., "La nova estructuració dels espectacles públics." *Treball* (12 August 1936): 3.

Anon., "La col·lectivització del públic." *Treball* 1, no. 20 (13 August 1936): 3.

Anon., "Els grans músics catalans al marge de la revolució." *Treball* 1, no. 21 (14 August 1936): 2.

Anon., "La revolució al teatre." *Treball* 1, no. 22 (15 August 1936): 2.

Anon., "Compositors i autors, creeu la cançó revolucionària!" *Treball* 1, no. 26 (20 August 1936): 3.

Anon., "Cap a la depuració del caciquisme a 'Ràdio Associació de Catalunya.'" *Treball* 1, no. 34 (29 August. 1936): 6.

Anon., "Eduard Toldrá, el gran compositor català s'ha allistat als rengles de les milícies." *Treball* 1, no. 36 (1 September 1936): 6.

Anon., "A propòsit del '14 de Juliol' de Romain Rolland. Música sàvia i música popular." *Treball* 1, no. 43 (9 September 1936): 5.

O. M., "L'orientació moderna de l'ensenyament artístic a l'escola nova." *Treball* 1, no. 44 (10 September 1936): 8.

Anon., "Problemes de sociologia musical. Música viva y música 'museal' I." *Treball* 1, no. 48 (15 September 1936): 5.

Anon., "El concert de Pau Casals." *Treball* 1, no. 48 (15 September 1936): 5.

Anon., "Problemes de sociologia musical. Música viva y música 'museal' i II." *Treball* 1, no. 49 (16 September 1936): 5.

Anon., "A propòsit del gran míting d'unificació cultural. Els intel·lectuals davant el feixisme." *Treball* 1, no. 53 (20 September 1936): 8.

Anon., "Orientacions per al C.E.N.U. Els mestres necessitem una formació revolucionària." *Treball* 1, no. 55 (23 September 1936): 5.

Anon., "Cap a la liquidació de la universitat burguesa. El problema universitari." *Treball* 1, no. 57 (25 September 1936): 12.

Anon., "Perspectives." *Mirador* 390 (9 October 1936): 7.

"Bases de discussió. Què és música revolucionària?" *Mirador* 391 (15 October 1936): 7.

"L'apoliticisme del músic." *Mirador* 394 (12 November 1936): 7.

"Vicissituds de la música moderna. El fracàs de la SIMC." *Mirador* 396 (26 November 1936): 6.

"Hanns Eisler. Un gran músic revolucionari." *Mirador* 400 (24 December 1936): 7 (published in Spanish translation as: "Hanns Eisler. Un gran músico revolucionario." *El ejército Popular* 4 (1937): 56–57).

"La Catalogne musicale." *Nova Iberia* 1, no. 1 (January 1937): 36.

"La renovació de la vida musical. Orientacions professionals." *Mirador* 402 (7 January 1937): 7.

"Una descoberta sensacional." *Mirador* 403 (14 January 1937): 7.

"Educació marxista. La teoria com a arma del proletariat." *Treball* 2, no. 153 (15 January 1937): 6.

"Què és música 'selecta'?" *Mirador* 404 (21 January 1937): 7.

"Noves formes de divulgació musical. Concert a la fàbrica Filatures Fabra i Coats." *Mirador* 405 (29 January 1937): 10.

"Perfils de músics revolucionaris. Alan Bush." *Mirador* 406 (5 February 1937): 9.

"Els crims del feixisme. José Antonio assassinat." *Mirador* 406 (5 February 1937): 9.

Anon., "Salutació a Pau Casals des de l'Alemanya feixista." *Mirador* 406 (5 February 1937): 9.

"Música a mida. Una conversa interessant amb el mestre Bernat." *Mirador* 407 (12 February 1937): 8.

Anon., "Els músics soviètics donen exemple." *Mirador* 411 (19 February 1937): 9.

"Beethoven 1827–1937." *Mirador* 414 (1 April 1937): 4.

"Temes de sociologia musical El crític musical en la societat capitalista." *Mirador* 416 (15 April 1937): 9.

"Ha mort el gran compositor i organista francès Charles Widor." *Mirador* 417 (22 April 1937): 9.

"La constitució de la secció 'Música' al Casal de Cultura. La lluita al front musical." *Mirador* 418 (29 April 1937): 8.

"A propòsit de la Banda Municipal de Madrid. Al Teatre Nacional de Catalunya." *Mirador* 420 (20 1937): 9.

"La veritable neutralitat de l'artista." *Treball* 2, no. 428 (2 December 1937): 3.

"Una composició de Rudolf Halffter en honor de la U.R.S.S." *Treball* (21 December 1937): 2

"A propósito de dos nuevas composiciones de Rodolfo Halffter [*Alerta, Para la tumba de Lenin*], *Hora de España* 1 (1938): 89–92.

"Ha mort el gran compositor francès Maurice Ravel." *Treball* 3, no. 455 (2 January 1938): 5.

"La formidable tasca creadora dels musics soviètics." *Treball* 3, no. 480 (1 February 1938): 3.

"En torno de una sociología de la música." *Música* 1, no. 3 (March 1938): 30–38.

"La música i el front popular." *Meridià* 1, no. 10 (18 March 1938): 7.

"*Las golondrinas* al Liceu." *Meridià* 1, no. 12 (1 April 1938): 7.

# Select Bibliography

Adorno, Theodor W. "Zur gesellschaftlichen Lage der Musik." *Zeitschrift für Sozialforschung* 1 (1932): 103–124 and 356–378.

Adorno, Theodor W. *Gesammelte Schriften,* vol. 18, edited by Rolf Tiedemann. Frankfurt am Main: Shurkampf, 1984.

Adorno, Theodor W. *Beethoven. Philosophie der Musik. Fragmente und Texte,* edited by Rolf Tiedemann. Frankfurt am Main: Suhrkampf, 1993.

Agulhon, Maurice. *Marianne au combat. L'imagerie et la symbolique républicaines de 1789 à 1880.* Paris : Flammarion, 1979.

Agulhon, Maurice. *Marianne au pouvoir. L'imagerie et la symbolique républicaines de 1880 à 1914.* Paris : Flammarion, 1989.

Agulhon, Maurice. *Les Métamorphoses de Marianne. L'imagerie et la symbolique républicaines de 1914 à nos jours.* Paris: Flammarion, 2001.

Aisa, Ferran. *Una història de Barcelona. Ateneu Enciclopèdic Popular (1902–1999).* Barcelona: Virus, 2000.

Alonso, Diego. "Unquestionably decisive. Roberto Gerhard studies with Arnold Schoenberg." In *The Companion to Roberto Gerhard,* edited by Monty Adkins. London: Ashgate Publishing, 2013.

Alonso, Diego. *La creación musical de Roberto Gerhard durante el magisterio de Arnold Schoenberg. Neoclasicismo, octatonismo y organización proto-serial (1923–1928).* PhD diss., Universidad de La Rioja, 2015.

Alonso, Diego. "From the People to the People: The Reception of Hanns Eisler's Critical Theory of Music in Spain through the Writings of Otto Mayer-Serra." *Musicologica Austriaca* (6 December 2019), http://www.musau.org/parts/neue-article-page/view/76

Alonso, Diego. "Transnational Networks of Communist Musical Propaganda in the Spanish Civil War." *Journal of War & Culture Studies* 14, no. 4 (2021): 1–25.

Alonso, Diego. "Kampflieder, Satiere, Homoerotik. Ludwig Renns 'nicht vertonte Texte' aus der Zeit des Spanischen Bürgerkriegs im Hanns Eisler Archiv." *Eisler-Mitteilungen* 72 (February 2022): 7–13.

Amo García, Alfonso del, ed., *Catálogo General del Cine de la Guerra Civil.* Madrid: Filmoteca Española, 1996.

Anon., ed. *Workers Songbook 1934,* vol. 1. New York: Workers Music League, 1934.

Anon., ed. *Workers Songbook,* vol. 2. New York: Workers Music League, 1935.

Anon., ed. *Chants révolutionnaires de divers pays,* vol. 3. Paris: Editions sociales internationales, 1937.

Arias, Fernando. *La Valencia de los años 30. Entre el paraíso y el infierno.* Valencia: Ayuntamiento de Valencia, 1996.

Asaf'ev, Boris Vladimirovič. *Muzykal' naja forma kak prozess*, vol 1. Leningrad, Muzyka, 1930.

Asholt, Wolfgang, Rüdiger Reinecke, and Susanne Schlünder, eds., *Der spanische Bürgerkrieg in der DDR. Strategien intermedialer Erinnerungsbildung.* Frankfurt am Main: Vervuert, 2009.

Aviñoa, Xosé. *Enric Morera*. Barcelona: Nou Art Thor, 1985.

Aviñoa, Xosé. *Història de la Música Catalana, Valenciana i Balear*, vol. IV "Del Modernisme a la Guerra Civil (1900–1939)." Barcelona: Ed. 62, 1999.

Ayats, Jaume. *Córrer la sardana: balls, joves i conflictes.* Barcelona: Rafael Dalmau, 2006.

Barjau, Santiago. "Un cartellista alemany a Catalunya 1933–1938." *Serra d'Or* 432 (December 1995).

Bauer, Yehuda. *My Brother's Keeper. A History of the American Jewish Joint Distribution Committee, 1929–1939.* Philadelphia: The Jewish Publication Society of America, 1974.

Beevor, Antony. *The Battle for Spain. The Spanish Civil War 1936–1939.* New York: Penguin Books, 2006.

Bendel, Oliver. *Das revolutionäre Arbeitertheater der Weimarer Zeit. Theater als Instrument kommunistischer Propaganda*. PhD diss., University Konstanz, 2004.

Bernhard Marx, Adolph. *Die Lehre von der musikalischen Komposition*, vol. 3. Leipzig: Breitkopf & Härtel, 1845.

Betz, Albrecht. *Hanns Eisler. Musik einer Zeit, die sich eben bildet.* Munich: text + kritik, 1976.

Betz, Albrecht. "Música, cinematografía, música filmica. Hanns Eisler en Mexico. 1939 1940." In *Mexico, el exilio bien temperado*, edited by Renata von Hanffstengel and Cecilia Tercero Vasconcelos, 297–302. Ciudad de Mexico: Gobierno del Estado de Puebla, 1995.

Beyer, Fernando. "Hanns Eisler in Mexico City." *Eisler Mitteilungen* 66 (2018): 4–11.

Blanco Rodríguez, Juan A. *El Quinto Regimiento en la política militar del PCE en la guerra civil.* Madrid: UNED, 1993.

Bleider-Staudt, Elke. *Die deutschsprachige Lyrik des spanischen Bürgerkriegs. Eine Untersuchung der Lebensform und lyrischen Sprache.* PhD diss., University of Tübingen, 1983.

Blick, Sally. "A Double Life in Hollywood: Hanns Eisler's Score for the Film Hangmen Also Die and the Covert Expressions of a Marxist Composer." *The Musical Quarterly* 93, no. 1 (2010): 90–143.

Boyd, Caled. *They Called me an alien. Hanns Eisler's American Years, 1935–1948.* PhD diss., Arizona University, 2013.

Brécy, Robert. *Florilege de la chanson révolutionnaire de 1789 au front Populaire.* Paris: Hier et Demain, 1978.

Breyer, Knud. *Hanns Eisler. Lieder für Singstimme und Klavier, 1922–1932.* Wiesbaden: Breitkopf & Härtel, 2020.

Brinkmann, Reinhold. "Kompositorische Maßnahmen Eislers." In *Über Musik und Politik*, edited by Rudolf Stephan, 9–22. Mainz: Instituts für neue Musik und Musikerziehung, 1971.

Brown, Royal S. "The Three Faces of Lady Macbeth." In *Russian and Soviet Music: Essays for Boris Schwartz*, edited by Malcolm Hamrick Brown, 245–252. Ann Arbor: UMI Research Press, 1984.

Busch, Ernst, ed. *Kampflieder der Internationalen Brigaden.* Barcelona: Brigadas Internacionales, 1937.

Busch, Ernst. *Spanien. 1936–39. So sangen die Kameraden der XI. Internationalen Brigade.* Berlin: Lied der Zeit, 1947.

Busch, Ernst. Lied der Bergarbeiter + Lied der Arbeitslosen (Stempellied). Homochord (H-3942); Gloria, Carl Lindström (G.O. 10605), 1930.

Cáceres-Piñuel, María. *El hombre del rincon. José Subirá y la historia cultural e intelectual de la musicología en España.* Kassel: Reichenberger, 2018.

Calmell, César. "El III congreso internacional de musicología en Barcelona 1936, a partir de la documentación guardada en el fondo Higni Anglès de la Biblioteca de Catalunya." *Anuario musical* 70 (2015): 161–178.

Cañaveras Garrido, Francisco. *Joaquín Villatoro. Vida y obra.* Córdoba: Ayuntamiento de Castro del Río, 1998.

Carbonell i Guberna, Jaume. *Josep Anselm Clavé i el naixement del cant coral a Catalunya (1850–1874).* Cabrera de Mar: Galerada, 2000.

Carroll, Peter N. *The Odyssey of the Abraham Lincoln Brigade. Americans in the Spanish Civil War.* Stanford: Stanford University Press, 1994.

Casal Chapí, Enrique. "Cancionero Revolucionario Internacional." *Hora de España* 9 (1937): 72–76.

Casal Chapí, Enrique. "Salvador Bacarisse." *Música* 1, no. 2 (1938): 27–53.

Celaya Álvarez, Laura. *Jesús García Leoz, un legado interrumpido (1904–1953).* Pamplona: Gobierno de Navarra. Fondo de Publicaciones, 2018.

Chaplin-Kyzer, Abigail. *Searching for Songs of the People: the Ideology of the Composers' Collective and its Musical Implications.* Master Thesis, University of North Texas, 2018.

Chiginskaya, Maria. "Lope de Vega de puntillas: el estreno del ballet *Laurencia* en Leningrado (1939)." *Anuario Lope de Vega. Texto, literatura, cultura* 22 (2016): 344–354.

Colli, Giorgio, ed. *Friedrich Nietzsche: Sämtliche Werke: kritische Studienausgabe*, vol. 9. Munich: Deutsche Taschenbuch, 1980.

Colomé, Gabriel. *La Olimpiada Popular de 1936: deporte y política.* Barcelona: Universidad Autónoma de Barcelona, 2008.

Crist, Elizabeth B. *Music for the Common Man. Aaron Copland during the Depression and War.* Oxford: Oxford University Press, 2005.

Csipák, Károly. *Probleme der Volkstümlichkeit bei Hanns Eisler.* Munich: Emil Katzbichler, 1975.

Cuevas, Sara. *La actividad musical de Joaquín Villatoro Medina*. Seville: Junta de Andalucía, 2015.

Dahin, Oliver and Erik Levi. *Eisler in England. Proceedings of the International Hanns Eisler Conference, London 2010*. Wiesbaden: Breitkopf & Härtel, 2014.

Davies, Alan. "The First Radio War. Broadcasting in the Spanish Civil War." *Historical Journal of Film, Radio and Television* 19, no. 4 (1999): 473–513.

Deeg, Peter and Oliver Dahin. "Meeting Marianne in Hilversum." in *Eisler Mitteilungen* 42, edited by Peter Schweinhardt et al., 12–15. Saarbrücken: Pfau, 2006.

Deeg, Peter and Jürgen Schebera. "Hanns Eisler auf Schallplatte." In *Eisler-Mitteilungen* 59, edited by Peter Deeg, 8–11. Saarbrücken: Pfau, 2015.

Denning, Michael T. *Cultural Front: The Laboring of American Culture in the Twentieth Century*. London: Verso, 1997.

Diezel, Peter, ed. *Erwin Piscator. Briefe*, vol. 1. Berlin: Diezel, 2005.

Dourado Bastos, Manuel. "Brasiliens Landlose entdecken Hanns Eisler." In *Eisler-Mitteilungen 50* (Die Nummer 50), edited by Peter Schweinhardt, 30–31. Saarbrücken: Pfau, 2010.

Dümling, Albrecht. "Schönberg und sein Schüler Hanns Eisler: Ein dokumentarischer Abriß." *Die Musikforschung* 29, no. 4 (1976): 431–461.

Dümling, Albrecht. *Lässt euch nicht verführen. Brecht und die Musik*. Munich: Kindler, 1985.

Dümling, Albrecht and Peter Gierth, eds. *Entartete Musik. Eine kommentierte Rekonstruktion*. Düsseldorf: Kleinherne, 1988.

Dümling, Albrecht. "Zwischen Autonomie und Fremdbestimmug: Die Olympische Hymne von Robert Lubahn und Richard Strauss." *Richard Strauss-Blätter* 38 (December 1997): 68–102.

Dümling, Albrecht. "Solidaritätslied." In *Brecht Handbuch*, vol. 2, edited by Jan Knopf and Joachim Lucchesi, 196–201. Stuttgart: Metzler, 2001.

Dunaway, David K. "Charles Seeger and Carl Sands: The Composers' Collective Years." *Ethnomusicology* 24, no. 2 (May 1980): 159–168.

Edmunds, Neil. *The Soviet Proletarian Musical Movement*. Bern: Peter Lang, 2000.

Eisler, Hanns. Score *Lied der Arbeitslosen (Stempellied)* für Singstimme und Klavier. Berlin: Verlag für Arbeiterkultur, 1931.

Eisler, Hanns. "Lectures on the Social History of Music" [1938/39], HEA (AdK), folders 2452 and 2727 (unpublished), quoted from Tobias Fasshauer's (unpublished) edition for the Hanns Eisler Gesamtausgabe, 34–36.

Eisler, Hanns. "Zeitungskritik." *Melos. Zeitschrift für Musik* 8, no. 3 (March 1929): 111–116 (the article is included in *Hanns Eisler. Gesammelte Schriften 1921–1935*, edited by Tobias Fasshauer and Günter Mayer, 92–97. Wiesbaden: Breitkopf & Härtel, 2007).

Eisler, Hanns. "Einiges über das Verhalten der Arbeiter-Sänger und -Musiker in Deutschland." In *Hanns Eisler. Gesammelte Schriften 1921–1935*, edited by Tobias Fasshauer and Günter Mayer, 214–232. Wiesbaden: Breitkopf & Härtel, 2007.

Eisler, Hanns. "Die Erbauer einer neuen Musikkultur." In *Hanns Eisler. Gesammelte Schriften 1921–1935*, edited by Tobias Fasshauer and Günter Mayer, 132–151. Wiesbaden: Breitkopf & Härtel, 2007.

Eisler, Hanns. "Neue Methode der Kampfmusik." In *Hanns Eisler: Gesammelte Schriften 1921–1935*, edited by Tobias Fasshauer and Günter Mayer, 155–156. Wiesbaden: Breitkopf & Härtel, 2007.

Eisler, Hanns. "Zur Krise der bürgerliche Musik." In *Hanns Eisler. Gesammelte Schriften 1921–1935*, edited by Tobias Fasshauer and Günter Mayer, 166–170. Wiesbaden: Breitkopf & Härtel, 2007.

Eisler, Hanns. "[Rundfunkmusik]. " In *Hanns Eisler. Gesammelte Schriften 1921–1935*, edited by Tobias Fasshauer and Günter Mayer, 99. Wiesbaden: Breitkopf & Härtel, 2007.

Eisler, Hanns. "Über moderne Musik." In *Hanns Eisler. Gesammelte Schriften 1921–1935*, edited by Tobias Fasshauer and Günter Mayer, 46–48. Wiesbaden: Breitkopf & Härtel, 2007.

Eisler, Hanns. "Einiges über die Lage des Moderne Komponisten I." In *Hanns Eisler. Gesammelte Schriften 1921–1935*, edited by Tobias Fasshauer and Günter Mayer, 246–252. Wiesbaden: Breitkopf & Härtel, 2007.

Eisler, Hanns. "Die Fortschritte in der Arbeitermusikbewegung." In *Hanns Eisler. Gesammelte Schriften 1921–1935*, 109–110. Wiesbaden: Breitkopf & Härtel, 2007.

Eisler, Hanns. "Die Kunst als Lehrmeisterin im Klassenkampf." In *Hanns Eisler. Gesammelte Schriften 1921–1935*, edited by Tobias Fasshauer and Günter Mayer, 121–131. Wiesbaden: Breitkopf & Härtel, 2007.

Eisler, Hanns. "Einiges über die Lage des modernen Komponisten II." In *Hanns Eisler. Gesammelte Schriften 1921–1935*, edited by Tobias Fasshauer and Günter Mayer, 315–319. Wiesbaden: Breitkopf & Härtel, 2007.

Eisler, Hanns. "Einiges über die Krise der kapitalistischen Musik und über den Aufbau der sozialistischen Musikkultur." In *Hanns Eisler. Gesammelte Schriften 1921–1935*, edited by Tobias Fasshauer and Günter Mayer, 279–284. Wiesbaden: Breitkopf & Härtel, 2007.

Eisler, Hanns. "Geschichte der deutschen Arbeitermusikbewegung seit 1848" [1934], In *Hanns Eisler. Gesammelte Schriften 1921–1935*, edited by Tobias Fasshauer and Günter Mayer, 191–203. Wiesbaden: Breitkopf & Härtel, 2007.

Eisler, Hanns. "Neue Methoden der Kampfmusik." In *Hanns Eisler. Gesammelte Schriften 1921–1935*, edited by Tobias Fasshauer and Günter Mayer, 155–157. Wiesbaden: Breitkopf & Härtel, 2007.

Eisler, Hanns. "Zur Avantgarde der Musik." *Die neue Weltbühne* 31, no 38 (19 September 1935): 1189–1192. (The text is reproduced in Eisler, "Einiges über die Lage des Modernene Komponisten II (Anlässlich des 13. Festivals der I. G. N. M.)" [1935] In *Hanns Eisler. Gesammelte Schriften 1921–1935*, edited by Tobias Fasshauer and Günter Mayer, 315–318. Wiesbaden: Breitkopf & Härtel, 2007.

Eisler, Stephanie and Manfred Grabs, eds. *Hanns Eisler. Gespräche mit Hans Bunge. Fragen Sie mehr über Brecht.* Leipzig: Deutsche Verlag für Musik, 1975.

Elsner, Jurgen. *Zur vokalsolistischer Vortragsweise der Kampfmusik Hanns Eislers.* Leipzig: Deutscher Verlag für Musik, 1971.

Fasshauer, Tobias. "Zur Krise der Volkstümlichkeit bei Hanns Eisler." In *Musik in der DDR. Beiträge zu den Musikverhältnissen eines verschwundenen Staates,* edited by Matthias Tischer, 26–49. Berlin: Ernst Kuhn, 2005.

Fasshauer, Tobias and Günter Mayer, eds. *Hanns Eisler. Gesammelte Schriften 1921–1935.* Wiesbaden: Breitkopf & Härtel, 2007.

Fasshauer, Tobias. "Fesche Märsche. Hanns Eisler und die Militärmusik." In *Eisler-Mitteilungen* 67, edited by Tobias Fasshauer, 5–21. Saarbrücken: Pfau, 2019.

Fauser, Annegret. *Sounds of War. Music in the United States during World War II.* Oxford: Oxford University Press, 2013.

Fava, Maria Cristina. "The Composers' Collective of New York, 1932–1936: Bourgeois Modernism for the Proletariat." *American Music* 34, no. 3 (Fall 2016): 301–343.

Fay, Laurel E., ed. *Shostakovich and His World.* Princeton: Princeton University Press, 2004.

Ferrando Morales, Àngel Lluís. *Carlos Palacio. Vivencia y pervivencia. Una aproximación a la figura y la obra de Carlos Palacio en el centenario de su nacimiento (1911–2011).* Alcoy: Ayuntamiento de Alcoy, 2014.

Fitzpatrick, Sheila. "The Lady Macbeth Affair: Shostakovich and the Soviet Puritans." In *The Cultural Front: Power and Culture in Revolutionary Russia.* Ithaca: Cornell University Press, 1992.

Fontelles i Ramonet, Albert. *La Cobla Barcelona (1922–1938) un projecte noucentista.* PhD diss., Universitat Autònoma de Barcelona, 2020.

Forcert, Arno."Scherings Beethovendeutung und ihre methodischen Voraussetzungen." In *Beitrage zur musikalischen Hermeneutik,* edited by Carl Dahlhaus, 41–52. Regensburg: Bosse, 1975.

Fuhr, Werner. *Proletarische Musik in Deutschland (1928–1933).* Göppingen: Alfred Kümmerle, 1977.

Gall, Johannes C. *Eisler goes Hollywood: das Buch Komposition für den Film und die Filmmusik zu Hangmen Also Die.* Wiesbaden: Breitkopf & Härtel, 2015.

Gall, Johannes C. *Hanns Eisler. A Cappella Choruses 1925–1932* (Wiesbaden: Breitkopf & Härtel, 2018).

Gan, Germán. "Germanic Fogs and Mediterranean Clarity in an Aesthetic Struggle. Spanish Music Criticism Facing Paul Hindemith's Music (1921–1936)." In *Music Criticism 1900–1950,* edited by Jordi Ballester and German Gan, 245–282. Turnhout: Brepols, 2018.

García Gómez, Arturo. *Teoría de la entonación. Sobre el proceso de formación de la música en la via y obra de Boris V. Asaf'ev (1884–1949).* PhD diss., Universidad Autónoma de Madrid, 2007.

García López, Sonia. *Spain is us. La guerra civil española en el cine del Frente Popular 1936–1939.* Valencia: Universidad de Valencia, 2013.

Garolera, Narcis, ed. *Josep M. de Sagarra, Obra complete.* Valencia: Eliseu Climent, 1994.

Garratt, James. *Music and Politics. A critical introduction.* Cambridge: Cambridge University Press, 2019.

Ginés Ramiro, Guillermo. "Poesía como método de propaganda activa. Guerra viva de José Herrera Petere." In *Métodos de propaganda activa en la guerra civil española,* edited by Emilio Peral and Francisco Sáenz, 115–146. Madrid: Iberoamericana, 2015.

Glanz, Christian. *Hanns Eisler. Werk und Leben.* Vienna: Steinbauer, 2008.

Glückauf, Erich. *Begegnungen und Signale. Erinnerungen eines Revolutionärs.* Berlin: Neues Leben, 1976.

González Lapuente, Alberto. "En el centenario de Enrique Casal Chapí." *Scherzo: Revista de Música* 24 (245) (2009): 150–151.

Gounout, André. *Die Rote Sportinternationale, 1921–1937. Kommunistische Massenpolitik im europäischen Arbeitersport.* Münster : LIT-Verlag, 2002.

Gounot, André. "El proyecto de la Olimpiada Popular de Barcelona (1936), entre comunismo internacional y republicanismo regional." *Cultura, Ciencia y Deporte* 1, no. 3 (2005), 115–123.

Gounot, André. "Barcelona gegen Berlin. Das Projekt der Volksolympiade 1936." In *Der deutsche Sport auf dem Weg in die Moderne. Carl Diem und seine Zeit,* edited by Michael Krüger, 119–130. Berlin: LIT-Verlag, 2009.

Grabs, Manfred, ed. *Hanns Eisler heute.* Berlin: Akademie der Künste. 1974.

Grabs, Manfred. *Hanns Eisler. Kompositionen, Schriften, Literatur. Ein Handbuch.* Leipzig: Deutscher Verlag für Musik, 1984.

Graham, Helen. *The Spanish Civil War. A Very Short Introduction.* Oxford: Oxford University Press, 2005.

Greeley, Robin Adèle. *Surrealism and the Spanish Civil War.* Yale: Yale University Press, 2006.

Grüneis, Christian. "Die Kantate Mitte des Jahrhunderts." In *Hanns Eisler zwischen Systemkonformität und musikalischem Anspruch,* edited by Christian Glanz and Annegret Huber, 13–114. Vienna: Mille Tre, 2015.

Günthart, Erich. "Der Tod von Hans Beimler und Louis Schuster in Ludwig Renns 'Der Spanische Krieg.'" *Zeitschrift des Forschungsverbundes SED-Staat der Freien Universität Berlin* 43 (2019): 106–130.

Gur, Golan. "Classicism as Anti-Fascist Heritage: Realism and Myth in Ernst Hermann Meyer's Mansfelder Oratorium (1950)." In *Classical Music in the German Democratic Republic: Production and Reception,* edited by Kyle Frackman and Larson Powell, 34–57. Rochester: Camden House, 2015.

Haefeli, Anton. "Hanns Eisler und die Internationale Gesellschaft für Neue Musik." *Beiträge zur Musikwissenschaft* 23, no. 2 (1981): 104–113.

Haefeli, Anton. *Die Internationale Gesellschaft für Neue Musik (IGNM).* Zurich: Atlantis, 1982.

Haug, Wolfgang Fritz, ed. *Hanns Eisler. Das Argument. Zeitschrift für Philosophie und Sozialwissenschaften.* Berlin: Argument Verlag, 1975.

Häusler, Josef. *Spiegel der Neuen Musik. Donaueschingen Chronik- Tendenzen- Werkbesprechungen.* Kassel: Bärenreiter, 1996.

Heine, Christiane. "Salvador Bacarisse (1898–1963) en el centenario de su nacimiento." *Cuadernos de música iberoamericana* 5 (1998): 43–75.

Heister, Hanns-Werner. "Brecht/Eisler. Das Einheitsfrontlied." In *Vom allgemeingiiltigen Neuen Analysen engagierter Musik: Dessau, Eisler, Ginastera, Hartmann,* edited by Thomas Phleps and Wieland Reich, 91–102. Saarbrücken: Pfau, 2006.

Hermsdorf, Klaus, ed. *Exil in den Niederlanden und in Spanien.* Leipzig: Reclam, 1981.

Herzer, Manfred. "Schwule Widerstandskämpfer gegen die Nazis." In *Dokumentation der Vortragsreihe "Homosexualität und Wissenschaft",* edited by Shwulenreferat im AStA der FU Berlin, 222–226. Berlin: Rosa Winkel, 1985.

Hoffman, Ludwig and Karl Siebig. *Ernst Busch. Eine Biographie in Texten, Bildern und Dokumenten.* Berlin: Das Europäische Buch, 1987.

Holmes, Deborah. *Ignazio Silone in Exile: Writing and Antifascism in Switzerland 1929–1944.* Aldershot: Ashgate, 2005.

Iglesias, Antonio. *Rodolfo Halffter. Su obra para piano.* Madrid: Alpuerto, 1979.

Iglesias, Antonio. *Rodolfo Halffter (tema, nueve décadas y final).* Madrid: Fundación Banco Exterior, 1991.

Jena, Stefan. "Dabeisein ist alles. Die Musik zu den olympischen Spielen 1936." In *Feste. Theophil Antonicek zum 70. Geburtstag,* edited by Martin Eybl, Stefan Jena, and Andreas Vejvar, 265–285. Tutzing: Schneider, 2010.

John, Eckhard. *Brüder, zur Sonne, zur Freiheit. Die unerhörte Geschichte eines Revolutionsliedes.* Berlin: Ch. Links Verlag, 2018.

Kaden, Werner. *Signale des Aufbruchs. Musik im Spiegel der"Roten Fahne".* Berlin: Neue Musik, 1988.

Kantorowicz, Alfred. *Spanisches Kriegstagebuch.* Frankfurt am Main: Fischer, 1982.

Kelly, Elaine. *Composing the Canon in the German Democratic Republic: Narratives of Nineteenth-Century Music.* Oxford: Oxford University Press, 2014.

Kiladi, Maria. *The London Labour Choral Union, 1924–1940: A Musical Institution of the Left.* PhD diss., Royal Holloway, University of London, 2016.

Kirschenbaum, Lisa A. *International Communism and the Spanish Civil War. Solidarity and Suspicion.* Cambridge: Cambridge University Press, 2015.

Knepler, Georg. "Zur Frage der Widerspiegelung der Wirklichkeit in Beethovens Musik." *Musik und Gesellschaft* 2, no 3 (1952): 66–71.

Knilli, Friedrich. "Die Arbeiterbewegung und die Medien. Ein Rückblick." *Gewerkschaftliche Monatshefte* 25 (1974): 349–362.

Knopf, Jan, ed. *Brecht-Handbuch,* vol. 1. Stuttgart: Metzler, 2001.

Koestler, Arthur. *Ein spanisches Testament.* Zürich: Europa Verlag, 2012.

Kolb, Roberto. "Hanns Eisler, Silvestre Revueltas und die mexikanische Kampfliedkultur." In *Hanns Eisler. Ein Komponist ohne Heimat?*, edited by Hartmut Krones, 133–149. Cologne: Böhlau. 2012.

Kolb-Neuhaus, Roberto. *Silvestre Revueltas. Sounds of a Political Passion.* Oxford: Oxford University Press, 2023.

Krabiel, Klaus-Dieter. *Brechts Lehrstücke. Entstehung und Entwicklung eines Spieltyps.* Stuttgart: Metzler, 1993.

Kranz, Martin. "Wem die Stunde schlägt. Die Madrider 'Generation der Republik' im spanischen Bürgerkrieg am Bespiel von Rodolfo Halffter." In *"Form follows function": zwischen Musik, Form und Funktion*, edited by Till Knipper, Martin Kranz, Thomas Kühnrich, and Carsten Neubauer, 217–243. Hamburg: Bockel, 2003.

Kuleshova, Vera Vladimirovna. *Ispaniya i SSSR: kul'turnye svyazi 1917–1939.* Moscow: Nauka, 1975.

Labajo, Joaquina. "Compartiendo canciones y utopías. El caso de los voluntarios Internacionales en la Guerra Civil española." *Trans. Revista Transcultural de Música* 8 (2004) (accessed online).

Labajo, Joaquina. "La práctica de una memoria sostenible. El repertorio de las canciones internacionales durante la guerra civil española." *ARBOR. Ciencia, Pensamiento y Cultura* 187 (2011): 847–856.

Lammel, Inge. *Lieder der Agitprop-Truppen vor 1945.* Leipzig: Friedrich Hofmeister, 1959.

Lammel, Inge. *Das Arbeiterlied.* Leipzig: Philipp Reclam, 1980.

Lammel, Inge. *Und weil der Mensch ein Mensch ist.* Leipzig: VEB Deutscher Verlag für Musik, 1986.

Lammel, Inge. *Arbeiterlied–Arbeitergesang. Hundert Jahre Arbeitermusikkultur in Deutschland. Aufsätze und Vorträge aus 40 Jahren 1959–1998.* Berlin: Hentrich & Hentrich 2002.

Landon, Robbin. *Haydn: Chronicle and Works*, vol. 4. London: Thames and Hudson, 1994.

Larcati, Arturo. "Stefan Zweigs heimliche Liebe zur italienischen Literatur." In *Am liebsten wäre mir Rom! Stefan Zweig und Italien*, edited by Arturo Larcati, 31–53. Blaufelden: Königshausen & Neumann, 2019.

Lee, Kyung-Boon. *Musik und Literatur im Exil. Hanns Eislers dodekaphone Exilkantaten.* New York: Peter Lang, 2001.

Levi, Erik. "Hanns Eisler's Deutsche Sinfonie." In *Hanns Eisler. A Miscellany*, edited by David Blake, 181–202. Luxembourg: Harwood, 1995.

Loos, Helmut. "Arnold Schering und seine Beethoven-Analysen." In *Beethoven 4. Studien und Interpretationen*, edited by Mieczysław Tomaszewsky and Magdalena Chrenkoff, 239–255. Kraków: Akademia Muzczna, 2009.

López Rubio, Clara and Wolfgang Martin-Hamdorf. "El lacayo de Berlín, Bonn y Washington. La imagen de Franco en el cine documental alemán: el caso de *Unbändiges Spanien* (España Indómita)." *Archivos de la filmoteca* 42/43 (October 2002–February 2003): 100–117.

Lowry, Yana Alexandrovna. *From Massenlieder to Massovaia Pesnia – Musical Exchanges between Communists and Socialists of Weimar Germany and the Early Soviet Union.* PhD diss., Duke University, 2014.

Lucchesi, Joachim. "Solidaritätslied." In *Brecht Lexikon,* edited by Ana Kugli and Michael Opitz, 226. Stuttgart: Metzler, 2006.

Mann, Hendrik de. *Más allá del marxismo.* Madrid: Aguilar, 1933.

Masters, Giles. "Performing Internationalism: The ISCM as a 'Musical League of Nations.'" *Journal of the Royal Musical Association* 147 no. 2 (November 2022): 560–571.

Martín-Hamdorf, Wolfgang. "Del testigo presencial a la transformación poética. *Ispanija-España*: poesía, narrativa y propaganda." *Secuencias: Revista de historia del cine* 3 (1995): 60–77.

Mateos, Eladio. *Rafael Alberti y la música.* PhD diss., Universidad de Granada, 2003.

Matzigkeit, Michael and Birgit Bernard, eds. *Fritz Lewy (1893–1950). Ein Leben für die Form.* Düsseldorf: Theatermuseum, Dumont-Lindemann-Archiv, 2002.

Mayer, Günter, ed. *Hanns Eisler. Musik und Politik. Schriften 1924–1948.* Leipzig: Deutscher Verlag für Musik, 1973.

Mayer, Günter. *Weltbild. Notenbild. Zur Dialektik des musikalischen Materials.* Leipzig: Philipp Reclam, 1978.

Mayer, Otto. *Cançoner Revolucionari Internacional,* vol. 1. Barcelona: Comissariat de Propaganda de la Generalitat de Catalunya, 1937.

Mazzetti, Elisabetta. *Thomas Mann und die Italiener.* Frankfurt am Main: Peter Lang, 2000.

McKinley, C. Alexander. *Illegitimate Children of the Enlightenment. Anarchists and the French Revolution (1880–1914).* New York: Peter Lang, 2008.

McLellan, Josie. *Antifascism and Memory in East Germany. Remembering the International Brigades 1945–1989.* Oxford: Oxford University Press, 2004.

Mendelson, Jordana. *Documenting Spain. Artists, Exhibition Culture, and the Modern Nation, 1929–1939.* Pennsylvania: The Pennsylvania State University, 2005.

Messer, August, ed. *Friedrich Nietzsche, Werke in 2 Bänden.* Leipzig: Kröner, 1931.

Meyer, Ernst H. "Aus der Tätigkeit der 'Kampfgemeinschaft der Arbeitersänger.'" In *Hanns Eisler. Sinn und Form. Beiträge zur Literatur,* edited by Deutsche Akademie der Künste, 152–160. Berlin: Akademie der Künste, 1964.

Meyer, Ernst H. "Die Vorherrschaft der Instrumentalmusik im niederländischen Barock. Eine unbekannte Blütezeit niederländischen Musik." *Tijdschrift der Vereeniging voor Noord-Nederlands Muziekgeschiedenis* 15, no. 1 (1936): 56–83.

Meyer, Ernst Hermann. *Kontraste, Konflikte: Erinnerungen, Gespräche, Kommentare,* edited by Dietrich Brennecke and Mathias Hansen. Berlin: Verlag Neue Musik, 1979.

Meyer, Ernst Hermann. *Musik im Zeitgeschehen*. Berlin: Deutschen Akademie der Künste, 1952.

Mikkonen, Simo. *State Composers and the Red Courtiers Music, Ideology, and Politics in the Soviet 1930s*. Jyväskylä: University of Jyväskyla, 2007.

Militärakademie "Friedrich Engels", ed. *Pasaremos. Deutsche Antifaschisten im national-revolutionären Kampf des spanischen Volkes*. Berlin: Deutscher Militärverlag, 1966.

Miravitlles, Jaume. *Episodis de la guerra civil española*. Barcelona: Portic, 1972.

Moore, Christopher Lee. *Music in France and the Popular Front (1934–1938): Politics, Aesthetics and Reception*. PhD diss., McGill University, 2006.

Morag, Josephine Grant. "On Music and War." *Transposition* [online 2020], hors-série 2. Available from: http://journals.openedition.org/transposition/4469 [Accessed 23 August 2022].

Moreda Rodriguez, Eva. "Why do orchestral and Band musicians in exile matter? A case study from Spain." *Music and Letters* 101, no. 1 (2019): 71–88.

Nelson, Amy. *Music for the Revolution. Musicians and Power in Early Soviet Russia*. Pennsylvania: The Pennsylvania State University Press, 2020.

Nobbe, Ernst. *Die thematische Entwicklung der Sonatenform im Sinne der Hegel'schen Philosophie betrachtet*. Würzburg: Triltsch, 1941.

Noeske, Nina and Matthias Tischer, eds. *Musikwissenschaft und Kalter Krieg: Das Beispiel DDR*. Cologne: Böhlau, 2010.

Oja, Carol J. "Marc Blitzstein's 'The Cradle Will Rock' and Mass-Song Style of the 1930s." *The Musical Quarterly* 73, no. 4 (1989): 445–475.

Opler, Daniel. "Music from the Vanguard. The Songs of the Composers Collective of New York, 1933–1936." *Journal for the Study of Radicalism* 10, no. 2 (Fall 2016): 123–152.

Orobon, Marie-Angéle. "Marianne y España. la identidad nacional en la Primera República Española." *Historia y política. Ideas, procesos y movimientos* 13 (2005): 79–98.

Ortiz-Echagüe Trujillano, Javier. "Una imagen para salvar la República: fotomontajes del pabellón español en la exposición internacional de París 1937." In *La comunicación durante la Segunda República y la Guerra civil*, edited by Antonio Checa Godoy et al., 471–484. Madrid: Fragua, 2007.

Palacio, Carlos. *Colección de canciones de lucha*. Valencia: Tipografía moderna, 1939.

Palacio, Carlos. "Erinnerungen an Hanns Eisler in Spanien." In *Hanns Eisler heute*, edited by Manfred Grabs, 67–69. Berlin: Akademie der Künste, 1974.

Palacio, Carlos. *Acordes en el alma*. Alicante: Institut Juan Gil-Albert, 1984.

Paynter, Maria Nicolai. *Ignazio Silone: Beyond the Tragic Vision*. Toronto: University of Toronto Press, 2000.

Peral Vega, Emilio. *Retablos de agitación política. Nuevas aproximaciones al teatro de la Guerra Civil española*. Madrid: Iberoamericana, 2013.

Peral Vega, Emilio. "Altavoz del frente": una experiencia multidisciplinar durante la Guerra Civil Española." *Hispanic Research Journal* 13, no. 3 (2012): 234–249.

Pérez López, Javier. *La música en las brigadas internacionales. Las canciones como estrategia de guerra*. PhD diss., Universidad de Castilla-La Mancha, 2014.

Pérez Castillo, Belén. "La transformación de un música en el exilio: Leopoldo Cardona." In *Huellas y rostros: exilios y migraciones en la construcción de la memoria musical de Latinoamérica*, edited by Consuelo Carredano and Olga Picún, 337–354. Mexico: Universidad Autónoma de Méxiko, 2017.

Pescatello, Ann M. *Charles Seeger: A Life in American Music.* Pittsburgh, University of Pittsburgh Press, 1992.

Phleps, Thomas. *Hanns Eislers Deutsche Sinfonie. Ein Beitrag zur Ästhetik des Widerstands.* Kassel: Bärenreiter, 1988.

Phleps, Thomas. "Der müde Soldat: Hanns Eisler und der Erste Weltkrieg." In *Musik bezieht Stellung. Funktionalisierungen der Musik im Ersten Weltkrieg*, edited by Stefan Hanheide, Dietrich Helms, Claudia Glunz, and Thomas F. Schneider, 403–428. Göttingen: V&R unipress, 2013.

Pike, David. *Deutsche Schriftsteller im sowjetischen Exil. 1933–1945.* Frankfurt am Main: Suhrkamp, 1981.

Potter, Pamela M. *Most German of the Arts. Musicology and Society from the Weimar Republic to the End of Hitler's Reich.* Yale: Yale University Press, 1998.

Pujadas, Joan, ed. *Sara Llorens. Epistolari (1901–1954).* Barcelona: Fundació Pere Coromines, 2004.

Pujadas, Xavier and Carlos Santacana. *L'altra olimpíada Barcelona'36: Esport, societat i política a Catalunya (1900–1936).* Badalona: Llibres de l'Index, 1990.

Ramírez Morcillo, Carlos. *Literatura y compromismo político. Experiencias y contenidos en José Herrera Petere.* PhD diss., Universidad de Castilla-La Mancha, 2017.

Ramírez Navarro, Antonio. *La fuerza de los débiles. Vida, prisiones y muerte de Vicente Talens Inglá (1892–1940).* Almería: Instituto de Estudios Almerienses, 2021.

Ramm, Valentina Iosifovna, ed. *International Collection of Revolutionary Songs.* Moscow: Moscow State Musical Publishing Office, 1933.

Reichel, Edward. "Ein Spanienkämpfer ohne Spanienbild: Ludwig Renn." In *Dresden und Spanien: Akten des interdisziplinären Kolloquiums, Dresden, 22.–23. Juni 1998*, edited by Christoph Rodiek, 179–189. Frankfurt am Main: Vervuet, 2000.

Reinecke, Rüdiger. *Gernika und der Luftkrieg gegen die spanische Republik (1936–1939) in der zeitgenössischen internationalen Literatur.* Bielefeld: Aisthesis, 2020.

Reininghaus, Frieder. "Über die Kunst zu erben und den Meister des Zitats. Hanns Eisler als Objekt und Subjekt der Rezeptionsgeschichte." *Österreichische Musikzeitschrift* 67, no. 4 (2012): 6–20.

Renn, Ludwig. *Krieg.* Frankfurt am Main: Frankfurter Societäts-Druckerei, 1928.

Renn, Ludwig. *Der spanische Krieg.* Berlin: Aufbau, 1955.

Requena Gallego, Manuel and Rosa Ma Sepúlveda Losa, eds. *Las Brigadas Internacionales. El contexto internacional, los medios de propaganda, Literatura y Memorias.* Cuenca: Universidad de Castilla-La Mancha, 2003.

Richard, Bernard. *Les emblèmes de la République.* Paris: CNRS Éditions, 2012.

Riemann, Hugo. *Große Kompositionslehre,* vol. 3. Berlin/Stuttgart: W. Spemann, 1913.

Rienäcker, Gerd. "Die 'Bauernkantate'. Eine Chronik über Spanien 1936?" In *Der spanische Bürgerkrieg in der DDR. Strategien intermedialer Erinnerungsbildung,* edited by Wolfgang Asholt, Rüdiger Reinecke, and Susanne Schlünder, 219–234. Frankfurt am Main: Vervuert, 2009.

Roig i Rosich, Josep M. *Història de l'Orfeó Català: moments cabdals del seu passat.* Barcelona: Abadía de Montserrat, 1993.

Ryjik, Veronika. "La recepción de *Fuente Ovejuna* en Rusia." In *Fuente Ovejuna (1619–2019). Pervivencia de un mito universal,* edited by Javier Huerta Calvo, 255–272. New York: IDEA/IGAS, 2019.

Saavedra, Leonora. "La sociología de la música de Otto Mayer-Serra." In *De Nueva España a México. El universo musical mexicano entre centenarios (1517–1917),* edited by Javier Marín-López, 195–214. Seville: Universidad Internacional de Andalucía, 2020.

Salazar, Adolfo. "Altaveu del Front. Cançó popular i cançó revolucionària." *Mirador* 392 (22 October 1936): 7.

S. J. [Salvat, Joan]. "El III Congrés de la Societat Internacional de Musicologia a Barcelona." *Revista musical catalana* 33, no. 389 (May 1936): 185–186.

Sánchez de Andrés, Leticia. *Pasión, desarraigo y literatura. El compositor Roberto Gerhard.* Madrid: Scherzo, 2013.

Sánchez Cervelló, Josep and Sebastián Agudo, eds. *Las Brigadas Internacionales. Nuevas perspectivas en la historia de la Guerra Civil y del exilio.* Tarragona: Universitat Rovira i Virgili, 2015.

Scammell, Michael. *Koestler: The Literary and Political Odyssey of a Twentieth-Century Skeptic.* London: Random House, 2009.

Schaber, Irme. *Gerta Taro: Fotoreporterin im spanischen Bürgerkrieg: eine Biografie.* Marburg: Jonas, 1994.

Schader, Luitgard. *Paul Hindemith. Sämtliche Werke,* vol VIII/2 (Sing- und Spielmusik II). Mainz: Schott, 2008.

Schebera, Jürgen. *Hanns Eisler im USA-Exil. Zu den politischen ästhetischen und kompositorischen Positionen des Komponisten 1938 bis 1948.* Berlin: Akademie Verlag, 1978.

Schebera, Jürgen. *Hanns Eisler. Eine Biographie in Texten, Bildern und Dokumenten.* Mainz: Schott, 1998.

Schebera, Jürgen and Maren Köster, eds. *Hanns Eisler, Briefe 1907–1943.* Leipzig: Breitkopf & Härtel, 2004.

Schebera, Jürgen and Maren Köster, eds. *Hanns Eisler, Briefe 1907–1943.* Wiesbaden: Breitkopf & Härtel, 2010.

Schebera, Jürgen. *España en el corazón.* Berlin: Bear Family, 2014.

Schenk, Dietmar. *Die Hochschule für Musik zu Berlin: Preußens Konservatorium zwischen romantischem Klassizismus und Neuer Musik 1869–1932/33.* Stuttgart: Steiner, 2004.

Schering, Arnold. "Musikalische Analyse und Wertidee." *Jahrbuch der Musikbibliothek Peters* 39 (1929): 9–20.

Schering, Arnold. "Zur Sinndeutung der 4. und 5. Symphonie von Beethoven." *Zeitschrift für Musikwissenschaft* 16, no 2 (1934): 65–83.

Schering, Arnold. *Beethoven in neuer Deutung*. Leipzig: C. F. Kahnt, 1934.

Schlüssel, Elizabeth. *Zur Rolle der Musik bei den Eröffnungs- und Schlussfeiern der Olympischen Spiele von 1896 bis 1972.* Hamburg: Diplomica GmbH, 2002.

Schmalfeldt, Janet. *In the process of becoming: analytic and philosophical perspectives on form in early nineteenth-century music.* Oxford: Oxford University Press, 2011.

Schmidt, Eberhard. *Ein Lied – ein Atemzug. Erinnerungen und Dokumente.* Berlin: Neue Musik, 1987.

Schneerson, Grigori, ed. *Pasaremos! Canciones de guerra. Испанские революционные песни.* Moscow: Art State Publishing House, 1938.

Schneerson, Grigori, ed. *антифашистские песни* (Antifascist songs), Moscow: ГОСУДАРСТВЕННОР МУЗЫКАЛЬНОЕ ИЗДАТЕЛЬСТВО (State Music Publishing House), 1939.

Schöne, Jens. *Die Landwirtschaft der DDR 1945–1990.* Erfurt: Landeszentrale für politische Bildung Thüringen, 2005.

Schüler-Springorum, Stefanie. *Krieg und Fliegen. Die Legion Condor im Spanischen Bürgerkrieg.* Paderborn: Ferdinand Schöningh, 2010.

Schwarz, Boris. *Music and Musical Life in Soviet Russia.* Bloomington: Indiana University Press, 1983.

Schweinhardt, Peter, ed. *Eisler Mitteilungen 37 (Eisler und die Schweiz).* Saarbrücken: Pfau, 2005.

Schweinhardt, Peter, ed. *Eisler Mitteilungen 42 (Eisler und die Niederlande).* Saarbrücken: Pfau, 2006.

Schweinhardt, Peter, ed. *Eisler und die Nachwelt.* Berlin: Breitkopf & Härtel, 2012.

Seguí i Francés, Romà. "Teresa Andrés y la organización Cultura Popular: una propuesta de coordinación bibliotecaria (1936–1938)." *Métodos de información* 2, no. 3 (2011): 127–154.

Serrano Betored, Pilar. *La influencia silenciada: Paul Dukas y la música española de la Edad de Plata.* PhD diss., Universidad Complutense de Madrid, 2019.

Shreffler, Anne C. "The International Society for Contemporary Music and its political context (Prague, 1935)." In *Music and International History in the Twentieth Century,* edited by Jessica Gienow-Hecht. New York: Berghahn Books, 2015.

Siebig, Karl. *"Ich geh' mit dem Jahrhundert mit". Ernst Busch. Eine Dokumentation.* Reibeck bei Hamburg: Rowohlt Taschen, 1980.

Silone, Ignazio. *Brot und Wein. Roman*, translated by Adolf Saager. Zürich: Oprecht & Helbling, 1936.

Solé i Sabaé, Josep Maria and Joan Villarroya. *España en llamas. La guerra civil desde el aire*. Madrid: Temas de Hoy, 2003.

Sponheuer, Bernd. "Angewandte Instrumentalmusik Hanns Eislers Kleine Sinfonie op. 29." *Die Musikforschung* 32, no. 3 (July/September 1979): 258–273.

Sponheuer, Bernd. "Anmerkungen zu der Kontroverse über Scherings Beethoven-Deutung in den 30er-Jahren." *Die Musikforschung* 58, no. 4 (2005): 341–352.

Stanley, Glenn. "Arnold Schering: ein Nazi-Musikologe? Dokumentation und Analyse." *Archiv für Musikwissenschaft* 70, no 2 (2013): 119–133.

Subirá, José. *El músico-poeta Clavé (1824–1874)*. Madrid: Imprenta Alrededor del mundo, 1924.

Subotnik, Rose Rosengard. "Adorno's Diagnosis of Beethoven's Late Style: Early Symptom of a Fatal Condition." *Journal of the American Musicological Society* 29, no. 2 (1976), 242–275.

Taube, Jakob. *Hans Kahle (1899–1947). Der vergessene Kommandeur der "Thälmann-Brigade".* Leipzig: Leipziger Universitätsverlag, 2017.

Teibler, Antonia. "Erstfunde mexikanischer Dokumente zu Hanns Eislers Gastprofessur am Conservatorio Nacional de Música in México D. F." In *Hanns Eisler. Ein Komponist ohne Heimat?*, edited by Hartmut Krones, 117–132. Vienna: Böhlau 2012.

Tellez Cenzano, Enrique. *La música como elemento de representación institucional: el himno de la Segunda República Española*. PhD diss., Universidad Complutense de Madrid, 2016.

Tolley, Thomas. *Painting the Cannon's Roar: Music, the Visual Arts, and the Rise of an Attentive Public in the Age of Haydn, c.1750 to c.1810*. Aldershot: Ashgate Publishing, 2001.

Tomoff, Kiril. *Creative Union: The Professional Organization of Soviet Composers, 1939–1953*. Ithaca: Cornell University Press, 2006.

Tremlett, Giles. *The International Brigades: Fascism, Freedom and the Spanish Civil War*. London: Bloomsbury, 2020.

Uhl, Michael. *Mythos Spanien. Das Erbe der Internationalen Brigaden in der DDR*. Bonn: J. H. W. Dietz, 2004.

Velasco-Pufleau, Luís. "The Spanish Civil War in the work of Silvestre Revueltas." In *Music and Francoism*, edited by Gemma Pérez Zalduondo and German Gan Quesada, 321–347. Turnhout: Brepols, 2013.

Vershinin, Konstantin, Andrej Tereshchuk, and Yuri Ignashov. "Algunos rasgos característicos de las canciones soviéticas sobre la Guerra Civil Española." *Mundo eslavo: revista de cultura y estudios eslavos* 18 (2019): 126–135.

Voigt, Boris. "Arbeitergesang zwischen bildungsbürgerlichem Ideal, Gemeinschaftskonstitution und proletarischem Kampf. Die Liedersammlungen des deutschen Arbeiter-Sängerbundes in der Zeit der

Weimarer Republik." *International Review of the Aesthetics and Sociology of Music* 51, no. 1 (June 2020): 59–100.

Voigt, Jochen. *Er rührte an den Schlaf der Welt. Ernst Busch. Die Biographie.* Berlin: Aufbau, 2010.

Weber, Horst. *I am not a hero. I am a composer. Hanns Eisler in Hollywood.* Hildesheim: Olms, 2012.

Weinert, Erich. *Camaradas. Ein Spanienbuch.* Berlin: Volk und Welt, 1956.

Werner, Abel. "Die versuchte Neutralisierung der 'Münzenberg-Kreise' durch die KPD-Abwehr im republikanischen Spanien." In *Globale Räume für radikale transnationale Solidarität,* edited by Bernhard H. Bayerlein, Kasper Braskén, and Uwe Sonnenberg, 467–492. Berlin: International Willi Münzenberg Forum, 2018.

Widmaier, Tobias, ed. *Paul Arma. Avantgarde und Arbeiterlied: Autobiographie 1904–1934.* Büdingen: PFAU, 2016.

Zauner, Waltraud. "Studien zu den musikalischen Bühnenwerken von Julius Bittner." *Studien zur Musikwissenschaft* no. 38 (1987): 135–214.

Zur Mühlen, Patrik von. *Spanien war ihre Hoffnung. Die deutsche Linke im Spanischen Bürgerkrieg 1936 bis 1939.* Berlin: Dietz, 1985.

Zur Mühlen, Patrik von. *Fluchtweg. Spanien – Portugal. Die deutsche Emigration und der Exodus aus Europa, 1933–1945.* Bonn: H. W Dietz, 1992.

# Index


1937 International Exhibition in Paris 96, 205

Adomian, Lan 170
Adorno, Theodor W. 5, 185
Alberti, Rafael 116–117, 144–146, 153, 161–162, 228
Albrecht, Erwin Fritz Bernhard 12
Alcantarilla Carbó, Alberto 230
Altavoz del Frente 77, 99, 115, 116–118, 133, 149, 153, 165
Anders, Günther 6
Antheil, George 170
antifascist modernism. *See* musical modernism and antifascism.
Aparicio, Antonio 100, 153, 231
Argenta, Ataulfo 112–113
Arma, Paul 65, 127, 145
Arendt, Hannah 6
Asaf'ev, Boris 194
atonal music 23, 107–109, 185
Aub, Max 100
Auden, Wystan Hugh 205
  *Spain 1937* 205
*Ay, Carmela* 211

Bacarisse, Salvador 20, 32, 149–152, 168, 229
  *Canto a la marina* (*Hymn for the Navy*) 149–152
  *Corrida de feria* (*Festive bullfight*) 168
Bach, Johann Sebastian 6, 193
Baker, Peter 127–128, 201 n. 67
*barricadas, A las* (*To the Barricades*) 57, 169
Bartók, Béla 195
Barcelona 1, 6, 14, 16–18, 21, 23, 29, 31–41, 49–51, 55, 59–60, 118, 123, 129–132, 139, 149, 192, 199, 200–201, 208, 212, 215, 233
  Casal de la Cultura 17, 23, 130–132
  Comissariat de Propaganda 17, 123–134, 195
  Eisler's visits 1, 18, 21, 39–41, 49, 60
  "Barcelona Section" of the ISCM 32–33
barretina 48, 96
battlefront 19–21, 59–61, 63, 111, 115, 119, 129, 153, 178, 221
battle songs 8–10, 16, 20
  by Eisler 11, 16, 21, 41, 49–50, 71–80, 107–138,208–209
  by others 12, 16, 17, 23, 63–67, 79–80, 104, 127, 139–180, 206, 212–214, 219, 227–228
    by Spanish composers 24, 63, 139–180, 227–228
    by Soviet composers. *See* battle songs *under* Soviet Union.
  civil war composition contest 155–156, 230
Bautista, Julián 168
  *Tres ciudades* (*Three Cities*) 168
Becher, Johannes R. 209
  *Mitte des Jahrhunderts* (*Mid-Century*) 209

Beethoven, Ludwig van 6, 90, 92
*Egmont* overture 192
Marxists readings of his music 184, 186–194, 203
Nazi readings of his music 187–190
sonata form 6, 192–194, 203
symphonies 187–192
Bely, Viktor 173
Bénichou, Georges 134
Berg, Alban 35, 39, 92, 107, 185–186, 198
*Lyric Suite* 186
Violin concerto 39
*Wozzeck* 35, 92, 186, 198
Bergamín, José 153
Berlin
1936 Olympic Games 18, 212
celebrations of the 20th anniversary of the beginning of the Spanish War 1, 204, 219–225
East Berlin 1, 25, 104, 204, 217, 221
Eisler's interwar circle of Marxist musicians 7–10, 39
Friedrich-Wilhelms-Universität. *See* Humboldt Universität zu Berlin.
Humboldt Universität zu Berlin 6, 203, 212
musical propaganda activities in pre-Nazi Berlin 7–14
Berlioz, Hector 184
Bittner, Julius 93–94, 99
*Der Bergsee* (*The Mountain Lake*) 93–94
Blake, Ben 136
Blanter, Matwej 174
Blitzstein, Marc 137, 170
Bloch, Ernst 197
Bloque Obrero y Campesino 14
Bolotin, Samuil Borisovich 134, 136
Brecht, Bertolt 84, 86, 90, 93–94
*Bauernkantate* (Peasant Cantata) 93–94, 218
*Bilder aus dem Kriegsfibel* (*Pictures from the Kriegsfibel*) 214–217
*Einheitsfrontlied* (*United Front Song*) 120
*Deutsches Sinfonie* (*German Symphony*) 93–94, 218
*Hangmen Also Die* 208
*Kriegsfibel* 214–217
*Mein Bruder, der Flieger* (*My Brother, the Pilot*). See *Spanisches Liedchen 1937.*
*Peasant Cantata.* See *Bauernkantata.*
*Solidaritätslied* (*Solidarity Song*) 139–143, 155
*Spanisches Liedchen 1937* (*Spanish Ditty 1937*) 204–207
Brigadas Internacionales. *See* International Brigades.
Bukofzer, Manfred 6, 9, 11, 39
*Kampfbundlied* (*Fighting League Song*) 11
*Lied der RGO* (*Song of the RGO*) 11
Busch, Ernst 3, 23, 25, 44f
as lyricist 25, 222–223
commemoration of the Spanish war in the GDR 204, 219
live and radio performances in Spain 129–133, 165
recordings 122, 159 n. 33, 223
works
*Abschied von Spanien* (*Farewell to Spain*) 25, 222–225
*Canciones de las Brigadas Internacionales (recording)* (*Songs of the International Brigades*) 159, 222–224
*Kampflieder der Internationalen Brigaden.* See *Songbook of the International Brigades.*
*Songbook of the International Brigades* 72, 76, 124, 137, 153
*Spanien.* See *Abschied von Spanien.*

Bush, Alan 24, 137, 173–174, 197
*Make Your Meaning Clear* 174

Caballero, Carlos 165–166, 230–231
Campo, Conrado del 144, 149, 153, 156
canon. *See* musical canon.
capitalism 4, 8, 15, 18–19, 24, 111–112, 139, 143, 181–186
and music 4, 8, 24, 111–112, 143, 181–186
Cardona, Leopoldo 156, 158–161, 168, 175, 230
Casal Chapí, Enrique 100, 153–155, 169, 212–213, 231
*Los campesinos* (*The Peasants*) 100, 153–155, 212–213, 231
Casal de la Cultura 17, 23, 130–132
Casasempere, Rafael 117, 156, 230
Catalan national identity 4, 14, 22, 48, 51, 55–57, 96, 211
*see also* barretina *and* sardana *and* "Barcelona Section" of the ISCM
Catalanism. *See* Catalan national identiy.
Catholic Church 25, 61, 86, 95–96, 103, 215–217
Chapí, Ruperto 114, 153
*La revoltosa* 114
Chardí Rusies, Salvador 110, 111, 120, 123 n. 31
Chopin, Frédéric 187
Club Internacional Antifascista 130
cobla 57
Comintern. *See* Communist International.
Comissariat de Propaganda de la Generalitat de Catalunya 17, 123–134, 195
*Nova Iberia* 123, 235
Communist International 4, 9, 18–22, 30–37, 83, 110–119
International Music Bureau 29–34
Red Sports International 40
campaigns against Trotskyism 83
Union of Revolutionary Theatre 136
Communist Party of Germany 5, 8, 12, 60–61, 68, 75, 78, 130, 145
activities in Spain 60–61, 130
Communist Party of Spain 4, 18, 19, 23, 55, 109–116, 156, 162
*Mundo obrero* 41, 55
Cultura Popular 115, 169
*see also* Orquesta y Coros Proletarios de Madrid
*Compañías de Acero, Las. See* Carlos Palacio.
Composers' Collective of New York 170–173, 197
Consejo Central de la Música 17, 149, 156, 181, 234
Copland, Aaron 24, 170, 172, 173
*Into the Streets, May First!* 172
coros confederales 162
Coslow, Sam 208
Corot, Alfred 144
Cowell, Henry 170
Crawford Seeger, Ruth 170
*cuatro muleros, Los (The Four Muleteers)* 80, 211

Davidenko, Alexander 114
Debussy, Claude 193, 198
DEFA (Deutsche Film AG) 211
"Degenerate Music" Exhibition 180
Dent, Edward J. 30–32
Dessau, Paul 65 n. 26, 79, 127, 131, 205–207, 219
*Guernika* 205
*Mein Bruder war ein Flieger* (*My Brother was a Pilot*) 206–207
*Spaniens Himmel breitet seine Sterne* (*Spain's Sky Spreads Its Stars*) 79, 131

Dudow, Slatan 139
  *Kuhle Wampe oder: Wem gehört die Welt?* (*Kuhle Wampe or: Who Owns the World?*) 139, 141
Dunayevsky, Isaak Osipovich 64, 114
Duncker, Hermann 6
Dukas, Paul 144
Editions Sociales Internationales 124 n. 34, 134–135
Eisler, Hanns
  collaboration with the International Brigades, 2, 19–21, 67–81
  collaboration with Herrera Petere 20–21, 61, 63–66
  "Eisler bass" 49, 143
  first visit to Spain 39–58
  interwar circle of Marxist music scholars 7–10, 39
  marxist views on music history 4–7, 181–186, 192–194
  relationship to Ludwig Renn 20, 22, 59–60
  relationship to Robert Gerhard 23, 29, 32–33, 107–109
  works about of the Spanish Civil War in the GDR 204–225
  *see also* attempt to move the 1936 festival to Moscow *under* International Society for Contemporary Music
Eisler, Hanns, works
  *Abschied von Spanien* (*Farewell to Spain*) 25, 222–225
  Anthem of the Communist International. *See Kominternlied.*
  *Auf den Straßen zu singen*, op. 15 109
  *Ballade vom Soldaten* (*Ballad of the Soldier*) 8
  *Ballade vom "Nigger Jim", Die* 131
  *Ballade zum § 218* (*Ballad about § 218*) 8
  *Bauernkantate* (*Peasant Cantata*) 21–25, 85–104, 205–206, 215
  Premiere in 1959 in Berlin 217–218
  *Baumvollpflücker, Die* (*The Tree Harvesters*) 132
  *Bilder aus dem Kriegsfibel* (*Pictures from the Kriegsfibel*) 25, 214–217
  *Comintern Song*. See *Kominternlied.*
  *Deutsche Sinfonie* (*German Symphony*) 22–25, 85–87, 102–104, 217–218
  *Deutsches Lied* (*German Song*) 131
  *Einheitsfrontlied* (*United Front Song*) 23, 64, 120–122, 131, 221
  *Faust* (opera project) 103
  Fifth Regiment of Popular Militias 22, 53, 61, 63–66, 104, 133, 153, 219
  *Hangmen Also Die* 25, 50, 208–209
  *Himne per a l'Olimpíada Popular* (*Hymn for the People's Olympiad*) 18, 22, 41–58
  *heimlische Aufmarsch, Der* (*The Secret Deployment*) 9, 11
  *Kampflied für die IAH* (*Battle Song for the Internationale Arbeiterhilfe*) 11, 16
  *Kominternlied* (*Comintern Song*) 9, 22, 23, 110–119, 171
  *Lied der Moorsoldaten* (*Song of the Peat Bog Soldiers*) 76, 131
  *Lied der Sichel* (*Sickle Lied*) 93
  *Lied der Tankisten* (*Song of the Tank Crewmen*) 25, 69, 220–222

*Lied vom 7. Januar, Das* (*The Song of 7th January*) 21–23, 69–72, 76, 79, 133, 136, 223–224
*Lied vom SA-Mann* (*Song of the SA Man*) 131
*Lieder und Kantate* (*Songs and Cantatas*) 223
*Linker Marsch* (*Left March*) 221
*Marcha del Quinto Regimiento (March of the Fifth Regiment)* 21–25, 65–67, 79, 133–137, 208–209, 219
*Maßnahme, Die (The Measures Taken)* 8, 23, 78, 109, 137
*Mitte des Jahrhunderts (Mid-Century)* 209
*Mutter , Die* (*The Mother*) 8, 90, 92
*No pasarán* (*They Shall Not Pass*) 21–23, 65–67, 133, 219
*Palmström* 108
Piano Sonata No 1, op. 1 107
*Rundköpfe und die Spitzköpfe, Die* (*Round Heads and Pointed Heads*) 93
*Solidaritätslied* (*Solidarity Song*) 9, 16, 21, 24, 72, 124, 127, 138–180, 211
*Solidarity Song.* See *Solidaritätslied.*
*Sonate in Form von Variationen,* Op. 6 35
*Song of the Hostages* 208–209
*Spanien.* See *Abschied von Spanien.*
*Spanisches Liedchen 1937* 25, 204–207
*Spartakus 1919* 11
*Stempellied* (*Stamp Song*) 9, 11, 71, 131
*rote Wedding, Der* (*The Red Wedding*) 9, 124, 131, 146, 171
*Unbändiges Spanien* (*Untamed Spain*) 210–212
*Und ich werde nicht mehr sehen das Land* (*And I Will No Longer See the Land*) 223
*Vier Klavierstücke,* Op. 3 108
*Vier Stücke für gemischten Chor,* op. 13 108–110
*Zeitungsausschnitte* 108
elitism and music 181–186, 196
Engels, Friedrich 4, 103
*Der deutsche Bauernkrieg* (*The German Peasants' War*) 103
Espinosa, Rafael 149, 165–168, 229, 231
*Alianza proletaria: Himno de las trincheras de Mieres* (*Proletarian Alliance: Hymn for the Trenches of Mieres*) 166
*Anthem of the International Brigades* 166
*Himno a Carlos Prestes* (*Hymn to Carlos Prestes*) 166
*Juventudes proletarias* (*Proletarian Youth*) 166
expressionism 24, 184–185

Falla, Manuel de 24, 117, 175–177, 195
Harpsichord Concert 176
*Himno marcial* (*Martyal Hymn*) 176
*retablo de Maese Pedro, El* (*Master Peter's Puppet Show*) 176
Fernández Blanco, Evaristo 230
First World War 9, 67, 184, 186
flamenco 80–81, 168, 206, 211
Franco, Franciso 76, 88–89, 211
Free German Cultural League 137
*Freie Deutsche Kultur* 137
French Revolution 43, 48, 198
Frenkel, Ilya 110
*Frente Popular* (Popular Front) 18, 22, 37, 43, 48–49, 57, 64, 75–76, 115, 120–123, 221

*Fuenteovejuna* (Lope de Vega's play) 100

Galeote, Pedro 228
García Leoz, Jesús 161–165, 168, 232
Garfías, Pedro 231
Garreta, Juli 57. See also *Juny* under sardana.
Gaster, Karin 13–14
Gerhard, Robert 23, 29, 32–38, 107–109, 138, 185
  *Catalan Songs* 34
German Communist Party. *See* Communist Party of Germany.
German Democratic Republic 1, 2, 131, 153f
  historiographical narratives 1, 21, 203–204
  film music 210–212
  films about the Spanish Civil War 210–214
    *Fünf Patronenhülsen* (*Five Bullet Casings*) 210
    *Mich dürstet* (*I Thirst*) 210
    *Unbändiges Spanien* (*Untamed Spain*) 210–212
    *Wo Du hin gehst* (*Where You Are Going*) 210
  Freie Deutsche Jugend 219, 222
  musical commemorations of the Spanish Civil War 219–225
  National People's Army 210, 219–222
  reception of the *Peasant Cantata* 217–218
German Society of Musicology 187
Glinka, Mikhail 101
Goebbels, Josef 180
Göhr, Walter 131
  *Kumpellied.* See *Lied der arbeitslosen Bergarbergmannes*
  *Lied der arbeitslosen Bergarbergmannes* (*Song of the Unemployed Miner*) 131–132
Grabs, Manfred 67, 219
Grosz, George 179
Guerra, Armand 229

Hába, Alois 29, 31, 38
Halffter, Rodolfo 20, 169–170, 195–196, 201, 231
  *Alerta* (*Alert!*) 170–171
  *Para la tumba de Lenin* (*For Lenin's Tomb*) 195–196
  relationship to Otto Mayer 169, 195–196, 201
Hans Beimler Medal 1, 2, 204, 222, 225
Haydn, Josep 90
Heartfield, John 179
Hegel, Georg Wilhelm Friedrich 192–194
Hellberg, Martin 212
Hemingway, Ernest 210
Hernández, Miguel 99
Herrera Petere, José 21–23, 53, 58, 61–64, 120–121, 232
  collaboration with Eisler 20–21, 61, 63–66
  *Marcha del Quinto Regimiento (March of the Fifth Regiment)* 21–25, 65–67, 79, 133–137, 208–209, 219
  *No pasarán* (*They Shall Not Pass*) 21–23, 65–67, 133, 219
Heydrich, Reinhard 208
Hindemith, Paul 7, 186, 195
Hollywood 25, 50, 100, 208–209, 214
*Hora de España* 201, 235
Hitler, Adolf 12–13, 16–17, 39–40, 74, 127–128, 189
  *Mein Kampf* (*My Struggle*) 16–17

Ibárruri "La Pasionaria", Dolores 112
International Brigades 19, 21, 25, 59–60, 63, 75, 78,122, 130, 136, 220
Anthem of the International Brigades 166
commemorative events in the GDR 210–212, 219
concert in Murcia 22, 61, 63, 69–78, 84, 103
German volunteers 1, 22, 61–62, 68, 71–84, 102
International Lenin School, Moscow 110
International Musicological Society 31, 39
International Society for Contemporary Music
1936 Festival in Barcelona 1, 22, 29–40
Eisler's attempt to move the 1936 festival to Moscow 22, 30–32
Internationale, The 44, 57, 114, 116–117, 169
Ivens, Joris 210
*Spanish Earth, The* 100, 210–211

Jacoby, Heinrich 6
jazz 44, 50, 143
*joven guardia, La* 114, 117, 119 n. 22
Juventudes Socialistas Unificadas (Unified Socialist Youth) 63, 111, 119, 162

Kahle, Hans 61, 68
*Kampfgemeinschaft der Arbeitersänger* 10–12, 16
*Kampflieder*. *See* battle songs.
*Kampfmusik* 7–10, 79, 93, 143, 221
Kochetov, Vadim 65, 136, 154, 174
*No pasarán* 136, 154
Krein, Alexander 101
*Laurencia* 101
Lamote de Grignon, Joan 32–33, 35
Lang, Fritz 25, 208
*Hangmen Also Die* 25, 50, 208–209
Lenin 4, 190, 195–197
Lewy, Fritz 55
Liszt, Franz 184, 187
Lubahn, Robert 18

Madrid 21, 22–23,59–64, 68–72, 76, 78, 83–85, 88–89, 112–119, 124, 137, 144–145, 149, 153, 156, 162–165, 195, 212
bombing of Madrid by the Condor Legion 85, 88, 89
conservatory 144, 149, 153, 156
Madrid front 60–61, 68–71, 76, 78
"Madrid Section" of the ISCM 32–33
*see also* Orquesta y Coros Proletarios de Madrid
Magritte, René 205
*Drapeau Noir, Le* (*The Black Flag*) 205
Mahler, Gustav 185
Malraux, André 98
Mancisidor Aquino, Tomás 118, 149
Mann, Thomas 86
*Marseillaise, La* 80, 103, 169
*Marcha fúnebre* (*Funeral March*) 114, 117, 119 n. 22
*Marianne Populaire, La* (*The People's Marianne*) 22, 43–52, 143
Marx, Adolf Bernhard 193
Marx, Karl 4, 118, 122
*Marxa de l'Exèrcit Popular. See* works *under* Ernst Hermann Meyer.
Marxist music historiography 4–7, 13, 17, 24, 184–203

Mateos González, Francisco 149
Mayer, Otto. *See* Mayer-Serra, Otto.
Mayer-Serra, Otto
  and the Barcelona Casal de la Cultura 130–133
  on Beethoven 186–194
  *Cançoner Revolucionari Internacional* (*International Revolutionary Songbook*) 123–129, 153, 170 n. 46
  career as musicologist in Berlin 3, 7, 233
  career as music writer in Barcelona 17, 199–201, 233–234
  early contacts to Eisler and his circle 6–7, 10
  Eisler's and Meyer's influence on his thought 4–7, 181–186, 192–194
  exile to Mexico 201–203
  exile to Spain 13–17
  Jewish origins and musicological training 6–7
  musical propaganda activities in Spain 14–17, 123–133
  *Panorama de la música mexicana desde la independencia hasta la actualidad* (*Overview of Mexican Music from Independence to the Present*) 202
  relationship to Rodolfo Halffter 169, 195–196, 201
  and the Soviet Union 196–199
  thoughts on musical modernism 185–186, 194–199
  thoughts on revolution and music 194–199
melodrama 85, 90, 92, 102, 205
Merenciano Bosch, Francisco 230
Meyer, Ernst Hermann 3, 7, 10, 13, 203, 231
  as composer of battle songs 9, 23–24, 125
  film music for *Wo du hin gehst* 25, 212–214, 231
  relationship to Otto Mayer-Serra 14–17, 182 n. 2
  works
    *1. Mai* (*1st of May*) 126–127
    *Auf die Straße!* (*To the Streets!*) 11, 16
    *Final Struggle, The* 127
    *Frau Kraemer* 127
    *Kampflied gegen Hitler* (*Battle Song against Hitler*) 12–13, 17, 127–128
    *Krieg* (*War*) 126
    *Labour's Marching Song* 127
    *Marxa de l'Exèrcit Popular* (*March of the People's Army*) 125–129
    *Refugees, The* 127
    *Schlaflose Nächte* (*Sleepless Nights*) 127
    *Strike in the West* 127
    *Solidarität* (*Solidarity*) 11
Mielke, Erich 210
militant music. See *Kampfmusik*
Ministry of Public Instruction and Fine Arts 155–156
*Mirador* (journal) 17, 108, 125, 128, 181, 187, 199–201, 234–235
Miravitlles, Jaume 51, 56
Miró, Joan 96, 99
  *Aidez l'Espagne* (*Help Spain!*) 96, 99
  *El segador. Pagès català en rebel·lia* (*The Reaper: Revolutionary Catalan Peasant*) 96
Mola, Emilio 153
montage 9–10, 16–17
Moraleda, Fernando 24, 175–176
  *Canción del falangista* (*Song of the Falangist*) 175–176
Morera, Enric 53, 55, 57

see also *La santa espina* under sardana
Mozart, Wolfgang A. 187
Murcia 21–22, 61, 63, 69, 71, 76–78, 84, 103, 115–117
concert at Teatro Romea 22, 61, 63, 69–78, 84, 103
Mussorgsky, Modest 195
*Pictures at an Exhibtion* 195
*Música* (music journal) 234
musical canon 4, 92, 131, 186–194
musical modernism 5, 24–25, 29–39, 139–180, 185–186, 194–199
and antifascism 24, 169–180, 194–199
*Musicografía* 181, 199–200, 234–235
music sociology 4–7, 181, 189, 201–203
Myaskovsky, Nikolai 198

Nazism 1, 6, 12–13, 19–22, 25, 29, 39–40, 50, 60, 68, 73, 78, 81, 85, 144, 180, 187–194, 208–209, 212
1936 Olympic Games in Berlin 18, 212
and musicology 39, 187–194
Condor Legion 23, 25, 85, 88–89, 102, 204–205
*see also* Hitler *and* Arnold Schering
Negrín, Juan 66, 122
neoclassicism in music 107–108, 149, 181, 195
Neruda, Pablo 89
*Neue Sachlichkeit* 186
New Musicology 203
Nietzsche, Friedrich 191
Nobbe, Ernst 194
Nüll, Edwin von der 6

octatonicism 170, 171, 175
Oliver i Sellarès, Joan 125, 231
Ordóñez, Carlos 230
Orfeón Gervasiense 118
*orfeós* (Catalan Choral Societies) 109, 118, 138
Orquesta y Coros Proletarios de Madrid 23, 112–114, 137, 145
Oropesa, Rafael 63–64, 232
*Himno del 5º cuerpo* (*Hymn of the Fifth Corps*) 63–64, 232

Palacio, Carlos 20, 23, 61, 66–67, 112, 114, 115, 117, 125, 129–133, 144, 149, 156–158, 162, 165–169, 175, 219, 229–231
*compañías de Acero, Las* (*Steel Companies*) 65–66, 116–117, 132, 149, 229
*Venguemos a los caídos* (*Avenge the Fallen!*) 155–158
*see also* Orquesta y Coros Proletarios de Madrid
*Partit Socialista Unificat de Catalunya* (Unified Socialist Party of Catalonia) 4, 17–19, 125, 129
*Treball* (organ of the party) 18, 125, 178, 181, 199–201, 234–235
pasodoble 63, 118, 175
Pasionaria, La. *See* Dolores Ibárruri.
peasants 21–25, 48, 63, 80, 84–89, 91–103, 111, 129, 153–154, 205–206, 212, 215–218
in civil war propaganda music 21–25, 85–103, 153–155, 205–206, 212–215, 231
Pedrell, Felipe 176
*Los Pirineos* (*The Pyrenees*) 176
Pemán, José María 176
People's Olympiad 18, 22, 40–42, 49–51, 54–57, 59, 209
Pere Quart. *See* Joan Oliver I Sellarès.
photomontage 96, 123, 178–180
Phrygian mode 141, 143, 151–152, 159–160, 164, 167–168, 206, 214
Picasso, Pablo 101, 205
*Guernica* 101, 205
Piscator, Erwin 32, 37
Prague 29–35, 38, 208

Prestes, Luis Carlos 228–229
Prince August Wilhelm of Prussia 12
Pokrass, Dmitry 114
proletarian movement and music 4, 7, 8–12, 23–24, 109, 111–115, 122, 137–138, 144–145, 156, 165–167, 168–173, 197–199, 228, 230–233

radio 4, 7, 20, 23, 34, 53–60, 115, 118–119, 129, 131–133, 137, 149, 156, 162, 198, 233
  Busch's radio performances in Spain 129–133, 165
  Ràdio Barcelona 55, 131
  Unión Radio, Madrid 115, 118
Ramos, Felíx Vicente 120–123, 156, 228, 230–231
Ramos, Manuel 228, 231
Rankl, Karl 11, 127
  *Chorstück für Naturschwärmer* (*Choral Piece for Nature Enthusiasts*) 11
Red Front 12, 112, 124 n. 37, 156
Reichenbach, Hermann 30–35, 38
Renau, Josep 96–111, 123, 162–163, 179, 210
  *Decreto 7 octubre 1936* (*Decree of October 7, 1936*) 96–97
  *Hoy más que nunca, Victoria* (*Today more than ever, Victory*) 162–163
  *Industria de guerra, potente palanca de la victoria* (*Military Industry, Powerful Lever of Victory*) 179
  *L'Agriculture espagnole reposait sur: Des salaires misérable, Une inique reparation de la terre* (Spanish agriculture was based on: Miserable wages, an unjust distribution of land) 96, 100
  *Unbändiges Spanien* (*Untamed Spain*) 210
Renn, Ludwig 3, 67–68
  as a lyricist 73–78
  as commander of the Thälmann Battalion 19
  as organizer of the concert in Murcia
  homosexuality 70, 81–82
  relationship to Eisler 20, 22, 59–60
  works
    *Der spanische Krieg* (*The Spanish War*) 69 n. 36, 77 n. 51, 80, 82, 124
    *Drüben in Deutschland herrscht Not* (*Over in Germany, Misery Reigns*) 74–79
    *In Spanien ist Revolution* (*It's Revolution in Spain*) 73–77
    *Lied vom 7. Januar, Das* (*The Song of 7th January*) 21–22, 67–72
    *Wir sind der Freiheit Soldaten* (*We Are the Solidiers of Freedom*) 75–76
Republican Air Force 161–162
revolutionary music 8, 170, 194–199
Revueltas, Silvestre 3 n. 4, 20 n. 53, 197
Richter, Horst 217–218
Riemann, Hugo 193
Rienäcker, Gerd 23, 102
Rimsky-Korsakov, Nikolai 101
Ripoll, Miguel 156, 158, 230
Ruera, Josep Maria 36

Sacharow, Wladimir 136
Sagarra, Josep María de 18, 22, 42, 50–57
Salas Viu, Vicente 228
Salazar, Adolfo 32, 39
Sands, Carl. *See* Charles Seeger.
sardana 55, 57, 211
  *Juny* 57
  *Santa espina, La* 57

Scarlatti, Domenico 195
Schechter, Boris 173
Schering, Arnold 187–190
Schiller, Friedrich 188
Schlesinger, Max. *See* Max Singer.
Schneerson, Grigori 129, 219, 228, 231
Schoenberg, Arnold 5, 23–24, 29, 107–108, 185–186, 195
Schumann, Robert 184
Second World War 1, 88–89, 137, 204, 208–209, 214
Seeger, Charles 128, 170–173
  *Mount the Barricades* 172
Serra i Moret, Manuel 13–14
Shaporin, Yuri 198
Shostakóvich, Dmitri 34, 36, 38, 198
  *Lady Macbeth of Mtsensk* 36, 198
  *see also* Shostakóvich affair *under* Soviet music
Shub, Esfir 136
  *Ispaniya* (*Spain*) 136
Siemsen, Hans 61
Sikorskaia, Tatiana Sergeevna 134, 136
Silone, Ignazio 85–89, 218
  *Brot und Wein* (*Bread and Wine*) 85–89, 102
  *Fontamara* (*Fontamara*) 102
Singer, Max 131
Social Democratic Party of Germany 8, 10
socialist realism 197, 203
Soviet battle songs. *See* battle songs *under* Soviet Union.
Soviet Union 19–20, 22, 24, 30–39, 83–84, 101, 104, 110–112, 114–115, 117–118, 129, 134–137, 152–153, 166–168, 173, 190, 194–195,197–200, 208, 218
  Association for Contemporary Music 30, 197
  Association of Proletarian Musicians 197
  battle songs 64, 110, 115, 136, 154, 166, 173–174, 231
  propaganda songs. *See* battle songs *under* Soviet Union.
  Shostakóvich affair 34, 198
  *Sovetskaya Muzyka* (USC journal) 197
  Union of Soviet Composers 31, 35, 197–198
*Sozialistische Einheitspartei Deutschlands* 209–210, 218–219
Spanish Communist Party. *See* Communist Party of Spain.
Sportintern. *See* Red Sports International.
*Sprechchöre* (Speaking Choirs) 22, 78
Stern, Jeanne 210–211
Stern, Kurt 61, 75–76, 83, 210
Strauss, Richard 18, 185, 197–198
  *Olympische Hymne* (*Olympic Hymn*) 18
  *Salomé* 185
  *Elektra* 185
Stravinsky, Igor 107, 198
symphonic music 21–25, 35, 36, 84–103, 112, 183–192, 197–198, 209, 212–14, 217–218
  by Beethoven 187–192
  by Soviet composers 197–198
Szabó, Ferenc 11, 136, 145 n. 12
  *Ernst Thälmann* 145 n. 12
  *Marcha de las Brigadas Internacionales* (*March of the International Brigades*) 136
  *Sowjetstern sei die Parole* (*Let the Soviet star be the slogan*) 11

Tapia, Luís de 116–117, 149–150, 229

Teatro Romea. *See* International Brigades. Concert in Murcia.
*Tendenzlied* 8–9, 10 n. 26
Thälmann Batallion 19, 21, 68–69, 73, 78
Thälmann, Ernst 145
Third International. *See* Communist International.
Thyssen, Franz 12
Toscanini, Arturo 86
*trece puntos de la victoria, Los* (*The Thirteen Points of Victory*) 122
Tschemberdschi, Nikolai 173, 219
twelve-tone composition 21, 25, 85, 94, 102, 204–206

Ulbricht, Walter 210
Unión Radio 115, 118
Universal Edition 107, 109, 139, 180
*Unsterbliche Opfer*. See *Marcha fúnebre.*

Valencia 21, 60–61, 66, 83, 130, 165, 195, 199–200
  Eisler's visit 21, 60–61, 83
Villatoro, Joaquin 20, 112, 114, 144–148, 160, 168, 175, 228
  *Himno a Thaelmann* (*Hymn to Thaelmann*) 114, 144–148
Vollmer, Karl 11, 127

Wagner, Richard 93, 114, 176, 184–187, 190, 193, 197
  *Rienzi* 114
*Warszawianka*. See *A las barricadas.*
Weber, Max 4
Webern, Anton 35, 107, 185
Weill, Kurt 186
  *Dreigroschenoper, Die* (*The Threepenny Opera*) 186
Weinert, Erich 25, 130, 136, 166, 219, 221, 229
  *Anthem of the International Brigades* 166
  German version of the *Marcha del Quinto Regimiento* 136, 219
  *Lied der Tankisten* (*Song of the Tank Crewmen*) 25, 69, 220–222
West Germany 204, 211, 218
Wexley, John 208
Wolpe, Stefan 9, 11
Workers Music League 124, 139, 172
World War I. *See* First World War.
World War II. *See* Second World War.

Yagüe, Juan 215

zarzuela 112, 115, 153, 234
Zweig, Stefan 86

www.ingramcontent.com/pod-product-compliance
Lightning Source LLC
LaVergne TN
LVHW012337100826
845148LV00018B/712

*9781837653188*